ARTISTS OF THE TUDC

THE PORTRAIT MINIATURE REDISCOVERED 1520-1620

ARTISTS OF THE TUDOR COURT

THE PORTRAIT MINIATURE REDISCOVERED
1520–1620

ROY STRONG

WITH CONTRIBUTIONS FROM
V. J. MURRELL

9 July–6 November 1983
THE VICTORIA & ALBERT MUSEUM
THIS EXHIBITION IS SPONSORED BY PEARSONS

On the cover:
ISAAC OLIVER
Unknown Melancholy Man
c. 1590–95
Reproduced by gracious permission of
Her Majesty the Queen
(Catalogue 268)

Frontispiece:
NICHOLAS HILLIARD
Henry Percy, 9th Earl of Northumberland
1590–95
The Rijksmuseum, Amsterdam
(Catalogue 266)

© Roy Strong and V. J. Murrell, 1983

DESIGNED AND PRODUCED BY THAMES AND HUDSON LTD
PUBLISHED BY THE VICTORIA & ALBERT MUSEUM 1983

Monochrome section printed in Great Britain by
BAS Printers Limited, Over Wallop, Hampshire
Colour section printed and Bound in Great Britain by
Balding and Mansell Ltd.
ISBN 0–905209–34–6

Contents

Preface · 7

Introduction: The Tudor Miniature: Mirror of an Age
by Roy Strong · 9

The Art of Limning
by V. J. Murrell · 13

Bibliography · 26

Technique and Practice: a display of limners' Tools
and Materials *by V. J. Murrell* · 28

THE CATALOGUE
by Roy Strong

Origins: Lucas Hornebolte · 34

Hans Holbein · 45

Survival: Levina Teerlinc · 52

Nicholas Hilliard · 58

Rowland Lockey · 92

Isaac Oliver · 97

Elizabeth I and the Limners · 117

Tournaments and Masques · 133

The Stuarts and the Limners · 143

The Cabinet Miniatures · 156

Index · 168

THE FRIENDS OF THE VICTORIA AND ALBERT MUSEUM

The Friends of the V & A receive the following privileges

FRIENDS £15 annually
FRIENDS (Concessionary) £10 annually for Pensioners
and full-time Museum staff

Free and immediate entry to all exhibitions with a guest
or husband/wife and children under 16

Free evening Private Views of major exhibitions
and new developments in the Museum

Quarterly mailings of Museum literature and News Letters

The opportunity to participate in trips abroad with
Keepers from the Departments

Discounts in the Craft Shop and on exhibition catalogues

CORPORATE FRIENDS £100 annually

Receive all the privileges offered to Friends, plus a
fully transferable Membership Card

BENEFACTORS £1000 donation, which may be directed
to the Department of the donor's choice

ASSOCIATES OF THE VICTORIA AND ALBERT MUSEUM

The Associates of the V&A are companies who pay a
minimum of £500 annually, covenanted for four years,
and who take a particular interest in the Museum and
have a close involvement with it.

ASSOCIATES

B.A.D.A.
The Baring Foundation
Bonas and Company Limited
Christie's
Commercial Union Assurance Company plc
Granada Group
Charles Letts (Holdings) Limited
Mobil
The Oppenheimer Charitable Trust
S. J. Phillips Limited
Rose and Hubble Limited
J. Sainsbury plc
Sotheby's
Thames Television Limited
Sir Duncan Oppenheim
Mrs Basil Samuel

BENEFACTOR FRIENDS

Sir Duncan Oppenheim
Mr Garth Nicholas

CORPORATE FRIENDS

Asprey and Company
Bankers Trust Company
Bonhams London
Colnaghi and Company
Coutts and Company, Bankers
Doulton and Company
Goldsmiths Company
John Keil Limited
Madame Tomo Kikuchi
Ian Logan Limited
Madame Tussaud's
Mendip Decorative and Fine Arts Society
Barbara Minto Limited
Phillips Auctioneers
RTZ Services Limited
Societe Generale
South Molton Antiques Limited
Spink and Son Limited
The Wellcome Foundation Limited

Preface

It is extremely appropriate that the Victoria and Albert Museum should stage a major exhibition on the subject of early portrait miniatures. Not only does the Museum house the National Collection of these precious objects but thirty-six years ago it put on a major pioneering exhibition to commemorate the four hundredth anniversary of the birth of Nicholas Hilliard. My former colleague, Graham Reynolds' work in 1947 signalled the beginnings of serious research on this subject. Since then his work has been enriched by that of a succession of scholars who have contributed, most notably Noel Blakiston and the late Erna Auerbach.

The present exhibition is inevitably very different from that of 1947 and presents to the public the fruits of a decade's research, the centre core of which has been an examination of the objects themselves in the Museum's Conservation Department. This has been a daunting task carried out under the aegis of my colleague, V. J. Murrell, Deputy-Keeper of Conservation, who has virtually created the technical study of these objects in scientific terms. The conclusions presented in this catalogue are the result of endless sessions looking at miniatures out of their frames under intense magnification. The results of this approach will quickly be apparent in the identification of the work of Lucas Hornebolte, Levina Teerlinc and Rowland Lockey, all important artists but virtually unheard of a generation ago. Through this approach we have also been able to radically alter many of the accepted datings of works by both Nicholas Hilliard and Isaac Oliver. I have tried to indicate the wider context into which these miniatures fit, in the sense that not one of these artists was ever solely a miniaturist. We have for too long viewed them through a distorting glass so that an attempt has been made to indicate the other types of work which they would have undertaken as a normal activity, things as varied as painting banners for funerals, colouring tombs, illuminating manuscripts and executing panel portraits.

Over the years my office has patiently borne the project and I would like to express my gratitude to Lindy Prys Roberts, and to Garth Hall, who initially acted as an assistant, a role later taken on by Stephen Calloway as the topic took its final shape. The Photographic Section of the Museum, in particular Sally Chappell and John Lee, has dealt admirably with the steady stream of miniatures from private and public collections. I would also pay tribute here to a succession of typists who waded through the endless versions of catalogue entries, in particular Pauline Cockrill who coped with the final version of the entire catalogue. John Westbrook undertook the strenuous task of indexing and checking the typescript with great thoroughness. This exhibition catalogue has the sad distinction of being the last to appear under the aegis of John Physick, Keeper of Museum Services.

The execution of the exhibition has been the work of essentially two people, Garth Hall and Paul Williams. The former has co-ordinated all aspects of putting on a great exhibition. The latter has faced up splendidly to the challenge of displaying these objects in exhibition terms with all the attendant problems caused by their fragility and their minute size. I would like finally to record my personal gratitude to a decade of working with V. J. Murrell. I shall miss those happy sessions in his workshop, snatched amidst a sea of administrative burdens, peering through that microscope. We both hope that the exhibition will convey to a wider public some of the excitement which we have felt as we unravelled the work of these artists of the Tudor Court.

ROY STRONG
Victoria and Albert Museum 1983

Acknowledgements

V. J. Murrell and I would like to express our gratitude to all those who contributed to the project either by lending to the exhibition or allowing their miniatures to come to the Victoria and Albert Museum for us to study. We list the collectors and collections and those who assisted in the enterprise. We extend equal gratitude to those who wish to remain anonymous.

Her Majesty The Queen
    Sir Oliver Millar KCVO, FBA, FSA, The Hon. Mrs Jane Roberts
Her Royal Highness Princess Juliana of The Netherlands
    A. F. Ubbels Esq.
The Dean and Chapter of St. George's, Windsor Castle
The Duke of Buccleuch and Queensberry, KT
    The Earl of Dalkeith
The Lady Ashcombe
The Countess Beauchamp, M.B.E., K[1]
The Duke of Devonshire and Trustees of the Chatsworth Settlement
The Lord Harlech KCMG
Lady Victoria Leatham and the Governors of Burghley House Preservation Trust
The Viscount De L'Isle VC, KG.
The Duke of Northumberland
The Earl of Pembroke
The Earl of Powis
The Marquess of Salisbury
The Marquess of Tavistock and Trustees of the Bedford Settled Estates
The Lord Tollemache
Society of Antiquaries, London
The Armouries: H.M. Tower of London
Visitors of The Ashmolean Museum
    Sir David Piper, Gerald Taylor Esq.
Major R. J. Berkeley and the Trustee of the 8th Earl of Berkeley deceased
The Bodleian Library, Oxford
    Steven Tomlinson Esq, J. A. Brister Esq.
The British Library: Department of Printed Books, Department of Manuscripts.
The British Museum: Department of Coins and Medals, Department of Prints and Drawings
The Master and Fellows of Emmanuel College, Cambridge
University of Cambridge Old Schools
College of Arms
Edinburgh University Library
Syndics of the Fitzwilliam Museum, Cambridge
    Professor Michael Jaffé, David Scrase Esq.
Brinsley Ford Esq, CBE, FSA
Greater London Council: The Rangers House, Blackheath
Mrs Eleanor Hamilton
George Howard Esq
The John Rylands University Library of Manchester
Major Malcolm Munthe and the Pennington Mellor Charity Trust
National Gallery of Scotland

National Maritime Museum, Greenwich
    Dr Basil Greenhill, W. W. Percival-Prescott Esq.
National Portrait Gallery
    Dr John Hayes, Robin Gibson Esq, Kai Kin Yung Esq.
National Museum of Wales
    Dr D. A. Bassett, Dr P. Cannon-Brookes, P. Rees Esq.
National Trust: Hardwick Hall
National Trust: Stourhead
    Anthony Mitchell Esq.
City Museum and Art Gallery, Plymouth
Public Record Office
Mrs P. A. Tritton, Parham Park
Walker Art Gallery, Liverpool
The Dean and Chapter of Westminster Cathedral
    Canon Oliver Kelly
Louis de Wet Esq
Simon Wingfield Digby Esq, Sherborne Castle

Bibliothèque Nationale, Paris
Kunsthistorische Museum, Vienna
'Mauritshuis', The Hague:
    Dr H. R. Hoetink
Nationalmuseum, Stockholm:
    Dr Per Bjurstrom, Dr Gorell Cavalli-Bjorkman
Rijksmuseum, Amsterdam:
    Dr J. W. Niemeijer
Royal Museum of Fine Arts, Copenhagen
V. de S Collection

Beaverbrook Foundation, Beaverbrook Art Gallery, Fredericton, New Brunswick
Cleveland Museum of Art, Ohio
E. Grosvenor Paine Esq.
Metropolitan Museum of Art, New York
Nelson-Atkins Museum of Art, Kansas City
Yale Center for British Art, New Haven
    Dr Duncan Robinson

We would also like to express our gratitude to many others who have dealt with enquiries and assisted with problems over the years. These include:
The Dowager Marchioness of Cholmondeley
Richard Allen Esq
Miss Janet Arnold
Claude Blair Esq
Miss Mary Edmond
Norman Evans Esq, Public Record Office
Mrs Daphne Foskett
Richard Green Esq.
Mrs Grace Holmes, Archivist to The Dean and Chapter of St. George's, Windsor Castle
Ronald Lightbown Esq
John Partridge Esq
Miss Lindsay Stainton, Department of Prints and Drawings, The British Museum
Maurice Tomlin Esq
Miss Hermione Waterfield

The Tudor Miniature: Mirror of an Age

ROY STRONG

PERHAPS the most famous miniature ever painted is Nicholas Hilliard's lyrical vision which we know as *The Young Man among Roses* (no. 263). Painted about 1587 it almost certainly depicts Elizabeth I's last favourite, Robert Devereux, 2nd Earl of Essex as her love-lorn swain. He leans against a tree wearing a suit of her colours of black and white, his hand symbolically placed on his heart, his figure encircled by the sinuous branches of the eglantine tree bearing its emblematic white flowers. It is an hypnotic image seemingly bearing within itself the quintessence of an age and yet we forget that it was unknown before 1910. I take this as a point of departure because the fact that we can stare at this Elizabethan miniature in a museum showcase or study it in books or in postcards has destroyed its prime role as a secret and revelatory image. Miniature painting or limning, as it was called in Tudor and Jacobean England, was an intensely private art, a unique contribution to the Renaissance unparalleled elsewhere in Europe, as unique to the court of the Tudors and early Stuarts as were the chalk drawings by the Clouets to that of the Valois dynasty.

Limning and Society

Court is the operative word because the art of limning pertained to the court from its origins. The fashion for portrait miniatures begins more or less simultaneously with the advent of the Reformation when England from the 1530's onwards went into virtual aesthetic isolation. As an art form it attained a dominance which would have been inconceivable if the links with everything that was going on in Italy had been preserved. As the century progressed limning came to occupy a role as an art form peculiarly expressive of Protestant England. When that aesthetic insularity was finally broken after 1620 limning entered a different phase with the advent of the miniature painter. On the whole thereafter it occupied a minor role in the history of painting and portraiture but for the century of the limners from about 1525 to 1620 it occupied the centre of the stage.

Until recently Tudor and Jacobean miniatures had been looked at through the eyes of collectors and connoisseurs or the historians of style. All of these approaches are, of course, valid ones but they fail to bring out the extraordinary nature of these objects and the important role that they played in the society of their age.

All the time that we look at them we need to bear in mind their original social setting, their rareness and preciousness, so difficult to recover amidst the glut of miniatures from later centuries amongst which they are so often placed; products of a period in which that art occupied a far minor role.

We are so used to seeing miniatures in serried ranks in a museum or country house showcase that their mystery has been totally destroyed for us. Destroyed too often by modern re-framing in inappropriate gilt which upsets the tonal balance.

From the outset miniatures were regarded as precious. They were put into turned ivory boxes like draughtsmen with crystals placed over them to protect them from dust in the same way that the lid prevented them from fading by exposure to light. Queen Elizabeth I we know kept hers in the innermost sanctum of the royal bedroom, each one carefully wrapped up with a label bearing the name of the sitter. The lid of Holbein's portrait of Anne of Cleves is elaborately carved in the form of a Tudor rose (no. 30) but most miniatures were kept in relatively simple boxes of a type in use right into the 1630's. The inventory of Charles I's collection spans the century of the limners and there is no doubt that what the cataloguer van der Dort is describing are the objects still in their original casing. Hornebolte's miniatures of Henry VIII from the mid-1520's which had been presented to the King by the Earl of Suffolk were in "white tournd Ivory boxes". So too was Isaac Oliver's miniature of James I's daughter Elizabeth over eighty years later listed as "in a white Ivory Box with a Christall over it".

By the 1570's, however, frames of stained ivory began to make their appearance. Perhaps the earliest of these to survive, and there seems no reason to doubt that it is contemporary, is the one containing a portrait of a Herefordshire girl, Jane Coningsby, dated 1574 (no. 63). It is turned in exactly the same way and the back is carved in a manner reminiscent of the Anne of Cleves case. Ebony frames became common by the close of the century, used to enclose the large cabinet miniatures on grounds of size alone but also utilised for smaller miniatures. This change in taste was reflective of the shadowed melancholy affected by the late Elizabethan and Jacobean ages. In Charles I's collection there is a full length of the second Earl of Essex "in a black frame", another of a lady "set in a big ebbone frame" and one of "a certein naked young mans picture to the waist . . . in a black wooddn tourn'd ebbone box with a Christall over it". All three were by Isaac Oliver.

By the 1630's miniatures even began to be framed as sets. Charles I had eight miniatures by various hands placed together into such a frame as "pictures of y^r Ma^{ts} progenitors": Henry VII, Elizabeth of York, Henry VIII, Katherine of Aragon, Anne Boleyn, Mary I, Edward VI and Elizabeth I. By that date miniatures had migrated from the bedside to the connoisseur's cabinet, a move reflective of the aesthetic revolution of the Jacobean and Caroline ages. We can evoke this ambience exactly in a surviving Caroline cabinet room, that built by Charles I's friend, William Murray, at Ham House.

The Green Closet with its allegorical ceiling by Francis Cleyn after Polidoro is a unique survival evoking the milieu of the Caroline aesthetes. Onto its green walls were banked not only small oil paintings but also miniatures by Hilliard and Oliver. Each wall had green curtains that were kept drawn over the pictures to prevent fading. Miniatures had become works of art to be collected and an acknowledged way of obtaining the King's favour was to present him with a miniature: "Item there was presented a Case with five little limned pictures to your Majesty by my Lady Killigrew to take choice thereof", reads a typical entry in the royal catalogue, "and your Majesty pleased to take one only".

A few enjoyed another, more public, existence as part of a locket or jewel. The earliest evidence that we have of a miniature being worn is in Levina Teerlinc's miniature of Catherine Grey, Lady Hertford. Painted in 1562–63 it records the Countess holding her infant child in an ambitious composition of a kind never essayed by Hilliard. The child had been conceived in the Tower into which the unfortunate Countess had been cast by Elizabeth for marrying Edward Seymour, Lord Hertford, whose miniature it must be that is suspended around her neck. The next reference is in a portrait of a lady called Lady Walsingham dated 1572 (no. 61) in which she actually holds a miniature in a jewelled locket which has a pendant pearl. This is hung at the end of a chain around her waist. The jewel has a lid and establishes the normal format for settings for miniatures, not only because the portrait likeness was intensely personal but also because the lid prevented fading. Original lockets are exceptionally rare and in this context were used as pledges of love between knight and lady, husband and wife, or as expressions of loyalty between sovereign and subject.

Sign and Symbol

This development of a symbolic role for the miniature only accelerated in the 1580's coincidentally with the cult of emblems and *imprese* which became such an essential feature of late Elizabethan and Jacobean thought, the expression of aims and ideals by way of esoteric image and motto. This accentuated the anti-naturalistic tendencies already strong in Tudor painted images. Onto the icon of rank expressed by dress, heraldry and inscription was overlaid representations of the physical world whose role was purely symbolic. The *Earl of Cumberland* (no. 216) appears as Queen's champion in allegorical star-studded armour and surcoat as he would have appeared in the tiltyard on her Accession Day. His emblematic shield proclaims he will be her challenger until earth, sun and moon pass into eclipse. In the distance a contracted view across to Westminster alludes to the mantle he inherited in the tiltyard of Whitehall Palace on November 17th 1590 when he took on the office of Champion. Twenty

years' later Lord Herbert of Cherbury (no. 273) reclines as a melancholic knight in a wood by a trickling stream in an elaborate symbolic presentation of himself in his dual role as a cavalier pursuing the *vita activa* and as a philospher seeking to practice the *vita contemplativa*.

Limnings played an extensive part in the etiquette of courtly love. That they did so depended on a platonised vision of the loved one the contemplation of whose external image was the beginning of a ladder of devotional ascent. These devotees are depicted consumed by the flames of their passion (nos. 163, 171) or with hand clasped to heart (no. 93). In one a young man has expressed his constancy by asking that he be depicted against the colour that embodied that virtue, black (no. 93). As the century draws to its close love melancholy is depicted. Oliver's gallant (no. 268) sits in a 'dump' or 'muse' with crossed arms and floppy black hat beneath a tree. Or another sitter (no. 161) with folded arms turns his eyes heavenwards while a rock and a ship amidst a stormy sea testify to his constancy.

The miniature of *Cumberland* (no. 216) establishes that many of them were conceived as commemorative. A whole series relates to the pageantry of the annual tournament held on Elizabeth I's Accession Day, when her knights tilted in her honour in allegorical guise. A similar group in the succeeding reign reflects and relates to the court masques, ladies in dresses designed by Inigo Jones or Henry, Prince of Wales *à l'antique* (no. 230) recalling his appearances in Jonson's *Barriers* of 1610 and the masque of *Oberon. The Fairy Prince* of the following year.

Limning and the cult of the Crown

One of the most striking features of the Tudor age was the accelerating cult of royalist symbols in the aftermath of the Reformation. As the century progressed and as the threats from without increased the images multiplied and at no period more forcefully than in the years leading up to the Spanish Armada. As the ideological confrontation between Protestant England and the Catholic powers moved to its dramatic climax images of the Virgin Queen multiplied into new media, medals, badges, engravings and woodcuts. At the same time miniatures of the Queen ceased to be unique objects, the result of a sitting by the monarch, but became rather images multiplied in the painter's studio and bestowed by the Queen. The gift by Elizabeth of a likeness of herself by Nicholas Hilliard must surely have been one of the ultimate accolades. That these images were generally presented unframed we know from a letter from Lord Zouche in 1598 who wrote "I would I could have as rich a box to keep it in as I esteem the favour great".

The celebrated Drake Jewel pinpoints the moment exactly when Government saw the miniature as a means of monarchical propaganda. On July 28th 1586 Sir Francis Drake's fleet returned in triumph to Plymouth after ten months pillaging Spanish colonies in the New World. On

April 2nd 1587 he set out again with orders to distress Spanish ships in their harbours, a voyage that culminated in the famous "singeing of the king of Spain's beard", when fireships destroyed much of the Spanish fleet, thus delaying the Armada for a year. Between those two dates the Queen gave Drake the miniature which he was to wear eight years later in his portrait. The jewel is of outstanding quality enamelled in white, opaque pale blue, pale green, mid-blue and with translucent enamels in other colours. The miniature within is a repetition and there are two others surviving of the same type (no. 192). Mass manufacture had for the first time set in.

By the closing decade of the reign Hilliard and his studio spent much of their time producing these royal portraits in which a rejuvenated image of the Queen, which bore no relationship to the raddled reality, was repeated and set each time into yet another arrangement of jewels and lace. Courtiers responded to the cult by expressing aspects of their devotion to her in the design of the lockets. In one (no. 205) she is celebrated as *Stella Britannis*, the Star of Britain, the front of the case being a star-burst of rubies and diamonds. In the Heneage or Armada Jewel (no. 208) this elaboration is taken to its highest pitch where the locket unfolds in layers moving through a paean in which Edmund Spenser's famous definition of the dual nature of the Queen is scrupulously observed. The exterior is her as "a most royall queene or empress", as Elizabetha Regina made visual in the proud Roman imperial profile image on the front. There she is Queen of England but on the reverse she is Governor of the Church and Defender of the Faith. Noah's ark is the traditional symbol of the Church which Elizabeth is praised in the motto for having guided safely through stormy waters. The locket opens to a vision of her as Spenser's "most vertuous and beautiful Lady", the heroine of the sonnets, epitomised in the idealised portrait of her and elaborated in the Rose enamelled on the reverse of the lid for, as the reign drew to its close, this symbolised not only the two roses of York and Lancaster that the Tudors had united, but became central to another aspect of the cult, the rose as the flower of Venus, goddess of love and beauty. We are contemplating Elizabeth in the words of the poet, John Davies, as "Beauty's Rose".

This obsession with the royal image did not die with Elizabeth. Everywhere European thought was moving towards the age of absolutism and the mystical cult of crowned heads reached new proportions as the sixteenth century turned into the next and as, in the aftermath of the terrible wars of religion, hopes centred on rulers such as Henry IV, who were built up as beings with almost superhuman powers. Elizabeth was one of these rulers in the aftermath of the Armada on whom such hopes were fastened. But we forget that the same hopes were focused also on her successor James I as he united England and Scotland and revived the ancient empire of Great Britain and assumed the leadership of protestant Europe. In fact the miniatures increase in number under James which is understandable in that he enunciated the doctrine of the Divine Right of Kings in which he sat on his throne as God's representative on earth. In this sense each miniature of James must be viewed as such a holy image.

The miniatures of the King are rarely of any brilliance of execution, for Hilliard found no inspiration in this untidy, flaccid Scot. So more and more of the miniatures are disappointing and hurried in execution or produced entirely by the workshop or feeble followers. An example of this (no. 238) charts the decline. The locket is of gold enamelled in white, opaque pale green and translucent red. The portrait is weak, not by Hilliard, although directly derived from his work. The imagery is also tired, the weary re-working of inherited symbols. The sun burst recalls the Star of Britain vision of Elizabeth and the Noah's ark we have already encountered on the Heneage Jewel. These tiny images played a role out of all proportion to their actual size. Limning seems to emerge as a fiercely nationalistic art suited to Protestant England, its monarchs and the new establishment that they created.

The sitters: from Crown to Court to City

The regal origins of this art form are central to its understanding. For the first fifty years or so miniatures remained almost exclusively a royal prerogative. Miniatures pertained to the crown, to the king and queen and to other members of the royal family or those who had married into it. The only exception to this rule was the oeuvre of Holbein who came late into the King's service as a salaried painter and who accepted commissions from outside the closed circle thus giving us an occasional glimpse of more humble members of the fabric of early Tudor society. Margaret Throckmorton (no. 29) was the wife of a country gentleman, Robert Pemberton of Pemberton in Lancashire. She had only the most distant connexions with the gilded world of the court where her family, the Throckmortons of Higham Ferrers, held only minor posts. The fact that she sat for her portrait miniature was startlingly novel in the 1530's and the stylistic evidence would indicate that it was executed before Holbein actually entered royal service in 1537.

In sharp contrast Lucas Hornebolte and his successor, Levina Teerlinc, never moved outside the Tudor family tree. We start inevitably with Henry VIII whom Hornebolte painted several times. We move on to the Queens: Catherine of Aragon (no. 6), Anne Boleyn (no. 14), or Catherine Parr, the King's sixth and last wife. So far no miniature of Henry's sister, Mary, who was married off to the decrepit Louis XII of France, has emerged, but there are two possible images of her second husband, Charles Brandon, Duke of Suffolk. His daughter, Frances, married Henry Grey, also Duke of Suffolk, and had three daughters, the celebrated blue-stocking Grey sisters, Jane, Catherine and Mary. The second,

Catherine, later to be Countess of Hertford, was painted more than once by Teerlinc (no. 38). In her cousin Mary's reign she appears as a tiny emaciated figure in a fur trimmed dress. Returning up the tree to the much-married Charles Brandon, Duke of Suffolk, there is a fourth wife, Catherine Willoughby, by whom he had two precocious boys, Henry and Charles, who were painted by Holbein. Both children were scholarly by nature, a fact alluded to in the one of Charles who has paper and pen before him. Both tragically died of the sweating sickness in 1551 at the ages of seventeen and fourteen. To these we can add miniatures of Edward VI and the young Elizabeth (no. 40) which take us on into the 1560's. Miniatures remained precious royal objects until a single event changed that: Nicholas Hilliard opening up shop in Gutter Lane off Fleet Street in the early 1570's. That was a revolution. Suddenly in the 1570's Hilliard was painting a broad spectrum of the aristocracy and gentry and as the reign progresses he extended even further out. By 1602 he was painting citizen's wives (no. 160). This huge change in the make up of the sitters enabled a window to be opened onto the faces of Elizabethan society and all this was the result of one fact, Hilliard was not, as his predecessors had been, a salaried artist in the employ of the crown. Of course, he worked for Elizabeth when she wanted him but he was not to be on the royal payroll until four years before her death. Hilliard had to make a living and for the first time anyone who could pay for a miniature was free to commission one. This simple economic fact therefore was to change the whole composition of the sitters and give us that unparalleled glimpse of the great ones of the age directly observed by him—Mary Queen of Scots, Drake, Raleigh, Bacon, Leicester, Cumberland, Essex. Isaac Oliver from the outset too accepted commissions from anyone and indeed many of his early sitters were the good citizens' wives of London in their tall hats, white stomachers and starched aprons. It was not until the middle 1590's that Oliver was patronised by the ruling classes. Up until then he was to rely for his patrons on the city.

This change went back to the abdication by the Crown of artistic patronage, the direct result of the careful husbanding of royal resources during the 1560's. Crown finances were put in order and one of the prices paid was the Queen was never, like her father, to be a direct patron of the arts. That responsibility was shifted onto the aristocracy. The policy had one disadvantage. It meant that it was difficult to control royal portraiture and from time to time government wrestled with this but to little avail. The only solution lay in a court painter with a large workshop, something to be achieved only with the advent of Van Dyck. But Gloriana's stinginess in the arts had resulted in the democratization of the miniature, thus giving us a breath-taking series of portraits which is why I have categorised the Tudor miniature as the true mirror of an age.

Limning and Reality

Why is it that after three hundred and fifty years these tiny images still exert so compulsive a hold over us? After having examined in laboratory conditions most of the few hundred that survive I can reply to that question with an answer that has all the potency of the obvious. These objects present the men and women of their age as they really were. That they do so springs from the accident of their technical tradition. A miniaturist only ever painted what he actually saw set before him. An elementary fact this may be but it accounts for the extreme power of these images, one that has a direct parallel with the sense of revelation we feel in the case of Victorian photographs. We peer through what might be described as a keyhole into Tudor and Jacobean England. The art of limning was grounded in the belief that this was an art whose aim was to record spontaneity of expression as though their subjects had been caught mid-stream in conversation which they often had. Edward Norgate, writing in the 1630's, was well aware of this when he wrote:

> "The party sitting by occasion of discourse to be sometimes in motion, and to regard you with a merry, jovial and friendly aspect, wherein you must be ready and sudden to catch at and steal your observations, and to express them with a quick and constant hand . . ."

A panel portrait or one on canvas needed processes far different, laborious ones, due to the slow drying nature of oil paint. The result by contrast is much more stiff and formal. Hilliard's rendering of James I's daughter, Elizabeth, Queen of Bohemia (no. 247) is pure enchantment, with its incipient smile and its freshness of characterization and quick detail such as the blue bell tucked into her bodice, when compared with the large formal portrait of her of the same date by Robert Peake. In addition miniatures, unlike oil paintings, have survived down to the present in the main untouched by the hands of later restorers. Always we have to accept fading due to exposure to light and the one missing ingredient is the silver and gold highlights which once shimmered giving the surface a sparkle. Age has oxidized these and we now see them blackened, a feature that can, in the case of portraits with a great deal of silver lace and jewellery, upset the balance of the original composition.

We cannot raise the dead from the grave to prove the accuracy of their physical reality but the fact the limners only painted what they saw can be corroborated occasionally by external evidence. When Hilliard painted the Earl of Cumberland in his tournament armour that armour must have been sent to the studio for it still survives, proving Hilliards accuracy in depicting it. This confirms that the costume we see in the miniatures actually existed. In those miniatures we are looking at the reality of the fabulous wardrobe of Elizabeth Tudor which must have been taken around to Hilliard and mounted onto a lay figure.

This is also the case with Oliver. We can prove this with one of his most spectacular miniatures painted in 1616, a year before he died. It is of Richard Sackville, 3rd Earl of Dorset (no. 276) a prodigal aristocrat, a family disaster, a spend-thrift and gambler who squandered a fortune and left a mountain of debt. Part of that squandering went on clothes. In 1617 an inventory was made of these and listed as item 10 we find: "one pair of Boulogne hose of scarlet and blue velvet the panes of scarlet laced all over with watchet silk silver and gold lace and the puffs of blue velvet embroidered all over with suns, moons and stars of gold". We only have to look at the trunk hose in this miniature to identify this item. The stockings also appear as "one pair of long watchet silk stockings embroidered". By 1617 the remainder of the suit which we see in the miniature had been disposed of, apart from one item that does not appear: "one pair of gloves with tops of tissue in colours embroidered with suns, moons and stars and edged with gold and silver lace".

The world of the limners came to an end more or less about 1620. Isaac Oliver died in 1617, Nicholas Hilliard two years later. Then follow in rapid succession the famous events that epitomise the aesthetic revolution that was to take the remote island of Britain into the mainstream of the European Renaissance: Inigo Jones's Whitehall Banqueting House, the commission for Rubens to paint its ceiling; the arrival of the painters Paul van Somer and Daniel Mytens, Van Dyck's first visit in 1621. Specialization also sets in. The limners of the age of Charles I, John Hoskins and Peter Oliver, were limners *only* and there is no evidence that they continued to do as their predecessors had done and run a workshop that accepted commissions as lowly as painting banners for funerals and tombs. They would have regarded that as demeaning, for the artists of the Caroline age wished to assert that their art belonged to the liberal as against mechanical arts. Limners henceforth ceased to be trades people turning their hand to tasks all across the spectrum and became instead gentlemen with intellectual pretensions linking their art to the new science of the post-Baconian era. It was an ethos very far removed from that in which Nicholas Hilliard and his antecedents had practiced and which led him to encapsulate the art of limning as one that "excelleth all other painting whatsoever . . . and is for the service of noble persons very meet, in small volumes, in private manner, for them to have the portraits and pictures of themselves, their peers, or any other foreign persons which are of interest to them". In short the century of the limners had come to its close.

The Art of Limning

V. J. MURRELL

Although it had its attractions, London in the sixteenth and early seventeenth centuries could have vied with any city in Europe for the unenviable distinction of being the most squalid, polluted, and dirty. Garbage, offal, and worse were dumped from houses and shops into the streets, which were very infrequently cleared. The new fuel, coal, was being used in fireplaces and chimneys which had been intended for burning wood and as a result the levels of sulphur and soot pollution were probably almost as high inside the houses as they were in the outer atmosphere. It is therefore hardly surprising that Hilliard and other early writers on miniature painting should appear to be almost obsessive over the cleanliness of the surroundings in which their precious art should be practised, and at a time when manners and standards of personal hygiene were very different from those to which we are accustomed today, should be equally particular over such details. Hilliard commends to the limner the most important precept of the art which is "cleanliness, and therefor fittest for gentlemen, that the practiser of limning be precisely pure and cleanly in all his doings, as in grinding his colours in place where there is neither dust nor smoke, . . . at the least let your apparel be silk, such as sheddeth least *Dust* or hairs wear nothing straight, beware you touch not your work with your fingers, or any hard thing, but with a clean pencil brush it, or with a white feather, neither breath on it, especially in cold weather, take heed of the dandruff of the head shedding from the hair, and of speaking over your work for sparkling of spittle, will never be helped if it light in the face or any part of the naked" and the painter is directed to work in a room "where neither dust, smoke, noise, nor stench may offend, a good painter hath tender senses, quiet and apt, and the colours themselves may not endure some airs, especially in the sulphurous air of sea-coal, and the gilding of goldsmiths . . .". Hilliard was perhaps the earliest artist to associate the discolouration of pigments with sulphurous pollution.

The artist had to be most particular over the lighting of his painting studio, and it must have been difficult to find a room which met Hilliard's specification in late medieval domestic buildings, the construction of which was such that each floor extended beyond the one below; an ideal arrangement for disposing of household slops into the street, but one which deprived the rooms on the lower floors of the full benefit of daylight. In his search for a room the artist would have been limited to the upper floors, especially where they overlooked an open space or garden. The room had to be more than 18 feet in length, in order that the limner should be at sufficient distance from his patron to be able to make a full-length portrait, and it had to have a very large window facing north-north-east without any obstructions to the light in the way of trees or walls. Apart from other things this room had to be furnished with a table for the artist at which to work, which had drawers in which he could store his reserve of dry pigments and other necessaries. The artist would place his easel upon this table. The easel would have an upright angled surface upon which the limner could place his work. Frequently such an easel would be supplied with drawers or shelves where the artist could arrange his shells of colour, brushes, and the tablets upon which he painted. Such an arrangement can be seen in the self-portrait by Simon Benninck of 1558. The table and easel were placed adjacent or near to the window with the light falling from the left. This was a practical arrangement, for the majority of artists were right-handed and if the light fell from the opposite side their painting hands would have cast a shadow, obscuring their minute works.

Because of the vulnerability of colours bound in gum arabic and the fine nature of their work, limners were extremely fastidious in their choice of pigments and the methods by which they were prepared for painting. A number of pigments which were acceptable in other types of painting were discarded because they were considered to be poisonous, chemically unstable, or because they were fugitive in daylight. In the sixteenth century it was no longer necessary for the artist to make his own pigments, for the majority were available in their crude form at the apothecary's shop. However, the adulteration of pigments in order to increase profits was not unknown, and it was necessary for the artist to be cautious in his purchases. Having acquired the raw pigments which were essential for the pursuit of his craft it was still necessary for the limner to prepare them to an impalpable powder, much finer than that used for other kinds of painting. Many of the pigments were prepared by grinding them with water on a flat, hard stone, using a stone muller; a long, tiring and very tedious procedure. Some pigments could not be ground because that process would reduce their brilliance. These had to be prepared by another lengthy process known as ''washing''. This entailed first crushing the pigment and then shaking it in a vessel with water, allowing the coarser pigment particles to settle before pouring off and drying the finest which remained suspended in the water. This process could be repeated up to seven times before the artist was satisfied that he had isolated the very finest of the pigment. The coarser pigment could be saved and used for oil painting. Once refined, the pigments were mixed with gum arabic and put into mussel shells ready for use. The amount of gum added to the colours was critical, for it had to be just sufficient to bind the particles together and make them adhere to the vellum. If too much gum was added the paint would become glossy and unsightly. Some pigments which tended to crack, either in the shell or on the painting, had a small amount of sugar candy (refined cane sugar) added to them. Occasionally ear wax would be added to a colour which would not lay well on the vellum. On the whole the pigments were basic and reliable. The earths such as the ochres and umbers and the minerals azurite, malachite, and lapis lazuli were used and were augmented with manufactured pigments such as white and red lead, vermilion and masticot (lead-tin yellow) and various carbon blacks. The white, ceruse, was also used and although that name was applied to various pigments at different times it seems likely that in the sixteenth century it was made by calcining a mixture of chalk and alum. Less fortunate were those pigments which relied for their colour on the staining properties of natural materials such as insects, resins and plants, for they were without exception fugitive in daylight. This group included the red lakes, pinks (yellow to brown colours) and blues, such as indigo and litmus, which are responsible for the faded appearance of so many early miniatures. The metals silver and gold were also reduced to very fine powder and used as paints.

The London brushmakers had a fine reputation, but there is evidence to suggest that some limners preferred to make their own. These pointed brushes were at that time called pencils and the hair used to make them was caliber which came from the tails of continental species of squirrel. The hairs were cut from the joints of the tail, sorted into sizes and tied into bundles with the tips of the hairs incurving. These hairs were then inserted into bird quills of appropriate diameters and then mounted on turned wooden or ivory sticks. The pencils varied considerably in size, but their common feature was that they had a full body of hair descending to a sharp point. The hairs from the last joint of the tail were used to make large pencils with splayed ends which were used when working, either to remove specks of dust from the shells of colours, or from the paint surface. The tablet upon which the limner painted his works was made by sticking the very finest parchment to a card; normally a playing card. At that time the reverse sides of playing cards were not printed with a design and were plain white. This side of the card would be prepared for attaching the parchment either by rubbing it with a stone or burnishing it with a dog's tooth mounted in a handle to remove any unevenness. The fine parchment (vellum) was then stuck to this surface with starch paste. This tablet was then placed under pressure until it was very nearly dry when it would be placed face down on a smooth stone and burnished at the back with the dog's or boar's tooth to ensure a perfect union between card and parchment. Because of the thinness of the parchment and the excellence of its attachment it has often been imagined that sixteenth century miniatures were painted directly on to card. The cyphers of the playing cards were normally left visible at the back and it is still a matter of conjecture as to whether the traditional symbolism of one of the various suits was deliberately chosen in order to reflect some attribute of the sitter portrayed. Although there often seems to be some symbolic relationship between the suit at the back of a miniature and the sitter portrayed on the front, an argument against the idea was innocently presented by Norgate when he observed that Hilliard and Oliver would have a number of tablets on hand already prepared with a flesh tone so that when they started a portrait it was only necessary to choose one of the right complexion for the sitter. On the other hand the traditional menace of the spade as a harbinger of death does seem to have been taken very seriously, for in the majority of instances when this suit was used for the backcard of an early miniature the spades have been deliberately and carefully painted over.

Having found a studio and supplied himself with desk and easel, paints and brushes, and painting tablets there were only a few more items to provide before the artist could begin to paint his portraits. It was useful to have at hand a sharp penknife or a pair of tweezers with which to remove specks of dust or hairs which might settle on the work while it was wet. A sheet of absorbent paper was essential not only to protect the vellum from the painting hand which might rest upon it, but also on which to test the flow of the pencil before applying colour. Apart from the dog's tooth used for burnishing the tablet, it was also necessary to have a weasel's or stoat's tooth mounted on a wooden handle with which to burnish small areas of gold paint. Finally, two pots of water were set at the artist's right hand; one in which to moisten the pencil before taking up colour, and the other for washing the brushes between each mixing of colour.

Hilliard's technical inventiveness assures him the place of exemplar of miniature painting at its most specialised, but before continuing to discuss his working methods it would be well to pause and consider his technical and stylistic inheritance from those 'cunning strangers' who had been enticed into service with Henry VIII. Although Hilliard claimed to have 'ever imitated' Holbein's manner of limning, it should be remembered that Holbein's miniatures were technically derivative and for the roots of the art we have to look back to Holbein's instructor in limning, Lucas Hornebolte. An examination of one of Hornebolte's first essays in portrait miniature painting, the Henry VIII at the Fitzwilliam Museum, confirms that the manner and technique of the limning were directly derived from the book illustration of the Ghent-Bruges school. In fact so great is the similarity that this might almost have been cut from the page of a book and stuck on to a piece of card.

Apart from the small modification that the parchment, which was thinner than that which was normally employed in books, had to be mounted on card, there was no technical difference between the methods employed by the Ghent-Bruges book painters and those of Lucas Hornebolte. This miniature is of especial value as a transitional work for the corners form spandrels in which are painted censing angels in touches of gold over brown ochre against a smoothly floated vermilion background. Such angels appear time after time in the borders of Flemish books, sometimes against smooth vermilion and at others against a miraculously smooth background of the pigment blue bice (azurite). This latter type of background was to become standard in portrait limning until Hilliard began to experiment with other colours. The special technique used for painting the features in this and other Hornebolte miniatures was again directly derived from the methods of the Flemish book painters and was to become standard in English limning. The area of the features was first covered with a very smooth ground of opaque pale flesh colour and the features were modelled over that using small strokes of transparent colour. Gold was used for painting jewels but was only applied in small touches over an ochre ground. This technique too derived from the *trompe l'oeil* jewels which appeared so frequently in the borders of Ghent-Bruges manuscripts. Other uses of gold were for painting the inscriptions of the blue backgrounds and the gold lines which encircled the portraits. These latter were painted over the bare vellum, a practice which continued until Hilliard's time. None of the gold paint used in these early miniatures was burnished. Although Holbein brought to the miniature his own inimitable genius as an artist and draughtsman, he worked strictly within the technical formulae established by Hornebolte, and Levina Teerlinc too worked with the same methods, although her poor draughtsmanship and her derivative compositions can only have served to debase the previously high artistic reputation of the English limning.

Hilliard's earliest miniatures of the 1570s conformed to the basic Flemish pattern and in describing his technical methods one is virtually recounting those of the earlier artists. The first stage in painting a miniature was to lay in the carnation ground. This ground was made by mixing white with toning colours in order to make a shade which matched the complexion of the sitter but was rather paler. This mixture was made to a rich consistency and then dashed quickly over the area to be occupied by the head, ensuring that the strokes overlapped well and that the paint did not begin to dry until all was laid. The carnation was then allowed to dry to a perfectly smooth even layer without a trace of brushwork. This effect was difficult to achieve and sometimes the painter was forced to remove a carnation and start again when it dried with a rough or bubbled surface. Therefore the wise artist would, like Hilliard and Oliver, have by him a stock of tablets prepared with various complexions so that he only had to choose the appropriate carnation and thus save valuable sitting time. The initial delineation of the features was carried out with a very faint red colour with the point of the pencil so that any errors in proportion could be corrected with a slightly stronger colour without any of these preparatory lines being obtrusive in the finished miniature. When the likeness had been established with these faint lines, the modelling of the features could be carried out with long hatching lines, similar to those used by engravers, the crisp hatches being overlaid with cross-hatches to simulate the kind of engraver's technique which Hilliard recommended as the pattern which should be observed in portrait limning. "Wherefor hatching with the pen in imitation of some fine well-graven portraiture of *Albrecht Durer*'s small pieces, is first to be practised and used, before one begin to *Limn*, and not to learn to limn at all, till one can Imitate the *Print* so well, as one shall not know the one from the other, that he may be able to handle the pencil point in like sort . . .".

The hair was roughed in with a transparent wash over the carnation, and was elaborated by drawing in the modelling with long sinuous lines. Once the head was delineated to the artist's satisfaction he would remove any excess carnation which extended beyond the contours of the head by wiping it off with a damp brush. If this was not removed it would mix into and sully the colours of the background and costume. The blue bice used for the backgrounds is a heavy, rather coarse pigment and difficult to work smoothly as a water-colour, so a special technique was used in applying it in two phases. First a weak mixture of the colour was used with a fine pencil to line around the contour of the figure and with the same watery mixture the whole area of background was washed in up to this line with a larger pencil. While this first layer was still quite wet a pencil would be loaded with a thick mixture of bice which was literally floated into the underlayer and which would dry to that incredibly smooth finish which is such a distinctive feature of sixteenth century limnings. Ruffs were modelled by hatching the lights and shadows with white and grey over a flat ground of off-white or pale grey. The main areas of costume were painted in much the same way, the shadows and lightenings being hatched with darker and lighter shades of the opaque middle tone which was first laid as a flat ground.

Hilliard's particular genius was for the invention of new techniques of miniature painting which would render more exactly the various textures of fabrics, the lustre of metals and the transparent beauty of precious stones. These techniques soon began to appear in his works of the 1570s and soon translated the limning from its previous role as a small portrait into something precious and jewel-like; a fitting counterpoint to the jewelled and enamelled picture box into which it was so often set.

Hilliard's fastidious attention to the rendering of textures is exemplified by his treatment of his white pigment, which he prepared in three grades, the coarsest being used for the carnation, the next for painting linen and the very finest for rendering satin. He also developed an extremely convincing method for painting the lace of ruffs. He achieved this by carefully drawing the design of the lace line for line with a brush very full of a thick mixture of white lead, virtually dribbling the paint on to the surface. When dry these lines stood up in relief as if they had been embossed on the surface, each one casting its own small shadow, thus representing the crispness of starched lace to perfection.

Hilliard was at his most inventive when it came to representing jewels. Earlier miniaturists painted pearls as flat grey circles highlighted with a touch of white. Hilliard's pearls were raised in a hemisphere of white lead, touched with the appropriate shadows, and crowned with a rounded touch of silver paint which was then burnished with a small tooth to stand as the highlight to a three-dimensional surrogate for a real pearl. Diamonds, too, were produced by using a method which reproduced something of the depth and reflective brilliance of the genuine stone. First a ground of silver paint was laid and burnished to produce a reflective ground. The cut of the stone was then drawn and shaded over this with transparent black and greys. It is sad that the beauty of Hilliard's pearls and diamonds is now so often marred by the inconstancy of the silver, which has tarnished to a jet black colour. However we can still see some of the glory of Hilliard's jewel painting in the transparent coloured stones which so often appear in his works; rubies, emeralds, sapphires, jacinths, garnets. Hilliard made these by first laying a reflective ground of burnished silver, and then modelling the shape of the jewel over that using a heated needle and turpentine resin stained with the appropriate transparent colour. The same technique served to represent the enamelled covers of picture boxes, and occasionally the transparent resin was laid over ordinary paints to represent a coloured enamel such as the George of the Garter Order. Hilliard used gold and silver paint in his miniatures with a lavishness unprecedented in the art and unlike earlier limners he burnished them so that instead of appearing as metallic coloured pigments they presented surfaces of gleaming metal. Unlike the earlier miniaturists, who painted the encircling gold lines of their works directly over the bare vellum, Hilliard painted a thicker gold line over the other colours of the miniature and then burnished it. Later in his career he adopted the practice of using an ochre ground for the line, giving added contrast and sparkle. Under magnification the calligraphic inscriptions on the backgrounds of his works can be seen to have been built up in quite thick gold before they were burnished. Hilliard's handling of the goldworks of jewellery is also very distinctive. First he would model the embossed shape of the gold using a thick ochre paint before adding the gold paint and burnishing it. Gold and silver were also used to represent armour, each being shaded with the appropriate transparent colour.

Hilliard was the first artist to challenge the convention of the plain blue background. Although he had flirted briefly with innovation in the 1570s in the Fitzwilliam portrait of a man dated 1574, when he used a brilliant green, his major break with tradition occurred in the mid-1590s when he introduced a red curtain in the background of his miniatures. At first these curtains appeared as if they had been freshly laundered, folded and ironed so that they hung in square folds, but later they were draped more loosely. Again a special technique was devised in order to express the swift but subtle transitions of light in draped satin. First the whole area of the background would be washed with a very pale watery mixture of red lake, and then, while this was still wet, a

Continued on page 25

1 MANNER OF NICHOLAS HILLIARD. Unknown Lady, 1595–1600. *Mrs P. A. Tritton, Parham Park.* (Cat. 111)

II LUCAS HORNEBOLTE.
Mary I as a Princess, 1525–29.
Private Collection. (Cat. 9)

III LUCAS HORNEBOLTE.
Catherine of Aragon, 1525–26.
The Duke of Buccleuch and Queensberry KT. (Cat. 6)

IV LUCAS HORNEBOLTE.
?Anne Boleyn, 1532–33.
The Duke of Buccleuch and Queensberry KT.
(Cat. 14)

V HANS HOLBEIN.
George Neville, Lord Abergavenny, c. 1535?
The Duke of Buccleuch and Queensberry KT. (Cat. 25)

VI HANS HOLBEIN.
?Margaret Throckmorton, Mrs Robert Pemberton,
c. 1536. *Victoria & Albert Museum.* (Cat. 29)

VII HANS HOLBEIN.
Elizabeth Grey, Lady Audley, c. 1540.
By gracious permission of Her Majesty The Queen.
(Cat. 31)

VIII HANS HOLBEIN.
Unknown Man, 1540–43.
Yale Center for British Art, New Haven.
(Cat. 36)

IX ATTRIBUTED TO LEVINA TEERLINC.
Unknown Lady, Possibly Elizabeth I as a
Princess, c. 1550.
*Yale Center for British Art,
New Haven.* (Cat. 37)

X ATTRIBUTED TO LEVINA TEERLINC.
An Elizabethan Maundy, c. 1565.
The Countess Beauchamp. (Cat. 42)

XI ATTRIBUTED TO LEVINA TEERLINC.
Catherine Grey,
Countess of Hertford, 1555–60.
Victoria & Albert Museum.
(Cat. 38)

XII NICHOLAS HILLIARD.
Francis, Duke of Anjou, 1581?
Kunsthistorisches Museum, Vienna. (Cat. 72)

XIII NICHOLAS HILLIARD.
Unknown Lady, 1572.
The Duke of Buccleuch and Queensberry KT.
(Cat. 60)

XIV NICHOLAS HILLIARD.
Unknown Lady, 1576.
Victoria & Albert Museum. (Cat. 67)

XV NICHOLAS HILLIARD.
Unknown Lady, 1590–93.
Victoria & Albert Museum. (Cat. 92)

XVI NICHOLAS HILLIARD.
Unknown Lady, c. 1590–93.
*The Duke of Buccleuch and
Queensberry KT.* (Cat. 94)

XVIII NICHOLAS HILLIARD AND ASSISTANTS. Charter authorizing Sir Walter Mildmay to found Emmanuel College, Cambridge, 11th January 1584. *Emmanuel College, Cambridge.* (Cat. 191)

XIX NICHOLAS HILLIARD.
Unknown Lady, 1602.
Victoria & Albert Museum.
(Cat. 104)

XX NICHOLAS HILLIARD.
Unknown Lady, c. 1600.
The Duke of Buccleuch and Queensberry KT. (Cat. 126)

XXI NICHOLAS HILLIARD.
Unknown Girl, 1609.
Victoria & Albert Museum on loan from the Olive Lloyd-Baker Estate. (Cat. 116)

XXII ATTRIBUTED TO JOHN DE CRITZ. Lucy Harington, Countess of Bedford as a Power of Juno in Ben Jonson's Masque, "Hymenaei", 1606.
The Trustees of the Bedford Settled Estates (Cat. 224)

XXIII ISAAC OLIVER. Edward Herbert, 1st Baron Herbert of Cherbury, 1610–14.
The Earl of Powis, Powis Castle. (Cat. 273)

XXIV ISAAC OLIVER.
Unknown Lady, 1595–1600.
The Duke of Buccleuch and Queensberry KT.
(Cat. 158)

XXV ISAAC OLIVER.
Unknown Man, c. 1610.
*Victoria & Albert Museum (Ham House
379–1948).* (Cat. 171)

thicker mixture was floated into it in the areas which were to represent shadow, the artist copying the folds of a satin curtain set up in his studio. After 1600 Hilliard developed a swifter method of achieving this effect by first floating a rich mixture of lake into the background and then, while that was still quite wet, lifting out the lights with the tip of a dry pencil.

Although Isaac Oliver adopted the majority of Hilliard's special technical effects, he used them sparingly and with greater reserve, the emphasis in his works being on realism and the expression of mood through colour and composition. However when there was a call for splendour and glitter Oliver could parade the whole range of Hilliard's decorative methods in such works as the 'Lady in masque costume' at the Mauritshuis. After Hilliard's death his jewel and drapery painting techniques had a final brief flowering in the early works of John Hoskins, during the 1620s.

Unlike most types of painting, limning was a very graphic art, closely related to drawing or printmaking, as Hilliard observed, the form being produced by making strokes with the point of the pencil. This graphic brushwork is always visible in the features of the sitters and because of the individuality of each artist's hand is a valuable aid to attribution. On close study it is apparent that the diversity of handling is very wide indeed. The features of Hornebolte's sitters appear to be bathed in soft diffused daylight with no strong transitions of light and shade. In order to achieve that effect he modelled the features over the carnation with short rather random hatches of pale red and grey. On the other hand, Holbein's treatment was more formal, the modelling which suggests the interior forms of the features being closely associated with crisp, firm contours. Although his modelling method is evident in the miniatures it can be seen more clearly in his portrait drawings, especially in those which remain unfinished. In these drawings it can be clearly seen that Holbein's method was to begin by modelling very faintly the interior forms of the features, gradually working towards the turning planes at the outer edges of the head and there establishing those firm contours, every inflection of which relates to the interior modelling. In his miniatures Holbein achieved this by using long, faint hatches which strictly relate to the interior modelling of the head and which intensify in tone as they approach contours of form. Teerlinc's modelling of the features is looser and more impressionistic than that of any other English limner, the technique being very similar to that which her father, Simon Benninck, used in his self-portrait. This manner of limning is quite unlike any other for it is carried out with the side of the pencil rather than the point. The flesh tones and shadows were laid on in transparent broad washes, with only the occasional hatched accent. When Hilliard wrote that he had always imitated Holbein's manner of limning it is evident that he meant that he had imitated Holbein's linearism, for their works had little else in common. Hilliard's linearism was, however, quite different from that of Holbein and probably was the result of his misunderstanding of the latter's working methods. Where

Holbein had arrived at his contours through a careful study of the internal forms, Hilliard worked in reverse starting with a carefully drawn outline and then inserting the internal forms into that framework using long hatches, often crossed, in the manner of the engraver. The result is that Hilliard's heads appear flatter because the outlines lack relationship to the interior modelling. Laurence Hilliard lacked the confidence as a draughtsman to work in his father's bold decorative manner and the features of his sitters are modelled in a weak stippling technique, while Roland Lockey, who was infinitely more talented, worked in a rough but vigorous hatching technique derived from, but not imitative of, Hilliard's manner. Isaac Oliver's brushwork was more varied and inventive than that of any other miniaturist before or since. In his early works modelled in heavy *chiaroscuro* he used broad hatches very densely grouped and startlingly bold in comparison with anything which had gone before. At the same time he could adopt a sensitive dotted stipple in such works as the two young girls in the Victoria and Albert Museum and the Woman, aged 30 in 1587 in the Collection of the Duke of Buccleuch. When Oliver wished to repress the evidence of the brushwork in miniatures such as the so-called "Frances Howard" in the Victoria and Albert Museum he could work in faint long and controlled hatches which were even finer than Hilliard's. Occasionally he would produce something quite unique, such as the *sfumato* "Head of Christ" in the Victoria and Albert Museum which is completely modelled in soft dotted stipples. Much of his latter work is characterised by thin, wiry hatches which are often lengthened into lines defining the turning edges of forms. The effect is one of nervousness and sensitivity. Although in his late works he could sometimes return to a rugged broad hatching in male portraits such as the Dr Donne at Windsor, in the main his technique was that which was part of his patrimony to Peter Oliver. The features in these late works are modelled very closely over the carnation in soft blended hatches of colour in which all sudden transitions of tone are carefully removed by constant reworking and by the addition of small amounts of white to the colours.

It is quite evident that Oliver's late technique, in which so much time and attention was paid to the soft modelling of the features, was the basis for Norgate's description of the sittings for a portrait miniature. One must assume that artists with more perfunctory face painting methods, such as Hilliard, would have taken far less time to complete a limning. The first sitting, which took from 2 to 4 hours, depending one presumes upon the speed of the artist and the patience of the sitter, was almost entirely concerned with the features and hair. After the artist had faintly drawn the main lines of the features with a very faint rose colour and had marked the position of areas of shadow, he could continue with a stronger colour to sketch in the pose of the figure. After this he would begin to dead-colour the features. This dead-colouring constituted the first broad working of the flesh tones, boldly hatched in with a fairly large pencil "not caring to be exact and Curious, but rather bold and judicious". The idea was to achieve a faintly painted likeness of the sitter which, although it would not stand close inspection, would appear satisfactory at a little distance. This work had to be advanced evenly so that at no time did one part of the features appear to be more finished than another. At the end of the sitting the middle tone of the hair could be broadly washed in. The second sitting of 6 to 8 hours, a whole day's work, must have been extremely tedious for the sitter. The first 2 hours were concentrated on the features, using a smaller pencil to close up the gaps and to soften any sudden tonal transitions. After this the artist would lay in the background and the basic ground tones for the ruff and the costume. When the intense colour of the background had been added the previous work on the face would appear pallid and dead, and the remainder of this sitting would be occupied with working over the features again, deepening the tones and intensifying the shadows. The basic floating of the hair would also be elaborated by hatching the shadows with a darker colour and adding such opaque heightenings which were necessary. By this time the exhausted sitter could be politely dismissed, and the artist would continue to polish and close up those parts of his work which did not require faithful observation from nature. The third and last sitting would last for 2 or 3 hours and was devoted first to the modelling with darker and lighter touches over their respective grounds of the ruff and the costume. Further attention would be paid to the features, deepening the shadows and closing up any imperfections. Lastly the special techniques for reproducing the gold, jewels and metals worn by the sitter would be introduced. The final sitting was then at an end, but no doubt the limner would have retained the miniature in order to write and burnish the gold inscription, to paint the gold line around its edge, to cut the oval from the rectangular tablet upon which he had worked, and to arrange the manufacture of its crystal glass cover and the locket or frame into which it would be set.

Bibliography

Age of Shakespeare, Whitworth, 1964. *The Age of Shakespeare*, Whitworth Art Gallery, University of Manchester, 1964.

Auerbach, *Hilliard*. Erna Auerbach, *Nicholas Hilliard*, London, 1961.

Auerbach, *Tudor Artists*. Erna Auerbach, *Tudor Artists*, London, 1954.

British Portraits, R.A. 1956. British Portraits, Royal Academy, 1956/7.

Chamberlain, *Holbein*, 1913. Arthur B. Chamberlain, *Hans Holbein the Younger*, London, 1913.

Edinburgh, 1975. *A Kind of Gentle Painting, An Exhibition of miniaturists by the court artists Nicholas Hilliard and Isaac Oliver*, Scottish Arts Council Exhibition, Edinburgh, 1975.

Foster, *Catalogue*, 1921. J. J. Foster, *A Catalogue of Miniatures, the property of His Grace the Duke of Northumberland*, London, 1921.

Ganz, *Holbein*, Paul Ganz, *The Paintings of Hans Holbein*, London, 1950.

Goulding, *Welbeck*. Richard W. Goulding, "The Welbeck Miniatures belonging to His Grace the Duke of Portland", *Walpole Society*, IV, 1916.

Hind, *Engraving*, I. Arthur M. Hind, *Engraving in England in the Sixteenth and Seventeenth Centuries*, I, *The Tudors*, Cambridge U.P., 1953.

Hind, *Engraving*, II. Arthur M. Hind, *Engraving in England in the Sixteenth and Seventeenth Centuries*, II, *The Reign of James I*, Cambridge U.P., 1955.

Holbein, Queen's Gallery, 1978. *Holbein and the Court of Henry VIII*, Queen's Gallery, 1978/9.

Holbein, R.A., 1950. *Catalogue of the Exhibition of Works by Holbein and Other Masters of the 16th and 17th Centuries*, Royal Academy, 1950/1.

Kennedy, *Buccleuch*. H. A. Kennedy, *Early English Portrait Miniatures in the Collection of the Duke of Buccleuch*, ed. C. Holmes, The Studio, 1917.

Long, *British Miniaturists*, 1929. Basil S. Long, *British Miniaturists 1520–1860*, London, 1929.

Millar, *Walpole Society* XXXVII, 1960. Oliver Millar, "Abraham van der Doort's Catalogue of the Collections of Charles I", *Walpole Society*, XXXVII, 1960.

Millar, *Walpole Society*, XLII, 1972. Oliver Millar, "The Inventories and Valuations of the King's Goods 1649/51", *Walpole Society*, XLII, 1970/72.

O'Donoghue, *Catalogue*, 1894. F. M. O'Donoghue, *A Descriptive and Classified Catalogue of Portraits of Queen Elizabeth*, London, 1894.

Parker, *Holbein*, 1945. K. T. Parker, *The Drawings of Hans Holbein in the Collection of H.M. the King at Windsor Castle*, London, 1945.

Pope-Hennessy, Lecture, 1949. John Pope-Hennessy, *A Lecture on Nicholas Hilliard*, London, 1949.

Princely Magnificence, 1980. *Princely Magnificence, Court Jewels of the Renaissance*, 1500–1620, Victoria and Albert Museum, 1980.

Queen's Pictures, 1977. *The Queen's Pictures*, Queen's Gallery, 1977.

Reynolds, *Connoisseur's Complete Period Guides*, 1968. Graham Reynolds, "Portrait Miniatures", *The Connoisseur's Complete Period Guides*, ed. R. Edwards and L. G. G. Ramsay, London, 1968, pp. 189–229.

Reynolds, *Miniatures*. Graham Reynolds, *English Portrait Miniatures*, London, 1952.

Reynolds, *Walpole Society*, XXXIV, 1958. Graham Reynolds, "Portraits by Nicholas Hilliard and his Assistants of King James I and his Family", *Walpole Society*, XXXIV, 1952/4, pp. 14–26.

Strong, *Hilliard*. Roy Strong, *Nicholas Hilliard*, London, 1975.

Strong, *The English Icon*. Roy Strong, *The English Icon. Elizabethan and Jacobean Portraiture*, London, 1969.

Strong, *Portraits of Queen Elizabeth I*. Roy Strong, *Portraits of Queen Elizabeth I*, Oxford, 1963.

Strong, *The Cult of Elizabeth*. Roy Strong, *The Cult of Elizabeth*, London, 1977.

Strong, *Tudor and Jacobean*. Roy Strong, *Tudor and Jacobean Portraits*, National Portrait Gallery, London, 1969.

Vertue, *Notebooks*. *Vertue Notebooks*, Walpole Society, XVIII, XX, XXIV, XXVI, XXIX, XXX, 1930–55.

V & A., 1947. Graham Reynolds, *Nicholas Hilliard and Isaac Oliver. An Exhibition to commemorate the 400th Anniversary of the birth of Nicholas Hilliard*, Victoria & Albert Museum, 1947.

Walpole, *Anecdotes*, ed. Wornum, 1849. Horace Walpole, *Anecdotes of Painting in England*, ed. James Dallaway and R. N. Wornum, London, 1849.

Williamson, *Catalogue*, 1906. G. C. Williamson, *Catalogue of the Miniatures in the Possession of J. Pierpont Morgan*, 1906.

Winter, *Elizabethan Miniatures*. Carl Winter, *Elizabethan Miniatures*, London, 1943.

Technique and Practice: A display of limner's tools and materials

II

This display has mainly been reconstructed from contemporary documentary sources, drawing heavily on the British Library Manuscript Harl.6376. (vii)

(a) Central to the display is the portable paint box-cum-easel illustrated in Harl. 6376.

(b) Although the miniature set up in the easel-lid of the paint box is not contemporaneous with the other paintings in this exhibition it does illustrate the timeless technique of faintly drawing the first outlines of the features over the carnation. It also shows the miniature at a stage before the oval was cut from the rectangular tablet.

SAMUEL COOPER

I Barbara Villiers, Duchess of Cleveland, c. 1665.

Victoria & Albert Museum (446–1892)
Vellum stuck to prepared card, 95 × 69 mm, $3\frac{3}{4} \times 2\frac{11}{16}$ in.

This miniature came from a pocket-book containing loose finished and unfinished miniatures by Susanna Penelope Rosse and unfinished miniatures by Samuel Cooper.

LITERATURE: Graham Reynolds, *Samuel Cooper's Pocket-Book*, 1975.

(c) Within and around the portable paint box are mussel shells smeared with pigments ground with gum arabic ready for painting portrait miniatures.

(d) Pencils for limning are displayed both inside the painting box on the spike provided for them, and at the right of the box. These pencils are made from dark squirrel hair set in bird quills of various sizes and mounted on wooden sticks.

(e) Beside the box there is a concave circular palette made of mother of pearl.

(f) The materials which were used in constructing the painting tablet are displayed together; the thin vellum and the playing card to which it was attached.

Playing Cards

British Museum, Department of Prints and Drawings (Queen of Spades, 1874–11–14–156, King of Hearts, 1874–11–14–137)

(g) Two burnishers are displayed, mounted on wooden sticks. The smaller is the canine tooth of a stoat for burnishing small areas of gold. The larger is the canine tooth of a large dog which would have been used for burnishing larger areas of gold and the vellum and card tablets.

NICHOLAS HILLIARD

II Unknown Lady, 1575–80

Victoria & Albert Museum (P.8–1947)
Vellum stuck to a playing card with three spades showing at the reverse, oval, 39 × 32.5 mm, $1\frac{9}{16} \times 1\frac{9}{32}$ in.

Both Reynolds and Auerbach date this miniature c. 1580, but the small ruff and closely dressed hair are more typical of the years before 1580. Federigo Zuccaro's drawing of Elizabeth I dated 1575 is a very close parallel for dress (Strong, *The English Icon*, p. 164 (108)) as are a number of ladies by Gower (e.g. *ibid*, p. 174 (121)). The oval shape, however, first appears in 1577 and the miniature could have been painted in France.

V. J. Murrell suggests that this is not, as has been assumed, an abandoned miniature but probably a demonstration piece kept in the studio. The evidence for this is, in particular, the carelessness in the preparation of the vellum which has been crudely trimmed and fails to reach the upper edge of the playing card upon which it has been mounted. This latter would have obviated its possibility as a finished portrait. Whether this is so or not the miniature gives us a vivid insight into Hilliard's working methods of the late 1570's. It represents a state of completion which would probably have been achieved during the second sitting. The modelling of the features over the carnation ground in transparent hatches of red and brown is not completed. The hair has been loosely washed over the carnation to indicate its disposition, but it awaits more detailed linear treatment. The ruff is almost complete; worked up with transparent grey over a white ground, and its lace raised in thick white. The background has been taken only so far as the first thin wash of blue bice, and awaits the second, thick floating of that colour which would result in the dense, smooth and brilliant blue which was typical of sixteenth-century miniatures. At this stage the costume has been indicated with dark lines of brown and black over the vellum, below which there are faint signs of graphite underdrawing.

COLLECTIONS: Bequeathed by E. Peter Jones, 1948, previous history unknown but conceivably this is the miniature recorded at Strawberry Hill: 'A lady's head, by Hilliard, unfinished: bought at Mr Lovibonde's' (*Description of the villa at Strawberry Hill*, 1774, p. 22).

LITERATURE: Auerbach, *Hilliard*, p. 85, pl. 45, 294 (41).

ANONYMOUS

III *A very proper treatise, wherein is briefly sett forthe the arte of Limming, etc.*

Printed by Richard Tottill, 1573. Fol. xii.
British Library. (1044.H.38.)
Printed on paper.

Apart from its present interest as the first English printed book on an art subject it stimulated a great deal of interest in the sixteenth century, six editions being printed by 1615. Unlike many early manuscripts it is an instruction manual, rather than a mere collection of recipes. Although the subject matter is illumination rather than portrait limning many of the techniques are similar, and it is a useful guide to the transitional technical period which saw the emergence of the portrait limning for which there is no other documentation. Folio xii is of particular interest because it lists all the materials used in the art which for the most part were available from the apothecary's shop.

LITERATURE: *The Art of Limming* (facsimile), 1932.
The Arte of Limming (facsimile), 1977.

NICHOLAS HILLIARD

IV **Unknown Lady**, c. 1590–93

> *The Fitzwilliam Museum, Cambridge (PD.209–1961)*
> Vellum which has been relaid on modern card, rectangular, 182 × 122 mm, 7⅛ × 4¹³⁄₁₆ in.

Hilliard's only surviving large full-length miniature of a lady, albeit unfinished. This miniature is of particular interest as the only surviving incomplete full-length miniature by Hilliard and demonstrates his somewhat erratic approach to the finishing of such large works. The features and hair have been taken to an advanced stage, whereas the white dress and ruff are only partly worked up in detail. On the other hand the velvet curtain background has been finished and at that stage the work has been abandoned either at the whim of the artist or the sitter. The miniature has suffered considerably from flaking and the restoration of the costume.

Initially the full-length concept must spring from Gheeraerts and two full-lengths of ladies in white dresses formerly at Ditchley are close parallels (Strong, *The English Icon*, pp. 295–6 (297–8)). The pose of tucking the hand behind is repeated in Segar's portrait of Lady Essex, c. 1590 (*ibid.*, p. 222 (183)). Reynolds and Auerbach date the miniature c. 1590 and the hair is painted in the pre-1593 free manner, thus giving us a tighter dating. All Hilliard's large-scale miniatures are of sitters of exceptional wealth and social status. The lady would have been of the rank, for instance, of the Countess of Essex.

COLLECTIONS: Dr Louis C. G. Clarke; bequeathed to the Fitzwilliam Museum, 1961.

LITERATURE: Auerbach, *Hilliard*, pp. 128–32, pl. 99, 305 (99).

IV

UNKNOWN ARTIST, SEVENTEENTH CENTURY

V **Hans Holbein, after a self-portrait**

> *The Duke of Buccleuch and Queensberry KT*
> Vellum stuck to card, painted in tempera or oil.
> 42 mm, 1⅝ in. diameter.

There are a number of versions of this miniature including two more in the collection of the Duke of Buccleuch, one in the Wallace Collection, one which was until recently in the Mayer van den Bergh Museum, Antwerp, and another in oil in the collection of G. H. A. Clowes, Indianapolis. The likeness is confirmed by a self-portrait drawing in the Uffizi. The only version which can be claimed to have been painted during or very shortly after Holbein's life-time is that in the Wallace Collection which Graham Reynolds has recently discussed in detail and has described as a portrait of Holbein by Lucas Hornebolte (Wallace Collection Catalogue of Miniatures, 1980, pp. 33–39). There is no doubt that Reynolds was correct in attributing the miniature to Hornebolte, but it is also evident that it was not a portrait of Holbein by Hornebolte but a copy by Hornebolte after a lost self-portrait by Holbein. The evidence for this is that we know that Holbein was left-handed as is demonstrated by his drawings. However, the

VI

As the woodcut gradually replaced the illuminated book, illuminators had to develop other lines, of which the portrait miniature was a logical development. Benninck's self-portrait is important evidence of this phase and he was working producing detailed portrait miniatures in the 1520's. Paul Wescher in 1946 published a portrait of a monk sitting in a room holding his prayer book and what very reasonably is an earlier self-portrait dated 1525, in the Louvre.

Benninck has depicted himself, at the age of 75, tense, tired and hermit-like seated at his work easel onto which is pinned the beginnings of a miniature of the Virgin and Child. A window gives onto a view of a house and garden. The form of the easel is of interest. Set up on a table, it is slanted at the usual angle but has a series of racks built onto it at the left for holding colours and brushes.

Although this miniature belongs to the history of portrait miniatures in the Low Countries, it is crucial evidence as the work of Levina Teerlinc's father. A comparison with Teerlinc's Catherine Grey (no. 38) reveals the same thin washing technique. His daughter never inherited her father's powers as a draughtsman but she must be the vital link that binds Nicholas Hilliard in a line of descent from the Ghent-Bruges School.

INSCRIBED: *Below: SIMŌ . BINNIK . ALEXĀDRI. Fˢ | SEIPSV . PĪGERAT . ANO. AETATIS 75 | 1558*

COLLECTIONS: Acquired at some date by George Salting and passed with his collection to the V.&A., 1910.

LITERATURE: W. H. J. Weale, *Burlington Magazine*, VIII, 1906, pp. 355–57.
P. Durrieu, *La Miniature Flamande*, 1927, pl. 87, fig. 4.
T. H. Colding, *Aspects of Miniature Painting*, 1955, fig. 101.
Collection Lehman de New York, Musée de l'Orangerie, Paris, 1957 (150).
Paul Wescher, "Sanders and Simon Bening and Gerard Horenbout", *Art Quarterly*, IX, 1946, pp. 207–208.

Wallace Collection miniature and the other versions depict a right-handed artist. These versions therefore derive from a mirror-image of a left-handed artist; a self-portrait in fact. Although the original may have been an easel painting, and in the portrait we are denied a glimpse of the painting upon which he is working, the shortness of the pencil which he holds in his hand suggests a miniature. The background has been much restored.

COLLECTIONS: Part of the collection formed by Walter Francis, 5th Duke of Buccleuch.

LITERATURE: Kennedy, *Buccleuch*.

SIMON BENNINCK

VI Self-portrait, aged 75 in 1558

Victoria & Albert Museum (P.159–1910)
Vellum stuck to an oak panel, rectangular,
86 × 58 mm, $3\frac{3}{8} \times 2\frac{1}{4}$ in.

Two versions exist of the self-portrait, the second being in the Lehman Collection (Metropolitan Museum of Art, New York). Both are autographed and signed and technical examination side by side would be the only way of establishing which was the *ad vivum* portrait and which the repetition. Technical examination of the V & A's version revealed nothing which would suggest that it was the repetition. The main variation is that the Lehman version does not include the Gothic spandrels and thus must be identical with that included in a still-life painting by Frans Francken, dated 1619, now in the Rubenshuis, Antwerp (see S. Speth-Holterhoff, *Les Peintres Flamandes de Cabinet d'Amateurs au XVIIᵉ Siècle*, Brussels, 1957, p. 69, pl. 9, 10).

ANONYMOUS AND HENRY GYLES

VII *The Art of Limning either by the Life Landscape or Histories.*

The first part written before 1660, pp. 10–11.
British Library, (Harl. 6376.)
Manuscript on paper.

Sometimes described as a plagiarism of Norgate's first treatise (no. VIII) with additions, and once ascribed to Henry Gyles in its entirety, the real importance of this manuscript has been previously overlooked. There is no doubt that the latter part of the manuscript was written by Henry Gyles (1645–1709), the glass-painter of York. However, the earlier sections of the work on limning and an original dissertation on oil painting are written in a different hand, and the date 1664 is interposed between this section of the manuscript and the latter which was written by Gyles. Although the first part of the manuscript on limning relies for its structure and much of its wording on Norgate, the original parts were written by an artist who had worked in Hilliard's studio, who was able to comment on that artist's methods with the intimacy of a pupil and who recorded some techniques used by the master which did not appear in his own treatise or in either of those written by Norgate. Moreover his own comments on techniques show him to have been a very practised professional. There is some evidence to suggest that the sections on miniature and oil painting *may* have been written by John Hoskins, although the arguments are too lengthy to include here. However it is of interest to note that these earlier sections of the manuscript terminate with the date 1664, which is not written in the author's hand. John Hoskins died in 1664. Whatever conclusion may be reached on the authorship of the first part of this manuscript, it cannot possibly have been written by Gyles, who was born 26 years after the death of Hilliard and, because in a number of passages it quotes *verbatim* entries from both Hilliard and Norgate, that it was compiled by a very privileged person who had access to both Hilliard's and Norgate's manuscripts. The author's practicality is evidenced by his shrewd criticisms of certain methods suggested by the earlier writers. On page 10 there are instructions for making a 'Pocket Deske', a travelling paint box-cum-easel, illustrated with a rough sketch. Its purpose was for taking portraits in the sitter's house.

COLLECTIONS: Belonged to Henry Gyles in 1702, when it was lent to Sir John Middleton; sold to Parliament by the Countess of Oxford and her daughter, the Duchess of Portland, 1753.

LITERATURE: Martin Hardie (ed.), Edward Norgate, *Miniatura or the Art of Limning*, 1919.
R. D. Harley, *Artists' Pigments c. 1600–1835*, 1970.
J. Murdoch, J. Murrell, P. Noon, R. Strong, *The English Miniature*, 1981.

EDWARD NORGATE

VIII *An exact & Compendious Discours concerning the Art of Miniatura or Limning, the names, Nature and proparties of the Coullours, the orders to be observed in preparing & using them both for Picture by the Life, Landscape & Historyes.*

17th century. ff.10, p. 18.
British Library, (Harl. 6000.)
Manuscript on paper.

This manuscript, the original of which was written in c. 1620 at the behest of Sir Theodore Turquet de Mayerne, was the earlier of Norgate's two treatises. It went astray and was plagiarised several times and it was not until 1648 that Norgate consulted his earlier notes and wrote a second version dedicated to the Earl of Arundel. Norgate, an amateur artist himself, had an extremely inquiring mind and the text proves that he was no stranger to the studios of Hilliard and Oliver. Many of Hilliard's techniques, which he had omitted from his own treatise were recorded for the first time by Norgate. On fol. 10, p. 18 Norgate recounts Hilliard's method for preventing the tarnishing of silver paint opposite the marginal note "ffor the making of Liquid Silver". The passage is transcribed as follows: "Only take this observacon, that when your Silver eyther with Long Keeping or Moystures of the Ayre will become

starved, tarnished, and rustie, yow must to prevent this inconvenience before yow lay your Silver, Lay or cover over the place with a little *Juice of Garlicke*, which will keepe it ever fayre and bright, and this Secret I had from *Mr Hilliard*."

COLLECTIONS: Possibly in the collection of George Vertue; sold to Parliament by the Countess of Oxford and her daughter, the Duchess of Portland, 1753.

LITERATURE: Philip Norman (ed.), "Nicholas Hilliard's Treatise Concerning 'the Arte of Limning', with Introduction and Notes by Philip Norman LL.D.", *Walpole Society*, I (1911–12).
R. D. Harley, *Artists' Pigments c. 1600–1835*, 1970.
J. Murdoch, J. Murrell, P. Noon, R. Strong, *The English Miniature*, 1981.
M. K. Talley, *Portrait Painting in England: Studies in the Technical Literature before 1700*, 1981.
Martin Hardie (ed.), Edward Norgate, *Miniatura or the Art of Limning*, 1919.

NICHOLAS HILLIARD

IX *A Treatise Concerning the Arte of Limning.*

A copy of Hilliard's lost original treatise of c. 1600 by an unknown scribe made in 1624, to which has been appended a section described as "A more compendious discourse concerning ye art of liming", probably derived from Edward Norgate's first manuscript on the techniques of portrait miniature painting which was written in c. 1620, ff.8v–9r.
Edinburgh University Library (MS La.III. 174.)
Manuscript on paper.

The earlier part of this manuscript which, from internal evidence, was certainly copied from Hilliard's original notes for a manual on portrait miniature painting is of great importance for not only is it the earliest work on miniature painting, but it also reveals the attitudes and working methods of one of the masters of the art. Hilliard wrote his manuscript at the request of Richard Haydocke who, in the introduction to his *A Tracte containing the Artes of curious Paintinge Carvinge & Buildinge* (Oxfod, 1598), a translation of Lomazzo's *Trattato dell'arte della pittura* (Milan, 1584), mentioned that he had prevailed upon Hilliard to write a treatise on limning. Hilliard's brief excursion into the literatue of art was evidently a failure. His manuscript had nothing of the order and logical development of those of Edward Norgate, which were written in c. 1620 and 1648, and is a rambling document which ends suddenly and impatiently with a dismissive *vale*, and then re-opens with a series of brief notes on subjects which Hilliard had evidently forgotten to include in the main text. Haydocke's enthusiastic expectation was not realized, and the work was never completed nor published.

At the left folio 8 verso is exposed, and in the lower third opposite the marginal note "Blewes", there is a section devoted to blue pigments which were used for limning which is transcribed as follows: "Blewes for Limning the darkest and highest Blewe is Ultermaryne of Venice of the best, I have payed iii s viii d a Carrett which is but fower graines, xi£ x s the ounce, and the worst which is but badd will cost ii s vi d the Carret vii £ x s the ounce. In steed wherof wee use smalt of the best, blewe byces of divers sorts, some paler then other, some of seaven or six degrees one above another. Theise may be grinded, but better broken lyke Ammel in a stone morter of flint excelent smouthe, with a pestel of fflint o Aggat well stirred till it be fine with gume watter only, and washed, soe have yo many sorts, and all good, shadowinge blews are Litmouse and Indy Blewe, and flory, theese need no washing, nor litmouse any grinding, but steeped in lee of sope ashes, use gume at discretion as aforsaid."

COLLECTIONS: George Vertue: Strawberry Hill after 1757; Patrick Fraser Tytler, 1842; David Laing.

LITERATURE: Horace Walpole, *Anecdotes*.

Philip Norman (ed.) "Nicholas Hilliard's Treatise Concerning 'The Arte of Limning', with Introduction and Notes by Philip Norman, LL.D.", *Walpole Society*, I (1911–12).

Martin Hardie (ed.), Edward Norgate, *Miniatura*, 1919.

Auerbach, *Hilliard*.

John Pope-Hennessy, *Lecture*, 1949.

John Pope-Hennessy, "Nicholas Hilliard and Mannerist Art Theory", *J.W.C.I.*, 1943.

Rosamund D. Harley, *Artists' Pigments c. 1600–1835*, 1970.

R. K. R. Thornton and T. G. S. Cain (ed.), Nicholas Hilliard, *The Arte of Limning*, 1981.

J. Murdoch, J. Murrell, P. Noon, R. Strong, *The English Miniature*, 1981.

M. K. Talley, *Portrait Painting in England: Studies in the Technical Literature before 1700*, 1981.

JOHN GWILLIM

X *The way how to lymme & howe thow shalt lay thy colours & make syse for lymminge or to cowche thy gold upon velome or parchement taken out of a booke of ye righte honourable Oliver Lorde St. John of Bletsho, in comitat: Bedforde.*

Written before 1582, f.53.
Victoria & Albert Museum Library
Manuscript on paper.

The title above is misleading for it only refers to the first section of the work devoted to manuscript illumination. The work is a collection from various sources on different methods of painting. Apart from illumination, it includes sections on panel painting, washing on paper (a technique using transparent colours, often employed for tinting prints and maps), painting wood sculpture and gilding on timber, staining pictures on taffeta or satin for use as hangings, and instructions for producing the formalized colouring of heraldic emblems.

The importance of this manuscript is that it includes information on many, but not all, of the variety of activities which would have been expected of a painter (a member of the Painter-Stainers' Company) in the sixteenth century.

From handwriting comparison it is quite certain that this manuscript is an early notebook of the John Gwillim, Rouge Croix pursuivant at arms, whose *A Display of Heraldrie* was published in 1610. Gwillim's manuscript upon which the book was based is in the British Library.

Fol. 53 contains a list of pigments and gums which were available in the late sixteenth century, together with their prices. The page is transcribed as follows:

The prises of all coloures used in the arte of payntinge.

White leade	1.lb		iii.d
Vermilion	1.lb	v.s	
Green byse	1.lb	v.s	
Blewe byse	1.lb	vi.s	viii
Verdigrese	1.lb	iii.s	
Yealowe orkament	1.lb		xii.d
Generall	1.lb	iii.s	iiii.d
Lampeblacke	1.lb	ii.s	
Masticotte	1.lb	vi.s	viii.d
Sinop. Toppes	1.lb	v.s	
Sinop. Lake	1.lb	x.s	
Ceruse	1.lb		xii.d
Red Orkament	1.lb		viii.d
Lytmose	1.lb		xii.d
Rosette	1.lb		xvi.d
Inde Blewe	1.lb	iiii.s	
Smalte	1.lb		
Sape greene	1.lb		vi.d
Red leade	1.lb		iiii.d
Verditer	1.lb	vi.s	viii.d
Gomme Arabicke	1.lb		xii.d
Gomme Alkanet	1.lb	iii.s	iiii.d

COLLECTIONS: Sir George Nayler, Garter King of Arms (1764?–1831); sold Sotheby 1832; Sir Thomas Phillips; belonged to T. Thorp in 1935.

LITERATURE: R. D. Harley, *Artists' Pigments c. 1600–1835*, 1970.

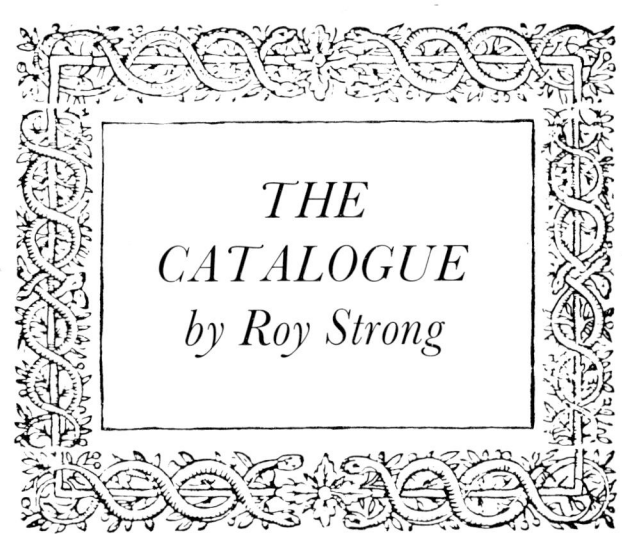

THE
CATALOGUE
by Roy Strong

Origins: Lucas Hornebolte, c. 1490/5–1544

c. 1490/5. Born. Trained in his father, Gerard Hornebolte's workshop

1525. September. First appearance in the royal accounts, by which time he was in England. He received an annuity of £62. 10s. p.a., until his death

1531. Specifically referred to as King's Painter

1534. 22nd June. Grant for life of the post of King's Painter

1544. Death of Lucas Hornebolte

LUCAS HORNEBOLTE came with his father and his sister, Susanna, to England in the middle of the 1520s. The portrait miniatures begin with a suddenness at precisely that date with a series of Henry VIII and his first Queen, Catherine of Aragon (nos. 5, 6). The family came from Ghent and was, with the Bennincks, the leading exponent of the Ghent-Bruges school of illuminators. In the case of the Tudor court their arrival needs to be placed into the perspective of a pattern of patronage which stretched back to the accession of Henry VII in 1485, namely a desire by the early Tudors to emulate the court of Burgundy. This motive cut right across the arts from architecture to music, from literature to painting.

The role of an artist at the Tudor court was never a narrow one. Gerard, the father, had been court painter to Margaret of Austria, Regent of the Netherlands. He was famous as an illuminator, having contributed to two of the most celebrated manuscripts of the period, the *Sforza Book of Hours* and the *Grimani Breviary*, but he is known to have run an atelier painting panel pictures besides providing designs for the decorative arts. Items so far attributed to him in England are all manuscripts (no. 2) of which the two most important are an *Epistolary* and *Lectionary* for Cardinal Wolsey.

We owe to Carel van Mander the fact that Lucas painted portrait miniatures for he records that he taught Holbein. This cannot mean that this was the only activity that Lucas pursued, but it is the only documented one. The annuity granted to him by Henry VIII is so huge that he must have occupied the key position as court painter for a period of almost twenty years. As an annuity would automatically rule out itemized accounts we are left with conjecture as to what precisely that other work was. On the basis of what his father did in the Low Countries his field of activity cannot have been a circumscribed one. It must have included panel painting and designs for the decorative arts. As we have no means of knowing how the workshop was organized or his proficiency in other fields such attributions must remain tentative. Hilliard, later, was never to be as good a painter in oil as in watercolour. In the case of Hornebolte a series of portraits assigned to the Cast Shadow Workshop could be his.

No satisfactory explanation has yet been found for the sudden emergence of the portrait miniature set within a turned ivory box. Detached single miniatures were known in the Low Countries in the late fifteenth century but the series of miniatures by Hornebolte of members of the royal family were a quite new departure. In France Jean Clouet reached a similar format in the circular portrait miniatures in *Les Commentaires de la Guerre Gallique* (1518–20) but there is no evidence that Hornebolte ever saw them and they are still firmly part of a manuscript. The missing link may lie in three lost works of art, the portrait miniatures of François I and the Dauphin and his brother, probably by Jean Clouet, sent to Henry VIII by Madame d'Alençon in 1526. The coincidence between the arrival of these miniatures, which caused a minor sensation at the Tudor court, and the beginning of the series of Hornebolte miniatures of Henry VIII and Catherine of Aragon at the same time is more than suggestive.

There are twenty three miniatures in all attributable to Hornebolte. All save one, (see no. v) that are certainly of identifiable sitters, and most are, are of members of the royal family. They fall into two distinct groups, those before the middle of the 1530s which stem from Burgundian court portraiture as exemplified by Bernart van Orley or Mabuse and those that betray the impact of Holbein. From first to last they remain constant in technique and handling. Apart from two (nos. 5, 6), they are circular. The ground is always blue and there is usually an encircling gold line and a somewhat awkward inscription. The portrait is rendered over an opaque wash of pink, the 'carnation', by a brush in red and grey lines in a manner exactly as in a woodcut. The sitters have a family resemblance, sharing slightly pouting lips and pop-eyes. From the outset, apart from repetitions, these miniatures were painted directly *ad vivum* with no preliminary drawing, a feature that was to be the essence of the English limning tradition and establishes Hornebolte as the founding father of the English miniature.

SELECT BIBLIOGRAPHY

T. H. Colding, *Aspects of Miniature Painting*, Copenhagen, 1953, pp. 58–65.
Auerbach, *Tudor Artists*, pp. 41–6, 50–51.
Hugh Paget, "Gerard and Lucas Hornebolte in England", *Burlington Magazine*, CI, 1959, pp. 396–402.
Strong, *Renaissance Miniature*, pp. 12–44.

ARTIST UNKNOWN

1 Illumination in Bernard André's "Grace Entière du Gouvernement d'un Prince", 1500

The British Library, Department of Manuscripts (Royal MS 16. F.11 (4))
Vellum, 37½ × 26 cm, 14¾ × 10¼ in.

The manuscript, from the old Royal Library, is open at an illumination at the beginning of a poem by Bernard André, the blind poet of Toulouse, whom Henry VII brought back with him to England and set at the head of his literary household. In 1496 he became tutor to Arthur, Prince of Wales formulating an education for him along the lines of that in use at the court of Burgundy. The poem *Grace entière* relates to that programme which makes virtue the goal of the prince, as against nobility or wealth.

The manuscript is illuminated by a Flemish hand working in England in the *scriptorium* created by Henry VII subsequent to his establishment of a Royal Library in 1492 with a Librarian, Quentin Poulet, from Lille. He recruited illuminators from the Ghent-Bruges School and eventually formed an *atelier* to provide manuscripts for this new Royal Library at Richmond Palace. Lucas Hornebolte fits into this series of artists imported from the Netherlands to work for the Tudor Court.

The inset scene shows the poet presenting his manuscript to Prince Arthur, and, in addition, the Prince is seen at Mass in the background. Such a scene is clearly based on observation from life, although it has been worked up in the studio. The faces are portraits with a border in the Ghent-Bruges manner of naturalistic flowers and birds but also interspersed with symbols of the new Tudor dynasty. The progression from this to the portrait miniature was a short one.

COLLECTIONS: The old Royal Library; transferred to the British Museum, 1757.

LITERATURE: Gordon Kipling, *The Triumph of Honour. Burgundian Origins of the Elizabethan Renaissance*, Sir Thomas Browne Institute, Leiden, 1977, pp. 16–20, 31–40.

ATTRIBUTED TO GERARD HORNEBOLTE

2   Patent for Cardinal College, Oxford, 5th May, 1526

Public Record Office (E.24/6/1)
Pen and brown ink and wash, 27.2 × 26.9 cm, 10¾ × 10⅝ in.

It was Erna Auerbach who first suggested the attribution of a group of three drawings on letters patent, connected with Cardinal Wolsey's colleges at Oxford and Ipswich, to Gerard Hornebolte, the father of Lucas. In the accounts covering the period Michaelmas 1528 to 1529 there are payments concerning these documents which include the sum of 16sh. 8d. "To Gerarde" (*Tudor Artists*, p. 42). Although it cannot be proved that this payment is necessarily to Gerard Hornebolte all three documents, this from 1526 and two others from 1529 (ibid., pl. 13 (a–b)), are so startlingly different from anything that precedes them that it would be difficult not to accept a connexion. Henry VIII is depicted enthroned, clasping the orb and sceptre, a formal frontal majesty image, with heavy robes falling into carefully arranged and delineated folds on to the ground. The style of the throne, with its flanking columns and shell niche, indicates distant Italian Renaissance influences.

LITERATURE: Auerbach, *Tudor Artists*, pp. 40–43.

GHENT-BRUGES SCHOOL

3   Hours of the Virgin, late XVth century

British Library, Department of Manuscripts (Additional MS 35, 314)
Vellum, 15.9 × 10.8 cm, 6¼ × 4½ in.

A manuscript typical of those produced by the Ghent-Bruges School of illuminators of which the Horneboltes, father and son, were two leading exponents at the opening of the sixteenth century. T. H. Colding was the first to point out the stylistic and technical relationship between these manuscripts and the miniature of Henry VIII in the Fitzwilliam Museum, Cambridge (no. 5). There is, in fact, no difference between the technique used in illumination and that used by Hornebolte to paint his miniatures. The Hours of the Virgin exhibited here is open at a page with a Crucifixion scene and border in the stock Ghent-Bruges manner, painted in lines of gold over an ochre ground and the two angels censing in the spandrels are composed and executed in exactly the same manner as those in the miniature of Henry VIII (no. 5).

COLLECTIONS: Rothschild Bequest.

PROBABLE ATTRIBUTION TO JEAN CLOUET

4   The Dauphin François, 1525–28

H.M. The Queen
Vellum, 62 cm, 2⅝ in. diam.

Jean Clouet (d. probably 1541), court painter to François I, was the most important exponent of the vogue for portraits that began on the new King's accession in 1515. His most celebrated series of miniatures is in a French manuscript entitled *Les Commentaires de la Guerre Gallique*, dating from 1518 to 1520, which depicts heroes of the Italian campaign, the *Preux de Marignan*. They are portraits worked up from chalk drawings from life and, as in the case of Hornebolte's miniatures, show the sitter with head and shoulders silhouetted against a blue background within a gold border. Their relationship to Hornebolte's works, which they precede by five to eight years, has often been commented upon by scholars.

Hornebolte cannot have seen that manuscript, but we know that in 1526 miniatures, almost certainly by Clouet, were sent to the court of Henry VIII in two lockets, each elaborately decorated with a symbolic programme, containing portraits of François I and his two sons, the Dauphin François and Henri, Duc D'Orléans. (See G. Lebel, "British-French Artistic Relations", *Gazette des Beaux-Arts*, I, 1948, pp. 272–73.) They caused a great stir at the Tudor court and it is a likely hypothesis that their arrival must have some connexion with the series of miniatures of Henry VIII that begin in the period 1525–26.

The present miniature cannot be identical with one of those sent but is accepted by Peter Mellen as being connected with it. There is a drawing at Chantilly that may have been a model but it could equally be based on a missing drawing. The fact that Clouet worked his

5   6

miniatures up from drawings could not have been deduced by Hornebolte as the English limning tradition worked from life.

COLLECTIONS: Provenance unknown.

LITERATURE: Peter Mellen, *Jean Clouet*, London, 1971, p. 234 (135).

LUCAS HORNEBOLTE

5   **Henry VIII**, 1525–26

The Fitzwilliam Museum, Cambridge
Vellum stuck onto plain card, 33 × 48 mm,
$2\frac{1}{8} \times 1\frac{7}{8}$ in.

First attributed by T. H. Colding to Hornebolte in 1953, it was subsequently rightly designated by Reynolds as the "key piece" for the reconstitution of his *oeuvre*. The portrait, painted shortly after Hornebolte's arrival in England, which is *ad vivum*, depicts Henry VIII in the thirty-fifth year of his age in 1525–26 and is therefore one of the earliest, if not the earliest, surviving portrait miniature.

The border of intertwined H and K, for Henry VIII and Catherine of Aragon and censing angels Colding pointed out, both stylistically and technically, can be paralleled directly in manuscripts of the Ghent-Bruges School (no. 3). This captures the portrait miniature at its emergent stage, though it quickly became an independent art form in its own right. The lettering, never Hornebolte's strongest point, is typical in its clumsy placing and the doublet, which was once silver-grey, has tarnished due to the oxidization of the silver.

Two repetitions with variant costume are in the Royal Collection (*Holbein*, Queen's Gallery, 1978 (89)) and in the Buccleuch Collection.

INSCRIBED: On either side of the head: + *HR* + / + *VIII* + / + *AN* + / + *XXXV* +.

COLLECTIONS: Stated erroneously by J. C. Robinson to have been in the Strawberry Hill collection but no mention of it can be found in the numerous accounts and sales; first recorded in the Hollingsworth Magniac collection, 1862, and later the sale, Christie's July 4th 1892 (lot 183); purchased for the Buccleuch collection whence it passed to the Fitzwilliam Museum, 1949.

LITERATURE: J. C. Robinson, *Notice of the Principal Works of Art in the Collection of Hollingsworth Magniac*, London, 1862, p. 103 (193).
Kennedy, *Buccleuch*, pl. VII.
C. Winter, *The British School of Miniature Painters*, London, 1948, p. 7, pl. 1(a).
T. H. Colding, *Aspects of Miniature Painting*, Copenhagen, 1953, pp. 63–65, pl. 100.
Reynolds, *Connoisseur: Complete Period Guides*, 1968, pp. 190–91, pl. 69A.
E. Auerbach, "Some Tudor Portraits at the Royal Academy", *Burlington Magazine*, XCIX, 1957, p. 13.
Hugh Paget, "Gerard and Lucas Hornebolte in England, *Burlington Magazine*, CI, 1959, pp. 396–402, pl. 44.
Auerbach, *Hilliard*, pp. 50–51, pl. 1; 287 (1).

LUCAS HORNEBOLTE

6   **Catherine of Aragon**, 1525–26

The Duke of Buccleuch and Queensberry KT
Vellum stuck onto a plain card, rectangular,
54.5 × 48 mm, $2\frac{1}{8} \times 1\frac{7}{8}$ in.

Catherine of Aragon (1485–1536), daughter of Ferdinand and Isabella of Spain, married Henry VII's eldest son, Arthur, in 1501. When he died, in 1502, she was married to his brother, Henry, on his accession in 1509. He began proceedings against her for divorce in 1526. She was separated from her daughter Mary and confined to a series of country houses until her death in 1536, three years after her husband's marriage to Anne Boleyn.

One of the most important portraits of Henry VIII's first Queen to survive, certainly painted *ad vivum*. The series of portrait miniatures of Catherine can be very closely dated since they must follow Hornebolte's arrival in England and cannot be later than 1529 when Catherine last publicly appeared with the King. As they are conceived as pendants, or companions, to ones of the King they should be the same date, c. 1525–26. This is Catherine at forty, matching a description of her in a report of 1531: "Her Majesty is not of tall stature, rather small. If not handsome she is not ugly; she is somewhat stout and has always a smile on her countenance" (*Calendar State Papers, Venetian, 1527–33*, p. 287).

This is a particularly striking instance of Hornebolte's style with characteristic bold modelling of the features and pouting scarlet lips. It is unusual in showing the hands; the left arm supporting a pet marmoset on a chain while she holds a morsel of food in her right hand. There is abrasion on the forehead and the costume. Circular head and shoulders repetitions of this are in the Buccleuch and E. Grosvenor Paine Collections.

COLLECTIONS: Conceivably in the collection of Queen Caroline at Kensington Palace (*Catalogue*, p. 22 (no. 147 (8))): "Katherine of Aragon, Queen of Spain, in a square"; first certainly recorded in the Buccleuch collection, 1866, previous history unknown.

LITERATURE: *Archaeologia*, XL, 1866, pp. 73–74. Strong, *Tudor and Jacobean*, I, p. 40; II, pl. 74.

LUCAS HORNEBOLTE

7 Henry VIII, 1525–26

The Duke of Buccleuch and Queensberry KT
Vellum stuck to a playing card with part of a diamond showing at the reverse, circular, 48 mm, 1⅞ in. diam.

This has all the mechanical qualities of a repetition from a studio pattern based on the Fitzwilliam miniature (no. 5). Its condition is good, with only a few slight abrasions to the face and some small restorations in the background. A varnish, similar to that on no. 8 has been removed.

This is one of three miniatures of Henry VIII given to Charles I by the Earl of Suffolk. Although it is numbered 48 on the reverse it is in fact the larger of the two identical miniatures listed by van der Dort who states that it is the same size as the one with the beard but larger than the one identical with it: "Item don upon the right. lighte a Third the – / like bignes King Henry the 8ts picture in a tourn'd / white Ivory round Box being without a Beard / in a black Capp, and a little gold Cheine about his / neck, in an Ash cullor'd wrought dowblett in a furr'd / Cloake and purple sleeves whereby alsoe written wth / golden letters his name and Age / 35 /".

INSCRIBED: On either side of the head: *H.R. | .VIII.: | .AN ETATIS | .XXXV.* Reverse: a label inscribed in the hand of Abraham van der Dort: *48| In the Cubbord| with ye cabo| nett roome at| whithall: 1638.*

COLLECTIONS: Given to Charles I with two other miniatures of Henry VIII by Theophilus Howard, 2nd Earl of Suffolk; recorded by van der Dort, 1638 (Millar, *Walpole Society*, XXXVII, 1960, p. 114 (no. 47); possibly Charles II inventory, c. 1662–85 (no. 452): "Henry .8. aged 35 yeares"; James II

7

(no. 604): "King Henry the Eighth with a jewel in his cap, a limning in an ivory frame"; William III: "Henry VIII. a Jewel in his cap; the frame ivory"; seen by Vertue, 1734, at Kensington Palace: "Henr. VIII. A°. AEt. XXXV" (*Notebooks*, IV, p. 67); purchased for the Buccleuch collection from Colnaghi's who were disposing of the collection of a Mr Sarson (letters of October 1882 from Andrew McKay to James Stewart, Buccleuch Archives).

LUCAS HORNEBOLTE

8 Catherine of Aragon, 1525–26

National Portrait Gallery, London (4682)
Vellum stuck onto a plain card, 39 mm, 1½ in. diam. See no. 6.

At one time the miniature was varnished, which makes it difficult to be emphatic that it is a repetition, but the general quality places it in that category. Although the later varnish has been removed, subsequent restorations obscure the original face-painting. The inscription presupposes that it is a pendant to one of Henry VIII.

INSCRIBED: On either side of the head: *+REGIN | A+KA | THER| INA+ | +EIVS+ | +VXOR.*

COLLECTIONS: Sold anonymously, Sotheby's June 9th 1969 (lot 67).

LITERATURE: *The King's Good Servant, Sir Thomas More*, National Portrait Gallery, 1978 (36).

LUCAS HORNEBOLTE

9 Mary I as a Princess, 1525–29

Private Collection
Vellum stuck onto modern plain card, 40 mm, 1 9/16 in. (sight measure) diam.

The earliest identifiable portrait of Mary Tudor, depicting her at about the age of ten. The severe restoration of the face, however, precludes stating definitely that it is from

9

10

life. In 1527 she was recorded as being "so thin, spare and small as to render it impossible for her" to be married in the next three years" (*C.S.P.*, *Venetian*, *1527–33*, p. 58). This description matches exactly the miniature whose identity is further secured by the large jewel on her bodice bearing an English inscription "EmPour", i.e. "Emperour", referring to her uncle, Charles V. Although undated, the miniature must belong to the group painted shortly after Hornebolte's arrival and is unlikely to have been painted much after the Divorce proceedings began in earnest in 1529.

COLLECTIONS: Sold unattributed in London in 1972, and subsequently given to the present owner in the same year.

LUCAS HORNEBOLTE

10   ?Charles Brandon, Duke of Suffolk,

c. 1530

Louis de Wet Esq.
Vellum stuck to plain card, circular, 40 mm, 1 in. diam.

Charles Brandon, Duke of Suffolk (d. 1545), soldier and statesman, rose rapidly in Henry VIII's favour from his accession. Created Duke of Suffolk, 1514, he secretly married, 1515, the King's sister, Mary, widow of the French King François. Supported the King in the Divorce proceedings and took part in several military expeditions to France, including the capture of Boulogne, 1544.

Two versions of this miniature are extant although the second version is not inscribed (rep. Reynolds, *Connoisseur: Complete Period Guides*, 1968, pl. 69 (c)). Condition makes it impossible to state certainly which is the *ad vivum* version. Edward Stafford, 3rd Duke of Buckingham (1478–1521), the traditional indentification, cannot be the sitter as it must be someone of the highest rank aged forty-eight c. 1530. All Hornebolte's miniatures are of royal or quasi-royal sitters. The only man who would fit the bill is Charles Brandon, Duke of Suffolk. His birthdate is unknown but, in the late certain portrait of him c. 1540–45 (Strong, *Tudor and Jacobean*, II, pl. 604–5), of which several versions are extant, he is very old with totally white hair and beard, seeming well into his sixties. To be Suffolk, before he grew a beard, he would have to have been born therefore in the early 1470s. A portrait, close in date but still bearded, is

the double one with his wife at Woburn (*ibid*, pl. 606); the likenesses are perfectly compatible. Beards, as the portraits of Henry VIII testify, were grown and shaved off at periodic intervals according to fashion and whim.

The edge of the miniature has been trimmed and the left hand side of the face restored. The crimson doublet has faded to a dull yellow.

INSCRIBED: On either side of the head: $+A\mathring{N}+ \ / \ XLV\mathring{I}\mathring{I}\mathring{I}$; on the reverse it is recorded that it came from the Stowe sale.

COLLECTIONS: In the collection of the Dukes of Buckingham at Stowe; sold at the Stowe sale, March 15th 1849 (lot 52); bt. Lord; subsequent history unknown until purchased in a sale at Fernand Fievez, Brussels, 1948; acquired by the present owner, 1978.

LUCAS HORNEBOLTE

11   The Emperor Charles V, 1525–30

Victoria & Albert Museum (P.22—1942)
Vellum remounted onto modern card, circular, 42 mm. $1\frac{5}{8}$ in. diam.

The miniature is after a portrait of the Emperor Charles V from the studio of Bernart van Orley still in the Royal Collection (O. Millar, *The Queen's Pictures*, London, 1977 pl. 3). In the 1542 inventory of Henry VIII's pictures it is recorded as showing the Emperor "his doublet being cutt and a rosemary braunch in his hand". Henry VIII was married to the Emperor's aunt Catherine of Aragon, and the oil portrait was doubtless sent as a gift.

This is not the only instance of Hornebolte making a reduction of an oil portrait and a similar piece exists of Henry VIII's grandmother, Margaret Beaufort, Countess of Richmond (no. 13). The alterations from the portrait are such as to contain the miniature within its circumference, e.g. the hat brim is noticeably smaller. By the advent of the Divorce proceedings demand for a miniature of the Emperor would have evaporated. It should therefore date to the last years of the 1520s.

INSCRIBED: On the reverse the number: *276*.

COLLECTIONS: Sir Hans Sloane (1660–1753); recorded in his inventory under no. 276 as "Philip the 2^d of Spain painted in

13

11

14

miniature by Oliver"; passed with his collection to the British Museum in 1754; transferred along with twenty-two other miniatures to the V. & A., 1934.

LUCAS HORNEBOLTE

12 Henry VIII, c. 1530

Collection V. de S.
Vellum stuck onto a playing card with one diamond showing at the reverse, circular, 30 mm, $1\frac{3}{16}$ in. diam.

One of a pair of miniatures, the other being of the King's grandmother. Margaret Beaufort (no. 13). It has all the qualities of a repetition. It is in virtually mint condition and preserves a portrait of the King predating Holbein's entry into royal service. The King's beard is greying and his face is wrinkled suggesting a date early in the 1530s.

INSCRIBED: On either side of the head: *·REX· | ·HENRI· | CVS· ·OCTA | VVS·.*

COLLECTIONS: Purchased by the present owner's grandfather on 22nd February 1913 from G. C. van Meurs; previously in the possession of the van den Heuvel family in The Hague.

LUCAS HORNEBOLTE

13 Margaret Beaufort, Countess of Richmond and Derby, c. 1530

Collection V. de S.
Vellum stuck onto a playing card, with one diamond showing at the reverse, circular, 30 mm, $1\frac{3}{16}$ in diam.

Margaret Beaufort (1443–1509), daughter and heiress of John, 1st Duke of Somerset, married Edmund Tudor, Earl of Richmond by whom she had Henry VII. Noted as a patroness of learning.

The miniature is a pendant to one of her grandson (no. 12) and based on the only known portrait type of her, probably by Maynard, of which numerous versions exist (Strong,

Tudor and Jacobean, I, pp. 20–21; II, pl. 34–36). As with his miniature of Charles V (no. 11) Hornebolte has executed a portrait after an existing painting. These two miniatures may be survivors from a larger group that included further members of the Tudor dynasty, or the appearance of the Countess may be due to the absence of a Queen during the serious phase of the Divorce proceedings from 1529 until the advent of Anne Boleyn in 1533. The miniature is basically in good condition with its derivative status accounting for the relative coarseness of characterization. The dress is that of a widow or a vowess and the original portrait was probably executed c. 1500.

INSCRIBED: On either side of the head: *MARGA | RETA ·MATER | ·ILLVS | TRISSIMI | REX | HÊRICVS | VIIˢ.*

COLLECTIONS: See no. 12.

LUCAS HORNEBOLTE

14 ?Anne Boleyn, 1532–33

The Duke of Buccleuch and Queensberry KT
Vellum stuck onto card, which has a relatively modern card glued over it at the back, circular, 41 mm, $1\frac{5}{8}$ in. diam.

Anne Boleyn (1507–36), daughter of Sir Thomas Boleyn, later Earl of Wiltshire and Ormond, became Henry VIII's mistress in 1527. He secretly married her in January 1533 and, after his marriage to Catherine was declared null, she was crowned. In September she gave birth to Elizabeth. Three years later she fell from favour and was executed.

There are two versions of this miniature. The second, in the Royal Ontario Museum, Toronto, was attributed to Hornebolte by Reynolds. It is slightly larger and bears an inscription giving the age of the sitter as twenty-five. The Toronto miniature was called Jane Seymour and the Buccleuch version Katherine of Aragon and only subsequently Jane Seymour.

This identification as Jane Seymour is difficult to sustain. In the first instance, the features are at total variance with Hornebolte's authentic miniature of her (no. 17) which corresponds exactly to Holbein's portraits. In addition, the age given on the Toronto miniature, twenty-five, would mean, if the date of Jane's birth as 1509 is acceptable (it comes from a miniature by Hilliard (no. 107)) that the miniatures were painted before Henry's marriage to her in May 1536 and about one fact there can be no doubt, it is a queen. Duplicates only exist of royal personages and the missing Queen from Hornebolte's gallery is Anne Boleyn who was born in 1507 and would have been twenty-five in 1532–33. In 1533 she was crowned, gave birth to Elizabeth and was at the apogee of her influence. Her features, generally known through workshop versions of a lost original portrait (Strong, *Tudor and Jacobean*, II, pls. 8–9), are perfectly compatible with those in the miniature, although the clothes are different. Sanuto, the Venetian ambassador, states that her eyes were black but in her portraits they are brown, as in the miniature.

The condition of the miniature is good, although there is some restoration on the forehead and cheek and minor damage of various kinds to the blue background.

COLLECTIONS: Stated by Horace Walpole to have been given by Charles II to the Duke of Monmouth; purchased at his daughter, Lady Isabella Scott's sale; Strawberry Hill collection as Katherine of Aragon (*A Description of the Villa at Strawberry Hill*, 1774, p. 84); 14th Day of the Strawberry Hill sale, 10th May 1842 (lot 65); purchased by Mr W. Blamire; his sale 9th November 1863 (lot 137); purchased for the Buccleuch collection.

LITERATURE: Walpole, *Anecdotes*, ed. Wornum, 1849, I, p. 94 (as Katherine of Aragon).
Archaeologia, XL, 1866, pp. 74, 82.
Chamberlain, *Holbein*, II, p. 237.
Kennedy, *Buccleuch*, pl. VII.

LUCAS HORNEBOLTE

15 Henry FitzRoy, Duke of Richmond, 1534–35

H.M. The Queen
Vellum stuck to a playing card with two hearts verso, circular, 43 mm, 1$\frac{11}{16}$ in. diam.

Henry FitzRoy, Duke of Richmond (1519–1536) was the son of Henry VIII by Elizabeth Blount. In 1525, at the age of six, he was made K.G., created Earl of Nottingham, Duke of Richmond and Somerset and appointed Lord High Admiral. On November 25th 1533 he married Mary Howard, daughter of Thomas, 3rd Duke of Norfolk. He died at St. James in July 1536.

First attributed by Graham Reynolds to Hornebolte in 1956, the portrait is clearly *ad vivum*. The Duke has a typical youthful Tudor face strongly reminiscent of portraits of his father as a young man. During the period when the portrait was painted Richmond, although illegitimate, was Henry VIII's only surviving male child, a fact emphasized by Mary being declared illegitimate and the birth of Elizabeth in September 1533, events which pushed Richmond to the centre of the Tudor family stage. The dress is unusual, depicting the Duke in a nightcap and open-necked shirt or nightdress making it conceivable that Hornebolte painted him in bed during one of his frequent

illnesses. This is one of Hornebolte's finest characterizations. The miniature has suffered abrasion in some areas.

INSCRIBED: On either side of the head: *HENRY, DVCK. OFF RICHMOND | ÆTATIS SVAE XV$_0$*.

COLLECTIONS: Probably Charles II to whom it was given by Lord Aubigny; inventory, c. 1662–85 (no. 442): "Henry Duke of Richmond in small Limbning. 0.2. Given by the Lord Dubigny"; Horace Walpole (*A Description of the Villa at Strawberry Hill*, 1774, p. 45); Strawberry Hill sale 20th Day 17th May 1842 (lot 3); purchased Jarman; C. Sackville Bale collection, sold 23rd May 1881 (lot 1418); purchased for the Royal Collection.

LITERATURE: *British Portraits*, R.A., 1956 (605).
Reynolds, *Connoisseur: Complete Period Guides*, 1968, p. 190.

LUCAS HORNEBOLTE

16 Henry VIII, c. 1537

Private Collection
Vellum stuck to plain card, circular, 49 mm, 1$\frac{15}{16}$ in. diam.

Formerly this miniature was attributed to Holbein but the technique is that of Hornebolte and the work of a right-handed artist. Holbein was left-handed. The head is identical with that in Holbein's portrait of the King in the Thyssen Collection and as initially conceived in the great wall-painting of 1537 in the Privy Chamber of Whitehall Palace (Strong, *Tudor and Jacobean*, II, pl. 307). Although both the hat and chain are identical, the costume is quite different. The painting, however, is spontaneous and lively and it could be the result of independent observation under the influence of Holbein as much as a copy of the head from the Thyssen Collection portrait. The miniature is in good condition, although the once silver doublet has oxidized.

INSCRIBED: On the backboard in the hand of the 2nd Earl of Oxford: "K. Henry 8th".

COLLECTIONS: In the collection of Edward Harley, 2nd Earl of Oxford (1689–1741); first recorded by Vertue, c. 1732: "K. Hen. 8" (Vertue, *Notebooks*, I, p. 41); Vertue's 1743 catalogue (60); Oxford's daughter Margaret married William Bentinck, 2nd Duke of Portland; thence by descent.

LITERATURE: Goulding, *Welbeck*, p. 55 (1).

LUCAS HORNEBOLTE

17 Jane Seymour, 1536–37

Sudeley Castle
Vellum stuck to a playing card with three hearts verso, circular, 45 mm, 1$\frac{25}{32}$ in. diam.

Jane Seymour (1509–1536), eldest daughter of Sir John Seymour of Wolf Hall, was lady-in-waiting to both

16　　　　　　　　　　　　　**17**

Catherine of Aragon and Anne Boleyn. She attracted the attentions of Henry VIII in 1535 and, subsequent to Anne's execution, married him in 1536, dying shortly after she gave birth to Edward VI.

This miniature bears a very early inscription identifying it as Jane Seymour, an identification which is supported by Holbein's famous likenesses of her to which it bears a striking resemblance (cf. Ganz, *Holbein*, pls. 136, 138). As in these she has grey-blue eyes and certainly not the brown ones of her predecessor as Queen (no. 14). There can be no doubt that Hornebolte was influenced by Holbein's portraits of her although, as in the case of Henry VIII, it is an independent portrait in which the figure is placed in a way typical of Hornebolte and certainly not of Holbein. The features are now damaged and much restored, even so, this is likely to have been an *ad vivum* miniature. Damage to the remainder of the miniature is, however, slight.

INSCRIBED: On the reverse a near contemporary inscription: *Quene Jane* (the *Q* has been clipped).

COLLECTIONS: Horace Walpole at Strawberry Hill (*Description of Strawberry Hill*, 1774, p. 83), 14th Day Strawberry Hill sale 10th May 1842 (lot 67), purchased by J. C. Dent of Sudeley.

LITERATURE: *Archaeologia*, XL, 1866, p. 84.

LUCAS HORNEBOLTE

18　Edward VI as Prince of Wales, 1541–42

The Duke of Buccleuch and Queensberry KT
Vellum stuck to a playing card with parts of three spades verso. Circular, 34 mm, 1⅜ in. diam., but now oval, 34 × 30 mm, 1⅜ × 1 3/16 in. (the projection of the curve of the remainder of the original gold lines at top and bottom produce a circle).

A sparkling likeness of Edward VI as a child, certainly painted from life. Retouching is minimal but includes probably the heightening of the doublet. The long-awaited male heir to the throne was much painted (see Strong,

Tudor and Jacobean, I, pp. 91–92), the earliest portrait being that by Holbein depicting the Prince at just over two years of age, presented to the King as a New Year's Gift on January 1st 1539/40. This is followed by a portrait from about 1542, for which a drawing, not unanimously accepted as by Holbein, is at Windsor (Parker, *Holbein*, 1945, pl. 71). Hornebolte's miniature falls between these two and records the fair, grey-eyed Prince at about the age of four, wearing a cameo jewel in his bonnet.

COLLECTIONS: Puchased from Colnaghi, 1844 (Buccleuch Archives).

LITERATURE: Kennedy, *Buccleuch*, pl. 22.

MORGAN WOLFF AFTER A DESIGN ATTRIBUTED TO LUCAS HORNEBOLTE

19　Third Great Seal of Henry VIII, 1542

Public Record Office (E.328/408)
Wax, 122 mm, 4.8 in. diam.

The payment to Morgan Wolff, goldsmith, is "for makinge workmanship and graveinge" (P.R.O.E. 315/251, f. 87ᵛ). The subject of who designed the Great Seals of the Tudor monarchs is an unessayed one apart from Hilliard's documented involvement in Elizabeth's Second Great Seal (no. 193). This presupposes that they were designed and in that instance the design was by the court limner. The Third Great Seal of Henry VIII is so strikingly close to illuminations of the King by Hornebolte and his workshop (nos. 20 & 21) that it would be reasonable to suggest that he was the author of the design for the seal. Its two predecessors were gothic and with this seal the image of the monarchy leaps forward and is presented in terms of the Northern Renaissance. It was probably the change in royal style, the result of the events of the 1530s, that prompted its commission. That change is incorporated into the obverse in the phrase: *ET. I TERA. ECCESIAE. AGLICANE. ET. HIBERNICE. CAPVT*. The portrait of the King on the obverse is of the Hornebolte type and he sits on a throne in the Renaissance style. The reverse or

20

counterseal, however, reworks its predecessors, depicting the King as a chivalrous warrior prince.

LITERATURE: A. Wyon, *The Great Seals of England*, London, 1887, p. 69.

LUCAS HORNEBOLTE AND ASSISTANTS

20 The "Liber Niger" of the Order of the Garter, c. 1534

THE DEAN OF WINDSOR as Register of the (Most Noble) Order of the Garter
Vellum, 420 × 300 mm, $16\frac{5}{8} \times 11\frac{7}{8}$ in.

The Order of the Garter as revived by the Tudor dynasty epitomized the cult of chivalry as a buttress to the Monarchy and was also seen as a rival to the *Toison d'Or* of the Dukes of Burgundy. The imitation of the *Toison d'Or* begun by Henry VII, who introduced the great collar of the Order, was continued by Henry VIII, who revised and clarified the statues, introducing the obligatory wearing of the Lesser George.

The *Liber Niger* or "Black Book" is the second Register of the Order containing its statutes in Latin, a history of its foundation and accounts of ceremonies in the reign of Henry VIII and Edward. It was a document close to the crown and executed about 1534 in the most sumptuous manner, a date deduced from the series of illuminations depicting ceremonies in that year, somewhat fancifully as the King himself was absent. The *Liber Niger* and its successor, the *Liber Ceruleus*, are crucial documents in the history of limning, for the original manuscript is directly in the Ghent-Bruges style with portraits executed initially in the Hornebolte manner and going on through subsequent reigns to give us illuminations by Levina Teerlinc and Nicholas Hilliard.

The manuscript is open at the first appearance of Henry VIII, depicted kneeling and praying in front of a low covered table on which a book lies open. This section of the page is certainly by Lucas Hornebolte and executed in exactly the same manner as the miniatures although, as one would expect, with slightly less finish. The border is less good in quality and, in common with others in the manuscript, is by another hand in the workshop. To the right, above the initial, there is a Madonna and Child and, at a distance, St George is shown with a green dragon. The top of the page is cut off.

LITERATURE: E. Auerbach, "The Black Book of the Garter", *Report of the Society of the Friends of St George's*, V, No. 4, 1977, pp. 149–53.
British Heraldry, British Museum, 1978 (No. 239).

LUCAS HORNEBOLTE

21   The "Valor Ecclesiasticus", 1535

Public Record Office (E.344/22)
Vellum

The "Valor Ecclesiasticus" or the King's Book was prepared in 1535 and contains the valuations of church property in England and Wales, bishoprics and benefices as well as monasteries and colleges. It was a direct consequence of the Act for First Fruits and Tenths which demanded a tenth of the net ecclesiastical incomes. The result is a document on the scale of the Domesday Book and the greatest single source of information on the economic position of the Tudor Church. It contains two illuminated title-pages, one from 1535, exhibited here, and a second from 1539. Both are by Lucas Hornebolte and both depict the monarch enthroned and flanked by officials, executed in watercolour with hatching typical of his style in red and grey and the usual pouting lips. This is one of a series of late Henrician initial portraits of the monarch likely to have been the product of the Hornebolte workshop. The drawing of the figures echoes closely that of those on the title-page of the 1539 Bible (no. 22).

AFTER A DESIGN ATTRIBUTED TO LUCAS HORNEBOLTE

22   Title border of "The Byble in Englyshe...," 1539

The British Library (C.18.d.1.)
Woodcut, 27 × 16.5 cm, $10\frac{5}{8} \times 6\frac{1}{2}$ in.

The relationship of this border to Hornebolte's illuminations of Henry VIII enthroned in the *Valor Ecclesiasticus* (no. 21) is too close not to postulate that it is also designed by him. The Great Bible which appeared in April 1539, translated by Miles Coverdale, was begun in Paris, because of the quality of French printing, but, due to the intervention of the Inquisitor General of France, was completed in England and issued by Richard Grafton and his partner, Whitchurch. This was to be the authoritative translation of the English Bible as conceived by Thomas Cromwell and issued under royal auspices. The King at the top distributes the scriptures, to the left to the clergy and, to the right, the laity. They, in their turn, pass the book down the ecclesiastical and secular social scale so that below people congregate and exclaim, *VIVAT REX*.

LITERATURE: R. B. McKerrow and F. S. Ferguson, *Title-page Borders in England and Scotland 1485–1640*, Bibliographical Society, O.U.P., 1932, p. 47 (45).
Hind, *Engraving*, I, p. 4.

23

CAST SHADOW WORKSHOP/HORNEBOLTE WORKSHOP

23   Edward IV, c. 1530

National Portrait Gallery (3542)
Oil on panel, 33 × 27.3 cm, $13 \times 10\frac{3}{4}$ in.

This is a typical example of thirteen portraits all from the same atelier which has been conveniently labelled the Cast Shadow Workshop. They include one of Henry V, two of Edward IV, eight of Henry VIII, using two different face-patterns, one of Jane Seymour and three of Edward VI as Prince. They can never have been more than workshop pieces, mass-produced under supervision, for decorating the new royal palaces arising in the 1530s. The format of the sitter tight in the panel and frame with his hands on a ledge before him is Netherlandish but from the 1520s and by the 1530s decidedly old-fashioned. The painting is schematic and stylized, each eyelash and hair being separately delineated. Further research may make the equation of the Cast Shadow Workshop with that of Lucas Hornebolte a correct one. For a discussion of the Cast Shadow pictures see Tudor-Craig, cited below, and Strong, *Renaissance Miniature*, pp. 42–44.

COLLECTIONS: Earls of Ellenborough at Southam Delabere; sold Sotheby's 11th June 1947 (lot 60).

LITERATURE: Strong, *Tudor and Jacobean*, I, pp. 86–87.
P. Tudor-Craig, *Richard III*, National Portrait Gallery, 1973 (p. 21–22).

24

CAST SHADOW MASTER/LUCAS HORNEBOLTE

24   ? **Margaret Pole, Countess of Salisbury**, c. 1530

National Portrait Gallery (2607)
Oil on panel, 62.8 × 48.9 cm, 24¾ × 19¼ in.

Margaret Pole, Countess of Salisbury (1473–1541) was the daughter of George Plantagenet, Duke of Clarence. She was married to Richard Pole and, in 1513, created Countess of Salisbury. As governess to the Princess Mary she was loyal to Catherine of Aragon and the pro-papal activities of herself and her sons led to her execution in 1541.

This portrait shows all the mannerisms of the Cast Shadow Workshop (no. 23) except that it is of far superior quality, an autograph likeness by the Master himself of an important sitter. It is unlikely to have been painted after 1533 when the Countess lost her position as governess to the Princess Mary and a date around 1530 would seem reasonable. Prior to cleaning the status of this portrait was uncertain but cleaning removed a later inscription and a coat of arms but established the authenticity of other items which indicate the identity to be correct. Dr Pamela Tudor-Craig suggests that the barrel at her wrist is a reference to her father's execution "in a butt of malmsey" and the W jewel suspended at the end of a ribbon to her brother Edward, Earl of Warwick, whose heir she was.

The relationship of this picture in its composition to Hornebolte's rectangular miniature of Catherine of Aragon (no. 6) is extremely close. The sitters are disposed within the painted surface in exactly the same way and the arrangement of the hands before the waist is the same, but in reverse. This picture could be the cornerstone to Lucas Hornebolte's oil painting style.

COLLECTIONS: Presumably descended to the Countess's grand-daughter, Winifred Pole, Lady Hastings, who married as her second husband, Thomas Barrington; Anne Barrington, his second daughter and co-heiress and wife of Charles Shales, to her daughter Essex Shales, wife of Richard Lowndes; descended to Colonel William Selby Lowndes of Whaddon Hall, Bletchley, Bucks; purchased from Messrs Knoedler, 1931, and presented by the N.A.C.F.

LITERATURE: Strong, *Tudor and Jacobean*, I, pp. 272–73.
P. Tudor-Craig, *Richard III*, National Portrait Gallery, 1973 (p. 5).

Hans Holbein,
1497–1543

Holbein's miniatures were all painted during his second visit to England.

1532. Returned to England from Basle
c. 1533–4. Patronized by Thomas Cromwell
1536. By this date known as a King's Painter
1537. Painted the wall-painting celebrating the Tudor dynasty in the Privy Chamber of Whitehall Palace
1538. Visits Brussels to paint Christina, Duchess of Milan
1539. Visits Germany to paint the daughters of the Duke of Cleves (no. 30).
1543. Death of Holbein

HOLBEIN is the odd man out within the limning tradition of Tudor England. It is Carel van Mander who records that Holbein learned to paint miniatures from Lucas Hornebolte and how he quickly outstripped him "in drawing, arrangement, understanding and execution". They must have come into contact while Holbein was working for Henry VIII's minister, Thomas Cromwell, whose miniature Holbein painted c. 1533–34 (Private Collection). At present there are sixteen miniatures which can be assigned to him. Of these fourteen have been subject to laboratory examination and can be accepted with complete confidence as the master's work not only on grounds of style but of technical similarity.

Holbein followed Hornebolte exactly in technique in every way except for one major difference, he applied to his miniatures the same sequence as he applied to his panel portraits, that is he did not paint direct from life but worked from a drawing. We can trace this process exactly in two miniatures exhibited here (nos. 26, 32), for which the original drawings actually survive. Holbein's miniatures begin like scaled down versions of his large scale portraits and it is only gradually that he responds compositionally to the format. He usually included the sitter's hands as an extension of character. His painting is not transparent as Hornebolte's but opaque and the essential ingredient is always the confining lines of the contours of the forms. The backgrounds are all blue as in the case of Hornebolte but his beautiful Renaissance lettering is invariably placed with an unerring sense of balance all too often missing from Hornebolte's work.

Although Holbein became one of the King's painters by 1536 his miniatures can, for the very first time, be of sitters outside the enclosed circle of the Tudor royal family and its collaterals. To this chance we owe some of his most moving portrayals of the humbler fabric of early Tudor society, the Ropers (nos. 27, 28) and the haunting Mrs Pemberton (no. 29).

SELECT BIBLIOGRAPHY
Ganz, *Holbein*, pp. 258–60.
Reynolds, *Miniatures*, 1952, pp. 3–7.
Strong, *Renaissance Miniature*, pp. 45–53.

25 George Neville, Lord Abergavenny, c. 1535?

The Duke of Buccleuch and Queensberry KT
Vellum stuck to a playing card in one heart verso, circular, 49 mm, $1\frac{15}{16}$ in. diam.

George Neville, 3rd Baron of Abergavenny (1460?–1535), was created Knight of the Bath by Richard III, fought for Henry VIII in France and was Constable of Dover and Lord Warden of the Cinque Ports.

Although the inscription is a later addition by Nicholas Hilliard in his characteristic calligraphy, the miniature is a perfectly authentic one by Holbein. No certain large-scale painting by him exists but the drawing, as in the case of Lady Audley (no. 32), does.

As Abergavenny died in June 1535 the drawing must have been made shortly before his death. The dating of the miniature is problematic. If done at the same time as the drawing it would date from c. 1534–35, which would fit perfectly well, as in concept it relates directly to one of Thomas Cromwell, c. 1533–34 (Ganz, *Holbein*, p. 258 (137)). These two probably formed Holbein's earliest essays in miniature painting. The possibility however that the miniature was slightly posthumous cannot altogether be eliminated. There are minor paint losses and the background is discoloured and scuffed.

INSCRIBED: To the left, later: *G Abergavenny*.

COLLECTIONS: Presumably by descent from the sitter to Mary Neville, only daughter and heiress of Henry, Lord Abergavenny, who married, 1574, Thomas Fane; their son, Francis, became 1st Earl of Westmorland; thence by descent; sold at the Apethorpe sale, Christie's 2nd June 1892 (lot 19); acquired for the Buccleuch collection.

LITERATURE: Chamberlain, *Holbein*, II, p. 222.
Kennedy, *Buccleuch*, pl. 11.
C. Winter, *Burlington Magazine*, LXXXIII, 1943, p. 266.
Ganz, *Holbein*, p. 258 (132).
Holbein, R.A., 1950 (184).

26 George Neville, 3rd Lord Abergavenny, c. 1535?

The Earl of Pembroke
Black and coloured chalks, touched with white, outlines reinforced in pen and ink, on pink prepared paper, 27.2 × 23.4 cm, $10\frac{3}{4} \times 9\frac{1}{4}$ in.

This is one of two instances where Holbein's original drawing survives as well as a miniature (for the second see no. 32). Holbein's miniatures follow the practice of Lucas Hornebolte exactly, except for the fact that he did not paint the sitter directly onto the vellum but applied to the format his usual method of portraiture by beginning with a drawing. His process of drawing moved from general

25

26

indications of the disposition of the features to final definite lines, a tradition distinctively North European, concerned with a literalness far removed from the idealizing tendencies of Renaissance Italy. Lord Abergavenny is depicted as an extremely old man. His birth date is uncertain but he was probably in his seventies. No feature is softened, for Holbein delineates exactly the warts and wrinkles on his face. No oil portrait certainly by Holbein's hand is known, although one is accepted by Ganz (*Holbein*, p. 243 (75)).

It is generally agreed, but cannot be proved, that Holbein made use of a device for tracing the outlines of the head on a piece of glass, an expedient to save his sitters the tedium of a long sitting and certainly not the result of inadequate draughtsmanship. Detailed though the drawings are, the portraits worked up away from the sitter also presuppose a remarkable visual memory on the part of the artist.

INSCRIBED: Later, bottom left: *LORD CROMWELL*; right: *HOLBEIN*.

COLLECTIONS: Once part of the series of Holbein drawings in the Royal Collection; these passed from the artist, probably by purchase, to Edward VI; on his death they passed by gift or purchase to Henry Fitzalan, Earl of Arundel; on his death, in 1580, they passed to his son-in-law, John, Lord Lumley; purchased with his library by Henry, Prince of Wales; from him to his brother, Charles I, who gave the book between 1627–30 to William, 3rd Earl of Pembroke in return for Raphael's St George and the Dragon; at this stage the Abergavenny drawing must have been retained, the sitter being a friend and contemporary of William, 1st Earl of Pembroke; thence by descent.

LITERATURE: Sidney, Earl of Pembroke, *A Catalogue of the Paintings and Drawings in the Collection at Wilton House, Salisbury, Wiltshire*, London, 1968, p. 94 (18).

HANS HOLBEIN

27 William Roper, 1536

Metropolitan Museum of Art, New York : Rogers Fund, 1950 (50.69.1)
Vellum stuck to card which has been backed with fabric, circular, 46 mm, 1$\frac{13}{16}$ in. diam.

William Roper (1493/8–1578) of Well Hall, Eltham, came of a Kentish family and was sixteen years in the household of Sir Thomas More, marrying his eldest daughter, Margaret, in 1521. Later he was M.P. in 1529, 1534, 1555 and 1557–8.

This is the only known portrait of William Roper and if, as is surely the case, it was painted simultaneously with that of his wife, it must date to the year 1536 and, together, they must represent some of the earliest fruits of Hornebolte's tuition of Holbein. The formula is exactly that of a life-scale portrait and is close to a dated circular portrait of an unknown man holding gloves dated 1535, also in the Metropolitan Museum of Art, New York (Bache Collection) (Ganz, *Holbein*, pl. 128). Even the placing of the lettering follows Holbein's customary practice during his second English period.

The connexion between Holbein and the Roper family would, of course, have been established during the artist's first visit. Husbands were not included by Holbein in the group portrait of the More family. The miniature is in good condition apart from slight damages at the edge and minor general flaking and abrasions.

INSCRIBED: On either side of the head: *A°N ÆTATIS | SVAE XLII*

COLLECTIONS: By descent in the Roper family; Lord Rothschild; Lord Carnarvon; Mrs Harry Goldman, New York; acquired 1950.

LITERATURE: *The Lyfe of Sir Thomas Moore, Knighte, written by William Roper, Esquire . . .*, ed. Elsie Vaughan Hitchcock, Early English Text Society, O.S., CXCVII, 1935, pp. xxxix–xlvii.
C. Winter, *Burlington Magazine*, LXXXII, 1943, p. 266.
Ganz, *Holbein*, p. 258 (134–35).
'*The King's Good Servant*', *Sir Thomas More*, N.P.G., 1977 (174).

29

HANS HOLBEIN

28 Margaret Roper, 1536

Metropolitan Museum of Art, New York: Rogers Fund, 1950 (50.69.2)
Vellum stuck to card which has been backed with fabric, circular, 46 mm, $1\frac{13}{16}$ in. diam.

Margaret Roper (1505–44), eldest and beloved daughter of Sir Thomas More, married William Roper in 1521. In 1526 she translated into English Erasmus on the Lord's Prayer. After her father's execution she rescued his head to bury it.

The age gives us the date 1536 when Margaret Roper would have been thirty and the resemblance to her likeness in the More Family Group is striking, although now the face is sad and careworn in the aftermath of her father's execution the previous year. Holbein's concept of her springs from his earlier one for again she is depicted holding a book, but this time closed. The formula is a typical one for female sitters during his second English period. Lady Godsalve (Ganz, *Holbein*, pl. 134) of about 1536 is almost identical in concept. In both these miniatures Holbein is literally scaling down from a large-scale image. In his later miniatures there is greater consideration for the form. In the case of Margaret Roper the pose would fit more naturally a rectangular format. The miniature is in good condition apart from slight losses and abrasions

INSCRIBED: On either side of the head: *A° ÆTATIS / XXX.*

COLLECTIONS: See no. 27.

LITERATURE: See no. 27.

HANS HOLBEIN

29 ?Margaret Throckmorton, Mrs Robert Pemberton, c. 1536

Victoria & Albert Museum, (P.40–1935)
Vellum stuck to a playing card with five hearts verso, circular, 52 mm, $2\frac{1}{16}$ in. diam.

Margaret Throckmorton (d. 1576) was daughter of Richard Throckmorton of Higham Ferrers. She married, at an unknown date, Robert Pemberton.

The identity depends on the coat of arms, mounted onto vellum stuck to a playing card which is inserted separately at the back of the miniature, bearing the year 1566, but the painting is 17th century in date. The arms are those of Robert Pemberton of Pemberton, Lancs and of Rushden (d. 1594) impaling those of his wife Margaret Throckmorton. There is nothing to disprove this identity and, indeed, the absence of jewellery and simplicity of her dress argue for modest rank. She was one of the younger daughters of a country gentleman but not without connections. Her aunt by marriage, or first cousin's wife, was Catherine, Lady Throckmorton, sister to Thomas 2nd Lord Vaux who sat for Holbein (information from the Hon Clare Stuart Wortley, 1935; Parker, *Holbein*, 1945, nos. 24, 30) and her Throckmorton cousins had posts at court. In spite of this a sitter of her rank is quite exceptional among early Tudor miniatures, but Holbein's sitters were never confined to the narrow range of Hornebolte's. The costume and pose are virtually duplicated in the portrait of a woman with a white coif at Detroit (Ganz, *Holbein*, pl. 123) which Ganz dates c. 1534. It is usual to date Mrs Pemberton c. 1540–43 but it is most closely related in introspection of mood to Holbein's Margaret Rorer of 1536. Both look back to the portraits of ladies of the More family and circle during Holbein's first period, for after he entered royal service in 1537 the treatment became progressively more iconic and the sitters wholly of the court.

The background is discoloured and a number of paint losses have been crudely restored.

INSCRIBED: On either side of the head: *·ANNO· / ETATIS·SVAE·23·*

Hans Holbein 47

COLLECTIONS: First recorded in 1865 when lent to the South
    Kensington Exhibition by Mr J. Heywood Hawkins; sold in
    the C. H. T. Hawkins sale, Christie's 13th May 1904 (lot 907);
    J. Pierpont Morgan collection; sold Christie's 24th June 1935
    (lot 125); purchased with funds from the Capt. H. B. Murray
    bequest and donations from the N.A.C.F. and Viscount
    Bearsted.

LITERATURE: R. Holmes, "A Miniature by Holbein", *Burlington
    Magazine*, V, 1904, p. 337.
Williamson, *Catalogue*, 1906, I, p. 8 (pl. 4).
Chamberlain, *Holbein*, II, pp. 228–29.
Winter, *Elizabethan Miniatures*, pl. 1.
Ganz, *Holbein*, p. 259 (140).

30

HANS HOLBEIN

30 **Anne of Cleves**, 1539

Victoria & Albert Museum (P.153–1910)
Vellum stuck to a playing card with part of a court
card verso, circular, 44.5 mm, 1¾ in. diam.

Anne of Cleves (1515–57), fourth Queen of Henry VIII,
was the daughter of John, Duke of Cleves. After the death
of Jane Seymour in 1537 she was considered as a possible
wife, although it was reported "I hear no great praise
neither of her personage nor beauty". As a result of
Thomas Cromwell's desire for England's alliance into
Protestant Germany the marriage treaty was signed on 24
September 1539. Although shortly after arrival Henry
deemed her "nothing so fair as had been reported" but the
marriage took place on January 6th 1540. In June when
Cromwell fell from power, Henry dropped the alliance
with the German princes and the marriage was declared
null. He then designated her King's "sister" and she settled
down to life in England, dying in Mary's reign.

The miniature is the most fully documented of the small
group of miniatures that can definitely be assigned to
Holbein's hand and can also be very precisely dated as the
documentation of Holbein's expedition to paint Henry
VIII's fourth bride is remarkably complete.

Subsequent to the death of Jane Seymour the King
remained a widower for two years until the political
situation at the opening of 1539 led to the serious
consideration of a marriage alliance with Protestant
Germany. In January 1539 Christopher Mont, a German
in Henry VIII's service, was sent to the Duke of Saxony
with various proposals, including one that the King might
marry one of the two unmarried daughters of the Duke of
Cleves. The proposal, however, must be seen to have been
initiated on the Cleves side and the King would not
proceed with the match until "they should send her picture
hither". The Duke of Saxony was unable to fulfil this
request because his court painter, Lucas Cranach the
Elder, was ill, but two portraits painted earlier may have
reached England in the summer. The English ambassadors
did not regard these portraits as at all satisfactory: "for to
see but a parte of theyr faces, and that under such a
monstruouse habyte and apparell, was no syght, neither of
theyr faces nor of theyr persones".

Holbein was despatched at the end of July and, reaching
the court at Düren early in August, had finished portraits

of both Anne and her sister Amelia by August 11th and
was back in England by the end of the month. Dr Wootten
wrote: "Your Grace's servant Hanze Albein hathe taken
th' effigies of my ladye Anne and the lady Amelye and
hath expressyd theyr imaiges very lyvely". Henry married
Anne at Greenwich on January 6th 1540 and divorced her
in July of the same year.

The problem to solve is what place the miniature
occupies in Holbein's working sequence. In the case of
Anne of Cleves there was an immense rush to complete the
picture, for normally a drawing would lead to a panel
painting, a lengthy process. In this instance the life-size
portrait (Louvre) is on parchment fastened down onto a
wood panel. In other words, due to shortness of time,
Holbein resorted to what means he could to achieve a life-
size portrait of the bride and the Louvre picture must be
the original drawing from life. The other medium which
could result in a likeness faster than the lengthy processes
and delays in drying out of paint-layers and glazes, would
have been a miniature. There would have been no
conceivable demand for such a thing of Anne after July
1540 and it seems reasonable to argue that Holbein
produced the two simultaneously. There is nothing
mechanical or derivative about the miniature as it is of an
outstanding quality with typical brilliance of
characterization, the pale face enlivened by brown eyes
and the details of dress rendered with customary exactitude
leaving no part of its structure to the imagination.

The turned ivory box in the form of a Tudor rose is the
only original box to survive from this period and no
parallel has yet been found. The condition is good
although the paint losses at the edge and the lack of a gold
edge-line suggest that it was trimmed to fit the box.

COLLECTIONS: First recorded in 1720 by George Vertue as follows:
    "a head of Anne of Cleves. painted Curiously a limning in a
    round Ivory box turn'd finely like a Rose with loose leaves. this
    done by Holbein, probably the picture that was done to show
    King Henry before she came over Mr. Alexander" (*Notebooks*,
    I, p. 65); it is not clear from this whether the Mr. Alexander
    was or was not its owner; next recorded by Vertue, 1732, when
    in the collection of Colonel James Seymour (1658(?)–1739):
    "The picture of Anne a Cleve I had another View of it in the
    Possession of Col. Seamor. it is a round Curious turnd Ivory

box the head only in full front. the ground blew. painted by Holbein. & supposed to be the Very picture showd to the King Hen. 8.-" (*Notebook*, IV, p. 45); Colonel James Seymour was father of the painter. Vertue records that he "drew and limned very ingeniously. he allways was conversant with the nobles & virtuosi of his Time all Lovers & practioners of the Arts of Painting Scripture graving &c – as well as mechanical works of Arts. had an infinite number of curious pictures, drawing & print of all kinds past thro' his hands was in great esteem" (*Notebooks*, III, p. 86); probably in the sale that followed his death it was purchased by the collector Thomas Barrett of Lee Priory, Kent (1698–1757) in whose possession Vertue records it c. 1739: "Anne a Cleve. a curious limning in an Ivory box finely turnd. done by Hans Holben" (*Notebooks*, IV, 1935–36, p. 156); engraved 1739 by Houbracken with slight variants and inscribed: *Holben pinxit. In the Collection of Thomas Barret Esqr*; descended to his son Thomas Barrett Brydges of Denton Court; during this period it is recorded at Lee, first in 1794 by Horace Wolpole (letter to the Misses Berry, 28th September 1794) and by Sir Thomas Croft in 1825 (letter of August 10th 1825 to his aunt, Elizabeth Croft, in the possession of the late Edward Croft Murray); sold in 1826 to a dealer named Tuck (Chamberlain, *Holbein*, II, p. 182); resold to Francis Douce, the antiquary (1757–1834); there it formed part of the Doucean Museum: "no 26 a beautiful miniature by Holbein, like the last, in an ivory box, but the cover elaborately carved so as to imitate the English rose, 1539" (*Gentleman's Magazine*, March, 1836, pp. 245ff.); passed to his second cousin, Lt-Col. Augustus Meyrick whose son bequeathed it to Miss Eleanor Davies (d. 1933) who sold it to George Salting; bequeathed with the Salting Collection to the V & A 1910.

LITERATURE: The miniature is referred to in all books on Holbein that refer to the Louvre portrait. None add anything to the basic documentation which is published in full in Chamberlain, *Holbein*, II, pp. 171–84.

HANS HOLBEIN

31 **Elizabeth Grey, Lady Audley**, c. 1540

H.M. The Queen
Vellum stuck to playing card with part of a heart verso, circular, 56 mm, 2½ in. diam.

Elizabeth Grey, Lady Audley (d. 1564), daughter of Thomas Grey, 2nd Marquis of Dorset and Margaret Wotton. She married in 1538 Thomas, Lord Audley of Walden who died in 1544, she then married, in 1549, George Norton.

There have always been problems as to the correct identity of the sitter, because there were two Audley families at court. Previously the sitter has been identified with Elizabeth Tuke wife of the 9th Lord Audley. He, however, did not succeed to the title until 1557. The suggestion that it is Elizabeth Grey, who became Lady Audley in 1538 is surely correct. An additional fact is the sitter's close link with the inner royal and quasi-royal circle who sat for miniatures.

The miniature is highly important as the drawing for it survives (no. 32). No life-scale portrait is known and it offers a direct insight into Holbein's working methods as

31

applied to portraiture on any scale. Unlike Hornebolte all Holbein's portraits began with a drawing from life from which he could execute either a panel picture or a miniature. The occasion of this miniature could have been Lady Audley's marriage in 1538 and the pose is the same formula repeated for a whole series of queens and court ladies during Holbein's second English period, turning the sitter to a three-quarter's view with hands clasped at the waist.

The costume has been extensively restored and there is some abrasion in the face and features.

COLLECTIONS: Possibly Charles II inventory, c. 1662–85 (no. 405): "A Dutch woman in a red garment holding boath her hands togeather. In small Limbning"; James II's catalogue (no. 615): "A limning of woman in red, with her hands before her"; temp. George I at Kensington (Stowe MS 567, f.8 "Une femme en Habit rouge"); first certainly listed as Lady Audley by Holbein in the Royal Library by Woltmann, 1866 (*Holbein und seine Zeit*, II, p. 248).

LITERATURE: Chamberlain, *Holbein*, II, pp. 222–23.
C. Winter, *Burlington Magazine*, LXXXIII, 1943, p. 266.
Ganz, *Holbein*, p. 259 (143).
Holbein, *Queen's Gallery*, 1978 (83).

HANS HOLBEIN

32 **Elizabeth Grey, Lady Audley**

H.M. The Queen
Black and coloured chalks, outlines reinforced in pen and ink, metal point in jewellery and writing at the bottom, on pink prepared paper, 292 × 207 mm, 11½ × 8⅛ in. (*Photograph*).
See no. 31

The second example of a drawing for which a miniature is extant. There is no known oil portrait. As in the case of Lord Abergavenny (no. 25) this gives a vivid insight into Holbein's working practices, in this instance via the annotations on the dress and the drawing of the jewellery. Norgate records, in the next century, that it was customary for a sitter to send the jewels and dress to the studio so that

Hans Holbein 49

34   **35**

the miniaturist could work on these details at his leisure. The dress is annotated *samet* (velvet) and *rot damast* (red damask) and the jewel at the front of her bodice with *rot* (red) *w* (for *weiss*, white), (?) *Gl* (for gold), and a small heart-shaped leaf for green. Even with these notes plus a retentive visual memory, it would seem difficult to believe that Holbein could have painted the detailed rendering of the gold work on the headdress and the embroidery on the neckline and sleeves without them being sent to his workshop.

INSCRIBED: At the top, later: *The Lady Audley*.

COLLECTIONS: See no. 26 for the early history; it seems that book of drawings was acquired by Charles II and is refered to as being in the Royal Collection again in 1675.

LITERATURE: K. T. Parker, *Holbein*, 1945, p. 51 (58); Holbein, *Queen's Gallery*, 1978 (44).

HANS HOLBEIN

33   ?Catherine Howard, c. 1540

H.M. The Queen
Vellum stuck to a playing card with four diamonds verso, circular, 62 mm, 2$\frac{15}{32}$ in. diam.

Catherine Howard (1520/21–42), niece of Thomas Howard, Duke of Norfolk, married Henry VIII in 1540. She was beheaded for adultery in 1542.

Two versions exist of this miniature, of which the second in the Buccleuch Collection was established in 1977 to be the repetition, also slightly clipped (Ganz, *Holbein*, p. 259 (142)). Research on Tudor miniatures before c. 1570 indicates a sitter of exceptional importance, as duplicates in the case of women exist only of Henry VIII's queens. Nothing certain is known of the Royal Collection miniature until it was recorded by Fraser Tytler in the 1840s when it appears as Queen Catherine Howard. It is conceivable that it is identical to one at Lee Priory along with that of Anne of Cleves recorded by Vertue in 1739. The Buccleuch version was seen by Vertue, c. 1736 when in the collection of Jonathan Richardson when he states it was "called Katherine Howard" (*Notebooks*, V, p. 116). It

was not, apparently so in the 17th century when Hollar engraved it (1646), then it was in the Arundel Collection and known as Mary, Duchess of Suffolk. It cannot, however, be her, as she died too early. As there is no known portrait of Catherine Howard such a suggested identification must remain unproven. On the other hand evidence in favour is considerably stronger than when I last considered it in 1969 (*Tudor and Jacobean*, I, p. 44): (i) Duplicates only exist of queens: Catherine Howard is the only one who fits. Authentic portraits discount the other queens. (ii) She is wearing at her neck the same jewel that appears in Holbein's Jane Seymour (*Princely Magnificence*, 1980 (P5)), a ruby above an emerald which would argue strongly for a subsequent queen. (iii) Janet Arnold points out that the pearls around the neckline could connect with Henry VIII's gift in 1540 to Catherine Howard of a "Square conteignyng xxxiij Diamondes and lx rubyes with an Edge of peerll conteignyng xxiij", (ibid., loc. cit.).

The Royal Collection version is from life and Holbein uses his usual formula for female portraits during this period. The technical examination carried out in 1977 dispelled any doubts cast upon its authenticity by Ganz and some other Holbein scholars. The silver in the dress has oxidized and the features have been restored.

COLLECTIONS: Conceivably that recorded, 1739, in the collection of Lee Priory, Kent (1698–1757), who also owned the Anne of Cleves (no. 30): "Katherine Howard a limning – by or (after rather H. Holben" (*Notebooks*, IV, p. 156); presumably acquired in the 1840s when Victoria and Albert embarked on their miniature collection; Fraser Tytler *List* (73 or another unnumbered one of the same sitter).

LITERATURE: Chamberlain, *Holbein*, II, p. 192–93.
Ganz, *Holbein*, p. 259 (141).
Strong, *Tudor and Jacobean*, I, p. 44.
Holbein, *Queen's Gallery*, 1978 (84).

HANS HOLBEIN

34   Henry Brandon, 2nd Duke of Suffolk, 1540–41

H.M. The Queen
Vellum stuck to a playing card with part of a king verso, circular, 55 mm, 2$\frac{5}{32}$ in. diam.

Henry Brandon, 2nd Duke of Suffolk (1535–1551), eldest son of Charles Brandon, 1st Duke of Suffolk and his fourth wife, Catherine Willoughby. He was educated with Prince Edward and subsequently at St John's College, Cambridge. With his brother (no. 35) renowned for their learning. Both died of the sweating sickness.

The inscription is confusing combining the age, five, with the date of the month when the portrait was painted, 6th September, with, below, the impossible year, 1535. This could refer to the sitter's birth on September 18th 1535 but it seems unlikely as the companion (no. 35) records the date of the portrait. Henry Brandon would have been five in 1540–41 and the miniatures must have been painted as a pair. Examination under intense magnification suggests that the date could have been altered. The miniature and the second one of his younger brother are part of a series bearing testimony to the intense interest in miniatures shown by the Dukes of Suffolk and their family (nos. 10, 35). As usual the composition is totally different from Hornebolte's and relates to Holbein's large-scale portrait of Prince Edward painted at exactly the same period (Ganz, *Holbein*, pl. 146). The motif of the arm resting on a table is a development of the familar ledge (e.g. Derich Born, 1533, ibid., pl. 107). A drawing of a mother, or nurse, with a baby and two boys (British Museum, Chamberlain, *Holbein*, II, pl. 32) shows one in an identical pose to the miniature, with an arm resting on the arm of a bench.

Both miniatures have always been accepted as by Holbein, apart from a doubt cast by Ganz and complete rejection by Schmid, both of which can be discounted. Technically they belong within the small group that are authentic. There is a restoration in the feather.

INSCRIBED: On the table right: *ETATIS.SVAE.5.6. SEPDEM.| ANNO | 1535*

COLLECTIONS: Presented by Sir Henry Fanshawe to Charles I and recorded by van der Dort (Millar, *Walpole Society*, XXXVII, 1960, p. 119 (nos. 64–65); sold by the Commonwealth and recovered at the Restoration; Charles II inventory, c. 1662–85 (no. 383); James II's catalogue (no. 646), temp. George I, at Kensington (Stowe MS 567, f./v as "Un Garson en Habit Raye" and "Un Garson avec un bonet Noir"); recorded by Vertue in 1720 and 1734 (*Notebooks*, I, p. 74; IV, p. 67; recorded Fraser Tytler, *List* (no. 21).

LITERATURE: Chamberlain, *Holbein*, II, pp. 224–26.
C. Winter, *Burlington Magazine*, LXXXIII, 1943, p. 266.
Ganz, *Holbein*, p. 259 (145).
Holbein, *Queen's Gallery*, 1978 (85–86).

HANS HOLBEIN

35 **Charles Brandon, 3rd Duke of Suffolk**, 1541

H.M. The Queen
Vellum stuck to a playing card with one club verso, circular, 55 mm, 2$\frac{5}{32}$ in. diam.

Charles Brandon, 3rd Duke of Suffolk (1537–51), second son of Charles Brandon, Duke of Suffolk and Catherine

36

Willoughby. With his brother (no. 34) celebrated for their learning and dying half an hour later than him of the sweating sickness.

For a general discussion see no. 34. The presentation of Charles Brandon with pen and paper reflects the precociousness for which the brothers were noted. Sitters depicted in the act of writing are a recurring formula in Holbein's portraits, from Erasmus (1523) onwards. The frontal pose with hands and papers with or without a ledge likewise recurs (Ganz, *Holbein*, pl. 105, 106, 130). There is a small restoration on the right shoulder.

INSCRIBED: On the paper: *ANN – | 1541 | .ETATIS SVAE 3 | . 10. MARCI.*

COLLECTIONS and LITERATURE: As no. 34.

HANS HOLBEIN

36 **Unknown Man**, 1540–43

Yale Center for British Art, New Haven (B 1974.2.58)
Vellum stuck to plain card, circular, 46 mm, 1$\frac{13}{16}$ in. diam.

Formerly attributed to Hornebolte by Reynolds. Technically, of course, it is perfectly compatible with his work, but compositionally it bears little relation. It does, however, fit well into the small group of miniatures that are certainly by Holbein. It is monumental in concept, graphic in treatment and there is also a profundity of characterization in the downcast eyes beyond Hornebolte's capabilities. The inscription is also typical of those on other Holbein miniatures, quite unlike ones by Hornebolte. The costume with bonnet and short-clipped hair is c. 1540 and close to that in Holbein's drawing of William Parr, 1st Marquess of Northampton which was almost certainly executed after 1541 or 1542 (see *Holbein*; Queen's Gallery, 1978 (53)). Some scratch marks and minor flaking.

INSCRIBED: On either side of the head: *ÆTATIS | SVE 35*

COLLECTIONS: Miss Dorothy Hutton, MVO; sold Sotheby's 1st June 1970 (lot 87).

LITERATURE: *British Portraits*, RA, 1956 (607).
Reynolds, *Connoisseur: Complete Period Guides*, 1968, p. 190, pl. 69B.

Hans Holbein 51

Survival: Levina Teerlinc, 1510/20–1576

37

38

1510/20. Born, one of the children of Simon Benninck, one of the chief exponents of the Ghent-Bruges school of illuminators

1546. Recruited into the service of Henry VIII with an annuity of £40 p.a., by which time she had married George Teerlinc

1551. Warrant to pay Teerlinc for a portrait of the Princess Elizabeth

1553. Presents Mary I with "a smale picture of the Trynite", the first of a series of New Year's gifts of pictures or limnings which continued until 1576

1576. Death of Levina Teerlinc

As in the case of Lucas Hornebolte the present exhibition is the first occasion when a group of miniatures has been assembled which can be attributed to Levina Teerlinc. As a person she is amply documented occupying a superior role in the royal household as gentlewoman to both Mary I and the young Elizabeth. To the latter she annually presented a limning each New Year's Day and these offer evidence not only that she painted single portraits of the Queen but ones of her in groups on progress or with her Knights of the Garter. Very few miniatures certainly datable to the years 1546–76 have so far emerged and, tempting as it would be to attribute all of them to Teerlinc, there were two other artists who are believed also to have practised limning. Richard Haydocke in 1598 states that both John Shute (d. 1563) and John Bettes (died before 1570) were limners. The former described himself as 'architect and painter', although we have no examples, and the latter was a distinguished author of panel portraits in a manner which presupposes study of, if not training by, Hans Holbein.

Nonetheless there is a convincing group of miniatures that emerge as the work of a single hand, one whose draughtsmanship is weak, whose paint is thin and transparent and whose brushwork loose. These centre on a miniature of an Elizabethan Maundy (no. 42) and a series of female portraits of members of the royal family, Catherine Grey (no. 38) and the young Elizabeth (nos 37, 40), all of which show the same compositional mannerisms and the same emaciated treatment of the figure. These, in their turn, relate to a series of manuscript illuminations in the same loose style (no. 45). Her role at court with its handsome annual annuity brought little pressure on her to commercialize as her successor, Nicholas Hilliard, was forced to do. Within this group of miniatures, feeble though they may be, there is, however, a degree of innovation in subject matter, in the use of new forms of inscription and in adopting the oval format, much of which was never to be brought to fruition by Hilliard. It is amongst the royal seals and other official, government promoted, printed images of the mid-Tudor monarchs that we are probably contemplating her originating hand. When she died in 1576 she was not replaced on the royal payroll. By then she was a solitary survivor of Henry VIII's

recruitment of artists from abroad and the direct line of connexion with the Ghent-Bruges line of illuminators was finally broken.

SELECT BIBLIOGRAPHY
Auerbach, *Tudor Artists*, pp. 75–77, 91, 103–6, 187–88.
Strong, *Renaissance Miniature*, pp. 54–64

ATTRIBUTED TO LEVINA TEERLINC

37 Unknown Lady, Possibly Elizabeth I as a Princess, c. 1550

Yale Center for British Art, New Haven
(B1971.2.59)
Vellum stuck to plain paper, circular, 48 mm, 1⅞ in. diam.

It would be tempting to attribute this to Hornebolte as the inscription is typical of his style, but detailed examination of the object would indicate this more probably to be the work of Levina Teerlinc, done soon after her arrival in England. The draughtsmanship is much weaker than anything by Hornebolte, the treatment of the features thin and transparent and the tiny arms are also a recurring feature in Teerlinc's female sitters. Teerlinc too was influenced by large-scale painters and this miniature reflects the work of Master John e.g. Mary I, 1544 (Strong, *The English Icon*, p. 76 (12)).

39

All the sitters for miniatures by the court limners come from a closely-knit royal circle which would probably narrow the identity of the possible sitter down to either Mary I, Elizabeth I as a princess, or one of their cousins, the three Grey sisters. The dress is of a type worn between the middle 1540s and the early 1550s. Mary I would have been too old and Lady Jane Grey only ten in 1547. This leaves Elizabeth who was eighteen in 1551. The earliest portrait of her is the famous picture in the Royal Collection (Strong, *Portraits of Queen Elizabeth I*, 1963, pl. I) depicting her between the ages of twelve and fourteen, c. 1542–47. There are no more certain portraits until the miniatures by Levina of the 1560s (nos 45, 46) when the Queen was in her late twenties or early thirties with a greatly changed appearance and dress. The Yale miniature follows the Royal Collection picture well as the face of a fully developed, tough teenager. She is wearing a highly important jewel with an *à l'antique* profile head, probably of a Roman emperor, in jet with the laurel garland and looped mantle worked in gold into which sprigs of acorns and cowslips have been tucked.

There are a number of appreciable paint losses in the background and flaking and discolouration. In addition there are minor losses in the hair and features.

INSCRIBED: On either side of the head: +*A° N+* | + *XVIII* +

COLLECTIONS: Miss Dorothy Hutton; sold Sotheby's 1st June 1970 (lot 87).

ATTRIBUTED TO LEVINA TEERLINC

38 Catherine Grey, Countess of Hertford, 1555–60

Victoria & Albert Museum (P.10–1979)
Vellum stuck to a plain card, circular, 35 mm, 1⅜ in. diam.

Lady Catherine Grey (1540–68), daughter of Frances, Marchioness of Dorset and Duchess of Suffolk and of Henry Grey, Marquis of Dorset and Duke of Suffolk and grand-daughter of Henry VIII's sister, Mary, Queen of France and wife of Charles Brandon, Duke of Suffolk. Together with her elder and younger sisters, Jane and Mary, enjoyed the status of Tudor princesses. Under Mary she first received the advances of the Duke of Somerset's son, Edward Seymour, Earl of Hertford. In 1560, without royal permission, she secretly married him, a fact which the imminent birth of a child brought to light. Sent to the Tower by Elizabeth, she was later, in 1563, transferred to confinement in the country where she died in 1568.

The miniature is in its original turned ivory box. The forehead has suffered from abrasion, the background is discoloured and there are paint losses at the edge. The identification as Lady Catherine Grey is secured by the very early inscription on the back of the miniature. A second version, very much repainted, of the same miniature but bearing the date 1549 is also in the V & A (P.21–1954). The date, however, is a later addition and the costume is typical of Mary's reign which would accord with the age of the sitter, about fifteen to twenty, c. 1555–60. The formula is derived from portraits by Hans Eworth and this relationship is clearer in the second version which is to the waist and includes the hands clasped together.

A third miniature of the same sitter, which may also be by Teerlinc, is at Belvoir Castle (Duke of Rutland) (Auerbach, *Hilliard*, pl. 8), depicting the Countess wearing a miniature of her husband and carrying her son in her arms. The dating can therefore be established as the child was born on September 21st 1561 and must be about a year to eighteen months in the miniature, i.e. late 1562 or early 1563. Large-scale paintings, probably derived from the miniature, exist of this, e.g. Audley End, Petworth, Syon and Trinity College, Oxford.

INSCRIBED: On the reverse in a late sixteenth century hand: *the La Kathe'* | *Graye.* | *Wyfe of Therle of* | *hertford.*

COLLECTIONS: Sold anonymously Sotheby's 25th June 1979 (lot 88).

ATTRIBUTED TO LEVINA TEERLINC

39 *Certain prayers to be used by the quenes heignes in the consecration of the crampe rynges*, 1553–58

Westminster Cathedral
Vellum, 206 × 154 mm, 8⅛ × 6 in.

The manuscript provides the order of service to bless rings for the healing of cramp each Good Friday, a practice established by the reign of Edward II. Once the monarch had finished prostrating himself before the cross in the chapel royal, he would go up to the altar and place on it an offering in new gold and silver coins. He would then redeem this by ordinary coins and from these talismanic rings were made which were believed to relieve muscular pains or spasms, and, more especially, epilepsy. Hence they were called cramp rings. By the Tudor period the ceremonial had changed and ready-made rings were offered at the foot of the cross and redeemed. One illumination in this manuscript shows Mary I kneeling before the altar within an enclosure with two golden dishes containing cramp rings resting on top of the railings. She is shown at the moment preceeding the action, in which she prays and simultaneously takes each of the rings and rubs them, after which they were sprinkled with holy water. The cramp ring ceremonial was revived by Mary but abandoned by Elizabeth.

The manuscript goes on to give the ritual for a second more familiar regal custom, continued by her successor, touching for scrofula, or the King's Evil. As was customary the monarch is shown seated while the young patient kneels and is touched twice by her. On the first occasion the Queen laid her bare hands on the sufferer, on the second, she made the sign of the cross over his sores, holding in her fingers a gold coin which was subsequently hung around the patient's neck. A Venetian describes Mary making each sufferer swear "never to part from the piece of money except in the case of extreme need".

Both ceremonies epitomized the Marian Catholic revival and both scenes are clearly based on actual observation of the ceremonies. The likeness of the Queen is also a portrait one. In addition to these scenes the manuscript contains a Crucifixion based on a stock Ghent-Bruges pattern, a royal coat of arms and borders adorned with swags of fruit, Tudor symbols, virtues and grotesque work. The latter is in the manner of a series of panels probably from Nonsuch Palace (E. Croft-Murray, *Decorative Painting in England 1537–1837*, London, 1962, pls. 17–20). There is also ornament based on Thomas Geminus's *Morysse and Damashin renewed and encreased very profitable for Goldsmythes and Embroiderars* (1548).

The style of the borders links it to a number of manuscripts (e.g. no. 45) and the attribution to Levina Teerlinc is a perfectly reasonable one. The draughtsmanship is weak, the painting thin with washes over the 'carnations' exactly as in the miniatures. The quality of the manuscript indicates that it was probably done in great haste to meet the Queen's programme of Catholic revival.

COLLECTIONS: Apparently seen by Thomas Hearne, c. 1700–25; owned by Cardinal Wiseman by 1851.

LITERATURE: *Notes and Queries*, 1st series, VII, 1853, p. 88.
Sir Henry Ellis, *Proceedings of the Society of Antiquaries*, 1st series, II, 1853, pp. 292–94.
W. Sparrow Simpson, "On the forms of prayer recited 'at the healing' or touching for the King's Evil", *Journal of the British Archaeological Association*, 1871, pp. 285–87.
R. Crawford, *The King's Evil*, Oxford, 1911, opp. p. 68.
R. Crawford, "The blessing of cramp-rings. A chapter in the history of the treatment of epilepsy", *Studies in the history and method of science*, ed. C. Singer, Oxford, 1917, I, opp. p. 178.

Marc Bloch, *The Royal Touch, Sacred Monarchy and Scrofula in England and France*, trans. J. E. Anderson, London, 1973, pp. 92–107; 181–82; 256 (6); 259 (19).
British Portraits, R.A., 1956 (598).

ATTRIBUTED TO LEVINA TEERLINC

40 ?Elizabeth I, c. 1565

H.M. The Queen
Vellum stuck to a playing card with four hearts at the reverse, circular, 45.5 mm, 1 $\frac{25}{32}$ in. diam.

This format, derived from Hans Eworth, is typical of Teerlinc, the frontal portrait with hands clasped before the sitter. The face has been entirely repainted and there are paint losses, abrasion and staining over the rest of the miniature. Nonetheless what remains constitutes a vestigial Teerlinc. The identity as Elizabeth can be questioned but the tradition goes back to the 1630s and agrees with the somewhat fragmentary iconography of the Queen before 1570.

COLLECTIONS: Conceivably in the Royal Collection from when it was painted; first recorded by van der Dort: "Item don upon the right lighte in a white Ivory Box/ wthout a Christall a Certaine Ladies Picture in her haire/ in a gold bone lace little ruff, and black habbitt/ lined wth white furr wth goulden Tissue sleeves/ wth one hand over another supposed to have bin -/ Queene Elizabeth before shee came to the Crowne"; the margin is annotated "don by an unknoune/hand" and the size is given as 2$\frac{1}{8}$ in. diam. (Millar, *Walpole Society*, XXXVII, 1960, p. 113 (no. 42)); Charles II inventory (no. 450) (temp 1662–85): "A woman in black bodies Ioined with furr embroidered sleeves, wth her hands before her. Limbning. In a small round Ivory frame"; sold anonymously Christie's April 10th 1962 (lot 94); acquired for the Royal Collection.

LITERATURE: O'Donoghue, *Catalogue*, 1894, p. 27 (7).
Auerbach, *Tudor Artists*, p. 76.

HANS EWORTH

41 Unknown Lady, 1557

The Tate Gallery (T.1569)
Oil on panel, 59.8 × 48.3 cm, 23$\frac{1}{2}$ × 19 in.

Hans Eworth (fl.1540–73) was by far the most distinguished portrait painter working in England in the middle of the sixteenth century. His background was Netherlandish and his earliest dated work appears in 1549, followed by a steady stream of pictures down to 1570 signed with the monogram HE. Although he held no official position he emerges as unofficial court painter to Mary I. He painted several portraits of her, including a miniature in oil (Strong, *The English Icon*, pp. 87 (23–24), 89 (7), 100 (44), 105 (52)) and it is significant that he seems to have fallen from favour on Elizabeth's accession.

Teerlinc was clearly familiar with Eworth's work. This portrait is a typical example of a recurring formula, the half-length with hands clasped before the waist. It was already utilized by Holbein in the late 1530s but in Eworth's hands the sitters are progressively turned more and more towards the onlooker until they finally face the spectator. Eworth would seem to be the likely source for Teerlinc's treatment of her half-length female sitters (see no. 40).

INSCRIBED: Top left: *HE; VIVRE POVR MOVRIR | MOVRIR POVR VIVRE*: top right: *ÆTATIS 29.|1557.*

COLLECTIONS: Percy Moore Turner by 1925; sold Christie's 3rd May 1929 (94); bt. Bellesi; sold to Mr Sully; with Wildenstein, New York by 1932; with M. H. Wildenstein, London, 1953; purchased, 1963.

LITERATURE: *Tate Gallery Report, 1963–64*, p. 23 (T.606). *Hans Eworth*, National Portrait Gallery, 1965 (6). Strong, *The English Icon*, p. 90 (28).

ATTRIBUTED TO LEVINA TEERLINC

42 An Elizabethan Maundy, c. 1565

The Countess Beauchamp, M.B.E., K[1]
Vellum stuck to card, originally square or rectangular but cut into an oval, 65 × 55 mm, $2\frac{3}{4} \times 2\frac{1}{4}$ in.

The miniature has been cut into an oval shape and mounted onto a card with a gold border. It is difficult to guess its original shape but the composition would suggest a square or more probably a rectangle. Although it is conceivable that this has been cut from an illuminated page, its minute scale would suggest that it ought to be identical with one of the series of miniatures presented by the artist to the Queen as a New Year's Gift during the 1560s, (listed in Strong, *Renaissance Miniature*, p. 55). Several of these depicted court scenes, including the Queen on progress and the Garter ceremonial. Like the Cramp Ring Manuscript (no. 39) it is the result of a direct observation of the ritual worked up subsequently in the studio. Teerlinc is unlikely to have been an innovator here. In 1556 Nicholas Lizarde presented Mary I with a "Table painted with the Maundy" (Auerbach, *Tudor Artists*, p. 146). As in the case of touching for the King's Evil and the Garter ceremonies, Elizabeth preserved those customary for Maundy Thursday in which she, in imitation of Christ, washed the feet of the number of poor women corresponding to her age. These are seen seated in two long rows on either side stretching from front to back with a gentlewoman standing behind each one. In the centre at the back stand the choristers with the Gentlemen of the Chapel Royal wearing copes. The Queen seems already to have worked her way down the line on the right hand side and, attended by her train of ladies, all wearing long white aprons, to be about to embark on the left. One of the old men in attendance is probably the Lord Chamberlain of the Household as he carries a white rod. The attenuated figures, awkward draughtsmanship and thin colour are familiar characteristics of Teerlinc.

The miniature is very abraded and has suffered from extensive flaking. Auerbach first pointed out its

42

relationship to the Ghent-Bruges School and suggested the attribution to Teerlinc, which is surely right.

COLLECTIONS: Part of the collection by Catherine Denne, wife of William Lygon, 1st Earl Beauchamp (1747–1816).

LITERATURE: Long, *British Miniaturists*, 1929, p. 211. Auerbach, *Hilliard*, pp. 53–54, 287 (6).

DERICKE ANTHONY AFTER A DESIGN ATTRIBUTED TO LEVINA TEERLINC

43 Great Seal of Mary I, 1553

Wax, 125 mm, 4.9 in. diam. *(Photograph)*

The payment for the making of the Great Seal of Mary I reads: "To Dericke Anthony graver of the mynt for the gravinge and making of the great seale of England and for the silver that made the same . . . 83[li] xv[s] (P.R.O. E. 405/484, f.71[v]) The gravers at the Mint were not designers but were skilled at carrying out the designs of others. The process for making seals must have varied. Hilliard drew patterns, made models and could even make the matrix as he was a goldsmith (no. 193) but this would not have been so in the case of his predecessors. The attribution of this seal to Teerlinc is tentative and she cannot have gone further than providing to the graver line drawings for the observe and reverse. Teerlinc was no great draughtsman and these images evoke her weak style. On the obverse Mary is depicted as a somewhat squat figure with an overlarge crown on her head seated on a throne with a fringed tester in an empty space. Below on the exergue is her motto: *TEMPORIS FILIA VERITAS*. The reverse posed problems for a queen regnant could not be depicted as a knight at arms, so Mary is represented riding side-saddle on a caparisoned horse, a formula to be re-worked by Hilliard for Elizabeth (no. 193).

LITERATURE: A. Wyon, *The Great Seals of England*, London, 1887, p. 73.

44

ATTRIBUTED TO DERICKE ANTHONY AFTER A
DESIGN ATTRIBUTED TO LEVINA TEERLINC

44 Great Seal of Elizabeth I, 1559

Public Record Office (SC 13/L5)
Wax, 122 mm, 4.8 in. diam.

Wyon remarks over this seal that "The artistic merit of the
seals, which, as we noticed, had been declining for some
time, here touches its lowest depths". It is a comment more
applicable to that of Mary (no. 43) than to this of
Elizabeth. No documentation for this seal has so far
emerged but it is likely to have followed precedent, having
all the mannerisms of that of Mary. The favour Teerlinc
enjoyed under Elizabeth, the close relationship of its design
to illuminations of the Queen enthroned attributable to her
(no. 45) and the fact that Elizabeth automatically turned
to a limner, Hilliard, to design her next seal, would suggest
a pattern and a connexion. The design of the obverse is an
improvement on its predecessor, the throne and canopy
filling the enclosure. The motto this time emphasizes the
Protestant revival: *PVLCHRVM PRO PATRIA PATI*. The
reverse virtually duplicates that of Mary but with the
interesting addition of serpenting branches of Tudor roses,
a motif to be developed by Hilliard in the Second Great
Seal (no. 193).

LITERATURE: A. Wyon, *The Great Seals of England*, London, 1887,
p. 76.

ATTRIBUTED TO LEVINA TEERLINC

45 Indenture between Elizabeth I and the Dean and Canons of St George's Chapel, Windsor, 30th August 1559

Public Record Office, London, (E.36/277)
Illumination, 10×8 cm, 4×3⅛ in.

The Poor Knights of Windsor were the reconstitution of
the medieval Alms-Knights as specified in Henry VIII's

will. Elizabeth duly established the Knights in the first
year of her reign who were to be "thirteen poor men,
decayed in Wars, and such like service of the Realm, to be
called *Thirteen Knights of Windsor*". (Elias Ashmole, *The
Institution, Laws and Ceremonies of the Most Noble Order of the
Garter*, London, 1672, pp. 158–65).

The indenture is closely related to the Cramp Ring
manuscript (no. 39) although it shows fewer signs of haste.
The borders contain identical motifs: arabesques
interspersed with Tudor symbols and arms with grapes,
gilly flowers and roses. The *Liber Ceruleus* of the Order of
the Garter contains pages and royal portraits in the same
manner of Mary, Philip and Mary and the young
Elizabeth, all attributable to Teerlinc. These illuminations
are on documents directly connected with the monarch.
They are technically executed in exactly the same manner
as the miniatures although the degree of finish can vary.

The formal portrait of Elizabeth is a type, as Auerbach
demonstrates, that became standard on official documents.
Teerlinc's role as the initiator of this image would seem
more than a logical one.

LITERATURE: E. Auerbach, "An Elizabethan Indenture",
Burlington Magazine, CXII, 1951, pp. 319–23.

LEVINA TEERLINC

46 New Year's Gift List, 1568

Society of Antiquaries, London (MS 538)

It was Levina Teerlinc's custom to present Elizabeth I with
a miniature annually, on New Year's Day. The surviving
Gift Rolls are a rich source of documentation for her work
giving evidence that she gave the Queen not only
miniatures of herself but also ones of her surrounded by her
court or even on progress. In 1568 she presented "a paper
paynted with the Quenis majestie and the knightes of the
order". As the entry does not refer to it as a picture or as
on card it seems likely that in this instance the gift took the
form of a detached illuminated page depicting Elizabeth

probably going in procession with the Knights of the Garter. Iconographically this would pick up a theme from the *Liber Niger* (no. 20) and anticipate Marcus Gheeraerts the Elder's engraving of 1576 (Hind, *Engraving*, I, pls. 52–56). These court scenes were not to be repeated by Hilliard.

LITERATURE: Strong, *Renaissance Miniature*, p. 55.

ATTRIBUTED TO LEVINA TEERLINC

47 Unknown Man, 1569

The Countess Beauchamp, M.B.E., K[1]
Vellum stuck onto card, oval, 39 × 32 mm,
$1\frac{9}{16} \times 1\frac{1}{4}$ in.

Technically identical in handling to a second miniature at Waddesdon of an unknown man enclosed in a celestial sphere also by Teerlinc and also dated 1569 (Strong, *Renaissance Miniature*, pl. 59). The sitter is wearing a white doublet slashed over red. The oval shape, which is authentic and not due to later clipping, is unique in Teerlinc's work and anticipates by a decade Hilliard's adoption of the form. The miniature is in very good condition.

INSCRIBED: On either side of the head: *27 | Año Dñi 1569*

COLLECTIONS: Part of the collection formed by Catherine Denne, wife of William Lygon, 1st Earl Beauchamp.

45

Nicholas Hilliard,
1547–1619

49

I BEGINNINGS, 1547–76

1547. Birth of Nicholas Hilliard, son of Richard Hilliard,
   an Exeter goldsmith
1557. Arrives in Geneva with the Bodley family seeking
   refuge from the Marian persecutions
1558. Presumably returned to London with the Bodleys
1562. Apprenticed to the Queen's goldsmith, Robert
   Brandon for seven years
1569. Became a freeman of the Goldsmiths' Company
1571. Earliest work as a practising miniaturist (no. 55).
   Also active both as a jeweller and goldsmith
1572. The Queen sits for Hilliard (no. 182)
1574. Designs a titlepage border (no. 65)
1576. Marries Alice Brandon (no. 77)

As in the case of virtually all Tudor artists the historical
facts about Nicholas Hilliard tell us little about the realities
of his training. What facts we do know about the young
Hilliard place him firmly in the context of west country
Protestantism amidst the prosperous urban middle classes.
A solitary miniature painted at the age of thirteen (no. 51)
indicates a precocious talent, conceivable links with the
Seymour family and that he had access by then to limnings
within the Ghent-Bruges tradition which he crudely tried
to imitate. Eleven years later he emerges with his first
dated miniature (no. 55) as a totally accomplished artist
working within a technical and stylistic format evolved by
Hornebolte and Teerlinc but with a talent far in excess of
theirs. Although, at the end of his life, he was to state that
he had always striven to imitate Holbein this was in fact
not the case. Hilliard's miniatures did not involve
preliminary drawings as Holbein's did. They were painted
directly from life onto the vellum before him.

In his *Treatise* he states that the miniaturist is grounded
in his art by copying engravings. The process of building
up his portraits is exactly that, of cross hatching and line
shading over a carnation ground. He was never to surpass
his portraits from the early 1570s for their sureness of touch
and frankness of characterization. In this aspect lay
Holbein's influence later to be eroded by the courtly
softness of the Clouets.

All the evidence points to a wide range of commissions
being undertaken by the Hilliard workshop: jewellery,
designs for woodcuts, panel portraits, decorative painting
as well as the miniatures. The broader aspect of his work
has always been obscured and needs to be emphasised as it
explains the trickle of miniatures. His proficiency in these
other spheres would have been variable and his panel
painting was decidedly inferior to his limning. Such
activities imply training in these skills by persons other
than Robert Brandon. Limning was such a covert
medium that it is likely that he was trained by Teerlinc. In
the case of oil painting he was heavily influenced if not
taught by the Master of the Countess of Warwick (no. 52).

After 1570 the miniature enters a new phase for Hilliard
was not a paid officer of the court and, as a result, was to
be in perpetual financial straits. As he operated as any
other tradesman or artificer, the status accorded artists in
backward Tudor England, he was open to any commission.
This fact resulted in the miniature as a portrait medium
being freely available for the first time to anyone who
could pay for it.

SELECT BIBLIOGRAPHY
Auerbach, *Hilliard*, pp. 1–10; 55–69.
Strong, *Renaissance Miniature*, pp. 63–74.

NICHOLAS HILLIARD

48   **Richard Hilliard**, 157(7?)

Victoria & Albert Museum (P.154–1910)
Vellum stuck onto card, the back of which has been
obscured by another card stuck to it at a later date,
circular, 41 mm, $1\frac{19}{32}$ in. diam.

Richard Hilliard (1518/19–1594), goldsmith of Exeter, was
of reformist bent and father of Nicholas.

The descent of this miniature is identical to that of the self-
portrait (no. 49) which, as in the case of the latter,
presupposes the miniature was painted in France or that
Hilliard was in England for a period during his known
time in France, if the date of 1577 is correct. V. J. Murrell
points out that the last figure of the date has completely
flaked away and that it could have been erroneously
restored. Auerbach (*Hilliard*, p. 2) establishes Richard's
birth to 1518/19 and, as he is fifty-eight in the miniature,
this would give us a date of either 1576 or 1577. If the
former it could work as having been painted just before the
artist left for France which was by July 1576.

Condition is generally good apart from flaking in the
background which has been restored with a paint that has
discoloured. The miniature was once set into a frame along
the lines of that still around Alice Brandon (no. 77) which
bore an inscription recorded by De Piles: *Ricardus Hilliardus
quondam vice-comes civitatis et comitatus Exoniae, anno 1560,
aetatis suae 58, annoq(ue) Domini 1577* (*Art of Painting*,
London, 1706, p. 431). This was discarded (see under
Nicholas No. 49) when it was inset into a snuff-box.

An eighteenth century copy is in the Buccleuch
collection (Auerbach, *Hilliard*, p. 293 (32)).

INSCRIBED: On either side of the head: *Aetatis suae 58 | Anno Dni. 157(?)* (restored to a 7) On a paper at the back of the frame an inscription by Lady Caroline Liddell: *Hilliard the | Father – painted by his | son – See an acc^T of these | pictures in H. Walpole's | anec. of pai(n)ting vol 1 art | Hilliard | These pictures were in the col | lection of the last and only Earl | of Leicester and were given by | him to the late field | Marshall ^Sir Robert | Rich | C E Liddell.*

COLLECTIONS: The descent is identical to the one of Nicholas (see no. 49).

LITERATURE: V & A, 1947 (13).
Auerbach, *Hilliard*, pp. 70–71, pl. 31; 292 (30).

NICHOLAS HILLIARD

49 **Self-portrait**, 1577

Victoria & Albert Museum (P.155–1910)
Vellum, stuck to card (the back of the original card is not visible, as a thick layer of later card has been glued to it), circular 41 mm, 1⅝ in. diam.

Hilliard painted his self-portrait while he was in France. As a miniature it has suffered extensive damage and restoration, both the right cheek and beard and ruff have been repainted and the warm tones of the face are restorer's work. In spite of this the brilliance and boldness of the characterization comes through with force so that we can understand the high esteem in which this miniature and the companion one of his father (no. 48) were held from their first appearance at the beginning of the eighteenth century.

Carl Winter, who first discussed the stylistic sources, referred to the influence of portrait medals by Germain Pilon which often show the bonnet touching the rim of the circumference, a view endorsed by Auerbach. This, however, was already a feature of miniatures painted before the French visit. It is the mood rather than the formula which echoes portraiture of the late Valois court. Painters there enjoyed a higher social standing than their English counterparts who were regarded as artificers and tradespeople. That he chose to paint himself at this moment reflects a period when he moved in French humanist circles and exchanged conversation with the poet Ronsard. The status enjoyed by painters at the Valois court must have come as a revelation to Hilliard and it must have been there surely that he first came into contact with the Renaissance concept of the artist. Exposure to the highly sophisticated attitudes of the art-loving court of Henri III and Catherine de' Medici prompted Hilliard to recognize his own genius.

The miniature of his father (no. 48) is also probably dated 1577 and shares the same descent from Nicholas's son, Laurence, and both were once inset into later frames on the lines of that still surrounding Alice Hilliard (no. 77). Possibly it was Laurence Hilliard who mounted the family portraits in this way. De Piles records the inscriptions on both. That on Hilliard ran: *Nicholas Hilliardus Aurifaber, Sculptor, & celebris Illuminator Serenissimae Reginae Elisabethae, Anno 1577. Aetatis suae 30* (*Art of Painting*, London, 1706, p. 431). Sometime before 1735 the frame and mount were

discarded when they were set, as Vertue records (see Collections) in a snuff box lid by the 7th Earl of Leicester. Two versions exist (Buccleuch and a private collection) of a self-portrait as a boy, dated 1560. One is certainly a later copy and the second of uncertain status, (Strong, *Renaissance Miniature* p. 66).

INSCRIBED: On either side of the head: *Ano Dni.|1577; Ætatis Suae |30;* above the left shoulder: *NH* in monogram (damaged).
On the back of the frame an inscription on part of their descent by the Hon Mrs Thomas Liddell: *Hilliard the | son painted by | himself – see the Father | These pictures were given | to me by Mrs Clavering | who had them originally from S^ir Robt Rich | 1843 C E Liddell.*

COLLECTIONS: This or both this and the one of Richard Hilliard (no. 48) are referred to in the will of Laurence Hilliard dated February 21st 1640 bequeathing to his son, Thomas, "by way of Leagacey my ^granFather(s) (pic) Hillyard his picture in an ivrey box with a Cristall vpponst" (Auerbach, *Hilliard*, p. 227) this originally read "my Fathars pic" and was altered to "my gran Fathar"; both are next referred to by de Piles in 1706 when in the possession of Simon Fanshaw: "There are, moreover, two wonderful pieces of his, now in the Possession of *Simon Fanshaw*, Esq; and by him valu'd, nor without reason, as 'tis the opinion of some good Judges, at above 50 Guineas each, tho'not much bigger than a Crown-Piece. One of these is the Picture of our Artist himself, with this / inscription in Gold Letters round it. |*Nicolaus . . .*| The other is the Picture of his Father . . . These two pictures in *Miniature* are so Masterly done, that not only the Faces are finely colour'd, and naturally with a good *Rilievo*; but that almost each single Hair is express'd." (De Piles, *The Art Of Painting*, London, 1706, pp. 430–31 and Vertue, *Notebooks*, II, p. 129); both were acquired by John Sidney, 6th Earl of Leicester (1680–1737) and passed on his death to his brother Jocelyn Sidney, 7th and last Earl of Leicester (d. 1743); these facts are recorded by Vertue when he saw them at Leicester House in 1735 and in addition he records: "the writeing round these two pictures and the gilt mettal Frames first made for them was taken away and the two pictures sett in a gold Snuff box – by the present Earl of Leicester who had them from his Brother. but I wish them to be returned into their old Frames again" (Vertue, *Notebooks*, IV, p. 80); Walpole records that the Earl of Leicester gave the snuff box to Field-Marshal Sir Robert Rich, Bt, (*Anecdotes of Painting in England*, London, 1782 ed, I, p. 257 note); descended from Sir Robert Rich, 4th Bt, (1685–1768) to his son, Lt-General Sir Robert Rich, 5th Bt, (1714–85); they passed from him to a Mrs Clavering who gave them to her niece, Caroline Elizabeth (d. 1890), eldest daughter of George, 5th Viscount Barrington, in 1843 on her marriage to the Hon Thomas Liddell; she, in turn, gave them to her niece, Mary Frances (d. 1913), daughter of William, 6th Viscount Barrington, and wife of Alfred Sartoris; she sold them at Christie's 27th June 1906 (lot 76); bt. Hodgkins; acquired by George Salting and bequeathed by him with his collection to the V & A, 1910.

LITERATURE: Winter, *Elizabethan Miniatures*, pl. 111 (a).
V & A, 1947 (14).
Auerbach, *Hilliard*, pp. 70–71, pl. 30, 292 (no. 29).
Strong, *Hilliard*, pl. 1.

50

NICHOLAS HILLIARD

50   Sir Thomas Bodley, 1598

The Bodleian Library, Oxford
Vellum stuck onto card, 51 × 42 mm, 2 × 1⅝ in.

Sir Thomas Bodley (1545–1613), diplomat and scholar, was taken to Geneva during the Marian persecutions. Returned to England, 1558; educated at Magdalen College, Oxford; fellow of Merton College, 1564; MA, 1566. Travelled abroad, 1576–80; MP for Plymouth, 1584; for St Germans, 1586; employed in diplomatic missions by the Queen. Sent as resident in the Hague, 1589–96. Returned and founded the Bodleian Library, Oxford, 1598 which opened, 1602.

The Bodleys were an Exeter family of a strongly Protestant persuasion and had gone into exile during Mary's reign. On 8th May 1557 their arrival in Geneva is recorded in the *Livre des Anglais*. The family then included the ten year old Nicholas Hilliard. This link with the Bodley family places Hilliard firmly into the Puritan orbit of Elizabethan society and during his stay in Geneva he must have learned French which accounts for the ease with which he later spent three years in France.

This miniature was painted in 1598, the year Sir Thomas Bodley founded his library in Oxford showing that the association of the two men was active forty years on. In the same year Richard Haydocke dedicated his translation of Poalo Lomazzo's *Tratto dell'arte de la pittura* to Bodley in which he refers to Hilliard and which led to the miniaturist writing his *Treatise* (no. IX).

INSCRIBED: On either side of the head: *Año Dm̄i 1598 | Ætatis Suae 54.*

COLLECTIONS: Dukes of Buckingham at Stowe; sold 15th March 1849 (lot 89).

LITERATURE: V & A, 1947 (67).
Roy Strong, "Queen Elizabeth, the Earl of Essex and Nicholas Hilliard", *Burlington Magazine*, CI, 1959, p. 146.
Auerbach, *Hilliard*, pp. 135, pl. 115; 307 (116).

NICHOLAS HILLIARD

51   Edward Seymour, Duke of Somerset, 1560
Probably after Levina Teerlinc, c. 1547–50

The Duke of Buccleuch and Queensberry KT
Vellum stuck to plain card, circular, 33.5 mm, 1 5⁄16 in. diam.

Edward Seymour, Duke of Somerset (1506?–1552), son of Sir John Seymour and brother of Jane Seymour, created Earl of Hertford 1539, and Lord High Admiral 1542, became Lord Protector on Edward VI's accession, 1547 carrying through a new phase of religious reform, until he was deposed in 1550. Executed on a charge of conspiracy, 1552.

This miniature presents many problems but there seem to be no firm reasons for rejecting its attribution, although it pre-dates any of Hilliard's miniatures by a decade. In the first instance, the portrait is posthumous and should be after a likeness of Somerset as Protector, i.e. c. 1547–1550. The circular form would indicate that the original is likely to have been a miniature and that it was probably by Levina Teerlinc. Technically it has no connexion with Hilliard's style in its fully formed expression after 1570 but must take its place as an effort by a thirteen year old at miniature painting. Needless to say it is crude and clumsy but there are elements that reflect understanding of the Ghent-Bruges tradition: the features and hair are worked over a "carnation" ground and the red lips directly recall Hornebolte. The background, which is gold washed over an ochre ground, is unusual if not unique. The lettering reveals no trace of his later calligraphic style. In general the miniature is in good condition apart from very minor losses.

The Hilliard family were strongly Protestant and Nicholas's father had been a staunch ally of Somerset against the Prayer Book Rebellion of 1549. The miniaturist was later to paint and work for Somerset's son, the Earl of Hertford (Strong, *Renaissance Miniature*, pp. 67, 75).

INSCRIBED: In the border: *EDWARDE DUKE OF SOMERSET. ANNO DOMINI 1560 NH* (in monogram). On the back of the miniature a faint near contemporary inscription: *King Edward | yᵉ 6ᵗʰ | Governor.*

COLLECTIONS: Part of the collection formed by Walter Francis, 5th Duke of Buccleuch (1806–1884).

LITERATURE: Kennedy, *Buccleuch*, pl. V.
V & A, 1947 (3).
Auerbach, *Hilliard*, p. 56, pl. 12; 288–9 (12).
Strong, *Tudor and Jacobean*, I, p. 295; II, pl. 576.

MASTER OF THE COUNTESS OF WARWICK

52   Unknown Lady, 1567

The Lord Tollemache
Oil on panel, 68 × 53.3 cm, 26¾ × 21 in.

A group of eight portraits from the 1560s has emerged as the distinctive work of one painter, for convenience identified as the Master of the Countess of Warwick. It is conceivable that he may be identifiable with Nicholas Lizarde (d. 1571), a painter of French extraction who was Serjeant Painter from 1554 and who certainly presented subject pictures to Mary I as New Year's gifts (Auerbach, *Tudor Artists*, pp. 145–46). These portraits are all far more iconic than Hans Eworth's, with highly stylized drawing of the hands and fingers, the features treated in a flat linear manner, with lighting from the front and a stress placed on an exact rendering of jewels and costume. This portrait, which may be of Dorothy Wentworth, Mrs Tollemache, is a typical example of his work. It is a very short step from portraits of this type to the oil portraits by Nicholas Hilliard executed in the early 1570s of the Queen. He was clearly heavily influenced by the Master of the Countess of Warwick and the possibility of some training in painting on panel in his studio cannot be excluded as a hypothesis.

INSCRIBED: Top left: *AN°. DNI / 1567*; top right: *ÆTATIS SVÆ 43*

COLLECTIONS: By family descent.

LITERATURE: E. K. Waterhouse, *The Collections of Pictures in Helmingham Hall*, 1958, p. 17 (31).
Strong, *The English Icon*, p. 109 (57).

JOHN DE BEAUCHESNE AND JOHN BALDON

53 *A Booke containing divers sortes of hands*, London, 1571.

The Pepys Library, Magdalen College, Cambridge (Photograph)

The title of the work goes on to state that it gives scripts "as well the English as French secretarie with the Italian, Roman, Chancelry & Court hands". Beauchesne's work was a copybook and ran into several editions down to 1602. Hilliard's miniatures from their outset in 1571 reveal him as an expert calligrapher using an italic script with occasional bold flourishes above and below the line, often purely for decoration. Hilliard must have been trained by a writing master and the script he uses is closest to the italic in Beauchesne's book which was originally issued in 1570.

LITERATURE: Ambrose Heal, *The English Writing Masters*, London, 1931, p. 127; information from Miss Irene Whalley.

HANS EWORTH

54 **Anthony Browne, 1st Viscount Montague**, 1569

National Portrait Gallery (842)
Oil on panel, 96.2 × 67.6 cm, 37⅞ × 26⅝ in.

Anthony Brown, 1st Viscount Montague (1526–92), eldest son of Sir Anthony Browne, remained a staunch Catholic although loyal to the Queen, enjoying office under Mary but no public career of importance under Elizabeth whom he entertained at Cowdray, 1591.

Hans Eworth (fl. 1540–73) was by far the most talented painter working in England during the 1560s and he had virtually been court painter to Mary I but was dropped by Elizabeth. His patrons in the 1560s were all noted as Catholic sympathizers as in the case of Lord Montague. Eworth's work along with that of a second Netherlandish artist, Steven van der Muelen (fl. 1543–68), must have been familiar to the young Hilliard. Although increasingly stylized and formalized in presentation, the tradition stemming from Holbein of vigorous unbiased characterization of sitters still remained strong. Hilliard's earliest miniatures from the early 1570s show the influence of Eworth (on Eworth see Strong, *The English Icon*, pp. 83–106; van der Muelen, pp. 119–34).

INSCRIBED: To right, only visible fully in x-ray: *ÆTATIS XL / (MDL) XIX*.

COLLECTIONS: The sitter's daughter married Jane, daughter of Thomas Sackville, Lord Buckhurst, Earl of Dorset; first recorded at Buckhurst, seat of the Earls De La Warr, c. 1884; sale of Edward Adolphus, 12th Duke of Somerset, Christie's 28th June 1890 (lot 19).

LITERATURE: Strong, *Tudor and Jacobean*, I, pp. 225–26.
Strong, *The English Icon*, p. 104 (50).

NICHOLAS HILLIARD

55 **Unknown man**, 1571

Private Collection
Vellum, which has been damaged and stuck to a later card, circular, 45 mm, 1¾ in. diam.

The earliest surviving miniature by Hilliard as he began his career subsequent to his apprenticeship to Robert Brandon, terminated in 1569. Although damaged this early work shows him in complete control of his technique and the circular shape, soon abandoned in favour of an oval, directly relates to the format of miniatures that can be attributed to Levina Teerlinc.

The damage is to the vellum at the top and bottom of the miniature which has resulted in it being laid down on a later card. It was neither attributed nor identified in Vertue's 1743 catalogue. In the 1880 inventory it appears as "Called the Earl of Morton by J Bettes" and Goulding pointed out a resemblance to a portrait of Oliver St John, 1st Baron St John of Bletso (Strong, *The English Icon*, p. 136 (91)). There are no grounds for these identifications as it is too young a man at too late a date for both of the suggestions.

INSCRIBED: On either side of the head: *Anno Dm̄ 1571. / Ætatis Suae.35*.

COLLECTIONS: Edward Harley, 2nd Earl of Oxford (1689–1741); not identifiable in Vertue's list of c. 1732; first recorded in Vertue's catalogue of 1743 (113); Oxford's daughter married William Bentinck, 2nd Duke of Portland; thence by descent.

LITERATURE: Goulding, *Welbeck*, p. 65 (18).
V & A, 1947 (5).
Auerbach, *Hilliard*, p. 61, pl. 16; 289 (14).
Strong, *Tudor and Jacobean*, I, p. 271.

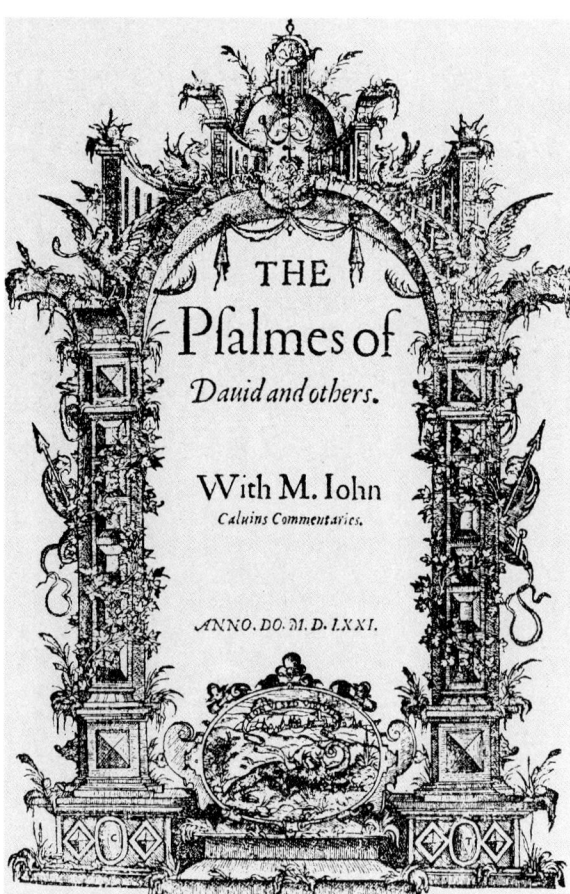

56

58

?CHRISTOPHER TRESSELL AFTER A DESIGN
ATTRIBUTED TO NICHOLAS HILLIARD

56   Title border, 1571

> *The Psalmes of David and others. With M. Iohn Calvins
> Commentaries*, London, 1571

> *The British Library (1107.E.24)*
> Woodcut

McKerrow and Ferguson in 1932 pointed out that
stylistically the design of this border was identical to one
signed by Nicholas Hilliard (no. 65) in 1574 and also cut
by C.T., probably Christopher Tressell. This is even more
in the Roman ruins genre exemplified by the work of
Hieronymus Cock in which ruined architecture sprouts
greenery. At the bottom there is a cartouche containing an
emblem which seems to depict a wild animal, probably a
panther, sprawling with a dragon and the motto *NON VI
SED VIRTVTE*. Hilliard in his *Treatise* (ed. Thornton and
Cain, p. 75) writes of the painter's role in setting forth
"emblem, impresa, or other device whatsoever". This title
border shares with no. 65 many of the same features,
including the exploding cannon-balls at the top.

LITERATURE: R. B. McKerrow and F. S. Ferguson, *Title-page
    Borders used in England and Scotland 1485–1640*, Bibliographical
    Society, O.U.P., 1932, pp. xxxvi–xxxvii; 116 (133).

NICHOLAS HILLIARD

57   Unknown man, 1572

> *The Fitzwilliam Museum, Cambridge (3899)*
> Vellum stuck to a playing card with three spades
> showing at the reverse, circular, 46 mm, $1\frac{27}{32}$ in.

Formerly wrongly called Edward Courtney, Earl of Devon,
V. J. Murrell points our that the lack of the sitter's age
could indicate that it has been removed. It is possible,
however, that it was never inserted. There is some flaking
in the collar and ribbon and small restorations in the
beard. The interpretation of the sitter is highly reminiscent
of the formalized male portraits by Hans Eworth during
the 1560s (e.g. Strong, *The English Icon*, pp. 94 (34); 95
(36) and no. 54).

INSCRIBED: On either side of the head: *Año. Dm̄. 1572· | Ætatis Suae*
    [blank].

COLLECTIONS: Part of the collection formed by Walter Francis, 5th
    Duke of Buccleuch (1806–1884); acquired, 1942.

LITERATURE: Kennedy, *Buccleuch*, pl. III.
V & A, 1947 (7).
Auerbach, *Hilliard*, pp. 63, pl. 19; 289 (17).

NICHOLAS HILLIARD

58   Unknown man aged 24, 1572

> *Victoria & Albert Museum (P. 1–1942)*
> Vellum stuck to a playing card with three hearts at
> the reverse, rectangular, 60 × 48 mm, $2\frac{3}{8} \times 1\frac{7}{8}$ in.

One of a pair of miniatures of husband and wife, the latter
being still in the Buccleuch collection (no. 59). This one of
the husband has been extensively restored, especially on
the face and ruff. Nonetheless it and its companion are rare
instances in Hilliard's work of rectangular miniatures.
Reynolds' (*Miniatures*, 1952, p. 18) points out the influence
of Mor, and Pope-Hennessy that of Clouet and French
court portraiture (*Lecture*, 1949, pp. 17–18) but the portrait

59

60

formula could equally have been derived from Hans Eworth who was still working in the 1570s (Strong, *The English Icon*, pp. 92 (31', 94 (34) and no. 54). The format must have been dictated by the client, presumably to create some form of diptych, oval and circular miniatures lending themselves more readily to setting in lockets or ivory boxes. The liveliness of characterization suggests familiarity already with French portrait drawings by Clouet. The form of "s" in the inscription of this and no. 59 is not repeated

In 1864 the miniature was unattributed but identified as James Stuart, 1st Earl of Moray, an identification that cannot be sustained because of the age of the sitter.

INSCRIBED: On either side of the head: *Ætatis sue. XXIIII | Ano.,* *1572.*

COLLECTIONS: Part of the collection formed by Walter Francis, 5th Duke of Buccleuch (1806–84); first recorded in 1864; purchased and presented by the N.A.C.F. 1942.

LITERATURE: L. Caldesi & Co. and Amelia B. Edwards, *Photographic Historical Portrait Gallery*, London, 1864, pl. XLVII (1).
Kennedy, *Buccleuch*, pl. XII.
Winter, *Elizabethan Miniatures*, pl. II (b).
V & A, 1947 (8).
Pope-Hennessy, *Lecture*, 1949, p. 18, pl. VIII, IX.
Auerbach, *Hilliard*, pp. 61–2, pl. 7; 289 (15).
G. Reynolds, *Apollo*, LXXIX, 1964, p. 283, pl. 8.
Strong, *Hilliard*, pl. 2(b).

NICHOLAS HILLIARD

59   Unknown lady aged 18, 1572

The Duke of Buccleuch and Queensberry KT
Vellum stuck to a playing card with four spades visible at the reverse, rectangular, 54 × 45 mm, $2\frac{1}{8} \times 1\frac{13}{16}$ in.

Companion to no. 58, the face has been very heavily restored but the costume, which is brilliantly rendered is, in

the main, in good condition. Both the dress and the pose of the figure are closely paralleled in portraits by George Gower during the same years (Strong, *The English Icon*, p. 171 (114 dated 1572), 172 (117 dated 1573). The sitter wears a blue bodice, gold embroidered partlet and a surcoat patterned in black on black. The bodice is ultramarine as against the blue used for the background.

INSCRIBED: To the left and along the top: *.Etatis. suae. XVIII | Año. Dni. | 1572.*

COLLECTIONS: See no. 58.

LITERATURE: Auerbach, *Hilliard*, pp. 62–3, pl. 18, 289 (16).

NICHOLAS HILLIARD

60   Unknown lady, 1572

The Duke of Buccleuch and Queensberry KT
Vellum stuck to a playing card with two clubs at the reverse, the right edge trimmed as though to fit a hinged locket, circular, 49 mm, $1\frac{15}{16}$ in. diam.

A fine early miniature using the circular format inherited from Hornebolte and Teerlinc and the strongly drawn head suggests the direct influence of Holbein. It is technically closely related to the rectangular portrait of a young man also from 1572 (no. 58) and both inscriptions include an inverted number 5. The dress would indicate a sitter of modest social status. The clipping is original, so that the miniature might fit a locket. Restoration, in the main, is in the areas of the ruff and black costume.

INSCRIBED: On either side of the head: *Ætatis Suae .52. | Año Dni* *.1572.*

COLLECTIONS: Part of the collection formed by Walter Francis, 5th Duke of Buccleuch (1806–1884).

LITERATURE: Kennedy, *Buccleuch*, pl. 111.
Auerbach, *Hilliard*, pp. 62, pl. 20; 290 (18).

63

61

GEORGE GOWER

61   **Called Lady Walsingham**, 1572

The Viscount De L'Isle VC, KG
Oil on panel, 83.9 × 63.5 cm, 33 × 25 in.

This is the earliest life-scale portrait to record the wearing
of a portrait miniature. A miniature, almost certainly by
Levina Teerlinc from the middle 1560s of Catherine Grey,
Countess of Hertford (Auerbach, *Hilliard*, pl. 8), gives an
earlier instance.

    The identity of the sitter is not known but she holds up a
miniature, presumably of her husband, which she wears
suspended at the end of a ribband from her waist. The
miniature is circular and set within a jewelled locket. It is
impossible to tell whether it is by Hilliard or Teerlinc but is
a visual document recording the extension of the
availability of the portrait miniature to those outside the
royal and quasi-royal family circle.

    The portrait is one of a series from the 1570s attributable
to George Gower (see no. 62).

INSCRIBED: On either sie of the head: *AN° DNI 1572 | ÆTATIS
    SVAE 22.*

COLLECTIONS: Acquired by the present owner's grandfather.

LITERATURE: L. Cust, "Hans Eworth", *Walpole Society*, II, 1913,
    p. 38.
Strong, *The English Icon*, p. 171 (114).

GEORGE GOWER

62   **Elizabeth Cornwallis, Lady Kytson**, 1573

The Tate Gallery (6091)
Oil on panel, 68.3 × 52.1 cm, 26⅞ × 20½ in.

Elizabeth Cornwallis was daughter of Sir Thomas
Cornwallis, of Brome Hall, Suffolk and wife of Sir Thomas
Kytson, of Hengrave Hall, Suffolk.

One of the three documented and dated pictures by
George Gower (fl. 1540–1596) who was appointed Serjeant
Painter to Elizabeth I in 1581. Gower emerges as a
fashionable portrait painter simultaneously with Hilliard in
the early 1570s and portraits reasonably attributable to
him can be identified from this period and into the eighties.
Their quality is bordering at times on coarse but there is
always a very great stress on strong and direct
characterization, particularly noticeable in his portraits of
women which are close in feeling to Hilliard's equally
forceful female sitters from the seventies before his
approach was softened by France. The colour too is high in
key in Gower's portraits.

    Hilliard must have been familiar with Gower's work and
it is likely that Hilliard's absence in France for two years
led to the Queen turning to Gower for her portraits. A
recently cleaned version of the 1579 Sieve Portrait (Strong,
Portraits of Queen Elizabeth I, p. 66 (44)) emerges as certainly
by him. It is conceivable that Hilliard's unreliability lost
him the post of Serjeant Painter when it fell vacant in 1581.

64 *Nicholas Hilliard*

INSCRIBED: Top left-hand corner: *AN° DNI 1573 | aetatis suae 26*; and below a later inscription: *LADY KYTSON*.

COLLECTIONS: Descended with Hengrave Hall, the seat of the Kytsons; first recorded, c. 1797; sold Hengrave Hall sale, 1953 (lot 1648).

LITERATURE: E. Farrer, *Portraits in Suffolk House (West)*, 1908, p. 178 (24).
J. W Goodison, "George Gower", *Burlington Magazine*, XC, 1948, pp. 261–64.
M. Chamot, *British School Concise Catalogue*, Tate Gallery, 1953, p. 86 (6091).
Strong, *The English Icon*, p. 169 (112).

NICHOLAS HILLIARD

63 Jane Coningsby, Mrs Boughton, 1574

Private Collection
Vellum stuck to a playing card with part of a "court" card visible at the reverse, circular, 44 mm, $1\frac{3}{4}$ in. diam.

Jane Coningsby (b. 1553), daughter of Humphrey Coningsby, and sister of Sir Thomas Coningsby (d. 1625), of Hampton Court, Hereford. By 1572 she was wife of William Boughton (d. 1596) of Little Lawford, Warwickshire. After his death she married a William Medeley.

One of the most outstanding of Hilliard's early miniatures, bold in its treatment of the features in a direct unfussy linear manner. The assurance in the placing of the figure and in the painting reflect a rapid advance in confidence within two years. Jane Coningsby is one of the earliest of Hilliard's identifiable sitters, establishing at once that his clientele extended beyond the previous tight royal and quasi-royal circle. Although the sitter was daughter to the Queen's Gentleman Treasurer, she was only the young wife of a country gentleman. The features are probably faded and the silver oxidized but, apart from a little minute flaking and a small stain above the right shoulder, it is in splendid condition. The miniature is mounted in a contemporary turned stained ivory frame.

INSCRIBED: On either side of the head: *Anno Dni. 1574. | Ætatis Sua.21.*

COLLECTIONS: Descended in the sitter's family to her four-times-great-grand-daughter, Theodosia, wife of Sir Egerton Leigh of High Leigh, Cheshire; their daughter married John Ward of Guilsborough Grange, Northants; it descended to their fourth son, John, who adopted the names of Boughton and Leigh; sold from the estate of his descendant, A C Ward-Boughton-Leigh, Sotheby's 24th March 1980 (lot 105).

LITERATURE: V & A, 1947 (10).
Auerbach, *Hilliard*, pp. 68, pl. 25; 291 (22).

NICHOLAS HILLIARD

64 Margaret Douglas, Countess of Lennox, 1575

Rijksmuseum, Amsterdam, on loan to the Mauritshuis, The Hague
Vellum stuck onto card, circular, 45 mm, $1\frac{3}{4}$ in. diam.

Margaret Douglas, Countess of Lennox (1515–78), daughter of Archibald Douglas, 6th Earl of Angus by Margaret Tudor. Brought up with the Princess Mary, she married Matthew Stuart, Earl of Lennox in 1544 and was instrumental in securing the match of her son Henry Stuart, Lord Darnley, to Mary, Queen of Scots, for which Elizabeth imprisoned her.

Auerbach first pointed out that this miniature tallied with the description of one of Margaret Douglas, Countess of Lennox in the collection of Charles I. It matched it in every way except that the age, fifty-three, mentioned by van der Dort, seems never, as far as can be seen, to have been inserted. The entry reads as follows: "The Third Picture being upon blew grounded card written about the yeare of our Lord wth gould letters 1575 and alsoe her age, 53, being the Lady Marg^{t} Duglas, Aunt to Queene Mary of Scotland in a black and white mourning widdows habitt a – little plaine ruffe" (Millar, *Walpole Society*, XXVII, 1960, p. 111 (34)).

The features correspond exactly with those in the full length portrait of her in the Royal Collection, painted three years earlier (Strong, *Tudor and Jacobean*, II, pl. 393–94).

The miniature must have been painted after the release of the Countess from the Tower just before the winter of 1575–76. She had been imprisoned for her complicity in the marriage of her second son, Charles, to the Countess of Shrewsbury's daughter, Elizabeth Cavendish. As the grand-daughter of Henry VII by his daughter, Margaret Tudor, the Countess belonged to the circle to which the miniature as a portrait-form most pertained. Its importance is emphasized in the use of the expensive pigment ultramarine for the background. Slightly reduced in size there is retouching in the background to the left. It is interesting that the Countess went to the young Hilliard rather than Levina Teerlinc who was still active.

It is conceivable that a second version of this miniature once existed which bore the age of the sitter and was therefore identical with that in Charles I's collection and a very damaged version is in the Fitzwilliam Museum (3851) called Anne, Lady Hunsdon. It uses ultramarine for the background but it seems so coarse that it is difficult to believe that Hilliard's hand lurks beneath the present surface. It came from the C. H. T. Hawkins collection at Bignor Park and passed to the Pierpont Morgan collection (sold Christie's 24 June 1935 (lot 103)).

INSCRIBED: On either side of the head: *Año Dn̄ 1575 | Ætatis Svae* (age missing).

COLLECTIONS: Possibly Charles I, the sitter's great grandson (see above); one was listed as being in Queen Caroline's collection (*A Catalogue . . .*, p. 25 (5)) which bore the age, 53); first certainly recorded in the Dutch Royal Collection, 1815–21.

LITERATURE: Auerbach, *Hilliard*, pp. 68, pl. 28; 291 (25).
All the Paintings in the Rijksmuseum, Amsterdam, Olivetti, 1976, p. 757 (A 4723).

?CHRISTOPHER TRESSELL, AFTER A DESIGN BY
NICHOLAS HILLIARD

65   Title border, 1574

The Common Places of the most famous and renowned Divine Doctor PETER MARTYR . . . Translated and partlie efathered by Anthonie Marden . . ., London, 1582

The British Library
Woodcut, 294 × 186 mm, $11\frac{9}{16} \times 7\frac{5}{16}$ in.

The title border was first used from 1574 onwards for a whole series of publications. Below the medallion of the slain lamb at the top it is signed NH and on the scrolling emerging from the urn below there is the date. It was McKerrow and Ferguson who first attributed this to Hilliard whose initials it bears in a form that occasionally he used on his miniatures (no. 51). The title border also bears the initials CT, probably identifiable with a certain Christopher Tressell, Treasure or Tress, a Dutchman, described in 1582 as "a carver to the printers".

The art of limning was learned by being grounded in copying woodcuts so that his very training ensured that Hilliard would have been proficient in preparing designs in that medium. The original design would have been lost in the process of being cut. In this instance the title border is for religious books and consists of a pair of Solomonic twisted columns embraced by vines springing from an urn below. At the top there is a fireball and architectural cartouche work in the Roman ruins genre of the type exemplified by the engravings of Hieronymous Cock. The most noticeable stylistic feature is the serpentining spiralling nature of the design and its preoccupation with decorative excrescences.

LITERATURE: R. B. McKerrow and F. S. Ferguson, *Title-page Borders used in England and Scotland* 1485–1640, Bibliographial Society, O.U.P., 1932, pp. xxxvi–xxxvii; 127 (148).
E. Auerbach, "More Light on Nicholas Hilliard", *Burlington Magazine*, XCI, 1949, p. 167.
Auerbach, *Hilliard*, p. 321 (191).

NICHOLAS HILLIARD

66   ?Charles Howard, Baron Howard of Effingham, Earl of Nottingham, 1576

Cleveland Museum of Art, Ohio
Vellum stuck onto card, 49 × 46 mm, $1\frac{15}{16} \times 1\frac{13}{16}$ in.

Charles Howard, 2nd Baron Howard of Effingham and 1st Earl of Nottingham (1536–1624) rose rapidly in royal service: Lord Chamberlain, 1583–85, Lord High Admiral, 1585–1618, in charge of the fleet in the sea battle against the Armada, created Earl in 1596 and ambassador to Spain, 1605.

A fine miniature, (it cannot be Northampton as it is now called), for which a highly likely Howard candidate (which its provenance would indicate) is Charles Howard, Baron Howard of Effingham, later Earl of Nottingham. He was in his thirty-ninth year in 1576 matching the inscription and a person of high birth and connexions rising rapidly in the 1570s. In January 1573 he succeeded his father as Baron Effingham and was installed a Knight of the Garter on 24th April 1574. The chain around the neck of the sitter is of a type which presupposes that the Lesser George of the Garter is at the end of it, paralleled in portraits of both Leicester and Sussex at the same period (Strong, *Tudor and Jacobean*, II, pl. 379–380, 615–16). Howard appears in Marcus Gheeraerts' engraved Procession of Knights of the Garter from the same year 1576, and the likeness is perfectly compatible (Hind, *Engraving*, I, pp. 116–17; pl. 55). The next portrait is a full length in Garter robes with his arms carrying the Lord Chamberlain's wand of office he held from 1583–85 (J. B. Speed Art Museum, Louisville, Kentucky). Then follows Thomas Cockson's engraving c. 1596–1603 (Hind, *op. cit.*, I, pl. 127). A certain miniature attributed to Lockey (no. 129) depicts him in his sixty-ninth year, 1605.

The miniature is a striking and vigorous one with a grey doublet and black hat with white plumes, gold chain and lettering. There is some flaking from the brim of the hat and retouching to the left.

INSCRIBED: On either side of the head: *Año Dn̄i, 1576 | Ætatis Suae.39.*

COLLECTIONS: The Howards, Earls of Carlisle at Castle Howard; sold from the collection of Viscount Morpeth at Sotheby's 14th May 1959 (lot 14); gift of Mrs A. Dean Perry in memory of Mr and Mrs B. Greene, 1940.

LITERATURE: Lord Hawkesbury, *Catalogue of Portraits, Miniatures, etc at Castle Howard*, p. 68 (4).
Auerbach, *Hilliard*, pp. 69, pl. 29; 292 (27).
Strong, *Tudor and Jacobean*, I, pp. 236–37 (for his iconography).

NICHOLAS HILLIARD

67   Unknown lady, 1576

Victoria & Albert Museum (P. 27-1977)
Vellum stuck to a plain card, circular, 37 mm, $1\frac{15}{32}$ in. diam.

An early and brilliant miniature by Hilliard in superb condition. As the year 1576 runs from April 1st 1575/6 to March 31st 1576/77 this miniature could have been painted in France. Hilliard travelled to France between July 15th and December 8th 1576 and was still in Paris with his wife in February 1578. The sitter and her dress look English, so that the miniature was either painted just before he left, or is of an English lady in, for instance, the embassy in Paris. In concept and handling it is closest of all to the only other miniature of comparable quality, from this period *Jane Coningsby*, 1574 (no. 63).

The dress is that of a lady of the gentry and aristocratic classes and may be closely paralleled in portraits by George

67

Gower during the 1570s (Strong, *The English Icon*, p. 174 (no. 120)). There are slight paint losses at the edges and the features are faded and silver oxidized.

INSCRIBED: On either side of the head: *Ano Dn̄i 1576 | Ætatis Suae. 31.*

COLLECTIONS: With S. J. Phillips, London; sold from the collection of the late Greta S. Heckett, Sotheby's 5th November 1977 (lot 122).

LITERATURE: *Four Centuries of Portrait Miniatures, Catalogue of the Heckett Collection*, 1954 (no. 27), pl. II.
Auerbach, *Hilliard*, p. 335 (289).
Art at Auction 1976–77, p. 274 rep.

NICHOLAS HILLIARD

68 Robert Dudley, Earl of Leicester, 1576

National Portrait Gallery, London (4197)
Vellum stuck to a playing card with part of an unidentified picture card showing at the reverse, painted over with black watercolour, circular, 44 mm, 1 11/16 in.

Robert Dudley, Earl of Leicester (1532?–88), the son of John Dudley, Duke of Northumberland, rose rapidly to favour under Elizabeth; created High Steward of Cambridge University, 1562; Baron Denbigh and Earl of Leicester, 1564, and Chancellor of Oxford University, 1564. Entertained Elizabeth with "The Princely Pleasures of Kenilworth" in 1575, but incurred her wrath over his marriage to Lettice Knollys. He commanded the expedition to assist the United Provinces against Spain, 1585, became Governor General and was recalled in 1587.

A fine *ad vivum* miniature with the features in an especially good unfaded condition, with little damage, the gold chain would have had the Lesser George of the Garter suspended from it which he received in 1559. Leicester was a notable patron of the arts and letters: the year before this miniature was painted he seems to have been instrumental in bringing over Federigo Zuccaro. From the outset he was interested in Hilliard, who in 1571 prepared a "booke of portraitures" for him; in 1582 the Earl interceded for him at Court and many of the artist's children bore names in honour of the Dudleys. Another version of this miniature is in the Harcourt collection. Laurence Hilliard refers to a

miniature of Leicester in his will in 1640: "the Earl of Lestars picture in a yet box draune in his Cloake with a Cap and Fethar" (Auerbach, *Hilliard*), p. 227).

INSCRIBED: On either side of the head: *Ano· Dn̄i· 1576· | Ætatis Suae 44·*

COLLECTIONS: A. Staal, Amsterdam; sold anonymously (Bernard Stadel), Christie's 21st February 1961 (lot 90); purchased with contributions from the N.A.C.F. and an anonymous donor, 1961.

LITERATURE: Strong, *Tudor and Jacobean*, I, p. 194.

II HILLIARD IN FRANCE 1576–78/9

1576. Hilliard leaves for France in the train of the Queen's ambassador, Sir Amyas Paulet.
1577. Recorded as *valet de chambre* in the household of Francis, Duke of Anjou.
Travelled south to the court of Marguerite de Valois at Béarn.
1578. Executed woodcut portraits of the Duke and Duchess of Nevers.
Stays in the house of the court painter to the French Queen, Louise of Lorraine.
1578/9. Returned to London sometime between the end of August 1578 and 14th July 1579.

Hilliard spent almost three years in France. He went there, he said, to obtain money and knowledge. Money, in Hilliard's case, was a perennial problem but "knowledge" requires explanation. In 1575 one of Hilliard's key patrons, Elizabeth's favourite, Robert Dudley, Earl of Leicester (no. 68), had brought over the Italian painter, Federigo Zuccaro. He did not stay but Hilliard must have felt distinctly inadequate and provincial in comparison. Italy was virtually closed to the Protestant English in the aftermath of the excommunication of the Queen, whereas relations with France at that juncture were cordial. Hilliard could speak French and it is unlikely that he went there without some form of introduction or some existing connexion. He would have been exposed to the Valois court at its sunset apogee, the palaces of Fontainebleau, the Louvre and the Tuileries in their pristine glory covered in the decorative work of the School of Fontainebleau. Although the leading court portraitist, François Clouet, had died a short time before, Antoine Caron was the most influential member of a whole team of artists who serviced members of the art-loving Valois dynasty. The lavish patronage of the arts by this bankrupt monarchy must have made the extreme parsimony of the Elizabethan court all the more striking. None the less it is surprising that its effect on Hilliard was to be so minimal. The influence of the chalk portrait drawings by Clouet on Hilliard's miniatures after about 1580 has long been recognized. They are reflcted in the close-ups and above all in the softness and feminity of characterization both in his male as well as his female portraits. In a way French court art weakened Hilliard's style and eroded the Holbeinesque toughness which make his earliest miniatures his most outstanding. The experience of France came too late – he was thirty – and where one would have expected a dramatic change and development in style in a younger man in Hilliard's case very little happened. The years in France cannot have been a success. While he was away his position with the Queen had been jeopardized by her patronage of Gower.

SELECT BIBLIOGRAPHY: N. Blakiston, "Nicholas Hilliard as a Traveller", *Burlington Magazine*, XCI, 1949, p. 169.
N. Blakiston, "Nicholas Hilliard in France", *Gazette des Beaux Arts*, LI, 1958, pp. 297–300.
Auerbach, *Hilliard*, pp. 11–16, 70–76.
Strong, *Renaissance Miniature*, pp. 75–81

ANTOINE CARON

69 Water Festival at Fontainebleau

National Gallery of Scotland, Edinburgh (D767)
Graphite, pen and wash, 316 × 464 mm, $12\frac{1}{2} \times 18\frac{5}{16}$ in.

One of a series of six drawings which seem to have been conceived as a set depicting festivals at the Valois court between 1564 and 1573. All the festivals portrayed took place in the reign of Charles IX and the drawings served as the basis for the series of eight tapestries now in the Uffizi. These rearrange and alter the content of the drawings and superimpose a frieze of portrait figures designed to glorify Henri III (no. 71) and his brother, Francis, Duke of Anjou (no. 72).

Recent research points to the fact that these drawings were done in retrospect. The latest event that they certainly depict is the reception given to the Polish Ambassadors in the gardens of the Tuileries in 1573. Those for which the subject matter can be identified seem to be reconstructions and abridgements, based on descriptions compiled at a later date and even, in some cases, shifting the location of a particular spectacle to introduce a royal palace. In this instance an attack on an island by combatants in fancy dress is in progress on the pond at Fontainebleau. In February 1564 Charles IX's *Grand voyage de France* was prefaced by a series of elaborate fêtes staged there. No surviving evidence exists either to prove or disprove that this was one of them.

It is likely that Hilliard visited Fontainebleau during his stay in France. About a decade later he was to draw on his memories for his celebrated miniature of the *Young Man among Roses* (no. 263), the pose for which derives directly from figures by Primaticcio among the stucco and frescoes which made up its decoration.

Valois court festivals were closely studied in England and the earliest, somewhat awkward, attempt at imitation was the series of entertainments given by Hilliard's patron Robert Dudley, Earl of Leicester at Kenilworth in 1575.

COLLECTIONS: Given to the Royal Scottish Academy by David Laing, 1879; transferred to the National Gallery.

LITERATURE: J. Ehrmann, "Caron et les Tapisseries de Florence", *Revue des Arts*, I, 1952, pp. 27–30.
J. Ehrmann, *Antoine Caron, peintre à la cour de Valois* (1521–1599), Geneva, 1955, p. 35.
J. Ehrmann, "Les Tapisseries de Valois au Musées des Offices", in *Les Fêtes de la Renaissance*, ed, J. Jacquot, Paris, 1956, p. 94.
J. Ehrmann, "Dessins d'Antoine Caron pour les Tapisseries de Valois au Musée des Offices", *Bulletin de la Société de l'Histoire de l'Art Français*, 1956, pp. 116–17.
Frances Yates, *The Valois Tapestries*, London, 1959, pp. 3, 69.
S. Beguin, *Il Cinquecento Francese*, Milan, 1970, pl. XXV.
L'Ecole de Fontainebleau, Grand Palais, 1972 43).
V. E. Graham and W. McAllister Johnson, *The Royal Tour of France by Charles IX and Catherine de' Medici. Festivals and Entries 1564–6*, University of Toronto, 1979, pp. 59–60.

?FRANÇOIS CLOUET

70 Catherine de Medici, c. 1555

Victoria & Albert Museum (P.26–1954)
Vellum stuck onto card, oval, 60 × 44 mm, $2\frac{3}{8} \times 1\frac{3}{4}$ in.

Catherine Medici (1519–89), married the future Henri II in 1533. She became Queen in 1547 and subsequent to the death of her husband in 1559 became Regent.

François Clouet (c. 1515–72) succeeded his father, Jean, as being portraitist to the Valois court. He not only executed chalk drawings and oil paintings but also miniatures. The latter fact we know from a document dated 1572 in which he is mentioned as having painted a miniature of the Queen, Elizabeth of Austria: "Portrait qu'il peignit dans un petit tableau d'or" (L. Dimier, *Histoire de la Peinture de Portrait en France au XVIe siecle*, Paris, 1924, I, p. 99). This miniature of Catherine belongs to a small group attributable to Clouet which includes one of Mary, Queen of Scots (Royal Collection) and two of Catherine and her son, Charles IX, in a jewelled locket (Kunsthistorisches Museum, Vienna).

The tradition of miniature painting practised by François Clouet followed that established by his father in being worked up from drawings. This miniature is probably based on a version of a drawing in the British Museum (*Crayons Français de la collection de M. G. Salting*, ed. E. Moreau-Nelaton, pl. xxxii) which is attributed also to Clouet. Hilliard would have probably seen miniatures by Clouet, but it was only the oval shape which he adopted. Apart from the process of painting a portrait, Clouet's approach was quite different. It was not linear, as was Hilliard's, but aimed at a far more three-dimensional realistic effect: the features being loosely built up with little strokes of the brush over a brownish red flesh tone. There is no use of real gold and silver for the highlights or any attempt to simulate jewels. The attitude to pictorial space is a Renaissance one, emphasized by the trick of the hands being extended over the gold border. The miniature is a rare likeness of Catherine before her widowhood after which she invariably dressed in widows weeds. She is depicted in a black dress trimmed with white fur, a lattice work of jewels over her partlet, a jewelled French hood and a feather fan in her hand.

70

72

The miniature is framed in one half of a seventeenth-century portrait box of turned wood stained black. In the other half there is a portrait of James I by John Hoskins (P.27–1954).

COLLECTIONS: With H. E. Backer, 1954.

LITERATURE: V & A archives.

STUDIO OF FRANÇOIS CLOUET

71   Henri III, c. 1571

Bibliothèque Nationale, Paris: Cabinet des Estampes, (Na 21 rés. f. 92)
Drawing, crayon on paper, 32 × 22 cm, $12\frac{5}{8} \times 8\frac{11}{16}$ in.

The drawing depicts the future Henri III (1551–89) as Duke of Anjou and is a copy or version of two made by François Clouet during the negotiations for his marriage to Elizabeth I. One drawing was of the head only (*Les Clouets*, cited below, pl. XXVIII) and the other *en pied*. The first was sent with a letter from the Queen Mother, Catherine de'Medici to La Mothe Fénélon, the French ambassador in England and the second followed, arriving in London on July 9th.

Pope-Hennessy first pointed out (*Lecture*, 1949, pp. 18–19) the relationship of the doll-like figures in Hilliard's large-scale cabinet miniatures (nos. 263ff.) to this drawing. Unlike Hilliard's portraits, however, the Clouet drawing shows a perfect understanding of correct perspective. The elongated stylized treatment of the figure is a typical ingredient of late Valois court art of which Hilliard would have seen an abundance during his two years in France.

LITERATURE:: L. Dinier, *Les Clouets*, Paris, 1924 (473).
J. Adhémar, *Les Dessin Français au XVIᵉ Siècle*, Lausanne, 1954, pp. xxi–xxiii; 132 (60).

Les Clouet et la Cour des Rois de France, Bibliothèque Nationale, Paris, 1970 (41).

NICHOLAS HILLIARD

72   Francis, Duke of Anjou, 1581?

Kunsthistorisches Museum, Vienna
Vellum stuck onto card, oval, 48 × 39 mm, $1\frac{29}{32} \times 1\frac{1}{2}$ in.

Francis, Duke of Alençon and later Anjou (1554–1584), fourth son of Catherine de'Medici and Henri II.

Hilliard is recorded as *valet de chambre* to Anjou in 1577 and there are two miniatures by him of the Duke. The one in the Musée de Condé, at Chantilly is the earlier, painted during the period in which he was in the Duke's service (Auerbach, *Hilliard*, pl. 36). The Kunsthistorisches Museum miniature is later and Hilliard painted a second version of it in a lost prayer book which he illuminated during the height of the negotiations for the Queen's marriage to the Prince (a facsimile of the manuscript is in the British Library, see Auerbach, *Hilliard*, pp. 78–79, pl. 39–40; Strong, *Portraits of Queen Elizabeth I*, p. 102 (9)). The most likely occasion for the painting of this miniature was during Anjou's visit to England from November 1581 to February 1582.

Examination under magnification would suggest that the face was the result of one sitting, showing evidence of great haste. The clothes, a black bonnet with a pink and white feather and a grey doublet with chains of pearls and jewels, were obviously finished at a later date. Its condition is very abraded.

COLLECTIONS: Part of the collection formed by the Archduke Ferdinand of Tyrol (1529–95).

LITERATURE: Auerbach, *Hilliard*, pp. 79; 294 (40).

STUDIO OF FRANÇOIS CLOUET.

73 Marguerite de Valois, c. 1572

*Bibliothèque Nationale, Paris: Cabinet des Estampes,
(Na 22 res. pl.XXX.)*
Drawing, crayon on paper.

Marguerite de Valois (1552–1615), daughter of Catherine
de'Medici, married Henri, King of Navarre in 1572, the
occasion of the Massacre of St Bartholemew. She was
extremely close to her brother, Anjou (no. 72). During the
summer of 1577 both he and the English embassy travelled
south to Poitiers. Marguerite reigned briefly over a court in
her husband's principality of Béarn until she returned to
Paris in 1582. The Queen of Navarre had connexions with
a painter called Jacques Gaultier who designed the
decorations for her entry into Bordeaux in September 1578
and became painter to the city in August 1579. Gaultier
knew Hilliard and sent him greetings in a letter written to
Francis Bacon's brother, Anthony, in January 1593.
Gaultier's son was probably Leonard Gaultier, the
engraver, supposedly the son-in-law of Antoine Caron, the
most important artist working for the Valois court (see
Noel Blakiston, "Nicholas Hilliard and Bordeaux", *The
Times Literary Supplement*, 28th July 1950, p. 469; Auerbach,
Hilliard, p. 14).

The drawing was made at about the time of her
marriage. Henri of Navarre's mother, Jeanne d'Albret
wrote to her son on 8th March 1572 saying that she was
sending him "sa peinture". Clouet's chalk drawings had an
immense influence on Hilliard, particularly the ones of
women, softening his previous interpretation and leading
him to emphasize their charm, sexual allure and femininity,
a formula he applied henceforth to his English sitters.

LITERATURE: *Les Clouets & La Cour des Rois de France*, Bibliothèque
Nationale, Paris, 1970 (47)

NICHOLAS HILLIARD

74 Marguerite de Valois, Queen of Navarre, 1577

Private Collection
Vellum stuck to card, oval, 56×44 mm, $2\frac{3}{16} \times 1\frac{3}{4}$ in.

Marguerite de Valois (1552–1615), daughter of Henri II
and Catherine de'Medici. Married Henri of Navarre,
1572; devoted to her brother, Alençon; escaped from St
Germain to Guyenne, 1576; voyaged to Flanders, 1577;
held court with her husband at Nérac, 1578–82; confined
to the Chateau d'Usson by Henri IV, 1599; returned to
Paris.

Previously this has been called "Mademoiselle de Sourdis"
but there is no basis for this identification. The features are
without doubt those of Marguerite de Valois, dressed as
usual in the height of fashion for which she, along with
Elizabeth I, was renowned (for portraits of Marguerite see
F. A. Yates, *The Valois Tapestries*, London, 1959, pl. 2
(c–d)). Hilliard was in the service of her brother, Alençon,
later Anjou. Both he and the English embassy went as far
south as Poitiers in the summer of 1577 and it is likely that

74

this included a visit to the Navarre court at Béarn.
Hilliard, we know, was a friend of Marguerite's painter,
Jacques Gaultier (Auerbach, *Hilliard*, pp. 13–14). A
portrait of the Queen of Navarre would be entirely
explicable during this period when she and her brother
were politically in alignment. The face has been damaged
and restored and there is some flaking in the costume.

INSCRIBED: To the left: *Anō Dnī. 1577.*

COLLECTIONS: C. H. T. Hawkins sale, Christie's 16th May, 1904
(lot 1050); Pierpont Morgan Collection; sold Christie's 24th
June 1935 (lot 101); bt. Dr Beets; sold Fred. Muller, 9–11th
April 1940.

LITERATURE: Williamson, *Catalogue*, I, (no. 23).
Auerbach, *Hilliard*, p. 293 (34).

NICHOLAS HILLIARD

75 Louis de Gonzague, Duke of Nevers and Henriette de Cleves, Duchess of Nevers, 1578

Bibliothèque Nationale, Paris, Department des Imprimés,
Woodcuts, oval, 29×26 mm, $1\frac{1}{8} \times 1$ in.

Louis de Gonzague, Prince of Mantua (1539–95), captain
of a hundred men-at-arms, married Henriette de Cleves in
1565. He was created Duke of Nemours in 1566.

In 1578 the Duke and Duchess of Nevers had made a deed
of covenant for the dowries of daughters on their
marriage, an event which was marked by a formal vellum
document decorated with woodcuts of the donors. The two
oval portraits, but not the surround, are by Hilliard. No
less than two French artists had produced blocks that had

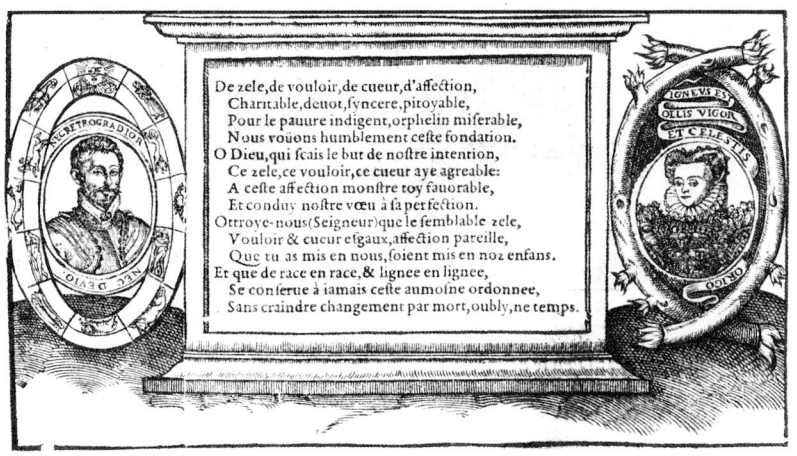

75

77

been unacceptable and Hilliard was brought in to replace them through the offices of the humanist, Blaise de Vignère. These two ovals are the only certain woodcuts actually designed and cut by Hilliard. Both adopt the oval format and the portrait of the Duchess is particularly close to his miniature of the previous year of Marguerite de Valois (no. 74) and to woodcuts of Queen Elizabeth in the 1580s.

LITERATURE: Henri Bouchot, "La Preparation de la publication d'un livre illustré au XVIe siècle" *Bibliothèque de l'Ecole de Chartes*, LIII, 1892, pp. 612 ff.

L. Dimier, *Histoire de la Peinture de Portrait en France au XVIe siècle*, Paris, 1924–26, I, pp. 125–27.

L. Dimier, *French Painting in the 16th Century*, London, 1904, p. 254.

Williamson, *Catalogue*, I, p. 24.

J. Adhémar, *Inventaire des Fonds français Graveurs du 16me siècle*, Paris, 1939, p. 403.

E. P. Goldschmidt, "Nicholas Hilliard as Wood Engraver", *The Times Literary Supplement*, August 9th 1947, p. 403.

E. Auerbach, "More Light on Nicholas Hilliard", *Burlington Magazine*, XCI, 1949, p. 166.

N. Blakiston, "Nicholas Hilliard in France", *Gazette des Beaux-Arts*, LI, 1958, pp. 298–300.

Auerbach, *Hilliard*, pp. 73–74; 321 (192–93).

A. FAVYN

76 *The Theater of Honour and Knighthood*, London, 1623

Victoria & Albert Museum Library (44-A-57)

One of the most important events at the Valois court during the years that Hilliard was in France was the creation by Henri III of the Order of the Holy Spirit. This new chivalrous Order was designed to be a vehicle of Counter Reformation piety and bind its aristocratic members in loyalty to the monarchy. Its ceremonies were held in the Church of the Augustines and a great picture was painted and placed in the church which, according to Favyn, corresponded closely to the Great Seal of the Order

displayed here which depicts Henri III enthroned in robes of state attended by officers of the Order with the Dove and tongues of fire of the Holy Spirit descending upon him. The iconography of the Holy Spirit with its descending rays onto the head of the monarch may be the source of Hilliard's presentation of Elizabeth on the reverse of the Great Seal (no. 44).

LITERATURE: Frances A. Yates, *The French Academies in the Sixteenth Century*, London, 1947, pp. 156–57.

NICHOLAS HILLIARD

77 **Alice Brandon, Mrs Hilliard**, 1578

Victoria & Albert Museum (P.2–1942)
Vellum stuck to card and subsequently stuck to a larger, circular piece of card upon which the outer band of inscription and decoration has been painted, almost circular, 59 × 57.5 mm, $2\frac{5}{16} \times 2\frac{1}{4}$ in.

Alice Brandon (b. 1556–d. before 1608), daughter of Robert Brandon, the Queen's goldsmith, married Nicholas Hilliard in 1576 and bore him seven children, Daniel, Elizabeth, Francis, Laurence, Lettice, Penelope and Robert.

This delightful miniature was definitely painted while Hilliard was in France and is recognized as the prime instance of a more direct contact with the portraiture of François Clouet. Its sensitivity and feminine charm reflects very fully the impact of French portraiture which, particularly in the chalk drawings, aimed at catching fleeting expression.

The face has been damaged, with restoration to the forehead. There is a degree of flaking and the usual fading and oxidizing of the silver. This retains a frame of a type which at one time was also added to both the miniatures of Nicholas and Richard Hilliard (nos. 48, 49). It would seem highly likely that this decorative border was added by Laurence Hilliard. The inscription refers to Alice as *UXOR PRIMA*, Hilliard's first wife which would indicate that the Nicholas who married Susan Gysard in 1608 was the

Nicholas Hilliard 71

miniaturist (Edmond, *Limners and Picture-makers*, p. 68).

This is a rare instance of Hilliard signing with a monogram NH.

INSCRIBED: Above the shoulders: *NH* (in monogram); on either side of the head: *Ano Dni | * Æ*S*S*. 22.*

On the mount over the arms left of Hilliard and right of Brandon and the inscription: +*ALICIA · BRANDON NICOLAI HILLYARD · Q | VI PROPRIA MANV DEPINXIT VXOR PRIMA.*

COLLECTIONS: The miniature is not referred to in Laurence Hilliard's will as are those of her husband and father-in-law (see no. 48) which supposes a different descent; it was purchased together with another Hilliard by Walter Francis, 5th Duke of Buccleuch, in 1869; thence by descent; acquired through the *N.A.C.F.* 1942.

LITERATURE: C. Holmes, *Burlington Magazine*, VIII, 1906, p. 316.
Kennedy, *Buccleuch*, pl. XII.
Winter, *Elizabethan Miniatures*, pl. III (b).
V & A, 1947 (15)
Pope-Hennessy, *Lecture*, 1949, p. 18, pl. XI.
Auerbach, *Hilliard*, pp. 72–3, pl. 33; 293 (33).
Strong, *Hilliard*, pl. 3 (b).

STUDIO OF FRANÇOIS CLOUET

78   Marguerite de France, Duchesse de Savoie, after a portrait c. 1560

The British Museum, Department of Prints and Drawings (1910–2–12–56)
Graphite and coloured chalks, 32.8 × 23.5 cm, 12⅞ × 9¼ in.
Marguerite de France, Duchesse de Savoie (1523–74), daughter of François I.

A drawing typical of the type produced by the Clouet studio which Hilliard must have seen and which certainly deeply affected his approach to female sitters. What is more surprising is that contact with this soft graphic style had no other effect on Hilliard at all and his drawings continued in the manner he had learned through copying engravings and woodcuts.

COLLECTIONS: Part of collection of French portrait drawings assembled by Ignatius Hugford (1703–78); Salting Bequest, 1910.

79

III HIGH ELIZABETHAN, 1578/9–1593

1578. Hilliard moves into the house in Gutter Lane off the Strand in which he was to live for the next thirty-five years.
1578–88. Six children born.
1582. The Earl of Leicester intercedes for him with Sir Walter Mildmay.
1584. Draft monopoly for manufacturing portraits of the Queen in which George Gower excludes Hilliard from all the media except "in small compasse in lymnynge".
1584–86. Engaged jointly with Dericke Anthony, graver to the Mint, in making a second Great Seal.
1591. Rewarded by the Queen with a gift of £400. Robert Brandon, his father-in-law, dies and cuts Hilliard and his children out of his will.

The 1580s were Hilliard's heyday. Although George Gower and not Hilliard was appointed to the lucrative post of Serjeant Painter in 1581, royal patronage clearly continued and statistically this was to be by far Hilliard's most productive decade. The sitters included virtually every major figure of the period from the imprisoned Queen of Scots (no. 79) to Sir Walter Raleigh (no. 81). In the field of limning he had no competitors. Rowland Lockey was an apprentice in his workshop and it was not until about 1586–87 that Oliver became his pupil. Although Oliver was active as a miniaturist from 1587 onwards it was not until the early 1590s that Hilliard was threatened by his pupil's brilliant precosity. Throughout the eighties in addition large-scale painters adopted the Hilliard aesthetic: John Bettes, William Segar (no. 218) and Robert Peake (no. 204). Even Gower responded in his formalized images of Elizabethan court ladies (no. 85).

This was also a period of isolationism as England went to war with Spain and both France and the Low Countries were embroiled in civil war. At no time during the sixteenth century were the achievements of Renaissance Italy to be more remote and inaccessible. The result was that the anti-naturalistic tendencies of Hilliard's work were heightened rather than diminished as the modelling of features became progressively reduced to a few diagrammatic lines and the attention to elaboration of the jewels and dress became a major preoccupation. Technically the miniatures remain as assured as ever and only at the close of this period do we sense signs of the decline to come. The first traces of this coincide with the advent of Oliver which resulted in uneasy experiments. The first was an attempt at small full-length miniatures, a format immediately found to be unsatisfactory and abandoned. The second was the cabinet miniatures, the large full lengths starting with the *Young man among Roses*. They, however, were shortly to reveal the artist's limitations but for the years around the Armada Hilliard's archaic style reflected exactly Elizabethan England at its heroic height.

SELECT BIBLIOGRAPHY: Auerbach, *Hilliard*, pp. 16–26, 87–131. Strong, *Renaissance Miniature*, pp. 92–101

NICHOLAS HILLIARD

79   **Mary Queen of Scots**, 1578/9

H.M. The Queen
Vellum stuck to a card, with another card glued over that, oval, 43.5×36.5 mm, $1\frac{23}{32} \times 1\frac{7}{16}$ in.

Two versions survive of this miniature, the second being in the Victoria & Albert Museum ((P.24–1975) rep. Auerbach, *Hilliard*, pl. 38) which technical examination in 1976 established was without doubt a repetition. This reverses the order first postulated by Lionel Cust in 1903 and accepted by everyone, including myself in 1969. The Royal Collection version is *ad vivum*. Not only is it more sensitive in its rendering of the Queen's features but the use of ultramarine as against the more usual blue bice for the background establishes it as the more costly object. A third version of uncertain status was last recorded in 1889 (Auerbach, *Hilliard*, p. 294 (39)).

The iconography of Mary Queen of Scots is one of the most complex of all sixteenth-century figures, in the main not for the number of portraits executed during her lifetime, but due to the hundreds of posthumous likenesses manufactured after her political resurrection on the accession of her son, James VI, in 1603. From 1569 Mary was in the custody of the Earl and Countess of Shrewsbury and resided at one or other of their houses. In 1575 there is a reference to the manufacture of miniatures of her abroad for distribution to adherents in England which indicates that the production of portraits of her was hedged with difficulties. Two years later comes a reference to a sitting for what must have been a miniature. On August 31st Mary wrote to her agent in France, the Archbishop of Glasgow: "Je pensois faire accompagner la presente d'un portraict de sa Majeste, mais le peintre ne luy a sceu donner sa perfection avant le partement de cette despeche" (for all this see Strong, *Tudor and Jacobean*, I, p. 220).

This sitting cannot have been for Hilliard who did not, as far as we know, return from France before August 1578. The earliest life-scale portrait using this face-pattern is dated 1583 (Blair Castle, Duke of Atholl) and the type was known to engravers before 1603. The date 1578 is the one that appears on the full-length versions of this type produced during the Jacobean period in considerable numbers (e.g. National Portrait Gallery no. 429). Stylistically both the Royal Collection and V & A miniatures are from the late seventies and the dress would also be correct. There is no evidence to establish that the miniatures were painted in 1578 and they are more safely

assigned to the period immediately following Hilliard's return from France. The wired veil appears in portraits of Elizabeth I only from c. 1580 onwards, making even a date in the very early eighties a possibility. The veil, as it appears here, is in its early less formalized manner of wiring as in the Sieve Portrait of Elizabeth (Strong, *Portraits of Queen Elizabeth I*, pl. X). This sitting and portrait was probably the origin of the vast out-pouring of portraits of all sizes of Mary usually labelled as the "Oudry" or "Sheffield" type.

There is slight flaking on the head-dress and the ruff which has been restored. The features are faded.

COLLECTIONS: Possibly Charles II inventory, c. 1662–85 (421): "Mary Queene of Scotland, in a gold ovall case. In small Limbning"; James II catalogue (606): "A little limning of Mary Queen of Scots in a gold case"; probably at Kensington, temp. George I: "La Reine Marie d'Ecosse en Habit blanc" (Stowe MS 567. f 8^v); listed by Vertue in the Closet at Kensington, 1720: "a hed of Mary Quen Scots a Coppy of that at St Jameses whole length" (*Notebooks*, I, p. 74); and again, 1734 (*Notebooks*, IV, p. 67); Fraser Tytler lists a number of miniatures of Mary Queen of Scots in his *List* compiled in the 1840s.

LITERATURE: Auerbach, *Hilliard*, p. 294 (38) but for previous literature on this topic see Strong, *Tudor and Jacobean*, I, p. 220.

ATTRIBUTED TO NICHOLAS HILLIARD

80   **Compartments used in Thomas Bentley's "The Monument of Matrones"**, 1582

The British Library (G12047)
Woodcuts

McKerrow and Ferguson list no less than twenty-eight head and foot pieces related to this series which must have been commissioned for use first in Thomas Bentley's *The Monument of Matrones*, 1582 which was never completed so that not all the compartments were used. Twenty-seven, however, of the head and foot pieces are to be found also in folio editions of Edmund Spenser's *Faerie Queene* and other works by him printed by H. Lownes for M. Lownes in 1609 and 1611–13. Thomas Bentley's book contains "seven severall Lamps of Virginitie", a series of private devotions in the main by Theodore Beza, whose central section is a dialogue between God and His chosen and pure virgin, Elizabeth I. The borders are unusually elaborate and are flanked with portraits of holy women and queens, including *Elizabetha Regina*.

McKerrow and Ferguson link these compartments stylistically to a formidable series which they believe to have been cut by C.T., Charles Tressell, whose signed title page of 1574 was designed by Hilliard (no. 65). Any association of Hilliard as the designer of these borders must be tentative but it is not impossible. The title page coat of arms with its strapwork, indented swags of drapery and serpenting branches of greenery are very close to those on the Emmanuel College Charter (no. 191). Holy women as subject-matter was certainly in Hilliard's orbit in the

82

83

1580s. In 1584 he presented the Queen as a New Year's Gift with "a faire Table conteyninge the history of the fyve wise virgins and the fyve foolysshe virgins" (B. L. Egerton MS 3052).

LITERATURE: R. B. McKerrow and F. S. Ferguson, *Title-page Borders used in England and Scotland 1485–1640*, Bibliographical Society, O.U.P., 1932, pp. 145–46.

NICHOLAS HILLIARD

81   Sir Walter Raleigh, c. 1585

National Portrait Gallery, London (4106)
Vellum stuck onto card, oval, 48 × 41 mm,
$1\frac{7}{8} \times 1\frac{5}{8}$ in.

Sir Walter Raleigh (1552?–1618), military and naval commander, author and favourite of Elizabeth I was knighted in 1584 and pioneered the colonization of Virginia. Fell from favour on his marriage, 1592; took part in the Cadiz and Azores expeditions. Deprived of office by James I and imprisoned on a charge of conspiracy, 1603; he was released to voyage for gold and executed on his return for attacking the Spanish.

Formerly known as Henry Howard, Earl of Northampton, its true identity was established in 1948 by C. S. Emden by comparison with an old oil copy of the type. Although undated the costume is c. 1585, during which period Raleigh was friendly with Lord Thomas Howard (see no. 83), ancestor of the Howards of Castle Howard and Morpeth. Auerbach's dating of the miniature to 1588 cannot be substantiated. The presentation of the sitter is very frenchified in feeling, close in mood to the *mignons* of the court of Henri III whom Hilliard knew. Although the dress is French in style with its bonnet at the back of the head, its huge cartwheel ruff and its pink scarf swagged with pearls, the interpretation must have reflected the years in France and perhaps even more the great embassy of 1581 to England for the Anjou marriage. The features are faded and the silver highlights oxidized. There is considerable flaking.

LITERATURE: Lord Hawkesbury, *Catalogue of Portraits, Miniatures, etc. at Castle Howard*, p. 68 (5).
Reynolds, *Miniatures*, 1952, pl. I.
C. S. Emden, *Oriel Papers*, Oxford, 1948, pp. 9–21; same author, *Oriel Record*, 1953, pp. 10–11.
Auerbach, *Hilliard*, pp. 95–96, pl. 68; 298 (65).
Strong, *Tudor and Jacobean*, I, pp. 255–56.

NICHOLAS HILLIARD

82   Possibly John, 2nd Lord St John of Bletso or Oliver, 3rd Lord St John of Bletso, 1586

Private Collection
Vellum stuck to a playing card with six spades verso, oval, 58 × 47 mm, $2\frac{1}{4} \times 1\frac{27}{32}$ in.

First described by Vertue c. 1721: "Sr Walter (*Henry* struck through) St John ancestor of the Present Lord St John. / a limning in poses. of the said Lord. inscribed about it. A^no Dom, 1586. Aeta. sui. 24. done by J. Oliver. not markt with his name. but seems to be in a juvenile manner. or like Hilyard limnings but better colourd" (*Notebooks*, I p. 108). The sitter is therefore an ancestor of the 10th Baron St John of Bletso and likely to be one of the sons of the 1st Lord, who married before January 1548/9 Agnes Fisher. The eldest son was John, 2nd Lord St. John (d. 1596) who sat on the trial of Mary, Queen of Scots. The second was Oliver, 3rd Baron (d. 1618). Exact birth dates for either are not known but the sitter in the miniature was born in 1552. Apart from slight damage to the edge, the miniature is in virtually mint condition. It is not only of fine quality but unusual in that Hilliard has allowed the black hat to intersect the usual gold border. The frame is a Bernard Lens pear-tree one.

INSCRIBED: On either side of the head: *Ano Dni: 1586* | *Ætatis Suae 24*:

COLLECTIONS: First recorded c. 1721 by Vertue when in the possession of the 10th Lord St John of Bletso (see above); acquired by Edward Harley, 2nd Earl of Oxford (1689–1741); recorded in Vertue's list, c. 1732 as 'St John' (*Notebooks*, IV, p. 63); referred to again in 1738: "another head of a Man (the same master) ano D^{ni}. 1586. aetat svae 24. a black hi crownd hat and laced square falling band" (*Notebooks*, IV, p. 153); Vertue's catalogue, 1743 (40); Oxford's daughter married William Bentinck, 2nd Duke of Portland; thence by descent.

LITERATURE: Goulding, *Welbeck*, pp. 63–64 (15). V & A, 1947 (31). Auerbach, *Hilliard*, pp. 96–97, pl. 70; 298 (67).

NICHOLAS HILLIARD

83 Man Clasping a Hand from a Cloud, perhaps Lord Thomas Howard, 1588

Victoria & Albert Museum (P. 21–1942)
Vellum mounted on to a plain brown card, which is probably a later addition, oval, 60 mm × 49.5 mm, $2\frac{3}{4} \times 1$ in.

Lord Thomas Howard, later 1st Earl of Suffolk and 1st Baron Howard de Walden (1561–1626) was the second son of Thomas, 4th Duke of Norfolk, executed in 1572. He served as a volunteer in the fleet sent against the Armada (1588); was commander in the Azores expedition (1591); admiral in the Cadiz expedition (1596) and in 1597, created Baron Howard de Walden. Although closely connected with Essex, he led the forces that besieged Essex House in 1601. In July 1603 he was created Earl of Suffolk; in 1614 became Lord-Treasurer and survived the disgrace of his daughter, the notorious Frances, in 1615 but eventually both he and his wife fell from power in 1618 for embezzlement. Humble submission to the King and the promise to repay brought a restoration to favour two years later.

There are two versions of this miniature, the second of which is in the possession of Dr Leslie Hotson who made it the subject of his book, *Shakespeare by Hilliard*, London, 1977. The existence of a repetition indicates that the sitter was of some social standing. A close comparison of both miniatures, accompanied by technical examination, should establish which is the *ad vivum*, although this one, in spite of the large amount of damage on the sitter's left cheek and the fading, is of high quality.

There can be no question that the sitter is not William Shakespeare, as Dr Hotson believes, an identification supported by wholly speculative arguments. Proof of identity must depend on provenance. The V & A version was known as Robert Devereux, 2nd Earl of Essex when in the collection of Sir Hans Sloane, again an identification that cannot be sustained. The Hotson version was part of a group of miniatures that belonged to the Howards of Naworth Castle and Castle Howard.

The only certain clue to the true identity is this Howard connexion and the now certainly identified Raleigh miniature. This leads us to Lord Thomas Howard. In 1591

Raleigh was appointed to serve under Lord Thomas on an expedition to the West Indies and he also attempted to reconcile Raleigh with Essex. Later serving under Essex on the Cadiz expedition he was closely connected with the Earl throughout this period. Howard was twenty-seven in 1588, the date of the miniature, during which period he was active in court fêtes, taking part in the Accession Day Tilts of 1584, 1585, 1586 and 1589 (Strong, *The Cult of Elizabeth*, pp. 206–7) and made his second marriage to Catherine, daughter and co-heiress of Sir Henry Knevet of Charlton, in 1583.

In 1588 Howard accompanied, as a volunteer, the fleet sent to oppose the Spanish Armada and in the attack off Calais displayed such courage that he was knighted at sea June 25th 1588, certainly an event to commemorate in a miniature. This brings us to the allegory of the symbolic linked hands. The sitter's right hand is raised clasping a female left hand issuing from a cloud with a ruff-cuff. A comparison with many other miniatures by Hilliard leaves it indisputable that this is a female and not a male hand as Hotson tries to argue (*Shakespeare by Hilliard*, op. cit. pp. 37 ff.) The formula is paralleled in Hans Eworth's portrait of Sir John Luttrell (1550) in which Peace, ensconced in the clouds, embraces his raised arm (Strong, *The English Icon*, p. 86 (no. 22)). Clasped hands are a common emblem of Concord and plighted faith:

Of Concord firme, the *Romans* in their coine,
This symbole gave, their peace abour to make,
That as their hands, as in one their hearts should ione,
And sooner first, they would their lives forsake . . .
(H. Peacham, *Minerva Britanna*, London, 1612, p. 135).

The *Hand-in-hand*, which *Plighted faith* implies . . .
(George Wither, *A Collection of Emblemes*, London, 1635, p. 166).

(Hotson, *op. cit.*, cites more, pp. 49–50). More confusing is the motto which no one has satisfactorily explained or translated. The Raleigh-Essex-Howard links during the mid to late 1580s would at least make this identification a possibility. Lord Thomas's role as a courtier, used to assuming the allegorical guise demanded of actors in the tiltyard, would also fit. Surviving portraits of him are much later in date and depict him as an older man. An early copy of a lost portrait of c. 1605 now in the National Portrait Gallery (no. 4572), depicts Lord Thomas as Earl of Suffolk aged about forty-five. The hair is brown streaked with grey and the beard is differently cut, darker and also streaked with grey. The hair matches the miniature in colour as do the grey eyes. (For a discussion of his meagre iconography see Strong, *Tudor and Jacobean*, I, pp. 359–60, II, pls. 685–88.) If it is Howard in the miniature it is Howard the young courtier, the budding naval Thomas and not the degenerate Jacobean courtier of the century that followed.

INSCRIBED: On either side of the head: *Attici amoris ergo.* | *Ano. Dni. 1588*

COLLECTIONS: This should be identical with a group of Hilliard miniatures sold in May 1726 from the collection of a writer, Mr Halstead: "there likewise several hds of Hilliard with writing about, gold letters. One of Leonard Dorns Aeta. 37. An°. 1591 . . . another Aeta. 33. 1611. the Earl of Essex. 1588. William Earl of Pembroke by Hoskins" (Vertue, *Notebooks*, II,

Walpole Society, XX, 1932, p. 13); the Essex could be this miniature (and not as assumed by Hotson (p. 202) the Naworth one) acquired by Sir Hans Sloane (1660–1753); this passed with his collection to the British Museum in 1754 (BM No. 3; Sloane 272) and it is recorded in the Sloane Inventory: "The picture of the Earl of Essex in whose hand is another coming from the clouds, supposed to be that of Queen Elizabeth, wrote upon Attici Amoris Ergo 1588 in miniature", purchased or valued at £2.2.0d; transferred to the V & A, 1939.

LITERATURE: Winter, *Elizabethan Miniatures*, p. 24, pl. IV (b).
V & A, 1947 (35).
Pope-Hennessy, *Lecture*, 1949, p. 23.
Auerbach, *Hilliard*, pp. 100, 299 (no. 73).
L. Hotson, *Shakespeare by Hilliard*, London, 1977, passim.

NICHOLAS HILLIARD

84 Unknown Lady, 1585–90

Private Collection
Vellum stuck to a playing card with four diamonds verso, oval, 54 × 42 mm, $2\frac{1}{4} \times 1\frac{11}{16}$ in.

A beautiful, unfaded miniature in virtually mint condition with only very slight flaking and oxidization of the silver. In the eighteenth century the sitter was called Queen Elizabeth, Goulding later suggesting Anne Morgan, Lady Hunsdon. Both identifications can be discounted. The only clue as to identity is the letter S that forms a repeat on the ruff. The splendour of the jewellery and costume indicate a lady of high rank. Someone like Mary Sidney, Countess of Pembroke (1561–1621) would fit who would have been about twenty-five to thirty in c. 1585–90. The only authentic portrait depicts her at sixty-seven in 1618 (Strong, *Tudor and Jacobean*, II, pl. 483) and is not irreconcilable.

This miniature derives closely from French chalk portrait drawings of the Clouet School both in their lively characterization and in the tight placing of head and ruff into the picture's surface.

COLLECTIONS: Edward Harley, 2nd Earl of Oxford (1689–1741); conceivably identical with an entry on a portrait of Queen Elizabeth in Vertue's list of c. 1732 'dito. a head' (*Notebooks*, IV, p. 41); Vertue's 1743 catalogue (25): 'A Lady's head . . . call'd Q. Elizabeth'; Oxford's daughter married William Bentinck, 2nd Duke of Portland; thence by descent.

LITERATURE: Goulding, *Welbeck*, p. 56 (4).
V & A, 1947 (26).
Auerbach, *Hilliard*, p. 94, pl. 66; 297 (62).

ATTRIBUTED TO GEORGE GOWER

85 Elizabeth Sydenham, Lady Drake, c. 1585

City of Plymouth Museum and Art Gallery
Oil on canvas, 108.1 × 81.4 cm, 42 × 32 in.

Elizabeth Sydenham, Lady Drake, daughter of Sir George

85

Sydenham, married Sir Francis Drake as his second wife in 1585; after his death she married, in 1597, Sir William Courtney of Powderham Castle.

This portrait is a typical example of the formalized portraiture practised by George Gower in the 1580's. Its climax was to be the Armada Portrait of the Queen at Woburn Abbey (Strong, *The English Icon*, p. 182 (135)). They are far less forceful than his portraiture in the 1570's and they relate to the highly decorative miniatures by Hilliard of female sitters during the same period. The life-scale portraits are devoid, however, of the intimacy that is the striking feature of the miniatures.

The relationship of Gower and Hilliard in the 1580's is a problematic one. There exists a draft monopoly from 1584 in which all images of the Queen in whatever media *except* limning were to be the province of Gower. Evidently the Serjeant-Painter was attempting to confine Hilliard's activities to painting miniatures. It was never put into practice but is hardly evidence of a happy relationship. Hilliard, in fact, was to be the predominating force in the creation of the royal image.

COLLECTIONS: Buckland Abbey, the Drake seat; probably passed via the sitter to Powderham, the seat of her second husband; on her death probably to Sir Francis Drake's godson, Francis Drake of Ash; his descendants inherited Shardeloes; Drake Heirlooms Settlement sale, Christie's 26th July 1957 (lot 127);

sold again anonymously Christie's 29th January 1965 (lot 75);
J. B. Gold; sold Sotheby's 7th July 1976 (lot 81).

LITERATURE: Strong, *The English Icon*, p. 181 (134).

87

THEODORE DE BRY

86 Section of the funeral procession of Sir Philip Sidney, 1587

Engraving, average size of plates, 194 × 380 mm,
7⅝ × 15 in. *(Photograph)*

Both in 1593 and 1594 two Painter Stainers petitioned for a monopoly in executing the decorative painting evoked by Elizabethan funerals (Auerbach, *Hilliard*, p. 27). In their letter to Lord Burghley of 1594 they ask for Hilliard to be included in the monopoly "so well knowne for his sufficiencie and care in his works". This phrase does not mean necessarily that Hilliard had done such work but neither does it exclude the possibility that he had. What it does make clear is that he was regarded as fully capable of it.

The most spectacular funeral of the Elizabethan age, excluding the Queen's, was that accorded to Sir Philip Sidney on 16th February 1587. The procession was drawn by Thomas Lant, later Portcullis Pursuivant and Windsor Herald, and engraved by Theodore de Bry. This a rare instance of an engraver giving the source of his design. Hilliard was known to Sidney (*ibid.*, p. 211), although there is no evidence as to who did the decorative painting for the funeral but engravings show that it consisted not only of heraldic banners but ensigns decorated with Sidney's *imprese* such as one covered in stars with the motto *Per tenebras* or another with the star-gazing fish, the uranoscopus with the motto *Pulchrum propter se*, (see K. Duncan-Jones, "Sidney's Personal *Imprese*", *Journal of the Warburg and Courtauld Institutes*, XXXIII, 1970, p. 322).

LITERATURE: Hind, *Engraving*, I, pp. 132–37.

NICHOLAS HILLIARD

87 Unknown Lady, 1585–90

Victoria & Albert Museum (P.2–1974)
Vellum stuck on to playing card with a queen showing on the reverse, oval, 46 × 39 mm,
1 3/16 × 1½ in.

One of the five Radnor miniatures still in its original turned ivory box (see nos. 93, 210). Datable on costume to c. 1585–90 this is a relatively unfaded miniature with only very slight flaking. It is of fine autograph quality, reflecting Hilliard's characteristic response to the charm of his young sitter. V. J. Murrell observes that the highlights of the pearls in the hair are deliberately painted with gold rather than, as was usual, with silver in order to heighten the warm reflections from the sitter's hair. It is another

instance of Hilliard's use of the "close-up" as a portrait formula.

The identity of the sitter ought to lie within the family of Elizabeth Stafford, Lady Drury. It could depict her daughter, Frances, wife of Sir Nicholas Clifford.

COLLECTIONS: This and no. 93 are the two earliest in date of a
   group of five miniatures that were acquired from the Earl of
   Radnor in 1974. The documentation on their history was first
   published by W. B. Squire and the Countess of Radnor in the
   catalogue of the collection at Longford Castle published in
   1909. They came with a memorandum listing other items, most
   now untraceable, on August 2nd 1796 when they were
   purchased by the 2nd Earl of Radnor from a Mrs Anne Lewis
   for £52.10s.

"Original Portraits of
Queen Elizabeth
Mary Queen of Scots
James 1st
Lord Darnly
Rizzo
and two others
A Letter written by Queen Elizabeth to her
Maid of Honor Lady Rich upon her unhappy Marriage –
A Letter from Lady Rich to her daughter –
A curious smelling Bottle (oval) Spoon –
Hair pins, Coins and sundry antiquities –
The Cabinet was given by Queen Elizabeth to
Lady Rich – And by her Ladyship it was given to
the family of the present Possessor – And has
never been in any other hands -"
This memorandum survives and of the items listed those which
also survive are five out of the seven miniatures and the two
letters which are still at Longford (information kindly
communicated by Lord Radnor). One letter (undated) is from
Lettice Rich, Lady Carey, to her mother, the celebrated
Penelope Devereux, Lady Rich. The second is from Queen
Elizabeth to Elizabeth Stafford, Lady Drury, on the occasion
of the death of her husband, Sir William, in 1589. Of the two
miniatures now missing, Squire records that one was set in a
brooch for a fancy dress ball.

The cabinet in which these things were kept, Squire records,
contained the following memorandum no longer traceable:

"The Cabinet was given by Q. Elizabeth to Lady Rich Maid
of Honour to Q. Eliz. Her Daughter marr'd Sir Cecil Wray.
Christ.
His daughter married in to Askew's Family. A Daughter of

Nicholas Hilliard 77

88

evidence to support this (Strong, *The English Icon*, p. 188 (136) dated 1587). On the other hand there is already visible a tighter handling of the paint reflecting Oliver's influence which would take the miniature on in date to c. 1590 which again is perfectly compatible with what is visible of the costume, (eg *Ibid*, p. 222 (183)).

COLLECTIONS: Purchased in 1945 from H. E. Backer, 1 Elm Tree Road, St John's Wood, London, who stated that he had acquired it by private treaty from a family said to have owned it for a long time; purchased from the funds of the R. H. Stevenson Bequest.

LITERATURE: V & A, 1947 (40).
Auerbach, *Hilliard*, pp. 101, pl. 76; 300 (75).

Askew's Family married my Grandf. Ashton. This was I think Aunt Ludlam's Account, 1739".

There are from this evidence two possible lines of descent. The first, more romantic but less likely, is from Penelope Devereux, daughter of Walter Devereux, 1st Earl of Essex, wife of Robert Rich, 2nd Lord Rich and later 1st Earl of Warwick and celebrated as Sidney's "Stella" and later mistress and subsequently wife of Charles Blount, Earl of Devonshire. For this to work the miniatures would have had to have passed via her first husband, whom she divorced in 1605, to his brother-in-law (by his second marriage to Frances Wray), William, husband of Lady Drury's daughter, Frances.

   The more likely descent is from Elizabeth Stafford, Lady Drury, who was Lady of the Bedchamber and the Privy Chamber to the Queen. In this instance the descent is: Elizabeth Stafford, wife of Sir William Drury of Hawsted, Suffolk; her daughter Frances, who married firstly, Sir Nicholas Clifford and secondly Sir William Wray (not Sir Cecil or Sir Christopher as on the memorandum); her daughter, Lady Ayscough; her daughter, Elizabeth, Lady Ashton; her daughter, Anne, Mrs Ludlam, aunt of the Mrs Anne Lewis who sold the miniatures to the Earl of Radnor.

LITERATURE: Countess of Radnor and W. B. Squire, *Catalogue of the Collection of the Earl of Radnor, 1909, II, p. 109 (2)*.
Pope-Hennessy, *Lecture*, 1949, p. 23.
V & A 1947 (41).
Auerbach, *Hilliard*, pp. 97–8, pl. 71; 298 (68).
Strong, "The Radnor Miniatures", *Christie's Review of the Season 1974*, ed John Herbert, 1974, pp. 254–57.

NICHOLAS HILLIARD

88   Unknown Lady, c. 1590

Victoria & Albert Museum (P.8–1945)
Vellum stuck on to a plain card, oval, 51.5 × 43 mm, 2 × 1 11/16 in.

The miniature was formerly wrongly identified as Mary, Queen of Scots. It is basically in good condition, apart from the usual fading and oxidization. Little of the costume is visible which poses difficulties in dating. Both Reynolds and Auerbach date it c. 1588 and indeed there is costume

NICHOLAS HILLIARD

89   Sir Christopher Hatton, 1588–91

Victoria & Albert Museum (P. 138–1910)
Vellum stuck to a playing card with four clubs showing at the reverse, oval, 56 × 43 mm, 2 3/16 × 1 11/16 in.

Sir Christopher Hatton (1540–91), Lord Chancellor, rose rapidly in the Queen's favour, became Captain of the Guard, 1572, vice-Chamberlain, 1578, High Steward of Cambridge University, 1588, and Lord Chancellor, 1587–91.

Hilliard's miniature of Hatton must have been painted between 1588, the year he was made K. G., the collar of which he wears, and his death. He wears the robes of Lord Chancellor which he became in 1587 and on the table to the left is the Chancellor's mace and seal bag. Hatton was famed for his good looks and Naunton refers to him as being "tall and proportionable" (*Fragmenta Regalia*, 1808 ed., p. 248). There is an important reference to Hatton in Hilliard's *Treatise* which should relate to this sitting. It occurs in his discussion of Dürer's theory of proportion in relation to the face:

"Therefore I will be bold to remember me of one, namely Sir Christopher Hatton, sometime Lord Chancellor of England, a man generally known and respected of all men amongst the best favours, and held to be one of the goodliest personages of England: yet had he a very low forehead, not answerable to that good proportion of a third part of his face . . ."

(*A Treatise Concerning Arte of Limning*, ed. R. K. R. Thornton and T. G. S. Cain, Carcanet New Press, 1981, p. 81).

The dating of this experiment with a full-length miniature on a minute scale as after 1588 makes it follow in date Oliver's earliest experiment of this type of scale dated 1587 (no. 137). As usual there is no grasp of the rules of scientific perspective, the lines of table and window going impossibly in opposite directions to and from a vanishing point. Hilliard abandoned this format almost immediately.

   This version is the *ad vivum* while at Belvoir there is a replica (V & A, 1947 (51)). In the latter the sun is shining through the window and there is a fireplace to the right. The overall height of the figure in the Belvoir version is just under two inches. In the case of the V & A's version, $2\frac{3}{16}$ inches, also the areas of green have flaked badly and been restored and the areas using lakes have faded. Recently a head and shoulders version related to the same sitting has come to light (Private Collection).

COLLECTIONS: Either this or the version at Belvoir, Stowe sale March 15th 1849 (lot 87); J. L. Propert Collection; purchased by Salting at the dispersal of his collection by the Fine Art Society, 1897; bequeathed with the Salting Bequest, 1910

LITERATURE: V & A, 1947 (50).
Auerbach, *Hilliard*, pp. 116–17, pl. 91; 303 (90).
Strong, *Tudor and Jacobean*, I, pp. 137–38.

91

JODOCUS HONDIUS

90 Hugh Broughton, *A Concent of Scripture*, London, 1590?

Victoria & Albert Museum Library
Engravings, normal page size, 17.8 × 11.8 cm, $7 \times 4\frac{5}{8}$ in.

Hugh Broughton (1549–1612), was a puritan and noted Hewbrew scholar. He shared one of his key patrons with Hilliard, Sir Walter Mildmay (see no. 264) who gave him an allowance for a lectureship in Greek at Cambridge although he subsequently settled in London receiving support, in particular from the Cotton family. The first illustrated edition of his *Concent* appeared in 1588 and was seen through the press by John Speed. The subject of the book was scriptural chronology and it evoked bitter controversy.

There are two editions of the *Concent* which are illustrated. One is with engravings by William Rogers (Hind, *Engraving*, I, p. 272 (21)) and the other with ones by Jodocus Hondius. Neither is dated but an illustrated edition is referred to as being in existence in 1591 and Hind argues that that was the one with engravings by Hondius upon which the Rogers engravings were based and largely copied. Broughton presented the Queen with a special copy of the *Concent* as a present on her Accession Day, November 17th 1589 and that might reasonably be suggested as a fitting occasion to prompt an illustrated edition.

Any connexion with Hilliard as the designer of these extraordinary engravings must inevitably be speculative. They shared a patron in Mildmay and if the illustrated edition was for the Queen, Hilliard would be a natural choice for their draughtmanship. Both men were of puritan persuasion. In addition the title page is a plagiary of the one signed by Hilliard in 1574 (no. 65) although this could, of course, be merely a copy. The aesthetic of the series of strange apocalyptic images within, however, is Hilliardesque being typically two dimensional and decorative with no sense of scientific perspective. They make use of a ground level across the front with a distant view beyond in the manner of Hilliard's Cumberland (no. 216). The vision of Rome as the whore of Babylon is like some extraordinary perverted variation of one of Hilliard's

miniatures of the Queen. Whoever their author, they belong firmly within the Hilliard orbit at its apogee in the isolationist years around the defeat of the Armada.

LITERATURE: Hind, *Engraving*, I, pp. 162–63 (13).

NICHOLAS HILLIARD

91 **Leonard Darr**, 1591

Private Collection
Vellum stuck to plain card, clipped at top edge as if to fit a hinged picture box, oval, 70 × 55 mm, $2\frac{3}{4} \times 2\frac{3}{16}$ in.

One of the few Hilliard miniatures to survive in mint condition giving us a powerful impression of the strength of colouring that is so often missing because of fading. The identity of Leonard Darr has yet to be satisfactorily resolved. Goulding suggested an equation, yet to be proved, with a certain Leonard Dare, merchant of Tavistock who was granted a licence to ship fish in October 1585 (*C.S.P., Domestic, Addenda, 1580–1625*, p. 156). The painting of the ruff is clearly influenced by Oliver.

INSCRIBED: One either side of the head: *Anō Ætatis. Leonardi Darr.37./Anō Dnī.1591*:

COLLECTIONS: Recorded by Vertue when sold from the collection of Mr Halstead or Halsted in May 1726: "one of Leonard Dorns Aeta.37.Anº.1591" (*Notebooks*, II, p. 13); Edward Harley, 2nd Earl of Oxford (1689–1741); recorded by Vertue, c. 1732 (Notebooks, IV, p. 41); Vertue's catalogue, 1743 (62); Oxford's daughter married William Bentinck, 2nd Duke of Portland; thence by descent.

LITERATURE: Goulding, *Welbeck*, p. 64 (16).
V & A, 1947 (53).
Auerbach, *Hilliard*, p. 134, pl. 109; 306 (109).

92

93

94

NICHOLAS HILLIARD

92 Unknown Lady, 1590–93

Victoria & Albert Museum (P.9-1947)
Vellum stuck onto a playing card with the six of
diamonds on the reverse, oval, 59 × 47 mm,
$12\frac{15}{16} \times 1\frac{7}{8}$ in.

The re-painted background and the fading make this
miniature strike the eye as less fine than, in fact, it is. Other
damage includes slight flaking of the right eye, the loss of
the red glaze from the rubies and oxidization of the silver.
The hair is still painted in the free linear style of the 1580s
and the miniature must therefore just pre-date the change
in manner established in the Unknown Lady of 1593
(no. 95). An almost identical dress appears in a portrait by
Gheeraerts dated 1592 (Strong, *The English Icon*, p. 291
(288)). Auerbach's dating c. 1595 therefore cannot be
sustained.

An eighteenth or nineteenth century metal frame is
inscribed on the back with an identification as Queen
Elizabeth which can be discounted.

COLLECTIONS: Mrs Wyndham Cook as Queen Elizabeth;
bequeathed by E. Peter Jones 1948.

LITERATURE: Auerbach, *Hilliard*, p. 133, pl. 100; 305 (100).

NICHOLAS HILLIARD

93 Unknown young man, 1590–93

Victoria & Albert Museum (P.3-1974)
Vellum stuck to a playing card with six hearts at the
reverse, oval, 50 × 42 mm, $2\frac{3}{4} \times 1\frac{5}{8}$ in.

One of the five Radnor miniatures (see nos. 87, 210) still in
its original turned ivory box. It is in very poor condition
with severe flaking of the shirt, abrasions to the features
and background, which is also damaged by water, and
very faded. Nonetheless the miniature is unique amongst
Hilliard's *oeuvre* in placing the sitter against a black

background. V. J. Murrell points out that the demand by
the sitter for this colour has caused Hilliard difficulties in
marrying it to the hair, resulting in a hard unbroken edge
in contrast to his usual ability to extend the hair over a
lighter background.

The young man looks about twenty and is presenting
himself as a lover. Black as a colour is emblematic of
constancy because it will take no other colour (see Leslie
Hotson, *Mr W H*, London, 1964, p. 211 for a list of
references to this). Both Reynolds and Auerbach date this
miniature to c. 1585 which, on grounds of the hairstyle, is
impossible. The hair is long and curly at the sides and
brushed away from the forehead, a fashion adopted by
young men at the opening of the 1590's (Strong, *The
English Icon*, 1969, p. 217 (175); 220 (179–80). The still free
calligraphic rendering of the hair dates it before c. 1593
when Hilliard's style changed.

No identity can be suggested but the miniatures, as a
group, relate to Elizabeth Stafford, Lady Drury.

COLLECTIONS: See no. 87.

LITERATURE: Countess of Radnor and W. B. Squire, *Catalogue of the
Collection of the Earl of Radnor*, 1909, II, p. 109 (4).
V & A, 1947 (27).
Auerbach, *Hilliard*, pp. 93–4; pl. 64; 297 (59).
Strong, "The Radnor Miniatures", *Christie's Review of the Season
1974*, ed John Herbert, 1974, pp. 254–57.
Strong, *Hilliard*, p. 30, pl. 9(a).

NICHOLAS HILLIARD

94 Unknown Lady, c. 1590–93

The Duke of Buccleuch and Queensberry, KT
Vellum stuck onto a playing card with inerted hearts
at the reverse, oval, 57 × 46 mm, $2\frac{1}{4} \times 1\frac{13}{16}$ in.

Apart from some restoration at the edge and oxidized
silver, the miniature is in very good condition and one of
the finest surviving from this period. The lady is evidently
of high rank with a bejewelled head-dress. Honeysuckle is

tucked into her hair, a thistle into the bodice of her dress and a rosebud on her ruff. It was formerly ascribed to Oliver and called Queen Elizabeth. The ruff and arrangement of the necklaces is virtually identical to those in an unfinished full length in the Fitzwilliam (No. IV).

Her hair is painted in the free manner of the 1580's and therefore dates this miniature before c. 1593, when Hilliard changed his style.

COLLECTIONS: Presumably part of the collection formed by Walter Francis, 5th Duke of Buccleuch (1806–1884).

LITERATURE: Kennedy, *Buccleuch*, pl. V.
V & A, 1947 (68).
Auerbach, *Hilliard*, pp. 140, pl. 123; 309 (125).

IV LATE ELIZABETHAN, 1593–1603

Before 1591 until
1603. Hilliard works on patterns for a third Great Seal which was never made
1595. The Earl of Essex assists Hilliard in repaying the mortgage on his house
1599. Granted an annuity of £40 p.a.
1600. The Privy Council intervenes and secures the renewal of the lease on his house in Gutter Lane from the Goldsmiths' Company. Hilliard in return agrees to paint a "faire picture in greate" of the Queen for the Company.

Hilliard was not only to be beset with increasing financial problems during the closing decade of Elizabethan's reign but, for the first time, he was faced with serious professional competition and, even more important, the onset of an aesthetic revolution. Rowland Lockey, his apprentice, was now a painter and miniaturist in his own right and seems at times to have worked in tandem with his old master. Isaac Oliver was a great problem. His infinite variety must have shown how stereotyped Hilliard's work had become. This is reflected, for example, in the loss of a major patron, Elizabeth's last favourite, Robert Devereux, 2nd Earl of Essex, who switched, c. 1596, to Oliver. About the same time Hilliard gave up painting large-scale miniatures not only because they must have taken so long to paint but because they showed his total inability to tackle even the basics of scientific perspective. He embarked, however, on minor innovations to meet the challenge. In 1593 he started painting his sitter's hair in the tight Oliver manner and the next year he introduced a new form of background, the folded velvet curtain (no. 96), although he was never satisfactorily to marry these with the inscriptions. Some of his work, however, now began to border on the perfunctory. Nothing, however, that he did could in fact meet the challenge of the change of aesthetic. In the 1590s the basic principles of Renaissance painting in addition to its critical vocabulary and attitudes were gaining acceptance amongst a new generation in an optical revolution as dramatic at the time as Picasso's *Damoiselles*

d'Avignon in our own age. Hilliard was never to come to terms with linear and aerial perspective let alone the whole apparatus of mannerist art theory which cast the artist as seer and purveyor of "ideas". In his treatise on the art of limning, begun at the instigation of translator of the Italian art theorist, Paolo Lamazzo, Richard Haydocke, Hilliard remains the tradesman artificer aspiring to gentility. It is hardly surprising that he never finished it.

SELECT BIBLIOGRAPHY
Auerbach, *Hilliard*, pp. 26–38, 131–46.
Lucy Gent, *Picture and Poetry 1560–1620*, Leamington Spa, 1981.
Strong, *Renaissance Miniature*, pp. 111–17

NICHOLAS HILLIARD

95 Unknown Lady, aged 26, 1593

Victoria & Albert Museum (P.134-1910)
Vellum stuck onto playing card with five spades showing at the reverse, oval, 58 × 48 mm, $2\frac{9}{32} \times 1\frac{29}{32}$ in.

Formerly called Mrs Holland, an identity attached to the miniature by a nineteenth century inscription on its reverse, it was also called Elizabeth, Lady Russell. Both identifications are purely speculative. In spite of its faded condition this is a fine *ad vivum* miniature and the earliest dated instance of Hilliard painting the sitter's hair not in the usual free manner but in imitation of Oliver with carefully marshalled tight brush strokes in ordered lines.

INSCRIBED: Around the top: *Anō Dñi. 1593. Ætatis suae. 26* and a fleur de lys. On the reverse in a nineteenth century hand: *Mrs – Holland | Maid of Honor in the | Court of Queen | Elizabeth | by Hilliard Senr.*

COLLECTIONS: In the collection of Samuel Addington in 1865 when lent to the South Kensington Exhibition as Mrs Holland; sold in his sale as Lady Elizabeth Russell, Christie's 26th April 1883 (lot 87); bought Warcham; J. Lumsden Propert Collection; purchased by Salting at the dissolution of that collection in 1897 by the Fine Art Society; bequeathed by Salting 1910.

LITERATURE: Winter, *Elizabethan Miniatures*, pl. 11 (a).
V & A, 1947 (60).
Auerbach, *Hilliard*, p. 133, pl. 102, 305 (102).

NICHOLAS HILLIARD

96 Henry Wriothesley, 3rd Earl of Southampton, 1594

The Fitzwilliam Museum, Cambridge (3856)
Vellum stuck to a playing card with three hearts showing at the reverse, oval, 41 × 32.5 mm, $1\frac{3}{8} \times 1\frac{9}{32}$ in.

Henry Wriothesley, 3rd Earl of Southampton (1573–1624), patron of poets, including Shakespeare, was during the

96

97

98

1590's closely associated with Essex and imprisoned for his part in the attempted coup of 1601. Released and received by James I with favour, being recreated Earl of Southampton and made K. G., he involved himself in overseas enterprises, in particular the Virginia Company.

The identification as Southampton is relatively recent but certainly correct, as both age and appearance fit. The next portrait is that at Welbeck Abbey, now on loan to the National Portrait Gallery (for a discussion of Southampton's iconography see Strong, *Tudor and Jacobean* I, pp. 299–300; II, pl. 589). By then he had grown a beard. The miniature is the earliest dated instance of Hilliard's new folded crimson curtain background painted in the wet-in-wet technique. From the start this presented difficulties to the artist over inscriptions which became confused against the multi-tonal curtain. The condition is good.

INSCRIBED: On either side of the head: *Anō: Dnī 1594. | Ætatis Suae.20.*

COLLECTIONS: C. Sackville Bale in 1865 at South Kensington when not identified ; Jeffery Whitehead, 1889; bequeathed by L. D. Cunliffe, 1937.

NICHOLAS HILLIARD

97 John Molle, c. 1595

The Pennington-Mellor Charity Trust
Vellum stuck onto card, oval, 47 × 39 mm,
$1\frac{7}{8} \times 1\frac{9}{16}$ in.

John Molle (d. c. 1640) of South Moulton, Devonshire, was treasurer to the English army in Brittany. Made examiner to the Council of the North by Thomas, Earl of Exeter. As tutor to the Earl's grandson, William Cecil, Lord Roos, he travelled with him to Italy in 1608. Arrested and imprisoned by the Inquisition for thirty years.

The portrait of the unfortunate John Molle is in exceptionally good condition with virtually no flaking and little fading. Although previously given the same date as the portrait of his wife, c. 1605, it is in fact earlier. The cut

of the hair with the love-lock hanging over the shoulder is paralleled in the miniature of Southampton (no. 96) dated 1594. At this period Molle was acting as a messenger for the Cecils. For a later 'companion' portrait of his wife see no. 117. There seems to be no reason to doubt the identity.

COLLECTIONS: Lord Clinton, 1905; the Hon Mrs Fane, 1940; Miss M Rivers-Bulkeley; sold Sotheby's 2nd April 1962 (lot 42); Lord Wharton.

LITERATURE: V & A, 1947 (97A).
Auerbach, *Hilliard*, pp. 195, pl. 151; 314 (157).

NICHOLAS HILLIARD

98 Sir Henry Slingsby, 1595

The Fitzwilliam Museum, Cambridge (3850)
Vellum stuck to card with another, gessoed, card stuck to it, oval, 84 × 63 mm, $3\frac{5}{16} \times 2\frac{1}{2}$ in.

Sir Henry Slingsby (1565–1634) of Scriven, Yorkshire, was knighted in 1602 and vice-president of the Council of the North in 1629. He married Frances, daughter of William Vavasour of Weston, Yorkshire.

A rare large oval offering, in addition, an early dated instance of the folded crimson velvet curtain background painted in the "wet-in-wet" technique. The introduction of this new type of background instead of the usual blue bice presented Hilliard with the problem of placing the lettering. It is not solved here satisfactorily by being inserted somewhat unhappily just above the shoulders. This is an excellent instance of the decline in quality that could occur: the portrait barely arises above the schematic.

Slingsby has an emblematic hat jewel of an open-petalled flower and the motto on a scroll *SEMPER IDEM*.

(Always the same). The allusion is to constancy and devotion, whether to God, Queen or his lady, and is a variant on the standard emblem of a flower opening its petals to the sun (e.g. Claude Paradin, *Devises Heroiques*, Lyons, 1557, p. 41; George Wither, *A Collection of Emblemes*, London, 1635, p. 209 with the couplet above: "Whil'st I, the *Sunne's* bright Face may view, / I will no meaner *Light* pursue").

The miniature is in good condition apart from the background which has craquelured and flaked in places.

INSCRIBED: On either side, above the shoulders: *1595 / AEs 35*. At the back in a seventeenth century hand: *Sr Henry Slingsby father to Sir Henry Slingsby beheaded by Oliver Cromwell.*

COLLECTIONS: The H. J. Pfungst collection; E. J. Pfungst sale, Christie's 14th June 1917 (lot 45); bequeathed by L. D. Cunliffe, 1937.

LITERATURE: *Catalogue of the Pfungst Collection*, 1914–18, V & A, pp. 12–13 (110).
V & A, 1947 (62).
Auerbach, *Hilliard*, p. 125, pl. 97; 304 (97).
Strong, *Hilliard*, pl. 12.

NICHOLAS HILLIARD

99 Unknown Lady, c. 1595–1600

The Fitzwilliam Museum, Cambridge (3898)
Vellum stuck to a playing card with hearts at the reverse, which have been overpainted with brown watercolour, oval, 73 × 53 mm, $2\frac{7}{8} \times 2\frac{3}{32}$ in.

The hair is painted in the carefully composed manner of post-1593 and is close in feeling to a miniature of the same date in the Buccleuch Collection. It was formerly called Anne Clifford, Countess of Dorset and Pembroke. The miniature is in good condition apart from minor damages, fading and oxidized silver.

COLLECTIONS: Part of the collection formed by Walter Francis, 5th Duke of Buccleuch (1806–1884).

LITERATURE: Kennedy, *Buccleuch*, pl. 13.
Winter, *Elizabethan Miniatures*, pl. 10a.
V & A, 1947 (47).
Auerbach, *Hilliard*, pp. 141–42, pl. 124; 309 (126).

NICHOLAS HILLIARD

100 Unknown Man, 1597

Victoria & Albert Museum (P.5-1944)
Vellum stuck onto a playing card with two hearts showing at the reverse, oval, 50 × 40 mm, $1\frac{31}{32} \times 1\frac{19}{32}$ in.

The miniature is a little tired in feeling and the hair is rendered in the typical tighter post-1593 Oliver style. The pose of the hand, clasping the cloak which is wrapped around the doublet, recurs in reverse in portraits by John

99

de Critz, in particulare his likeness of Sir Robert Cecil, the earliest instances of which are dated 1599 (Strong, *Tudor and Jacobean*, I, p. 275; II, pl. 538). The brilliant colours, pink, yellow, grey and blue, form a striking contrast to Oliver's sombre palette. I can offer no interpretation of the letter or monogram that appears in the inscription. These are a W and/or a combination of V and W, perhaps the sitter's initials.

Although the features are faded, the miniature is basically in good condition.

INSCRIBED: On either side of the head: *W Anō Dñi· 1957· / W Ætatis·22.*

COLLECTIONS: Bequeathed by Thomas Hugh Cobb, of The Manor, Davies Street, London, in 1944, previous history unknown.

LITERATURE: V & A., 1947 (66).
Auerbach, *Hilliard*, pp. 136, pl. 114; 307 (115).

WILLIAM ROGERS POSSIBLY AFTER A DESIGN IN THE MANNER OF NICHOLAS HILLIARD

101 Title-page to Sir Philip Sidney, *The Countess of Pembroke's Arcadia*, London, 1593

The British Library (C.21.D.21)
Woodcut, 244 × 157 mm, $9\frac{5}{8} \times 6\frac{3}{16}$

There was a connexion between Sir Philip Sidney and Hilliard, the latter records a conversation they had in his *Arte of Limning* (ed. Thornton and Cain, pp. 82–83) and although this is no reason to leap to the conclusion that he must have designed the title-page to the *Arcadia*, its design evokes what we know of Hilliard's spiralling style for title-borders.

Nicholas Hilliard 83

101

LITERATURE: R. B. McKerrow and F. S. Ferguson, *Title-page Borders used in England and Scotland, 1485–1640*, Bibliographical Society, O.U.P., 1932, no. 212.
M. Corbett and R. Lightbown, *The Comely Frontispiece. The Emblematic Titlepage in England 1550–1660*, London, 1979, pp. 59–65.

JOHN DONNE

102 Poems, by J. D. . . ., London, 1635

The British Library (1076.A.12.)

The Storme was a verse letter sent by John Donne to his most enduring friend, Christopher Brooke (1570–1628). It is followed by a second called *The Calm* and both described incidents in the 'Islands Expedition' to the Azores under Essex in the summer of 1597. The opening lines contain the most famous poetic tribute made to Hilliard:

. . . a hand, or eye
By Hilliard drawn, is worth an history
By a worse painter made . . .
(1. 4–5)

Donne on the voyage 'waited' on Hilliard's patron, Essex.

RICHARD HAYDOCKE

103 *A tracte containinge the Artes of curious Paintinge Carvinge & Buildinge*, Oxford, 1598

The British Library (C.104.6.25.)

Richard Haydocke (c. 1570–c. 1642) was educated at Winchester and entered in 1588, New College, Oxford. He became a Fellow in 1590, BA in 1592 and MA in 1595. After that date he travelled in Italy returning to become a Bachelor of Medicine in 1601. In 1605 he settled in Salisbury practising as a doctor.

Haydocke in the 1590s seems to have advised Hilliard's friend, Sir Thomas Bodley (no. 50) on the acquisition of art books for his library. In 1601 he gave to the Bodleian five books including an edition of Serlio, Vasari's *Vite* and Poalo Lomazzo *Trattato dell' arte de la pittvra* (Milan, 1584). The latter was a standard author for painters providing a massive encyclopaedia with precepts of all that an artist should know. This embodied a concept both of the artist and of what he produced that was unknown to Elizabethan England: painting as a liberal art fit for gentlemen, as a science based on cosmic and mathematical harmony and proportion and as the product of the *disegno interno* in the mind.

Haydocke's adaptation of this book, for it is not a literal translation, was a milestone in late Elizabethan England and the author was aware of this. He states his reason to be "the increase of the knowledge of the Arte".

In this *avant garde* ideological work Haydocke eulogizes Hilliard who might "strive for a comparison with the milde spirit of the worldes-wonder Raffaell Vrbine". He states that he has persuaded Hilliard to write a discourse on limning (no. IX). It is to be regretted that Haydocke did not know Isaac Oliver whose aesthetic milieu was one

The title-border relates closely to one for *Willobie his Avisa* (1594) which is signed WR, the initials of the English engraver, William Rogers (for whom see no. 201). The *Arcadia* programme was prepared by the editor of the text, Hugh Sanford, secretary to the Earl of Pembroke. At the top there is Sidney's crest, "a porcupine passant . . . quilled collared and chained". The bear and lion flanking the cartouche were the animals slain by the heroes of the Arcadia, the cousins Musidorus and Pyrocles, Princes of Macedon. These two are the figures facing each other across the page, the one to the left in his disguise as the Arcadian shepherd, Dorus, the other, in his disguise as the Amazon, Zelmane. Below, within a cartouche, is the emblem of the pig and the marjoram bush with the motto: *SPIRO NON TIBI* (I breathe (sweet scents) but not for thee).

The process of compiling a title-page involved three distinct people: the compiler of the iconography, the draughtsman or designer and the engraver. The elegant scrollwork, groteschi and swags are Fontainebleau in their derivation and not Netherlandish. Fontainebleau style borders in English books may well be the prime manifestation of the influence of Valois court art on Hilliard. It is important to recognise the Hilliardesque as a style not only in painting but in book design.

104

congenial to Lomazzo's view and far removed from the tradesman-artificer, Hilliard.

LITERATURE: F. Hard, "Richard Haydocke and Alexander Browne: Two half-forgotten writers on the art of painting", *PMLA*, 4, 1940, pp. 727–34.
J. Pope-Hennessy, "Nicholas Hilliard and Mannerist Art Theory", *Journal of the Warburg and Courtauld Institutes*, VI, 1943, pp. 89–100.
K. J. Höltgen, *Richard Haydocke: Translator, Engraver, Physician*, Bibliographical Society, 1978.
M. Corbett and R. Lightbown, *The Comely Frontispiece. The Emblematic Title-page in England, 1550–1660*, London, 1979, pp. 67–68.

NICHOLAS HILLIARD

104 Unknown Lady, 1602

Victoria & Albert Museum (P.26–1975)
Vellum stuck onto plain card, oval, 59 mm × 44 mm,
2 × 1 in.

A portrait clearly painted from life and in Hilliard's best direct, free manner. Oliver's influence is apparent only in the tight handling of the hair. There is no flagging in spontaneity of response or technical brilliance if a sitter interested Hilliard, which clearly this young woman did.

This is a rare miniature of a person not of the court but of the city. Typical of this dress is the tall black hat, smocked stomacher and apron. Comparison may be made with the watercolours of such a costume that appear in the *album amicorum* of the period (see J. L. Nevinson, "The Dress of the Citizens of London 1549–1640", *Collecteana Londiniensia*, Studies presented to R. Merrifield, London and Middlesex Archaeological Society, 1978, pp. 265–80). The dress is enlivened by naturalistic touches in the form of roses and flowers tucked into the corners of her neckline. The suggestion (Clifford-Smith cited below) that the *Vere* in the motto refers to the family of the Earls of Oxford can surely be discounted, together with the suggested identification as Elizabeth Trentham, second wife of Edward de Vere, 17th Earl of Oxford.

Conceivably the portrait commemorates a marriage as a gold ring hangs from a black thread attached to a yellow bow at her neckline. The enigmatic motto, "It seems and truely is" (?), would not exclude this interpretation. The miniature is in its contemporary turned ivory box, the lid of which is missing.

INSCRIBED: In gold around the top, left: *Videtur et Vere est*; right: *Anō Dn̄i. 1602*.

COLLECTIONS: With Danton Gerault; sold from the collection of Mr S. H. V. Hickson, Sotheby's 29th March 1965 (lot 75); previous history unknown; bequeathed to the V & A by Mrs Doris Herschorn, 1965.

LITERATURE: Edwina Clifford-Smith, "Hilliard, Heretics and Humphry", *Ivory Hammer*, 3, 1964–65, pp. 198–99.

NICHOLAS HILLIARD

Miniatures from the Bosworth Jewel, (105–108) c. 1600–1603

H.M. The Queen

105 Henry VII

Vellum stuck to a plain card, circular, 32.5 mm,
$1\frac{9}{32}$ in. diam. *(photograph)*

Recorded by van der Dort as "Inpris Done upon the righte lighte the / Picture of King Henry 7th in / a Black Capp. and scarfe with a redd / Garment and a redd roase in his right / hand". (Millar, *Walpole Society*, XXXVII, 1960, p. 116 (50)).

The miniature derives from a version of a standard portrait type of The King holding a rose (Strong, *Tudor and Jacobean*, I, p. 151; II, pl. 293). The inscription records the date of his death. It seems unlikely that this miniature goes back to an intermediary one by Hornebolte. There is some flaking of the costume, oxidization and restoration above the head and to the right hand.

INSCRIBED: On either side of the head: *Anō Dn̄i. 1509: | Ætatis Suae. 54*.

106 Henry VIII

Vellum stuck to a playing card with three hearts at the reverse, circular, 31 mm, $1\frac{7}{32}$ in. diam. *(photograph)*

Recorded by van der Dort: "Item don upon the wrong lighte the / second being King Henry the 8th in / a black Capp and white feather and / a little ruff in a white silver Tissue / doublett with a collar about his-/ shoulders". (Millar, *Walpole Society*, XXXVII, 1960, p. 116 (51).) Not derived from a miniature by Hornebolte but either directly or indirectly from Holbein's full length of Henry VIII in the Privy Chamber Group, of which numerous derivatives exist (*Tudor and Jacobean*, I, p. 158, Type V; II, pl. 309).

There is the usual oxidization and some restoration to small damages in the background.

INSCRIBED: One either side of the head: *1536 | Ætatis suae 46.*

107 Jane Seymour

Vellum stuck to plain card, circular, 31 mm, $1\frac{7}{32}$ in. diam. *(photograph)*

Recorded by van der Dort: "Item done upon the wrong light the-/ fourth and last picture in the said / Jewell Queene (space) in a black and-/ redd head dressing, and a carnation-/ habbitt and, 2 strings of pearls about / her necke". (Millar, *Walpole Society*, XXXVII, 1960, p. 117 (53)).

Not derived from the miniature by Hornebolte (no. 17) but based on the well-known Holbein portrait now in Vienna (Strong, *The English Icon*, p. 6, fig. 3). Hilliard's observation of the dress is particularly free in this miniature giving an identation to the neckline of the bodice which is totally at variance with the structure of the garment. It is basically in good condition with only slight flaking of the jewels, oxidization and modern restoration in the cap and on the left edge. This miniature is the only source for Jane Seymour's date of birth.

INSCRIBED: On either side of the head: *Anō Dnī 1536 | Ætatis suae 27.*

108 Edward VI

Vellum stuck onto a plain card, circular, 32 mm, $1\frac{1}{4}$ in. diam. *(photograph)*

Recorded by van der Dort: "Item the Third being King Edward the / 6th in a black Capp and white feather / and a little Roffe in a black habbitt / wth a Coller about his neck done / upon the right lighte". (Millar, *Walpole Society*, XXXVII, 1960, p. 116 (52)).

As in the case of the other three miniatures this is derived from a large-scale portrait, in this instance a version of that by William Scrots (Strong, *The English Icon*, p. 71 (6); *Tudor and Jacobean*, II, pl. 172–73). This has suffered more than the other three, the background having been extensively restored, some of the "carnation" ground has been scraped away, there is some flaking and the usual oxidization.

INSCRIBED: On either side of the head: *Ætatis suae. 14 | Regni.6.*

THE JEWEL: Van der Dort records the jewel as follows: "Item a ffowerfoul*dit* litle round goulden Jewell / with a litle pedant pearle hanging to it / which jewell on the out side is inamaled the / battell of Bason ffeilds (fofft inserted) Betweene Kinge Henry the 7.th and Crookd back. and on the other / Side of the Jewell the reed and white roase / ioyned togeether upon some greene ground = / within this Jewell are 4 limned pictures = / One being Kinge Henrie the 7th another Kinge / Henrie the 8th and his Queene Jane Seamor / And King Edward the 6th all without christalls / which Jewell was given to the Kinge by the

young Hilliard by the deceased Earle of / Pembrooks means *hu dilifferit te same | tu de King*". In the margin is the annotation: "done both Jew/ell & Pictures / By old Hilliard". (Millar, *Walpole Society*, XXXVII, 1960, pp. 116 (note 1)-17 (50–53)).

This is important in establishing that both the Jewel and the miniatures were by Hilliard. It must have been similar to the Armada Jewel with the obverse exterior with an enamelled picture of the battle of Bosworth opening to reveal Henry VII and Henry VIII and, on the reverse, a Tudor Rose on a green (the Tudor colours were green and white) ground opening to reveal Jane Seymour and Edward VI. Reynolds and Auerbach date them c. 1600–1610 on grounds of style. The content of the Jewel, which is a Tudor celebration totally irrelevant to the Stuarts, eliminates any date after 1603. The subject matter is also, by the exclusion of Mary, a eulogy of the Protestant succession. What is unusual is the absence of a miniature of Elizabeth I who is, by implication, the missing conclusion of the imagery and the living embodiment of the Tudor *pax* subsequent to the Wars of the Roses. This would suggest that the Jewel should have been made to present to her, conceivably commissioned as a gift on progress where such items were the natural culmination of any entertainment. The imagery, with its emphasis on the Wars of the Roses, reiterates the preoccupation with English history characteristic of the last decade as exemplified above all in Shakespeare's history plays.

Stylistically this set of miniatures belongs to a group painted in the technique of the last years of the reign. They are almost facile in quality.

COLLECTIONS: Descended from the artist to his son, Laurence Hilliard; passed from him via William, 3rd Earl of Pembroke to Charles I (see above); the Henry VII reappears in James II's inventory (no. 618) and William III's inventory (no. 84) the Jane Seymour appears in Stowe MS 567, f.9 temp. George I; the Henry VIII appears in James II's inventory (no. 616) and William III's inventory (King's Closet, no. 82) and in Stowe MS 567, f.8ᵛ; Vertue refers to all four at Kensington, 1720 (*Notebooks*, I, pp. 75–6); the Henry VII, Henry VIII and Jane Seymour are referred to again in Vertue's list of miniatures at Kensington Palace, 1734 (*Notebooks*, IV, p. 67) the Edward VI reappears in James II inventory (no. 607) and is recorded in the catalogue of Queen Caroline's Closet (*Catalogue of the Pictures in Queen CAROLINE's Closet. . .*, p. 22 (no. 147 (7)); Fraser Tytler *List*, 1840s (nos. 42, 49, 55 and 56).

LITERATURE: V & A, 1947 (81–84). Auerbach, *Hillard*, p. 151, pl. 137–40; 311–12 (142–45).

NICHOLAS HILLIARD

109 ?Elizabeth I, 1590–1600, possibly after a miniature of 1565–70 by Levina Teerlinc

Private Collection
Vellum stuck to plain card, circular, 40 mm, $1\frac{19}{32}$ in. diam.

V. J. Murrell points out that technically this miniature was executed c. 1590–1600. The evidence for this is the

109

thickness of the "carnation" ground, the use of a gold-over-brown edge line, and the employment of ultramarine in the background. In addition the dress is of a period before Hilliard began to paint miniatures. It can be paralleled in a number of portraits dated 1567 and 1569 (Strong, *The English Icon*, pp. 113 (61); 129 (129)).

Its size and the fact that it is circular might suggest that it is not a reduced version of an oil portrait but after a miniature by Levina Teerlinc. If this is the case it ought to depict the Queen at the close of the 1560s. Her features at that time were rapidly changing into those of a woman in her middle thirties, quite different from those in the very earliest portraits at the opening of the 1560s. In large-scale portraiture the equivalent type is the "Barrington Park" pattern (Strong, *Portraits of Queen Elizabeth I*, pp. 57–58 (nos. 12–22)).

The miniature is in exceptional condition, brilliantly fresh, with only the slightest paint losses around the edge and the usual oxidization.

COLLECTIONS: Hancock sale, 1858 (lot 1171); purchased for the 5th Duke of Portland.

LITERATURE: Goulding, *Welbeck*, p. 56 (3).

NICHOLAS HILLIARD PROBABLY AFTER LEVINA
TEERLINC

110 ?Edward Seymour, 1st Earl of Hertford and 1st Duke of Somerset, c. 1600, probably after a miniature by Levina Teerlinc, 1550

Victoria & Albert Museum (P.25–1942)
Vellum stuck to plain card, circular, 34 mm, $1\frac{5}{16}$ in. diam.
See no. 51

A superb late miniature by Hilliard unfortunately in a very damaged state, the blacks of the costume having severely flaked. The manner of painting is identical to that used in the portraits in the Bosworth Jewel (nos. 105/108) and in the Elizabeth in robes of state (no. 211). The sitter must be someone of great importance and the circular format and composition of the portrait would suggest that this is Hilliard copying a lost miniature by Teerlinc. This

importance is emphasized in the use of ultramarine for the background, a pigment reserved for the grandest commissions. If it were not for the date 1550 clearly inscribed upon it the resemblance to Thomas Seymour, Earl of Hertford is more than striking (Strong, *Tudor and Jacobean*, II, pls. 683–84). Seymour was executed, however, in March 1548/9. A miniature of him was recorded in the Stowe sale March 15 1849 (lot 145) which descended directly in the Seymour family. This must be the one formerly in the Buccleuch Collection (Kennedy, *Buccleuch*, pl. VIII). Miniatures up until Hilliard were only painted of those of the highest rank and the sitter who would fit neatly is a far more important man, Thomas's brother, Edward Seymour, Duke of Somerset, Edward VI's uncle and Lord Protector. The only certain portrait is the miniature painted by Hilliard aged thirteen and dated 1560 (no. 51), which is posthumous. It is a feeble work but the Seymour features are certain enough to identify him in the group portrait of Edward VI and the Pope (Strong, *Tudor and Jacobean*, II, pl. 678 to the King's immediate left). A portrait at Longleat (*ibid.*, pl. 575), an early copy of a lost original, is probably rightly him and bears an early inscription which there seems no reason to doubt.

Somerset actually fell from power in January 1549/50 and was consigned to the Tower for a short period being released in February, re-admitted to the Privy Council in April and his property restored. Optimism returned when his eldest daughter, Anne, was married to Warwick's son, in June.

Somerset was a massive patron of the arts and to sit for Teerlinc would be entirely comprehensible. His son, Edward, married into the Grey family, who were also painted by her. The Grey family were part of the royal family by extension through Henry VIII's sister, Mary, Duchess of Suffolk. The Seymours were related through the Protector's sister, Jane, Henry VIII's third queen.

INSCRIBED: On either side of the head: *Anno Dn̄ 1550 | Aetatis suae* (no age given).

COLLECTIONS: Transferred to the V & A from the British Museum, 1942.

MANNER OF NICHOLAS HILLIARD

111 Unknown Lady, 1595–1600

Mrs P. A. Tritton, Parham Park
Oil on canvas, 106.4 × 58.3 cm, 42 × 23 in.

There are two portraits certainly by this painter. Both are of the same sitter and the second is in the Metropolitan Museum of Art, New York (gift of J. Pierpont Morgan). The dresses in each are different but the jewels are identical, although re-arranged. Both pictures are of exceptional idiosyncratic quality strongly Hilliardesque and iconic for c. 1600 in view of the progressive trends of Gheeraerts. The work of the latter and of Robert Peake, John de Critz and Lockey is now reasonable definable which eliminates any possibility of their authorship.

The sitter is revealed to the onlooker by the device of a *trompe l'oeil* rendering of the curtain that it was usual to

III

114

1603. Accession of James I
1606. Petitions to trim the tomb of Elizabeth I
1608. Probably marries for a second time, Susan Gyzard
1613. Leaves his Gutter Lane workshop which he makes over to his son, Laurence, and moves to Westminster
1617. Granted a monopoly for twelve years to make, engrave and print portraits of the royal family
Imprisoned for debt in Ludgate
1618. December 24th. Makes his will
1619. January 7th. Buried in St Martins-in-the-Fields

Although Hilliard was to remain limner to the King until his death, fashion had in reality passed him by and the carelessness and summary execution that first appears in the 1590s accelerates. Statistically the miniatures go into decline indicating that there must have been a falling demand for what he had to offer. To meet this he began to experiment with more minor innovations. The folded velvet curtain backgrounds, first introduced in 1594, were replaced by ones of simple hanging velvets. More significantly he began to experiment with the borders of his miniatures, firstly in a quite tentative way by means of lines of brown, gold and ochre (no. 112) until, c. 1610–15, he evolved simulated jewelled ones with "sapphires", "rubies" and "emeralds" (No. 120). He must, however, have been acutely aware of Oliver's success and of the aesthetic revolution at the courts of Anne of Denmark and Prince Henry. That he was not entirely oblivious of the importance of the new fangled *chiaroscuro* is probably reflected in the cast shadows that appear in the miniatures (no. 121) and, at his best, he could meet the challenge of Oliver with a brilliant essay in the monochromatic (no. 158), totally at variance with his customary polychrome. In the terms of his period he lived to a great age, seventy-two, and his death was coincidental with that of the two chief exponents of the Hilliardesque in large-scale painting, William Larkin and Robert Peake. 1619 can indeed be taken as the terminal date of the age of Hilliard.

SELECT BIBLIOGRAPHY

Auerbach, *Hilliard*, pp. 38–42, 146–68.
Strong, *Renaissance Miniature*, pp. 130–33.

NICHOLAS HILLIARD

112 Unknown Man, 1603

Duke of Buccleuch and Queensberry KT
Vellum stuck to plain card, circular, 44 mm, $1\frac{23}{32}$ in. diam.

The identification as Henry Wriothesley, Earl of Southampton clearly cannot be sustained. Auerbach's

hang over pictures being looped up to one side. She stands before a familiar ingredient of late Hilliard miniatures, a velvet curtain with folds in squares. The lighting is Hilliardesque, direct from the front and the style linear and exact in its rendering of details such as the silkworms nibbling at mulberry leaves on the sleeves. The portrait belongs closely within the Hilliard orbit, although it would be difficult to attribute it directly to him on the basis of the certain pictures from the early 1570s. The miniatures probably give little idea as to how his large-scale painting style evolved over the intervening twenty-five years. That he was active painting large-scale portraits in 1600 we know from the fact he undertook to paint a "faire picture in greate" of the Queen for the Goldsmiths' Company (Auerbach, *Hilliard*, p. 29).

The portrait has been called Queen Elizabeth. It descended with the house which belonged to the Bisshopp family who revived in 1815 the Barony of Zouche. The last Lord Zouche was Edward, 11th Lord Zouche (1556–1625) who had no male heirs. His eldest daughter, Elizabeth, married in 1597 Sir William Tate of De la Pré Abbey, Northants. The date and her status as an heiress make her a candidate for the sitter.

COLLECTIONS: Passed with the house, seat of the Bysshopp family, the Barons Zouche, to Clive Pearson, 1922.

LITERATURE: Strong, *Country Life Annual*, 1966, pp. 44–45. *Parham Park, Picture Catalogue*, p. 6 (23).

conclusion that this is "not definitely Hilliard's work" with a suggestion of Laurence totally belies its fine quality. It is far superior to anything that can be associated with Hilliard's son. What is more, the gold outline has a brown one added beyond it, reflecting Hilliard's experimentation with borders which was to become a feature of his Jacobean work. The inscription is also characteristic. Although basically in good condition the doublet is entirely repainted and the right side of the ruff has been much restored.

INSCRIBED: On either side of the head: *Anō Dni·1603·* | *Ætatis suae·26·*

COLLECTIONS: Presumably part of the collection formed by Walter Francis, 5th Duke of Buccleuch (1806–1884).

LITERATURE: Williamson, *Portrait Miniatures*, 1904, pl. VI (3). *Burlington Magazine*, 1906, VIII, p. 317, Kennedy, *Buccleuch*, pl. XI. Auerbach, *Hilliard*, pp. 151, pl. 142; 312 (147).

NICHOLAS HILLIARD

113 Unknown Lady, 1605

The Marquess of Salisbury, Hatfield House
Vellum stuck onto card, oval, 45 × 38 mm, $1\frac{3}{4} \times 1\frac{1}{2}$ in.

A sparkling miniature of a young woman, to whose charm Hilliard has obviously responded, wearing a brown dress decorated with orange bows. There is a gold picture box or locket on her left breast and a tiny gold jewel in the form of a winged insect on her partlet. The miniature is in good condition apart from fading and oxidized silver.

Auerbach advances two possible identifications. The first is Robert Cecil's daughter, Frances, later wife of the 5th Earl of Cumberland. This would seem to be eliminated on grounds of age, as Frances would have been in her early teens in 1605 and the sitter is clearly older. The second is Audrey, Lady Walsingham, who was born in 1568, would have been thirty-seven in 1605 and therefore, in this instance, too old. The motto is amorous which places the miniature as a love token, something which is reinforced by the S with a line through it on either side. This does not, as Auerbach suggests, allude to the Earldom of Salisbury but is a contraction of *Esclave*, a form that occurs, for example, in the amorous correspondence of Elizabeth I with Anjou (information from Mr Robin Harcourt Williams).

INSCRIBED: On either side of the head: *S| qui bien ayme| tard oublie $|* *1605.*

COLLECTIONS: First listed by Holland in 1891.

LITERATURE: L. G. Holland, *A Descriptive and Historical Catalogue of the Collection of Pictures of Hatfield House and 20 Arlington Street*, 1891, case of miniatures (no. 9).
V & A, 1947 (90).
Auerbach, *Hilliard*, pp. 152–53, pl. 146; 313 (152).
E. Auerbach and C. K. Adams, *Paintings and Sculpture at Hatfield House*, London, 1971, p. 106 (114).

114 Frances Howard, Duchess of Richmond and Lennox, 1605–10

Victoria and Albert Museum (P.15–1941)
Vellum stuck onto a card which is painted on the reverse with a design of oval bands and scallops in ochre, brown and gold, oval, 32 × 26 mm, $1\frac{1}{4} \times 1\frac{1}{16}$ in.

Frances Howard (1578–1639) was the daughter of Thomas, 1st Viscount Howard of Bindon. Through her first marriage to a City merchant, Henry Pranell, she became a great heiress. In December 1600 she married as her second husband Edward Seymour, Earl of Hertford (1539?–1621), eldest son of Edward Seymour, 1st Duke of Somerset, Edward VI's Lord Protector. He died on April 6th 1621 and Frances married almost immediately the King's cousin, Ludovick Stuart, 2nd Duke of Lennox and Duke of Richmond (1574–1624). Ambitious and beautiful she was called the "double Duchess".

This portrait is a good example of Hilliard's sustained powers of observation in the new reign when his work, too often judged by repetitions and studio replicas of royal portraits, is held to go into decline. The portrait of the Duchess of Lennox is one of a number of miniatures that decisively reverse the judgement. It is from life and of high quality. Although undated the costume is of about c. 1605–10; the jewelled sash is paralleled in portraits of Elizabeth, Queen of Bohemia as a girl (no. 247).

Until recently the miniature was wrongly identified as Arabella Stuart, a fate likely to befall portraits of Elizabethan and Jacobean ladies wearing their hair loose as in the early portrait of Arabella at Hardwick Hall (Strong, *Tudor and Jacobean*, II, pl. 602). During recent technical examination the seventeenth century inscription was discovered. It was only partly decipherable and had been crossed out and replaced by a wrong identification as Elizabeth, Queen of Bohemia.

The discovery of this is important for the iconography of the Duchess of Lennox as a whole as her name is another one likely to drift onto Jacobean portraits. Previously the most certain likenesses were engravings published in her lifetime and inscribed as being her. One by Francis Delaram c. 1610–15 depicts her as Countess of Hertford (Hind, *Engraving*, II, pp. 229–30). A second, again by Delaram, is dated 1623 and records her as Duchess of Richmond and Lennox (ibid., II, p. 230, pl. 132(b)). A third issued in the same year is by Willem van de Passe (ibid., II, p. 293, pl. 178(c)). The first two are based on the full length portrait by William Larkin at Helmingham Hall (Strong, *The English Icon*, p. 320 (no. 235)), even to including the jewellery, albeit slightly rearranged. This must be before the artist's demise in 1617 and, from the costume, can be dated to c. 1615 so must therefore depict her as Lady Hertford. This is important because the Hilliard miniature emerges as the only certain likeness before that date.

INSCRIBED: On the back of the frame there is a piece of card with a 17th century inscription crossed through and only barely legible in parts: [Duch]ess of Richmo[nd] . . . |by Hilliard| . . . .|; and *Elizabeth . . .| . . . . . .| married to* [Frederick] *K. of Bohem*[ia] *1602.*

116

COLLECTIONS: Given by Mrs Samuel S. Joseph, 1941; no previous
history.

LITERATURE: V & A, 1947 (93).
Auerbach, *Hilliard*, pp. 156, 313–14 (no. 154).

MAXIMILLIAN COLTE

115 Tomb of Elizabeth I, 1605–7

Westminster Abbey (Photograph)

In 1606 Nicholas Hilliard wrote to Robert Cecil, Earl of
Salisbury petitioning that he might be commissioned to
trim the tomb of the late Queen: "as a Goldsmith, I
understand howe to set forthe and garnishe a pece of stone
woork, not with muche gylding to hyde the beauty of the
stone, but where it may grace the same and no more"
(Auerbach, *Hilliard*, p. 37). The letter implies that Hilliard
had already undertaken the trimming of tombs and such
work was carried out by his workshop. In this instance he
was unsuccessful for the sculptor Maximilian Colte's
brother-in-law, John de Critz, the Serjeant Painter, in fact
carried out the work (a transcript of the payment to de
Critz is in Vertue, *Notebooks*, I, p. 99).

Colte had made Elizabeth's funeral effigy in 1603 upon
which the head on the effigy must be based. It has no
kinship with Hilliard's Mask of Youth portraits of the
Queen.

LITERATURE: Strong, *Portraits of Queen Elizabeth I*, p. 152 (5).
Edmond, *Limners and Picturemakers, Walpole Society XLVII*, 1980,
p. 165.

NICHOLAS HILLIARD

116 Unknown Girl, 1609

*Victoria & Albert Museum on loan from the Olive Lloyd-
Baker Estate*
Vellum stuck onto card with a black painted band
verso obscuring the playing card cypher, oval,
55×45 mm, $2\frac{3}{16} \times 1\frac{3}{4}$ in.

A unique late use of the artist's monogram, NH. The
miniature is superb, with the interesting placing of the
figure before the gold edgeline and there is a cast shadow
to the left. The dress is of a purplish colour with gold
decoration emphasizing the face and very fair hair. Apart
from the faded features and oxidized silver, the miniature
is in outstanding condition.

INSCRIBED: On either side of the head: *Anō Dnī 1609. NH* (in
monogram) / *Ætatis Suae 10.*

NICHOLAS HILLIARD

117 Mrs John Molle, 1605–8

The Pennington-Mellor Charity Trust
Vellum stuck onto card, oval, 50×40 mm,
$1\frac{15}{16} \times 1\frac{9}{16}$ in.

Elizabeth, wife of John Molle. For her husband, see no. 97.

An outstanding late Hilliard miniature with a startling
colour combination of brilliant auburn hair against a
crimson curtain background. Apart from a little flaking on
the curtain it is in virtually mint condition. Hilliard was
always more responsive to his female than his male sitters
and this becomes increasingly evident in his late work.

The miniature descended as a pendant to one always
known as John Molle (no. 97). He was imprisoned in
Rome in 1608 by the Inquisition with this miniature of his
wife in his possession which was, subsequent to his death,
c. 1640, returned to England. If the miniature is her, and
there seems no reason to doubt it, it must have been
painted shortly before Molle left for Italy as the extremely
low-cut neckline to the bodice is more typical of c. 1610
than c. 1605.

COLLECTIONS: See no. 97.

LITERATURE: V & A, 1947 (97).
Auerbach, *Hilliard*, pp. 155, pl. 150; 314 (156).

NICHOLAS HILLIARD

118 Lady Elizabeth Stanley, 1605–10

Private Collection
Vellum stuck onto a playing card with three
diamonds verso, oval, 62×51 mm, $2\frac{7}{16} \times 2$ in.

Lady Elizabeth Stanley (1586–1633), was third daughter of
Ferdinando, 5th Earl of Derby. She married, in 1601,
Henry Hastings, 5th Earl of Huntingdon.

This is rather carelessly painted with flaking gum accretion
at the bottom and some of the silver oxidized. The
miniature is an allegory of constancy in love, the sitter's
hand is placed over her heart with two emblems on
constancy. To the left the sun's rays pierce a cloud with a
motto indicating that love is immutable although
appearances may change. To the right a pierced heart is
accompanied by a motto on the theme of once pierced,

117

120

always fixed. On the reverse is a short prayer. There seems no reason to doubt the identity. The dress is white embroidered with flowers.

INSCRIBED: To the left of the head: *facies mutabilis | sed amor stablis*; to the right: *semel missa | semp(er) fixa*. On the reverse: *Demitte michi deus | Parce Deus.*

COLLECTIONS: Horace Walpole (although not traceable at Strawberry Hill); given by him to Sir H. W. Huntingdon; part of the collection formed by Walter, 2nd Viscount Bearsted.

LITERATURE: Pope-Hennessy, *Lecture*, 1949, p. 24, pl. 25(a).
  V & A, 1947 (96).
Auerbach, *Hilliard*, pp. 154, pl. 147; 313 (153).
Strong, *Hilliard*, p. 32, pl. 15(b).

NICHOLAS HILLIARD

119 Henry Wriothesley, 3rd Earl of Southampton, 1610 15

E. Grosvenor Paine Esq.
Vellum stuck onto card, 51 × 41 mm, 2 × 1⅝ in.
See no. 96 for the sitter

Painted in James I's reign when Southampton was released from the Tower and restored to favour. He was made a Knight of the Garter in 1603, the Lesser George of which he wears in the miniature. The starched but still curving upstanding collar would indicate a date c. 1610–15 (Strong, *The English Icon*, p. 272 (255) dated 1608; *Tudor and Jacobean*, I, opp. p. 162 c. 1610; II, pl. 474 dated 1613). The painting is somewhat tired and mechanical in feeling. He wears a white doublet and is silhouetted against the usual crimson velvet curtain.

The miniature is faded with oxidized silver and some flaking of the curtain.

COLLECTIONS: E. Peter Jones; sold Sotheby's 3rd July 1958 (lot 66); again 5th March 1959 (lot 33).

LITERATURE: Strong, *Tudor and Jacobean*, I, p. 300; II, pl. 588.

NICHOLAS HILLIARD

120 Unknown lady, c. 1615

Private Collection
Vellum stuck to a playing card with two clubs verso, oval, 63 × 52 mm, 2¹⁵⁄₃₂ × 2¹⁄₃₂ in.

From its first appearance in the Earl of Oxford's collection c. 1732 it is listed by Vertue as "Qu. Scots in White" (*Notebooks*, IV, p. 41). This cannot be accurate but the strength of the tradition was such that the motto was eventually turned by Andrew Lang in 1906 into an anagram of "Marie Stouard", also stylistically the miniature cannot be earlier than about 1610–15. The most distinctive innovation by Hilliard during this period was the jewelled border of the type used here, paralleled exactly in the portrait of Prince Charles, 1614, at Belvoir (Auerbach, *Hilliard*, pl. 158) and an Unknown Man, 1616 (no. 121). The inclusion of the hands is also a feature of these miniatures. Everyone so far has placed the miniature into the 1580s to square with an identification with the Scottish Queen to whose portraits it bears little, if any, resemblance.

As an instance of Hilliard's final phase it belongs to a group that reverse any evidence of a decline in his powers. The elaborately bejewelled border in ochre, embellished with pearls and "jewels", sapphires, emeralds and rubies, is used to heighten the brilliant monochromatic concept of the portrait, an essay in silver and white of quite astonishing brilliance.

The sitter is reclining in a state bed, the curtain of which is visible to the right. Her cape is of ermine and the diaphanous wired head-dress and veil is edged with pearls and carefully arranged over the pillows that support her. It is clearly a lady of the highest rank and its iconography is quite without parallel in Hilliard's *œuvre*. The head-dress is of a type adopted by widows as can be seen in the full length at Bisham of Elizabeth Coke, Lady Russell (Strong, *The Cult of Elizabeth*, pl. 3) and in the same lady's tomb (*Walpole Society*, IX, 1921, pl. VIII). The allusion to the following of Virtue would fit the widow exactly.

On the reverse it is inscribed probably by Bernard Lens: *Nicˢ: Hillard | fecit.* The frame is a Bernard Lens pear-tree one.

INSCRIBED: At the top: *VIRTUTIS AMORE.*

COLLECTIONS: Edward Harley, 2nd Earl of Oxford (1689–1741);
first recorded c. 1732 (see above); Vertue's catalogue, 1743
(61); Oxford's daughter married William Bentinck, 2nd Duke
of Portland; thence by descent.

LITERATURE: Andrew Lang, *Portraits and Jewels of Mary Stuart.*
Glasgow, 1906, pl. V.
L. Cust and K. Martin, "The Portraits of Mary Queen of Scots",
Burlington Magazine, X, 1906, p. 40.
Goulding, *Welbeck*, pp. 58–9 (8).
V & A, 1947 (32).
Auerbach, *Hilliard*, p. 98, pl. 72; 298–99 (69).

NICHOLAS HILLIARD

121 Unknown man, 1616

> *Private Collection*
> Vellum stuck to a larger piece of plain card, upon
> which the border is painted, oval, 62 × 51 mm,
> $2\frac{7}{16} \times 2$ in.

One of the most outstanding of Hilliard's late miniatures,
in unfaded and virtually mint condition, apart from the
oxidization of the silver. The border with its inscription
and inset "jewels" is typical of his late style and to
emphasize the frame he has painted a cast shadow to the
left. Although the birth date fits, there is no other reason to
identify the sitter as Henry Carey, 2nd Earl of Monmouth
with the inscription alluding to the creation of Charles as
Prince of Wales in 1616. The burst of rays in the motto
could be for a sun equally as for a star. Whichever, within
the conventions of the miniature, the allusion is likely to be
the devotion of the young sitter to his lady, "Still one star
(or sun) shines for me". The amatory interpretation is
surely reinforced by the ring worn attached to a bracelet of
black ribbands entwined around the wrist. One
inexplicable feature is the *Quadragessimo* in the inscription
on the frame which can only make sense by referring back
to an event in 1576.

INSCRIBED: On the outer frame: *Quadragessimo | Ano Dni 1616 | Vera
Effigies | Aetatis Suae 20.*
On either side of the head: *+Encores vn* (burst of rays) | *Luy
pour moy.*

COLLECTIONS: Edward Harley, 2nd Earl of Oxford (1689–1741);
first certainly referred to as in his collection in 1738: "a small
Limning a Mans head I suppose by Hillyard Encore
un ☀ Luit pour moy vera Effigiis. aetatis suae 20.-
Quadragessimo An°. Dni 1616.- his left hand holding the string
of his Band". (*Notebooks*, IV, p. 153); Vertue's catalogue, 1743
(112); Oxford's daughter married William Bentinck, 2nd Duke
of Portland; thence by descent.

LITERATURE: *Burlington Magazine*, VIII, 1906. p. 323.
Goulding, *Welbeck*, pp. 62–3 (14).
V & A, 1947 (100).
Auerbach, *Hilliard*, pp. 161–2, pl. 159; 316 (187).

Rowland Lockey

ROWLAND LOCKEY (c. 1565–1616) was apprenticed to
Hilliard in 1581 and was certainly working as an artist in
his own right by the early 1590s. In that period he was
associated with his master in executing a commission for
Bess of Hardwick and in the Jacobean era he was
responsible for the mass manufacture of portraits for the
Long Gallery as it was reconstituted by Bess's son, Sir
William Cavendish. Several of these can be identified.
Lockey is important as he confirms an enlarged view of the
limner's sphere of activity because Hilliard must have
taught him not only to be a goldsmith but a painter of
portraits both on panel and on canvas, a miniaturist and a
designer of title–pages. This is the first occasion upon
which a group of miniatures has been brought together as a
possible *œuvre* for him. These, as we would expect, are all
in the Hilliard manner of the 1580s before he changed his
style, and the key document is the cabinet miniature of the
Family of Sir Thomas More (no. 267). This establishes
Lockey as a weak draughtsman and the paint strokes under
magnification are always muddled and smudgy. There are
indications that links with Hilliard for a period may have
been close and in the reign of James I he may have
occupied the role of convenient collaborator in producing
portraits of the royal family (nos. 240, 242, 245)). It is
important to remember that Lockey was an artist in his
own right and capable of painting distinguished sitters who
may have thought Hilliard too old, expensive or unreliable.

SELECT BIBLIOGRAPHY
Otto Kurz, "Rowland Lockey", *Burlington Magazine*, XCIX, 1957,
pp. 13–16.
Auerbach, *Hilliard*, pp. 254–62.
Strong, *The English Icon*, pp. 255–58.
Strong, *The English Miniature*, pp. 59–61.
Mary Edmond, "Limners and Picturemakers", *Walpole Society*,
XLVII, 1980, pp. 95–7.
Strong, *Renaissance Miniature*, pp. 136–41.

ATTRIBUTED TO ROWLAND LOCKEY

**122 Henry Percy, 9th Earl of
Northumberland**, 1590–95

> *The Fitzwilliam Museum, Cambridge (PD3–1953)*
> Vellum stuck to a playing card with three hearts
> showing at the reverse, oval, 51.5 × 63.5 mm,
> $2 \times 2\frac{1}{2}$ in.

The miniature uses all the techniques of Hilliard's studio
but has none of the incisive quality of the autograph

miniature (no. 266). There is no reason to doubt that it is other than contemporary and, although weak in execution, the artist has rearranged the background with its daisies, poppies, glove and open book with trailing pink ribbons in a decorative Hilliardesque manner. Auerbach and Reynolds acceptance of it as autograph can be discounted. In basically good if faded condition with some flaking on the collar, shirt and doublet.

The miniature came from Penshurst: Robert Sidney, 2nd Earl of Leicester married, in 1615, Northumberland's daughter, Dorothy Percy. This early copy could have been inherited or even commissioned by her from the original which must have descended in the male line and was seen in 1738 by Vertue in Northumberland House.

COLLECTIONS: Presumably descended through the sitter to his daughter, Dorothy Percy, who married Robert Sidney, 2nd Earl of Leicester; descended with Penshurst to the Lords De L'Isle and Dudley; passed to the Captain Bertram Currie Collection; sold Christie's, 27 March 1953 (lot 23); purchased with a donation from Mr E. Evelyn Barron and a contribution from the Friends of the Fitzwilliam Museum.

LITERATURE: G. Reynolds, *Connoisseur Complete Period Guides*, 1968, ed. R. Edwards and L. G. Ramsay, pl. 74.
Auerbach, *Hilliard*, pp. 120–21; pl. 95; 304 (95).
Strong, *Hilliard*, pl. 9 (b).
A. C. Judson, *Sidney's Appearance*, Indiana U.P., 1958.

ROWLAND LOCKEY

123 Margaret Beaufort, Countess of Richmond and Derby, 1598

The Master and Fellows of St John's College, Cambridge
Oil on panel, 180.1 × 115.9 cm, 71¼ × 45⅝ in.
See above, no. 13. *(Photograph)*

Rowland Lockey was not only active as a limner but as a painter of portraits in oil both on panel and canvas. It is important that he received this training from Nicholas Hilliard in the 1580s as part of his apprenticeship. This portrait is one of a series that are either signed or documented as Lockey's work. Although he accepted commissions for portraits a large amount of his work seems to have been copying and he was commissioned to do a considerable number for Sir William Cavendish of Hardwick between 1609–13 (Auerbach, *Hilliard*, pp. 255–56).

The portrait of Margaret Beaufort is a donor portrait, the Countess having founded the College in 1508 and could have been based on one recorded at St James's in 1549–50: "the picture of the Dutches of Richmounte and Darbie sitting upon her knees" (*Three Inventories of Pictures in the Collections of Henry VIII & Edward VI*, ed. W. A. Shaw, Courtauld Institute Texts for the Study of Art History, 1937, p. 62). The Countess is shown dressed as a widow or vowess, which she became in the lifetime of her last husband. The distinctive features of the dress are the barbe, worn slightly over the chin, the head-dress and mantle. She kneels beneath a cloth of estate embroidered

124

with Tudor emblems and the stained glass also contains the royal arms.

As a painter emerging from Hilliard's tuition Lockey shows as little grasp of the principles of Renaissance scientific perspective as his master. The picture shows the same naïve approach to pictorial space as Hilliard's full-length miniatures. The use of gold and the accent on decoration is also Hilliardesque. In spite of the window at the back the sitter is front lit.

INSCRIBED: On the back of the panel: *IMPENSIS IVLIANAE CLIPPESBIE GENERUSAE VIRGINIS NORFULCIENSIS*; and: *Rolandus Lockey pinxit Londini*.

COLLECTIONS: Presented by Juliana Clippersby or Clipesby, daughter and heiress of John Clipesby of Clipesby, Norfolk, in 1598, the year of her marriage to Sir Randolph Crew.

LITERATURE: J. W. Goodison, "Cambridge Portraits, I", *Connoisseur*, CXXXIX, 1957, p. 215.
Strong, *Tudor and Jacobean*, I, pp. 20–21.
Strong, *The English Icon*, p. 256 (236).
P. Tudor-Craig, *Richard III*, National Portrait Gallery, 1973 (P.7).

ATTRIBUTED TO ROWLAND LOCKEY

124 Unknown Lady, 1595–1600

E. Grosvenor Paine Esq.
Vellum stuck onto card, oval, 48 × 41 mm, 1⅞ × 1⅝ in.

Very close indeed to the treatment of the ladies in Lockey's *More Family Group* (no. 267) with the same somewhat thick handling of the paint. The sitter is a lady of rank indicating Lockey's patronage by the gentry and aristocratic classes. The silver has oxidized and there are minute paint losses.

COLLECTIONS: Previous history unknown.

126

127

ATTRIBUTED TO ROWLAND LOCKEY

125 Unknown Man, 1599

The Duke of Buccleuch and Queensberry KT
Vellum stuck to a playing card with two diamonds
showing at the reverse, oval, 46 × 39 mm,
$1\frac{13}{16} \times 1\frac{9}{16}$ in.

Auerbach categorized this in 1961 as "in the manner of
Nicholas Hilliard". Detailed examination confirms her
reluctance to accept it as autograph. It matches closely the
two heads of the younger generation of the More family in
the *Family Group* (no. 267), although they are on a smaller
scale. It has been restored in recent times on the forehead,
ruff and doublet. The inscription is pure neo-Hilliard with
elaborate flourishes to the capital A's and is identical in
format to that on a second miniature also attributable to
Lockey (no. 129).

INSCRIBED: On either side of the head: *Anō Dñi·1599·* | *Aetatis suae
.28.*

COLLECTIONS: Part of the collection formed by Walter Francis, 5th
Duke of Buccleuch (1806–1884).

LITERATURE: Auerbach, *Hilliard*, pp. 136, pl. 117; 307 (118).

NICHOLAS HILLIARD

126 Unknown Lady, c. 1600

The Duke of Buccleuch and Queensberry KT
Vellum stuck onto plain card, oval, 77 × 60 mm,
$3 \times 2\frac{3}{8}$ in.

This is the only instance where we have two versions of the
same miniature, one by Hilliard himself and the second, a
copy of it, attributable to Rowland Lockey (no. 127). The
miniature has been called Frances Howard, Duchess of

Richmond and Lennox but there are no grounds for the
identification. The sitter is obviously of high social rank
from the magnificence of her dress and the size of the
miniature which includes her right hand clutching a
flower. Against a background of a folded crimson curtain
Hilliard has set the figure in a dress of off-white,
embroidered in multi-colours and gold. The dress, with its
gauze puffs lining the ruff, belongs to the very final years of
the reign before the change of fashion with Anne of
Denmark (cf. Strong, *The English Icon*, p. 278 (264) dated
1599).

On initial encounter the miniature has the stiff qualities
of a repetition but it must be the *ad vivum*. The
exceptionally elaborate presentation of the sitter is close in
concept to the "Mask of Youth" miniature of the Queen at
Ham House (no. 209) which includes the same gesture of
the hand.

The miniature has undergone recent restoration in the
features, ruff and white bodice including the silver of the
pearls, which had oxidized, being overpainted white. All
the silver is oxidized and the features faded.

COLLECTIONS: Part of the collection formed by Walter Francis, 5th
Duke of Buccleuch (1806–84).

LITERATURE: Kennedy, *Buccleuch*, pl. 22.
V & A, 1947 (72).
Auerbach, *Hilliard*, pp. 140, pl. 121; 308 (123).

ATTRIBUTED TO ROWLAND LOCKEY

127 Unknown Lady, c. 1600

National museum, Stockholm (NMB 1694)
Vellum stuck onto card, oval, 76 × 60 mm, $3 \times 2\frac{3}{8}$ in.
See above, no. 126

Hitherto accepted by Reynolds and Auerbach as a replica
by Hilliard, this is a copy attributable to Lockey of a

miniature in the Buccleuch collection of an aristocratic lady. Under magnification it has all qualities of a copy, of observation at a remove. The hair is in Lockey's typically smudgy manner and his carelessness is revealed in having to add a piece of vellum to the left in order to complete the composition. It is very faded with flaking in the background and coronet and oxidized silver. There are a number of slight variants from the original in the embroidery of the dress and in the flower held.

COLLECTIONS: Purchased by Charles Sotheby from Colnaghi, 1861; Sotheby of Ecton Hall Collection; sold Sotheby's 11th October 1955 (lot 66).

LITERATURE: V & A, 1947 (73).
Auerbach, *Hilliard*, pp. 140–41; 308 (124).

ROWLAND LOCKEY AND CHRISTOPHER SWITZER

128 The Holy Bible . . . (The Bishops' Bible), 1602

The British Library (L.13.B.6.)
Woodcut

The title page is signed in the bottom two corners of the title compartment: *RL* and *CS*. It was McKerrow and Ferguson in 1932 who suggested that these stood for Rowland Lockey and Christopher Switzer. Christopher Switzer (active c. 1593–1611) worked as a line engraver and is eulogized by Francis Meres in his *Palladis Tamia*, 1598 (p. 287). Hind (*Engraving*, I, pp. 228–29) points out that we can assume that he was of Swiss origin and is almost certainly identifiable with the Christopher Switzer listed in the Return of Aliens in 1593, 1594, 1599 and 1600 and with the woodcutter who executed illustrations for Speed's *History of Great Britain* (1611–14) praised by the author as "the most exquisite and curious hand of our age".

The fact that he executed engravings does not mean necessarily that he designed them. His continental origins may account for the fact that he acknowledges the source for his design. What is important is that we should expect someone like Lockey who had been apprenticed to Hilliard to be capable of such work and other examples must exist, so far unattributed. It is also important to grasp the essentially co-operative nature of such a project for not only did it involve designer and engraver it also concerned the author of the complicated iconographic programme.

The commission was an important one, for the title page represents, as Corbett and Lightbown observe, a completely new departure for a title-page to an Elizabethan Bible. The publisher was, of course, the Queen's printer, Robert Parker, and for Lockey to be chosen is a significant reflection of his status as an artist and designer by 1602. The title-page was designed to match the series of continental biblical title-pages and, at the same time, not affront the very firm anti-idolatry stance of the established Church. The iconography must have been carefully compiled by a contemporary theologian or cleric. It presents the twelve tribes of Israel (left) confronting the twelve apostles (right), a numerological parallel possibly to demonstrate the inter-relationship of

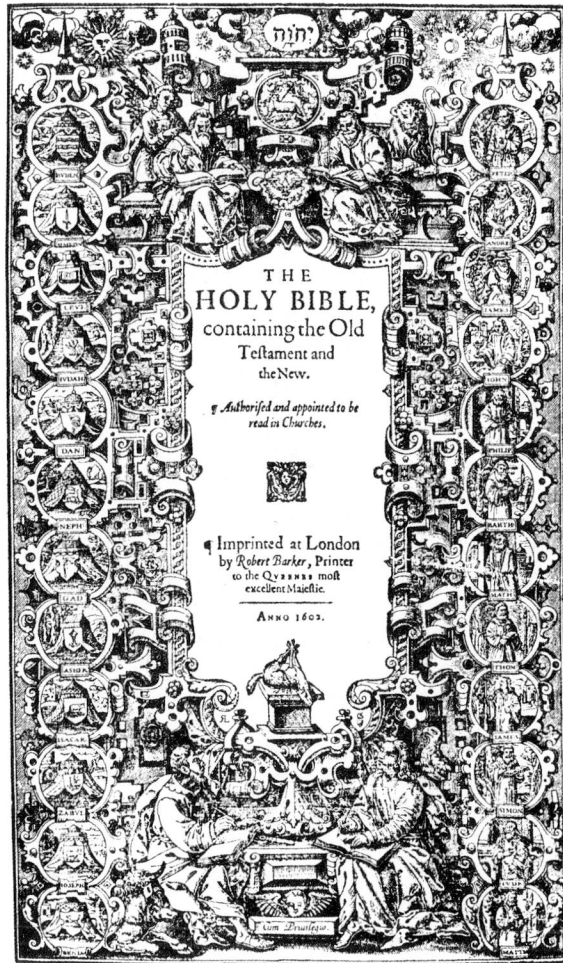

128

the Old and New Testaments. Around the central compartment are grouped the four Evangelists while at the top there is another innovation, the three Persons of the Trinity, probably a statement against anti-Trinitarian movements and a proclamation of Anglican orthodoxy. The ingredients of the title-page were re-used for the New Testament of the Authorized Version and by William Hole for the 1607 edition of the Genevan Bible.

LITERATURE: R. B. McKerrow and F. S. Ferguson, *Title-page Borders used in England and Scotland 1485–1640*, 1932 (no. 231).
M. Corbett and R. Lightbown, *The Comely Frontispiece. The Emblematic Title-page in England 1550–1600*, London, 1979, pp. 91–97.

129 Charles Howard, 2nd Baron Howard of Effingham and 1st Earl of Nottingham, 1605

National Maritime Museum, Greenwich
Vellum stuck to card which has been painted black verso, oval, 46 × 40.5 mm, $1\frac{7}{8} \times 1\frac{19}{32}$ in.

See no. 66.

A faded likeness of Nottingham in his sixty-ninth year. At one time this was wrongly called Lord Hunsdon although its identity was correct at an earlier date. Until now this has always been accepted as an authentic work by Hilliard, but it is certainly not by him. It is weak in handling, with a use of muddled brushstrokes to delineate the features typical of Lockey. The form of inscription for the date is identical to that in no. 125. There are losses at edge and to the plumes in the hat and the silver has oxidized.

COLLECTIONS: First recorded in the collection of Lady Betty Germain (1680–1769) in 1737: "Earl of Nottingham Admiral" (*Notebooks*, IV, p. 120); acquired by Horace Walpole (*A Description of the Villa at Strawberry Hill*, 1774, p. 82); Strawberry Hill sale 20th day 17th May 1842 (lot 4); purchased by the Duke of Buckingham; Stowe sale March 15th 1849 (lot 46); purchased by Rodd; C. Sackville Bale collection; sold 24th May 1881 (lot 1423); purchased by Walter Francis, 5th Duke of Buccleuch; acquired by the National Maritime Museum, 1942.

LITERATURE: Winter, *Elizabethan Miniatures*, p. 27, pl. X(b). V & A, 1947 (91).
Auerbach, *Hilliard*, pp. 153, pl. 145; 313 (151).

130 Unknown Man, 1612

The Duke of Buccleuch and Queensberry, KT
Vellum stuck onto plain card, oval, 53 × 41 mm, $2\frac{1}{16} \times 1\frac{5}{8}$ in.

Formerly called the Earl of Pembroke, Auerbach suggested a tentative attribution to Laurence Hilliard. It is, however, superior in quality to anything that has so far appeared as by him and it may be more certainly ascribed to Lockey. The white doublet which is embroidered in green, gold and other colours is in the lively tradition of direct observation. So far the earliest known Laurence Hilliard miniature is one dated 1622 (Auerbach, *Hilliard*, pl. 190) which is far more awkward and feeble in quality than this miniature. The face and ruff have been repainted and the silver has oxidized.

INSCRIBED: Around the edge: *Anō Dnī · 1612 · En · Vo · fi · Con · ma · Sub· ; Ætatis suae 30:*

COLLECTIONS: Part of the collection formed by Walter Francis, 5th Duke of Buccleuch (1806–1884).

LITERATURE: Auerbach, *Hilliard*, p. 232, pl. 194; 327 (228).

131 Called Catherine Carey, Countess of Nottingham, 1605–10

National museum, Stockholm (NMB 1582)
Vellum stuck onto card, oval 57 × 47 mm, $2\frac{1}{4} \times 1\frac{5}{8}$ in.

Auerbach recognized that this was in the Hilliard manner but not by him. Judging from the smudgy painting of the hair and the typical use of Hilliard techniques this miniature fits in with what might be grouped to form a nucleus for Lockey's work. Although faded and with oxidized silver, it is in an unusually good state and the crimson velvet curtain is in noticeably brilliant condition. The gesture of the hand on the heart appears in Hilliard's work in the 1580s (e.g. Auerbach, *Hilliard*, pl. 75), and suggests an amatory context for this miniature.

COLLECTIONS: Harry Seal Collection; sold Christie's 16th February 1949 (lot 105) as an Anne of Denmark by Hilliard.

LITERATURE: Auerbach, *Hilliard*, pp. 284; 334 (286).

Isaac Oliver, c. 1560–1617

I EARLY LIFE AND WORK, 1560–1596

c. 1560. Born about this date, the son of Pierre Olivier, a
    goldsmith of Rouen.
1568. Residing in London with his parents in Fleet Lane.
1577. Still recorded as resident.
1586. Signed and dated drawing of the *Lamentation*
    (no. 136) probably executed in Tournai.
1587. Earliest known portrait miniature (no. 137).

ISAAC OLIVER remains one of the most mysterious of all late
Elizabethan and Jacobean artists. Unlike Hilliard the
documentary facts about him are few and tantalizing,
especially in respect of his early life, a feature which he has
in common with Inigo Jones. Unlike Hilliard his
background was that of an impoverished emigré fleeing the
wars of religion in France and finding refuge in London.
He was there for something like a decade and then he next
appears abroad, if the reading of the date and
identification of the town name on his drawing of the
Lamentation is correct (no. 136). The importance of that
drawing can hardly be underestimated for it establishes
that Oliver was a fully trained artist when he went to
Hilliard to learn to paint miniatures and that his
relationship with him was that of master learning from
master and not that of pupil and master which has hitherto
been accepted. He would have been well into his twenties
when this happened and the evidence of his earliest
miniatures fully support that thesis. Although they make
use of Hilliard's techniques they have no other connexion
with him, epitomizing a totally new departure in the
limning story. If Oliver had served under Hilliard a seven-
year apprenticeship he would have emerged like Lockey
with an early style which would be a version of his master's
but he did not.

    It is what occurred in the lost years between 1577 and
1587 which is of such importance to discover. His work
indicates a familiarity with the art of the Low Countries, in
the case of the *Lamentation* with that of the 1560s and 70s
and in that of the miniatures with a portrait tradition in
the 1580s exemplified by the engravings of Hendrik
Goltzius. Another signed drawing (no. 135), which should
be an early one, establishes that he knew the work of the
School of Fontainebleau. Oliver as a young man belonged
to a class of the emigré community that constantly crossed
to and fro to the mainland. Evidence would suggest that he
left England and returned to France for his initial training
and that he then made his way northwards into the Low
Countries about the time of the outbreak of the most
savage of the wars of religion in France, those of the
Catholic League. It is conceivable that he somehow came
to England via the Low Countries during the period of
England's heaviest involvement in the war in the
expedition of Hilliard's patron, Leicester.

    Although we know more than we did thirty years ago
what little more that we do know raises more problems
than it solves. What is certain is that here we are dealing
with an artist trained on the mainland of Europe within

132

the tradition of the Renaissance. This meant that he moved
from accomplishments and assumptions totally unknown to
Hilliard and his contemporaries: ones such as drawing
from the nude model, that a drawing was a work of art in
its own right, that the art of painting was based on a
mastery of *chiaroscuro* and of linear and aerial perspective.
He must have felt completely isolated in the Elizabethan
London of the late 1580s. From the start there is a
dramatic break with Hilliard as he applies these principles
initially to his earliest sitters, mainly it seems members of
the citizen class and, as we get into the early 1590s, those of
the court. For the latter he tempers what must have seemed
an almost brutalist approach with touches of the
Hilliardesque. At this period he was admitted to paint the
Queen, an encounter which has left us arguably our
greatest likeness of her, although from the sitter's point of
view it was a failure.

SELECT BIBLIOGRAPHY
The literature on Oliver is very meagre and I list the main works
here:
Reynolds, *Miniatures*, pp. 22–9.
Auerbach, *Hilliard*, I, pp. 232–54.
Mary Edmond, "Limners and Picturemakers", *Walpole Society*,
    XLVII, 1980, pp. 72–81.
Strong, *The English Miniature*, pp. 62–8.
Strong, *Renaissance Miniature*, pp. 142–85.

?HENDRIK HONDIUS

132 Isaac Oliver, c. 1610

*British Museum, Department of Prints and Drawings
(O 8-118)*
Engraving, 20.5 × 12 cm, 8⅛ × 4¾ in. (plate),
15.8 × 11.7 cm, 6¼ × 4⅝ in. (plate).

Hind states that this plate was published (or printed) if not
engraved by Hendrik Hondius (1573–after 1649), an

136

engraver who worked in the main in The Hague but possibly visited Cologne, Paris and London. The engraving forms the last in a series of portraits of artists published about 1610 in The Hague entitled *Pictorum aliquot celebrium, praecipae Germaniae Inferioris, Effigies*.

Hind assumes that the original of the engraving must have been of the same date as the self-portrait miniatures of c. 1590 (nos. 133, 134). This, on the contrary, is an independently observed portrait of the miniaturist, older and wearing costume of the Jacobean period. It is conceivable that it goes back to a drawing supplied by Oliver himself. On the table to the left lie his palette and brushes and a series of portrait miniatures. The fact that Oliver was included in such a publication is an indication that his fame must have been to a degree international Constantine Huygens refers to Oliver's works which he had seen on visits to his son, Peter: "Oliverus, Britannus celeberimus, cuius stupendas tabulas apud aemulum parentis filium Londini alibique non paucas vidi" (A. G. H. Bachrach, *Sir Constantine Huygens and Britain: 1596–1687*, Sir Thomas Browne Institute, 1962, p. 144, note 2).

LITERATURE: Hind, *Engraving*, II, p. 398 (71).

ISAAC OLIVER

133 Self-portrait, c. 1590–95

National Portrait Gallery (4852)
Vellum stuck to plain card, oval, 62 × 50 mm,
$2\frac{7}{16} \times 1\frac{15}{16}$ in.

One of the two self-portraits from the same period, the other being in the Royal Collection (no. 134). The pose and presentation are close to portraits by the Antwerp painter, Hieronimo Custodis, working in England at this period (Strong, *The English Icon*, p. 199 (152)). The miniature is in excellent condition.

Another portrait of Oliver was engraved by H. Hondius and describes him as *Anglus, Pictor* (no. 132).

COLLECTIONS: First recorded by Vertue, c. 1726–27 when in the collection of Colonel James Seymour (1658(?)–1739), collector, limner and father of the painter (*Notebooks*, II, p. 47); presumably in the sale that followed his death purchased by the collector Thomas Barrett of Lee Priory, Kent (1698–1757); his sale, Horace Walpole at Strawberry Hill (*Description of the Villa . . . at Strawberry Hill*, 1774, p. 84); sold Strawberry Hill sale May 9th 1842 (13th day) (lot 85); bought by the 13th Earl of Derby; sold Christie's June 8th 1971 (lot 79); purchased by the National Portrait Gallery.

LITERATURE: H. Walpole, *Anecdotes*, Ed. Wornum, 1849, I, p. 178.
George Scharf, *A Catalogue of the Collection of Pictures at Knowsley Hall*, 1875, p. 229.
V & A, 1947 (135).
Elizabethan Image, Tate Gallery, 1969 (149).

ISAAC OLIVER

134 Self-portrait, c. 1590–95

H.M. The Queen
Vellum stuck to plain card, oval, 45 × 36 mm,
$1\frac{3}{4} \times 1\frac{5}{16}$ in.

Very much in the vein of the 1587 unknown lady (no. 137) but painted with far greater assurance. For the minute scale it is executed with bravura in his typically free early manner, similar in handling to the full length *Melancholy Man* (no. 268). The concept is close to portraits by Hieronimo Custodis (e.g. Edward Sheldon, 1590, Strong, *The English Icon*, p. 199 (152)) during the same period. There is a small restoration in the ruff at the right.

INSCRIBED: Signed to the right in monogram: *10*.

COLLECTIONS: Dr Richard Mead (1673–1754); recorded by Vertue, c. 1726–27 (*Notebooks*, II, p. 47); purchased by Frederick, Prince of Wales; recorded by Horace Walpole when at Buckingham House (*Visits*, Walpole Society, XVI, 193, p. 79).

LITERATURE: H. Walpole, *Anecdotes*, Ed. Wornum, 1849, I, p. 78.
V & A, 1947 (136);
Van Dyck, Queen Gallery, 1968 (84).

ISAAC OLIVER

135 Moses striking the rock, before 1586

H.M. The Queen
Brown and grey wash and white, 21 × 33.3 cm,
$8\frac{1}{4} \times 13\frac{1}{4}$ in.

The dating of Isaac Oliver's drawings is extremely problematic but this is by far the most tentative and it should preceed that dated 1586 (no. 136). The composition which is divided between a sharply defined foreground and a distant vista with no middle ground is an arrangement which recurs in his miniature of an unknown melancholy young man, c. 1590 (no. 268). The figures and groups fail to co-ordinate as a composition and derive from familiar motifs of artists of the School of Fontainebleau. The group to the left of a female figure with four children is derived from charity groups (*L'Ecole de Fontainebleau*, Grand Palais, 1972 (nos. 57, 235, 238)); the sinuous figure to right is in the manner of Nicolò dell'Abate (ibid., nos. 1, 3); the group of *à l'antique* warriors to the left are reminiscent of the elegant warrior figures of Antoine Caron (e.g. ibid., nos. 34, 36, 37). The exotically shaped large vases recall those in *Le Sacrifice* in the Galerie François I (*La Galerie François Ier au Château de Fontainbleau*, Revue de l'Art, 1972, p. 91).

If this can be accepted as a drawing by Oliver made before 1586 it could never have been executed without first hand knowledge of Valois court art. Apart from the fact that Oliver is listed as child, with no age given, in London in 1568 we know nothing certain about him until the 1586 drawing (no. 136) and his first miniature dated 1587 (no. 137). The Fontainebleau style drawing would suggest that Oliver returned while he was still young and was trained as an artist in France. It establishes a totally different grounding from that of Hilliard. The signature, which seems perfectly authentic, is on different paper and has been cut-out and inset. It is difficult to explain the reason for this but the drawing is certainly by Oliver.

INSCRIBED: Signed on the inset: *Isac: Olivier Fec.*

COLLECTIONS: First recorded in James II's collection (no. 636): 'A drawing in black and white of the journeying of the children of Israel by Isaac Oliver'.

LITERATURE: A. Oppé, *English Drawings . . . in the Collection of H.M. The King at Windsor Castle*, London, 1950, pp. 79 (459). Strong, *Renaissance Miniature*, p. 144.

ISAAC OLIVER

136 The Lamentation over the Dead Christ, 1586

The Fitzwilliam Museum, Cambridge (PD5–1957)
Pen and ink, wash, watercolour and bodycolour, 210 × 280 mm, 8¼ × 11 in.

Although this drawing has been known since 1957, it was only in 1981 that examination under ultra-violet ray disentangled more of the very damaged inscription. This includes a date, the completely legible figures being *15* [ ] *6*, the third figure being either a *6* or an *8*. Six would be an impossibility giving us a date of 1586. There is also another word, very damaged indeed, the letters of which could most satisfactorily be read as *Tuarnicum*, which could be a variant of the Latinized version of the town of Tornai (e.g. *Thornva, Turnacum*) (I am indebted to David Scrase for the technical examination of the drawing and Ronald Lightbown for suggestions as to the interpretation of the final word).

Such a reading would fit in well with the noticeably Flemish mannerist nature of the composition which harks back to the 1560s and 1570s: overlarge figures and details such as the Magdalene's costume or the hat worn by the man supporting Christ. It is extraordinary how closely *The Burial of Christ* develops out of this (no. 181), although it was painted decades later, and unfinished at his death.

137

Oliver was apparently capable of returning and re-working his earlier compositions over a period of thirty years.

INSCRIBED: Signed in ink, lower right: *I. Ollivārus in* [ ]/ *Tuarnic* [*um*](?)/ *15* [ ] *6*.

COLLECTIONS: Bought in Lisbon, 1940, by Sr. José Casimiro Serrao Franco; sold Sotheby's 20th November 1957 (lot 66); presented by the Friends of the Fitzwilliam Museum.

LITERATURE: Friends of the Fitzwilliam, *Annual Report, 1957*, pp. 2–3;.
E. Croft-Murray, and P. Hulton, *Catalogue of British Drawings*, London, British Museum, 1960, I, p. 23 (under 11); *European Drawings from the Fitzwilliam Museum*, Pierpont Morgan Library, 1976 (125).
Strong, *Renaissance Miniature*, p. 146.

ISAAC OLIVER

137 Unknown Lady, 1587

The Duke of Buccleuch and Queensberry, KT
Vellum stuck to plain card, oval, 54 × 44 mm, 2 1/16 × 1 23/32 in.

The earliest identifiable miniature by Oliver bearing his monogram. First published by Auerbach in 1961, it depicts a citizen's wife wearing the characteristic tall black hat and there is no jewellery (see no. 160). The choice of the three-quarter-length, considered in parallel with Hilliard's work at the time, established Oliver's interest in experimentation with differing scales and portrait formats. Technically the miniature is directly within the Hilliard tradition but the only other link is the inscription with the characteristic bold flourishes to the capitals. The source is Hendrik Goltzius engravings of women, issued in the early 1580s, always depicted three-quarter length within an oval.

There is a little flaking and the features, ruff and the white bodice have been restored.

INSCRIBED: Signed to the right: *IO* (monogram). On either side of the figure: *Ano Dni 1587 / Aetatis suae. 20.*

139

140

138

COLLECTIONS: Part of the collection formed by Walter Francis, 5th Duke of Buccleuch (1806–1884).

LITERATURE: Auerbach, *Hilliard*, p. 236, pl. 195; 327 (230).

HENDRIK GOLTZIUS

138 Lady Françoise van Egmont, 1580

> The British Museum, Department of Prints and Drawings (Bartsche 168)
> Engraving, oval, 180 × 142 mm, $7\frac{1}{8} \times 5\frac{5}{8}$ in.
> Lady Françoise van Egmont (d. 1586) was the daughter of Lamoral, Count Egmont.

Goltzius' engravings of female sitters in a three-quarter length formula must have been the source for Oliver's earliest portrait miniature (no. 137).

LITERATURE: *Hendrik Goltzius 1558–1617. The Complete Engravings and Woodcuts*, ed. Walter L. Strauss, N.Y., 1977, I, p. 226 (no. 132).

HENDRIK GOLTZIUS

139 Hans Felbrier or Jacob Gyscher, 1582

> The British Museum, Department of Prints and Drawings (Bartsch 206)
> Engraving, oval, 94 × 72 mm, $3\frac{11}{16} \times 2\frac{13}{16}$ in.

The identity is uncertain, but this type of small oval portrait is typical of a whole series executed by Goltzius during the 1580s which must have been a decisive influence on Oliver's portrait miniatures. They always present the sitter within an oval, strongly lit at one side, casting the other side of the face and figure into deep shadow and emphasizing the contours of the face. This was to be the striking feature of Oliver's earliest male portraits epitomizing an approach totally at variance with that of Hilliard, whose sitters were lit from the front with a flat, even light designed to eliminate any excrescences on the face and reduce the features to a few formalized lines.

LITERATURE: *Hendrik Goltzius 1558–1617. The Complete Engravings and Woodcuts*, ed. Walter L. Strauss, N.Y., 1977, I, p. 266 (157).

ISAAC OLIVER

140 Diederik Sonoy, 1588

> *Collection of H.R.H. Princess Juliana of the Netherlands*
> Vellum stuck onto card, rectangular, 68 × 55 mm, $2\frac{5}{8} \times 2\frac{1}{8}$ in.

Diederik Sonoy (1529–1597) was an early partisan in the revolt against Philip II of Spain. Subsequent to the death of William the Silent he supported Robert Dudley, Earl of Leicester, as Governor-General against Prince Maurice of Nassau. Defeated, he emigrated to England and was granted fenland by the Queen, returning to settle in the Low Countries in 1593.

The identification of this miniature as the Dutch military commander Diederik Sonoy was made by E. Pelinck in 1966, on the basis of both the age and date on the miniature and by comparison with a slightly later portrait still in the possession of the family. Sonoy was allowed to settle in England in September 1588 so that the miniature must have been painted here. Pelinck also points out that Oliver committed a mis-spelling in *Verhouve* which should read *Ver tr ouve*; the motto then reads correctly in translation: *To trust without suspicion.*
　　The miniature is in relatively unfaded condition. Oliver is experimenting, this time with a return to the use of the rectangular shape with spandrels decorated with arabesques, a formula that harks back to Hornebolte's Henry VIII but is obviously derived more from contemporary portrait engravings. Both the approach to the sitter and the brushwork are diametrically opposed to Hilliard's work at the same period.

INSCRIBED: Around the edge: *Sonder erch, Verhouve. Ae Suae 59. A° . D^m . 1588. Isac^s Oliver^s f.*

COLLECTIONS: Part of the collection formed by Queen Wilhelmina.

LITERATURE: V & A, 1947 (121).
Auerbach, *Hilliard*, pp. 238, pl. 197; 328 (232).

Pelinck, "Portretten van Diederik Sonoy", *Jaarbuck Centraal Bureau voor Genealogie*, XX, 1966, pp. 146–48.

Mary Edmond, "An Isaac Oliver sitter identified" *Burlington Magazine*, August, 1982 p. 496.

ISAAC OLIVER

141 Unknown Man, 1588

Brinsley Ford, Esq., C.B.E., F.S.A.
Vellum stuck onto card, oval, 51 × 42 mm, 2 × 1⅝ in.

Oliver's earliest dated instance using dramatic *chiaroscuro*, casting the left hand side of the sitter's face into shadow. The miniature, the precursor of a whole series of brilliant male portraits in this manner, demonstrates the artist's enormous development in style and technique within a year. The brown hair is beautifully painted with fair highlights.

INSCRIBED: Around the edge on either side of the head: *Anno.Domini.1588. Etatis Suae 19.*

COLLECTIONS: J. Pierpont Morgan collection with no provenance; sold Christie's June 24th 1935 (lot 71).

LITERATURE: Williamson, *Catalogue*, 1906, I, p. 73 (76). Pope-Hennessy, *Lecture*, 1949, pl. XXXVII. V & A, 1947 (126).

ISAAC OLIVER

142 Peregrine Bertie, Lord Willoughby D'Eresby, c. 1590

Victoria & Albert Museum (P.5–1947)
Vellum stuck onto card, oval, 36 × 26 mm, 1 9/32 × 1 in.

Peregrine Bertie, Lord Willoughby d'Eresby (1555–1601), Commander in the Low Countries in succession to Leicester, 1587–89, defended Bergen against the Spaniards. In 1589–90 he aided Henri of Navarre. Poverty and ill-health led him to live abroad, 1590–96, returning as Governor of Berwick.

Purchased and, up until now, accepted as a work by Hilliard this miniature is almost certainly an early work by Oliver. The hair is painted in the style of Hilliard but the placing of the head, the scale and the use of stippling is quite different from his work. Willoughby returned to England from the Low Countries in March 1589; left in September for France, returning early in 1590 and leaving again in the same year to live abroad. The miniature belongs to this period and the francophile appearance of the sitter recalls Rabel's engraving of Henri IV (F. A. Yates, *The Valois Tapestries*, London, 1959, ed., pl. 2 (f)). There are minor losses at the edge and in the background.

INSCRIBED: On the reverse of the frame in a later, probably 18th century hand: *by Hilliard | Rt. Hon | Peregrine Bertie | Lord Willoughby | of Eresby Son | of Richard | Bertie Esq. by | Catherine Duchess | of Suffolk.* This is virtually repeated in a second

inscription and faintly on the reverse of the miniature itself: *Honble Peregrine Bertie.*

COLLECTIONS: Sold anonymously Sotheby's 24th July 1947 (lot 101); purchased with funds from the R.H. Stephenson Bequest.

LITERATURE: Auerbach, *Hilliard*, p. 310 (134) as Hilliard.

143

ISAAC OLIVER

143 ? A Member of the Barbor Family, c. 1590

Victoria & Albert Museum (887–1894)
Vellum stuck onto a playing card with two diamonds verso, oval, 37 × 29 mm, 1 15/32 × 1 13/16 in.

For the sitter see below.

Traditionally this miniature is of William Barbor, a grocer of Protestant persuasion who was saved from the stake by the accession of Queen Elizabeth in 1558. In remembrance of his delivery he is said to have had the Barbor Jewel made (V & A 859–1894) and both it and the miniature were bequeathed to the eldest of his sons to have a daughter called Elizabeth. In the case of the Jewel stylistically it belongs to the 1580s (*Princely Magnificence*, V & A, 1980 (41)). Barbor died in 1586 and so it is arguable as to whether it was made for him or not.

The miniature, however, cannot be him but is more likely to be one of his sons. It also cannot be by Hilliard, an attribution up until now unchallenged for it is executed in a stipple style which was used by Isaac Oliver. The portrait is not easy to date due to the lack of visible costume but the short hair and collar seem to indicate a date in the early 1590s (cf. Strong, *The English Icon*, p. 196 (147) dated 1589; 199 (no. 152) dated 1590). With its indications of architecture in the background and medallic profile format it anticipates Oliver's portraits of Prince Henry *à l'antique* (no. 230).

There are slight paint losses and scratches on the collar and losses, which have been restored, in the background and at the edge. The gold edgeline has been restored in places; faded features and oxidized silver. It is in a contemporary turned ivory case.

COLLECTIONS: In possession of the Blencowe family who inherited it by the marriage of the last Elizabeth Barbor to Henry Prescott Blencowe of Thorby Priory, Essex sometime after 1757; presented by Miss M. Blencowe, 1894.

LITERATURE: V & A, 1947 (30).
Auerbach, *Hilliard*, pp. 180, pl. 180; 297 (64).

ISAAC OLIVER

144 **Unknown Man**, 1590

Victoria & Albert Museum (P.37–1941)
Vellum stuck on to a plain card (the vellum is in two
pieces, a small, separate strip having been added to
the left edge by the artist), oval, 52 × 43.5 mm,
$2\frac{1}{16} \times 1\frac{23}{32}$ in.

Although faded, a superb *ad vivum* portrait by Oliver. The
use of shadow by means of the strong light cast from the
front left is already highly developed, totally different from
Hilliard's technique during the same period and vividly
reflecting the influence of Netherlandish art and the
engraved portraits of Goltzius. This is accentuated by the
cast shadow in the background, giving a three dimensional
chiaroscuro effect which the lettering, very much in Hilliard's
vein with flourishes to the A's, denies. The edge of the
miniature has been trimmed, thus losing most of the gold
line; in addition there are a number of small damages in
the background and minute paint losses to the costume.
The erroneous identification on the later frame as Francis
Bacon can be discounted.

INSCRIBED: On either side of the head: *Ano Dm̄ 1590 | Ætatis Suae
27.*

COLLECTIONS: Presented by Mrs Samuel S. Joseph, 1941, previous
history unknown.

LITERATURE: Winter, *Elizabethan Miniatures*, pl. IX (a).
V & A, 1947 (131).
Auerbach, *Hilliard*, pp. 238, pl. 199.

ISAAC OLIVER

145 **Girl aged four**, 1590

Victoria & Albert Museum (P.145–1910)
Vellum stuck to a playing card with half a red
cypher (heart or diamond) showing at the reverse,
oval, 54 × 43 mm, $2\frac{1}{8} \times 1\frac{11}{16}$ in.

146 **Girl aged five**, 1590

Victoria & Albert Museum (P.146–1910)
Vellum stuck to a playing card with part of a picture
(possibly a King) showing at the reverse, oval,
54 × 43 mm, $2\frac{1}{8} \times 1\frac{11}{16}$ in.

Originally oddly attributed to Levina Teerlinc, the correct
attribution being made by Carl Winter in 1943. These are
amongst Oliver's earliest surviving miniatures and already
establish him as an artist whose range and approach was to
be much more varied and complex than Hilliard.
Miniatures of children, other than royal ones, are of the
utmost rarity and the two girls must have been of
exceptional status. Williamson, not an infallible source,
states that when they were in the possession of C. H. T.
Hawkins they had with them a slip of paper stating that
they were painted at Greenwich in 1590 (Williamson,
Catalogue, 1906, I, p. 20). Salting, who bequeathed them to

the V & A had never seen this piece of paper, if, indeed, it
ever existed.
Justifiably, these miniatures quickly established
themselves as two of Oliver's most popular works.

INSCRIBED: (P.145–1910): On either side of the head: *Ano Dm̄.
1590/ Ætatis Suae. 5.* (P.146–1910): On either side of the head:
Ano Dm̄. 1590./ Ætatis Suae. 4.

COLLECTIONS: C. H. T. Hawkins sale, Christie's 13th to 17th May
1904 (908); bt. E. M. Hodgkins; bequeathed to the V & A
with the Salting collection, 1910.

LITERATURE: Williamson, *Catalogue*, 1906, I, p. 20.
J. J. Foster, *The Athenaeum*, May 13th 1911.
Simone Bergmans, "The Miniatures of Levina Teerlinc",
Burlington Magazine, LXIV, 1934, pp. 232–36.
Winter, *Elizabethan Miniatures*, pp. 26–27, pl. IX.
V & A, 1947 (141, 142).
Auerbach, *Hilliard*, pp. 236–38, 328 (no. 235).

ISAAC OLIVER

147 **Unknown Lady**, 1590–95

Collection of H.R.H. Princess Juliana of the Netherlands
Vellum stuck onto card, oval, 50 × 43 mm,
$2 \times 1\frac{11}{16}$ in.

A delightful portrait which, apart from fading, is in superb
condition. The sitter is a young woman in dress of the
citizen class (on which see no. 160). The miniature has
been slightly trimmed thus losing the gold edgeline. There
are no grounds for the traditional identification as Oliver's
wife.

COLLECTIONS: Part of the collection formed by Queen Wilhelmina.

LITERATURE: Edinburgh, 1975 (51) (wrong miniature reproduced
in the catalogue).

ISAAC OLIVER

148 **Unknown Man**, 1590–95

Collection of H.R.H. Princess Juliana of the Netherlands
Vellum stuck onto card, oval, 54 × 48 mm,
$2\frac{1}{8} \times 1\frac{5}{8}$ in.

There are no grounds for identifying this as a self-portrait.
It appears to have been reduced in size thus cropping the
top of the hat, in spite of this it is a fine portrait in good
condition, apart from fading and some scattered flaking.

INSCRIBED: In gold on the verso: *Anno Dnj 15 ( )* (missing due to
trimming) *Æ Svae* (left blank).

COLLECTIONS: Part of the collection formed by Queen Wilhelmina.

LITERATURE: V & A, 1947 (134).
Auerbach, *Hilliard*, pp. 238, pl. 198; 328 (233).

147　　　　　　　　　　　　**148**

ISAAC OLIVER

149 Unknown Lady, c. 1590–95

National Maritime Museum, Greenwich
Vellum stuck to a playing card with one club verso, oval, 52 × 43 mm, $2\frac{1}{32}$ × $2\frac{11}{16}$ in.

Formerly wrongly ascribed to Hilliard and identified as Queen Elizabeth it was first correctly exhibited as Oliver by Reynolds in 1947. The handling of the features is very close to the pattern of Elizabeth I (no. 199). This is Oliver painting in the Hilliard style for the court and there is a Hilliardesque explosion of lace, patterned fabric and jewels which makes such a marked contrast to the dramatic and severe portraits of men and citizens' wives from the same period. It was not until after his visit to Italy that Oliver was able to establish a more forceful treatment of his female sitters. The hair is painted in the free 1580s style of Hilliard, much at variance with the tight handling of the features. Considerably faded and with damage and restoration at the edges, the silver as usual is oxidized and the lack of an edgeline indicates a reduction in size.

COLLECTIONS: As Queen Elizabeth by Hilliard: Horace Walpole, Strawberry Hill (*A Description of the Villa at Strawberry Hill*, 1774, p. 82); C. Sackville Bale collection, sold 24th May 1881 (lot 1422); purchased by Walter Francis, 5th Duke of Buccleuch. Acquired by the National Maritime Museum, 1942.

LITERATURE: V & A, 1947 (147).

ISAAC OLIVER

150 Unknown Child, c. 1590–95

The Duke of Buccleuch and Queensberry, KT
Vellum stuck to a playing card with one spade showing at the reverse, oval, 43 × 35 mm, $1\frac{11}{16}$ × $1\frac{3}{8}$ in.

This is an unfinished miniature: the ruff is modelled but with no lace and the jewels are sketched in black and grey. The lack of a gold line and the proximity of the monogram

to the edge would indicate that the miniature has probably been reduced in size. This is a delightful likeness of an aristocratic girl between the ages of six and ten in costume of the early 1590s, very close in treatment to the pattern portrait of the Queen (no. 199) and sharing the same heavy black line delineating the upper lid and painting of the ruff. An old inscription identifying the sitter as Arabella Stuart can hardly be right as Arabella was born in 1575 and would be too old. The sitter is obviously of considerable rank and Oliver's approach to child portraiture has advanced rapidly from the two little girls of 1590 (nos. 145, 146), with their stiff, formal presentation.

The background has craquelured with resulting paint loss including that of the monogram, which is almost obscured. Despite losses on the dress and ruff, abrasions on the face and general fading, it remains one of Oliver's most intriguing early miniatures.

INSCRIBED: To the right, but very damaged *IO* (in monogram). On the reverse an early inscription: *[L]ady Arabella Stu[art]* / *I Oliver f.*

COLLECTION: Part of the collection formed by Walter Francis, 5th Duke of Buccleuch (1806–1884).

II ITALY, 1596

The only certain evidence that pin-points a visit to Italy by Isaac Oliver in 1596 is the inscription on the reverse of a miniature called Sir Arundell Talbot (no. 152). From that we know he was in Venice on May 13th and 14th of that year. Until now it has been generally accepted that this was his only visit to Italy but evidence may point to a return in the Jacobean period (no. 179). This makes another piece of documentation more difficult to interpret, the large-scale limning he made after Veronese's *Mystic Marriage of St. Catherine* (no. 151) which was in the collection of Charles I. There is no doubt, however, of the influence of Italy on his work on his return to England. Fontainebleau and Flanders are now overlaid by memories of the Venetian masters, but more particularly the works of the Milanese School in the aftermath of Leonardo, which would have appealed to the essentially mannerist vision of

152

153

Oliver with its preoccupation with light and shade and mystery.

For bibliography see Section I.

PAOLO VERONESE (1528–1588)

151 Mystic Marriage of St. Catherine, 1575

(Gallerie dell'Accademia, Venice) *Photograph*

Van der Dort's catalogue of Charles I's collection includes a copy of Veronese's *Mystic Marriage of St. Catherine*. (O. Millar, *Walpole Society*, XXXVII, 1960, p. 123 (1).) This was a limning about a foot high in an ebony frame and door to protect it from fading. The entry is annotated "bought by yor Ma^{ty} of Isack Oliver" which means that it must have been acquired when Charles I was Prince and before 1617, the date of Oliver's death. Assuming that Oliver did not return to Venice at a later date (see no. 179) this large-scale miniature must have been executed by him when he was in Venice in 1596. The entry states it "was first done in Italy and since over done and touched by Isack Oliver". It anticipates his own large-scale miniatures of religious subjects in the Jacobean period and may have inspired Charles I to commission Isaac's son, Peter, to execute the series of large-scale cabinet miniatures after the most famous pictures in his own collection.

ISAAC OLIVER

152 Called Sir Arundell Talbot, 1596

Victoria & Albert Museum (P.4–1917)
Vellum stuck to a playing card, with an inverted heart verso, rectangular (with clipped corners), 69 × 54 mm, 2$\frac{23}{32}$ × 2$\frac{5}{32}$ in.

The importance of this miniature lies in the inscription on the reverse, presumably by Oliver himself which, in translation, reads: "The 13th day of May 1596 at Venice done by Mr Isaac Oliver French man I.O. May 14th for £8". This is undoubtedly contemporary and is vital

evidence for establishing Oliver's visit to Italy during the 1590s. The miniature itself is unfinished, although bordered by a gold line, it has not been clipped down to size. It appears to be the fruit of probably two sittings, with only the beginnings of the hatching in of the features: the ear, for example, has been begun and the dress is also incomplete.

The reverse contains a much later seventeenth century inscription giving the identity of the sitter as a certain Sir Arundell Talbot. No evidence has yet appeared to support the existence of such a person and the sitter could, equally well, be an Italian.

INSCRIBED: On either side of the head: *Anno Domini 1595 | Ætatis M. Isacq Oliviero | Francese IO* (in monogram) *V.14. | da e8*; below in a later hand: *Viva & vera effigies | Arundelli Talbot | Equitis Aurati.*

COLLECTIONS: W. G. Eden, 253 Cromwell Road from whom it was purchased by Messrs Durlacher, 12th February 1909; sold from the H. P. Pfungst collection, Christie's 14th June 1917 (lot 57); acquired by the V & A under the Capt H. B. Murray Bequest.

LITERATURE: Winter, *Elizabethan Miniatures*, pl. XI (b). V & A, 1947 (149). Auerbach, *Hilliard*, pp. 244, pl. 209; 329 (244).

ISAAC OLIVER

153 Unknown Man, 1595

Collection of H.R.H. Princess Juliana of the Netherlands
Vellum stuck onto card, oval, 51 × 41 mm, 2 × 1$\frac{5}{8}$ in.

The background makes use of the expensive pigment ultramarine indicating a sitter of rank. Although damaged and faded, with flaking in the doublet at the bottom, this is an important miniature with striking affinities in handling to the so-called Sir Arundell Talbot (no. 152). The sitter does not appear to be Italian but is possibly a North European in Italy, probably Venice.

INSCRIBED: On either side of the head: *Anno Domini 1595 | Ætatis Suae 26.*

COLLECTIONS: Part of the collection formed by Queen Wilhelmina.

III OLIVER AND "CURIOUS PAINTING", c. 1596–1617

1598. Mentioned by Richard Haydocke (no. 103)
1599. Death of his first wife, Elizabeth
1602. Marries as his second wife Marcus Gheeraerts' sister, Sara
1605. Appointed "painter for the Art of Limning" to Anne of Denmark
1606. Marries a third time, Elizabeth Harding, the daughter of a court musician
1610. Possibly re-visited Italy (no. 179)
1612. Walks in the funeral procession of Henry, Prince of Wales
1617. Death of Isaac Oliver

Oliver, subsequent to his return from Italy, began to enjoy enormous success. Such success, which lasted until his death, has to be placed into the context of a change in atmosphere in the arts which was to be the most striking feature of the closing years of the century. "Curious painting", as it was referred to, had its followers, its advocates, above all among the literati, where references abound to the delights of *trompe l'oeil* and optical tricks of deception that worked from a premise of scientific perspective. The new generation was moving out of the line and colour of a basically medieval optical experience into the European mainstream. As a point of reference no other art form charts this aesthetic revolution more fully than Inigo Jones's scenery for the court masques from 1605 onwards. They educated the audience by placing before it a completely new visual repertory: landscape and seascape, cloud visions and architectural vistas all conceived within terms of single point perspective and a dramatic control of light to heighten illusion.

Oliver's work subsequent to 1596 needs to be firmly set within this milieu. Although the old Queen was to remain a bastion against change within her closed circle and her successor was to maintain it through inertia, Oliver was to receive a stream of patronage from clients anxious to adopt the *avant garde*, Essex, who abandoned Hilliard, Anne of Denmark and her son, Prince Henry. The work of this twenty years establishes Oliver as a far greater artist than Hilliard, one who could hold his own with some of the foremost mannerist artists of the northern courts. Every single miniature that he painted was approached as a separate problem and not, as in the case of Hilliard, as conformity to a formula. He began, certainly in some instances, with a compositional sketch. Within the miniature format there are also considerable differences in the scale chosen. The large scale cabinet miniature he returned to as a format throughout his life, exploiting a variety of shapes, the upright rectangular, the landscape and the large *tondo*. But even in the middle ranges the sizes can fluctuate in response to a sitter (no. 172). In terms of style he is painter as chameleon, as he not only experimented himself but was quite happy to become conservative in manner if it suited a client. The 1616 miniature of John Donne (no. 178) is painted in a Hilliardesque manner more suited to fifteen years previous. The Head of Christ (no. 175) is without parallel in being executed entirely in a stipple technique as though a deliberate statement against the Hilliard tradition. His sources too are eclectic revealing a wide knowledge and a retentive memory of what he had seen abroad: the unknown lady enveloped in veils is an essay in the Leonardesque, *Diana* (no. 174) recalls the mythological deities of Spranger or Cornelis van Haarlem, the head of Christ (no. 175) reveals a preoccupation with Correggio. The astonishing *Madonna and Child in Glory* (no. 179) even postulates a return to Italy and sight of the young Rubens' *Madonna della Vallicella*. And yet, simultaneously, he could as easily adopt the formula of a Jacobean icon master such as William Larkin (no. 277).

As in the case of his predecessors limning was not Oliver's only ability. He was a painter of subject pictures which are well documented but none of which have as yet come to light. He provided designs for engravers as his drawing for William Hole of Prince Henry testifies (no. 259). Above all he was the first person in England to execute drawings as works of art in their own right, a totally new idea in the Jacobean period. His *Nymphs and Satyrs* is yet another surprising work when it is set into the backwaters of provincial London, a visual manifestation of a frank eroticism only normally to be found in the literature of the period. Together with the *Madonna* (no. 179) they are evidence that Oliver in his final years was crossing from mannerism and experimenting with the baroque.

For the bibliography see under Section I.

MARCUS GHEERAERTS

154 Robert Devereux, 2nd Earl of Essex, c. 1596

The Trustees of the Bedford Settled Estates
Oil on canvas, 211.2 × 127 cm, 83½ × 54 in.
See no. 263 for the sitter.

Marcus Gheeraerts (fl. 1561–d. 1635) became the most fashionable portrait painter of the 1590s, quickly rising to eminence and court patronage, probably with the backing of Sir Henry Lee who commissioned the famous Ditchley Portrait of the Queen (National Portrait Gallery) in about 1592. In 1602 his sister became Isaac Oliver's second wife. Both artists represented a "new wave" in the 1590s and the fact that Essex, then at the apogee of his power, turned from William Segar (no. 218) and Hilliard (no. 220) to Gheeraerts and Oliver c. 1596 must have been of major significance. Gheeraerts' portraits, like Oliver's, must have struck the onlooker as vividly three-dimensional and realistic. The approach to Essex's head is close to that of Oliver's but his most striking innovation is to stand the Earl in an open landscape setting, on the seashore in allusion to the recent expedition to Cadiz, which is, presumably, the town seen burning in the distance. Gheeraerts remained *avant garde* throughout the 1590s and into the early part of the new century. Only after c. 1615 does he become stereotyped and retrogressive.

As in the case of the miniature of Essex (no. 155) this portrait must have been designed for mass production and many versions of varying quality and size are extant.

Isaac Oliver 105

154

COLLECTIONS: First certainly recorded at Woburn, 1727 (Vertue, *Notebooks*, II, p. 41).

LITERATURE: G. Scharf, *A . . . Catalogue of the Collection of Pictures at Woburn Abbey*, 1890, pp. 37–8 (50).
L. Cust, "Marcus Gheeraerts", *Walpole Society*, III, 1914, p. 33.
Strong, *The English Icon*, p. 297 (300).
Strong, *Tudor and Jacobean*, I, p. 116.

ISAAC OLIVER

155 Robert Devereux, 2nd Earl of Essex, c. 1596

National Portrait Gallery (4966)
Vellum stuck to plain card, oval, 51 × 41 mm, 2 × 1⅝ in.
See no. 263

Essex grew a beard on the Cadiz expedition of 1596 and on his return sat to Marcus Gheeraerts for the portrait now at Woburn that commemorates the event (no. 154) with the Earl facing to the right. Oliver's miniature faces the left and relates so closely to his later brother-in-law's life-scale likeness that the two probably went *in tandem*. It marks

Essex's break with Hilliard whom he had patronized until then and the acquisition by Oliver of a major patron. As in the case of the Queen, the transfer has startling results, producing a greatly different portrait image. Oliver presents Essex, not as the romantic Knight of the tiltyard or the naval commander, but as the grave statesman, with stress placed on his high forehead and penetrating gaze. Several versions of this miniature exist, some probably painted by Oliver in James I's reign when Essex's reputation was resurrected (at Burghley House, Chatsworth and in the Royal Collection). This, an autograph repetition, reflects Oliver's experimentation with other colour backgrounds during this period, here, opaque grey. It is in good condition apart from extensive restoration to the gold edge-line and background and some retouching on the doublet. The most important version must have been the full-length one now in a private collection (Williamson, *Catalogue*, 1906, I, p. 55 (51) which once belonged to Charles I (O. Millar, *Walpole Society*, XXXVII, 1960, p. 108 (23)).

COLLECTIONS: Sold by E. J. Clark, Sotheby's 26th November 1973 (lot 96).

LITERATURE: Strong, *Tudor and Jacobean*, I, pp. 116–17.

ISAAC OLIVER

156 Unknown Lady, 1595–1600

Victoria & Albert Museum (P.43–1941)
Vellum stuck to a playing card with part of a spade verso, oval 49 × 39 mm, 1 15/16 × 1 9/16 in.

Although very faded, this was once a marvellous portrait of a lady with Oliver's typical post-Italian motif of the enigmatic smile. The miniature has been clipped, which accounts for its tight feeling, especially where the hair is cut into. Reynolds' dating of c. 1590 seems therefore too early: style and presentation would indicate a date after the Italian visit to be more correct. It does not, however, belong to the very last years of the reign when gauze puffs were worn to edge the ruff-line. The necklace incorporates a repeating letter S. A second version exists with a variant costume in the Mauritshuis (Auerbach, *Hilliard*, pp. 242, pl. 205; 329 (240)).

COLLECTIONS: Given by Mrs S. Joseph, 1941.

LITERATURE: V & A, 1947 (144).
Auerbach, *Hilliard*, p. 242, pl. 205 (wrongly as a miniature in the Dutch Royal Collection).

ISAAC OLIVER

157 Unknown Lady, 1595–1600

Duke of Buccleuch and Queensberry, KT
Vellum backed with thin card, oval, 51 × 43 mm, 2 1/32 × 1 23/32 in.

This miniature was formerly called Catherine Knevett, Countess of Suffolk (born after 1563–1638), second wife of

155

157

158

Thomas Howard, Earl of Suffolk, whom she married in or before 1583. There are no grounds for this identification and indeed there is no known authentic likeness. The portrait bearing the earliest inscription is that by Larkin but it also cannot be substantiated (John Jacob, *The Suffolk Collection Catalogue of Paintings*, n.d. (no. 8)) and bears little resemblance to the miniature.

This is one of Oliver's most ravishing characterizations from the 1590s. The costume includes the interesting detail of the wire support for the ruff being visible. On the whole it is in very good condition, although the state of the edges would suggest that it has been cut down from its original size. There is restoration on the ruff, the face has been abraided on the forehead and cheek and, as usual, there is fading and oxidization. There is no sign of "the traces of a gilt signature" referred to by Auerbach.

INSCRIBED: To the left: *Infelix Spectator*.

COLLECTIONS: Presumably part of the collection formed by Walter Francis, 5th Duke of Buccleuch (1806–1884).

LITERATURE: Kennedy, *Buccleuch*, pl. XXII.
Burlington Magazine, LXXII, 1938, p. 223.
V & A, 1947 (156).
Auerbach, *Hilliard*, pp. 244, pl. 210; 329 (245).

ISAAC OLIVER

158 Unknown Lady, 1595–1600

The Duke of Buccleuch and Queensberry, KT
Vellum stuck to plain card, oval, 55 × 45 mm,
$2\frac{5}{32} \times 1\frac{3}{4}$ in.

One of Oliver's finest late Elizabethan miniatures aiming at an "opposite" tonal effect to Hilliard. The whole portrait, apart from the carnations, being an essay in white, silver and grey against a brown-black background. The only touch of gold occurs in the star-jewel at her throat. This monochromatic approach echoes the large circular miniature wrongly called the Countess of Somerset (no. 271). Formerly called Frances Walsingham, Countess of Essex, it bears no relation to what is probably the only

authentic likeness (Strong, *The English Icon*, p. 222 (183)). The piling high of the hair over a pad and the gauze puffs along the ruff edge are a feature of the last years of the decade, painted therefore after Oliver's return from Italy. There have been minor losses and oxidized silver highlights have been scraped off in some cases or overpainted with white in others.

COLLECTIONS: Part of the collection formed by Walter Francis, 5th Duke of Buccleuch (1806–1884).

LITERATURE: V & A, 1947 (162).

ISAAC OLIVER

159 Unknown Man, 1595–1600

Private Collection
Vellum stuck to plain card, oval, 52 × 43 mm,
$2\frac{1}{16} \times 1\frac{11}{16}$ in.

One of Oliver's most superb portraits from the close of the century with a profound concern for interpretation of character, a deep rapport with the sitter is reflected in the nervous quality of the brushwork. Apart from very minor losses the miniature is in good condition. The identification, made in the last century, as Thomas Howard, 2nd Earl of Arundel can be discounted. As usual the style of hair and collar is very difficult to date. Reynolds dates the miniature to c. 1590; the costume fits any date in the decade but the extreme maturity of its style and the rank of the sitter would indicate the second half.

INSCRIBED: Signed to the left over the shoulder in monogram: *IO*.

COLLECTIONS: Part of the collection formed by Robert Harley, 2nd Earl of Oxford (1689–1741); not identifiable in Vertue's list of c. 1731 (*Notebooks*, IV, p. 41); described but not named in his 1743 catalogue (7); Oxford's daughter married William Bentinck, 2nd Duke of Portland; thence by descent.

LITERATURE: Goulding, *Welbeck*, p. 70 (28).
V & A, 1947 (137).

ISAAC OLIVER

160 Unknown Lady, 1595–1600

H.M. The Queen
Vellum stuck onto card, oval, 76 × 57 mm, 3 × 2¼ in.

In Oliver's immediate post-Italian style with a virtuoso *sfumato* handling of light and shade in the manner of the Milanese school, Reynolds' dating of it to before the Italian visit cannot, therefore, be sustained. The sitter is a lady of the city wearing specifically bourgeois dress (see no. 137) with its typical peaked hat. Nonetheless, the miniature is of extreme richness making use of expensive ultramarine for the background, a rare feature, on account of the cost. Its scale is unusually large for a head and shoulders portrait and is typical of Oliver's experimentation during the 1590s. It is in exceptionally good and unfaded condition.

COLLECTIONS: Dr Richard Mead (1673–1754); engraved by
    Houbracken as Mary Queen of Scots, 1738; recorded by
    Vertue, c. 1740–41 (*Notebooks*, IV, p. 187); purchased by
    Frederick, Prince of Wales.

LITERATURE: H. Walpole, *Anecdotes*, ed. Wornum, 1849, I, p. 78.
L. Cust, *Notes on the Authentic Portraits of Mary Queen of Scots*,
    London, 1903, p. 140.
Passing references to it in studies of the iconography of Mary
    Queen of Scots occur in much of the literature listed in Strong,
    Tudor and Jacobean, I, p. 223.
V & A, 1947 (133).

ISAAC OLIVER

161 Unknown Melancholy Young Man,
c. 1595–1600

Private Collection
Vellum stuck to plain card (the left edge has been trimmed to fit a hinged box), oval, 72 × 52 mm,
2¹³⁄₁₆ × 2¹⁄₁₆ in.

One of the most extraordinary of all Oliver's miniatures and quite unprecedented iconographically in English painting, by 1854 it was called, for no sound reason, "The Prodigal Son". In van der Dort's catalogue it is listed as "a Certaine naked young mans picture" and also as St John. The softly crossed hands on the chest with the fingers extended and the upturned ecstatic gaze of the eyes are a common pose for the Madonna, or Saints in adoration, particularly in religious painting of a type we associate with the Counter Reformation. The combination of long hair, nudity, ecstatic gaze and crossed arms derives above all from late sixteenth-century representations of the penitent Magdalene as depicted by the Milanese School in the aftermath of Leonardo (see Everett Fahy, *The Legacy of Leonardo*, N.G. of Art, Washington, 1919, p. 106). The nudity, apart from Hans Eworth's *Sir John Luttrell* (Strong, *The English Icon*, p. 86 (22)), is unprecedented in British art.

    There seems to be no evidence for van der Dort's alternative of St John, beyond the fact that the apostle was depicted as a slightly effeminate young man with long hair. The miniature is quite clearly a portrait and belongs to the series of melancholy portraits of the 1590s depicting men

with arms folded or crossed. In the background there is a stormy sea with a ship tossed on the waves and a rock, both common emblems which gained their greatest currency later as part of William Marshall's image of Charles I in the *Eikon Basilike*. Both symbolize constancy and devotion in adversity. In the case of Charles I the reference is political and religious which would point to this sitter suffering not from the more usual love melancholy but melancholy of a religious kind. The miniature has been cut to fit a locket. The sitter's hair is extremely long and the absence of clothes makes dating unusually difficult. On balance the style of hair fits more logically into the 1590s. It is in good condition apart from slight flaking at the edges.

INSCRIBED: Signed in monogram *IO* to the right.

COLLECTIONS: Recorded in the collection of Charles I by van der
    Dort (67): "Item a Certaine naked young mans picture -/ to
    the wast holding both his hands Cross over -/ another upon his
    breast tourning his head -/ upwards towards his left shoulder in
    a black woodden / tourn'd ebbone box with a Christall over it,
    done -/ upon the (   ) light" (Millar, *Walpole Society*,
    XXXVII, 1960, (p. 120); and again: "A St John houlding
    Twoe / handes att his breast" *ibid*, (p. 217); dispersed in the
    Commonwealth sale reappearing in the collection of Edward
    Harley, Earl of Oxford (1689–1741); recorded by Vertue,
    c. 1732 (*Notebooks*, IV, p. 41); Vertue's Catalogue, 1743
    (no. 9); Oxford's daughter married William Bentinck, 2nd
    Duke of Portland; thence by descent.

LITERATURE: Goulding, *Welbeck*, p. 73 (34).
V & A, 1947 (191).
Auerbach, *Hilliard*, pp. 251, pl. 226; 331 (261).

ISAAC OLIVER

162 George Carey, 2nd Lord Hunsdon,
1601

The Trustee of the Will of the 8th Earl of Berkeley
Vellum stuck onto card, oval, 49 × 40 mm,
1¹⁵⁄₁₆ × 1⁹⁄₁₆ in.

George Carey, 2nd Lord Hunsdon (1547–1603), son of the Queen's cousin, Henry Carey, 1st Lord Hunsdon was MP for Hertfordshire, 1571, and for Hampshire, 1584, 1586, 1588–9 and 1592. In 1582 he was appointed Captain-General of the Isle of Wight which he re-fortified. On his father's death in 1596 he became Captain of the Gentlemen Pensioners, a member of the Privy Council and KG. In 1597 he was apppointed Lord Chamberlain of the Household.

In the last century this was attributed to Oliver but Auerbach in 1961 assigned it to Hilliard. This attribution cannot be sustained. The reason for it is the late use by Oliver of a Hilliard style inscription for the date and age, likely to have been a concession to the elderly sitter who was fifty-four in 1601. The miniature is unfinished, perhaps because it failed to please Lord Hunsdon. The head is finished and is of fine quality but the dress is only blocked

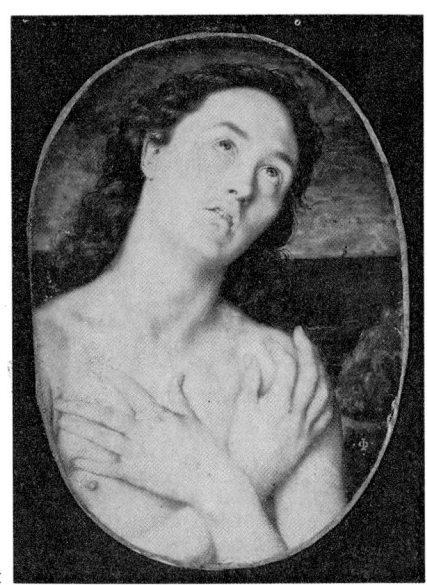

161

163

in as in the case of the so-called Sir Arundell Talbot (no. 152). Some flaking of the dress is evident, but otherwise it is in good condition. In the midst of so many unidentified sitters this one of a major court figure is important evidence of Oliver's advance in court circles by the close of the reign.

INSCRIBED: On either side of the head: *Ano Dni 1601 | Ætatis Suae ·54·*

COLLECTIONS: The sitter's daughter and heiress, Elizabeth, married Sir Thomas Berkeley of Berkeley Castle.

LITERATURE: Auerbach, *Hilliard*, pp. 138, pl. 119; 308 (121).

ISAAC OLIVER

163 **Unknown Man**, c. 1600

Victoria & Albert Museum (P.5–1917)
Vellum stuck to a playing card with one inverted heart at the reverse, oval, 66×51.5 mm, $2\frac{19}{32} \times 2\frac{1}{32}$ in.

The miniature was acquired as by Oliver, reattributed to Hilliard by Carl Winter in 1941 (V & A Archives) and finally accepted as by Oliver by both Reynolds and Auerbach. A detailed examination confirmed, on technical and stylistic grounds, that this indeed was by Oliver. The techniques which in particular mark it as his work are the stippling used in delineating the features and the naturalistic modelling of the folds of the shirt which is quite unlike Hilliard's impressionistic, graphic manner. The chiaroscuro and the adventurous iconography also place it decisively as Oliver's work.

As in the case of many of Oliver's miniatures it is difficult to date but the cut of the hair and moustache is identical to that in two portraits by Gheeraerts dated 1599 (Strong, *The English Icon*, pp. 278 (264), 280 (269)). I would favour as a date c. 1600. The iconography is of the flames of love and the sitter holds in his right hand what is

probably a picture box at the end of a chain. He has placed himself amidst flames in an emblematic manner that draws on common devices; the phoenix arising out of the flames, used as a device signifying varieties of resurrection, rebirth and chastity; the second is the salamander in the midst of flames. The general drift of possible meanings is caught in the verses accompanying a salamander emblem in George Wither's *A Collection of Emblemes* (1638), p. 30.

> This *Crowned Salamander* in the Fire,
> May therefore, not unfitly, signifie
> Those, who in *Fiery Chariots*, doe aspire
> *Elijah*-like, to *Immortality*:
> Or those *Heroicke-spirits*, who unharm'd
> Have through the Fires of *Troubles*, and *Affliction*,
> (With *Vertue*, and with *Innocence* arm'd)
> Walkt onward, in the Path-way, of Perfection.

The formula is repeated in a miniature by Oliver at Ham House (no. 171). Vaenius *Amorum Emblemata* (1608) which includes a salamander amidst the flames in a specifically amatory context:

> Love live In the fyre
> Unhu'rt amidds the fyer the Salamander lives
> The lover in the fyre of love delight doth take
> Where lover thereby to live his nouriture doth make
> What others doth destroy lyf to the lovers gives.

Or there is equally a parallel to the device of the flaming inverted torch with the motto *Qui me alit extinquit* (That which feeds me extinguishes me).

> Even as the waxe doth feede, and quenche the flame,
> So, love gives life; and love, dispaire doth give. . . .

(Geoffrey Whitney, *A choice of Emblemes and Other Devises*, Leiden, 1586, p. 183).

Once the sitter had adopted the device it became his *impresa* open to his own personal reading of its meaning.

The condition of the miniature is good apart from minor flaking and the silver paint being oxidized.

COLLECTIONS: W. C. Morland of Lamberhurst, Sussex by 1865
when lent to the S. K. Exhibition as Edward Courtney, Earl of
Devon; Henry J. P. Pfungst collection; sold Christie's 14th
June 1917 (lot 59); purchased from the funds of the Capt H. B.
Murray Bequest.

LITERATURE: *Catalogue of the collection of Miniatures lent in 1914–15 by
Henry J. Pfungst*, pp. 20–21.
Winter, *Elizabethan Miniatures*, pl. 6(b).
V & A, 1947 (64).
Pope-Hennessy, *Lecture*, 1949, pl. 20.
Reynolds, *Connoisseur's Complete Period Guides*, 1968, p. 227,
pl. 74(B).
Auerbach, *Hilliard*, pp. 136–7, pl. 118; 308(11a).

ISAAC OLIVER

164 Unknown Man, 1600–1605

Private Collection
Vellum stuck to a playing card with five diamonds
verso, oval, 52 × 42 mm, $2\frac{1}{16} \times 1\frac{5}{8}$ in.

A superb miniature with ravishing colour, a doublet of
grey and white decorated with shimmering silver
highlights. The use of the precious pigment ultramarine for
the background indicates a sitter of importance. As early as
1743 it was mis-identified as Sir Philip Sidney. There is
some damage: flaking in the collar and a stain on the
sitter's right temple. The silver is, as usual, oxidized and
there is some blackening of the lead white of the eyes and
collar.

INSCRIBED: Signed to the left: *IO* (in monogram)

COLLECTIONS: Part of the collection formed by Robert Harley, Earl
of Oxford (1689–1741); possibly that recorded by Vertue,
c. 1732: "a Mans hd" (*Notebooks*, IV, p. 41); Vertue's
catalogue, 1743 (no. 86) as possibly Sir Philip Sidney; Oxford's
daughter married William Bentinck, 2nd Duke of Portland;
thence by descent.

LITERATURE: Goulding, *Welbeck*, p. 68 (24).
V & A, 1947 (24).

ISAAC OLIVER

165 Jane Montgomerie, Duchess of Richmond and Lennox, c. 1605

Private Collection
Vellum stuck to card, oval, 52 × 42 mm,
$2\frac{1}{16} \times 1\frac{11}{16}$ in.

Jane Montgomerie, Duchess of Richmond and Lennox,
daughter of Sir Matthew Campbell of London and widow
of the Hon Robert Montgomerie.

A brilliant fresh, unfaded miniature which has been
reduced in size. The brushwork is in Oliver's agitated
manner, not in the least mechanical, with the background
painted in expensive ultramarine and it is probably

identical with that described as the Duchess of Richmond
as early as Vertue's c. 1732 list.

Richmond married three times: his third wife was
Frances Howard, the widowed Countess of Hertford (see
no. 271), whom he married in 1621 but it cannot be her.
Being a companion to one of the Duke dated 1603 by a
Hilliard follower, would make it a likeness of Lennox's
second wife, Jane Montgomerie.

The miniature has been reduced in size and there is
clumsy restoration of damage to the forehead with slight
flaking on the dress and the silver has oxidized.

COLLECTIONS: Edward Harley, 2nd Earl of Oxford (1689–1741);
first recorded in Vertue's list c. 1731 following one of the
Duke: "his Dutches" (*Notebooks*, IV, p. 41); Vertue's 1743
catalogue (no. 89) with no identity or artist; later called
Arabella Stuart; Oxford's daughter married William Bentinck,
2nd Duke of Portland; thence by descent.

LITERATURE: Goulding, *Welbeck*, p. 66 (21).

ISAAC OLIVER

166 Robert Cecil, 1st Earl of Salisbury, 1606–12

The Governors of the Burghley House Preservation Trust
Vellum stuck onto card, oval, 52 × 42 mm,
$2\frac{1}{16} \times 1\frac{11}{16}$ in.

Robert Cecil, 1st Viscount Cranbourne and 1st Earl of
Salisbury (1563–1612), second son of William Cecil, 1st
Lord Burghley, succeeded his father as Elizabeth's and
subsequently James I's "first" minister and played a
powerful role in securing Jame's accession in 1603.

The only known miniature of Robert Cecil and, curiously,
by Oliver in the light of the considerable correspondence
that exists between Cecil and Hilliard. Cecil, however, was
avant garde in his tastes in the arts, particularly during the
period of building first Cecil House in the Strand and, later,
Hatfield.

This miniature was given to Hoskins but is certainly by
Oliver and shows all the marks of being *ad vivum*. It cannot
have been painted before 1606 when he became a Knight
of the Garter. All Cecil's portraits, however, show him
exactly the same, carefully composed to conceal that he
was a hunch-back. The large-scale paintings can, with a
great deal of certainty, be associated with De Critz and
never change in format, except in attributes, the earliest
being dated 1599 (Strong, *Tudor and Jacobean*, I, p. 275).
The miniature, if it is from life, must have been conceived
from the outset to conform with this established image. The
underdrawing of the ruff is visible. Its condition is good
although there is retouching on the Garter ribbon. Another
miniature of Cecil is recorded at Strawberry Hill
(*Description*, 1784, p. 58). This was sold 10th May 1842
(lot 42) and passed to the Stowe collection and was sold
15th March 1849 (lot 51). It has not reappeared.

COLLECTIONS: Presumably by descent from the sitter's brother,
Thomas Cecil, 1st Marquess of Exeter; first recorded in W. H.
Charlton, *Burghley*, 1847, p. 259 (9).

164

167

170

ISAAC OLIVER

167 Unknown Lady, 1605–10

Private Collection
Vellum stuck onto card, oval, 54 × 44 mm
$2\frac{1}{8} \times 1\frac{3}{4}$ in.

An outstanding miniature by Oliver of a lady in hunting attire in the form of a masculine hat and doublet and looped Hibernian mantle. The colour scheme of black and orange give the miniature, which is in virtually unfaded state, a unique vibrancy.

COLLECTIONS: Part of the collection formed by Walter, 2nd Viscount Bearsted.

ISAAC OLIVER

168 Unknown Lady, Called Alice Spencer, Countess of Derby, c. 1610

Private Collection
Vellum stuck onto a playing card with two hearts verso, oval, 57 × 47 mm, $2\frac{1}{4} \times 1\frac{13}{16}$ in.

Alice, Countess of Derby (1556?–1637), daughter of Sir John Spencer of Althorpe, married first Ferdinando, 5th Earl of Derby and Second, in 1600, Sir Thomas Egerton, 1st Viscount Brackley, later Earl of Ellesmere. In her honour Milton wrote the *Arcades*.

The identity is unlikely. What is certainly an authentic portrait of the Countess of Derby at Stoneleigh Abbey (Lord Leigh), c. 1600, bears little resemblance to the sitter in the miniature. The picture includes coats of arms and SS for her maiden name, Spencer, woven into her ruff. The miniature in format is closely connected with a series of *à l'antique* profile images from the period around 1610 (nos. 225, 230).

As the hair is not a vehicle for an elaborate head-dress it is not a masque portrait. There are paint losses in the background, abrasion to the features, bosom and fur and the only earring has flaked.

COLLECTIONS: Part of the collection formed by Walter, 2nd Viscount Bearsted.

LITERATURE: V & A, 1947 (172).

ISAAC OLIVER

169 Unknown Man, 1610

Victoria & Albert Museum (P.129–1910)
Vellum stuck to a playing card with three spades verso, oval, 55 × 41 mm, $2\frac{5}{32} \times 1\frac{5}{8}$ in.

A striking miniature which, apart from slight flaking around the edge, is in excellent condition. It is a particularly good instance of the relationship of Oliver's portraits to the series of large-scale portraits by William Larkin, executed simultaneously, which set out to achieve the same glossy, startling effect (e.g. esp. Strong, *The English Icon*, p. 327 (349)). The identity as John Donne can be discounted.

INSCRIBED: Signed and dated to the right. *IO* (in monogram); *1610*.

COLLECTIONS: S. Addington sale Christie's 26th April 1883 (lot 96); J. Lumsden Propert Collection; purchased at its dispersal, 1897, by George Salting and bequeathed by him with his collection to the V & A, 1910.

ISAAC OLIVER

170 ?Elizabeth, Lady Willoughby D'Eresby, later Countess of Lindsey, 1610–15

Private Collection
Vellum stuck to card which has been attached to a larger vellum oval upon which the inscription has been written, oval, 55 × 43 mm, $2\frac{3}{16} \times 1\frac{11}{16}$ in.

Although the additional inscription is early, the miniature cannot depict Catherine Bertie, Baroness Willoughby

Isaac Oliver 111

171

The affectation of the antique looped mantle recurs in several portraits c. 1610 (Strong, *The English Icon*, pp. 300 (306–7); 315 (325–26)). The motto, *Alget qui non ardet*, states that he becomes cold who does not burn and, presumably, the flames are ones of passion. As a formula it is a reworking by Oliver of an earlier motif (see no. 163). The fact that the miniature does not appear before the 1911 inventory makes it unlikely that it was ever part of the Ham House collections, conceivably it could have been removed to Ham from Helmingham when the house passed to the Tollemaches. Its condition is good.

COLLECTIONS: First certainly recorded in an inventory of 1911 (information from Mr M. L. Tomlin).

ISAAC OLIVER

172 **Unknown Man**, 1614

Collection of H.R.H. Princess Juliana of the Netherlands
Vellum stuck onto card, oval, 54 × 41 mm,
$2\frac{1}{4} \times 1\frac{5}{8}$ in.

Formerly wrongly identified as the Duke of Buckingham, this is a fine miniature on a large scale. The sitter is attired in black with a plum coloured cloak swathed around him standing against a grey background. There is a marked chiaroscuro effect as the face catches the light to the left while the other side is cast into shadow. It is in outstanding condition apart from fading and some flaking at the edges.

INSCRIBED: To the right: *1614/30/IO* (in monogram).

LITERATURE: Williamson, *History*, 1904, I, pl. XIII (4); Edinburgh, 1975 (73).

d'Eresby in her own right and fourth wife of Charles Brandon, Duke of Suffolk. She died in 1580. It is also unlikely to be her daughter-in-law, Mary de Vere, daughter of John, 16th Earl of Oxford, wife of Peregrine Bertie, Lord Willoughby d'Eresby. A more possible candidate would be Elizabeth, daughter of Edward Montagu, 1st Baron Montague of Boughton, wife of Robert, Lord Willoughby d'Eresby, later 1st Earl of Lindsey. The costume seems closer to c. 1615 (Strong, *The English Icon*, p. 285 (nos. 278–79).

This miniature is a rare instance of Oliver using the wet-in-wet technique crimson velvet curtain background. There is damage in the hair to the left; dark striations in the flesh carnation; oxidized silver and fading.

INSCRIBED: A later inscription reads: *CATHERINE: LADY WILLOUGHBY OF ERESBY DUTCHESSE DOWAGER OF SUFFOLK.*

COLLECTIONS: Bequeathed by Lady Sophia Osborne (d. 1746), third wife of William Fermor, Baron Leominster, to her daughter-in-law, Henrietta Louisa, wife of Thomas Fermore, 2nd Baron Leominster and 1st Earl of Pomfret; Vertue records this, c. 1748: "a limning in an oval a Ladys head dishevilled hair – fair and curiously done by . . . (Oliver I think)" although the inscription was different (*Notebooks*, V, p. 68); subsequent history unknown until acquired, 1929, by Walter, 2nd Viscount Bearsted.

LITERATURE: V & A, 1947 (174).

ISAAC OLIVER

173 **Elizabeth Harding, Mrs Oliver**, 1610–15

Private Collection
Vellum stuck to a playing card with three clubs verso, oval, 52 × 42 mm, $2\frac{1}{16} \times 1\frac{5}{8}$ in.

Elizabeth Harden or Harding (1589–buried between 1628 and 1640), daughter of James Harding, a court musician married Isaac Oliver in 1606 and bore him six children. After his death she married a mercer, Pierce Morgan.

One of the finest miniatures Oliver ever painted. It is undated and the dating can only be done on costume. Embroidered jackets of this type are a feature of Jacobean dress and they appear most frequently in portraits from c. 1610–15 (Strong, *The English Icon*, pp. 301 (309); 330 (354); 331 (356)). Reynolds' dating of the miniature c. 1595 is surely far too early. Oliver married three times and the sitter must be his third wife, Elizabeth Harden or Harding, whom he married at Isleworth in 1606. (Mary Edmond, "Limners and Picturemakers", *Walpole Society*, XLVII, 1980, pp. 74–6.) The directness and joyous

ISAAC OLIVER

171 **Unknown Man**, c. 1610

Victoria & Albert Museum (Ham House 379–1948)
Vellum stuck to card extended by another piece of card glued to the back, presumably to fit the miniature into its later seventeenth century turned ebony frame, oval, 52 × 44 mm, $2\frac{1}{16} \times 1\frac{11}{16}$ in.

A brilliant miniature with the sitter draped in an *à l'antique* mantle and surrounded on all sides by gold and red flames.

172

173

175

informality spring from a knowledge of the tradition of Dutch portraiture that was at exactly this period producing Frans Hals's earliest work. It is also a remarkable instance of Oliver's control of colour, the whole being conceived in white and grey with touches of silver, including the abandonment of a blue background in favour of grey. There is a little flaking at the edges, the lead whites have blackened, the features faded and the silver oxidized.

This does not appear to be identical with the portrait of his wife recorded in Charles II's inventory, c. 1662–85 (393): "Isaac Oliver, Isaac Oliver's wife in a Ruffe".

COLLECTIONS: Edward Harley, Earl of Oxford (1689–1741); Vertue's Catalogue, 1743 (no. 81): "The Wife of Isaac Oliver, Limner, done by himself"; Oxford's daughter married William Bentinck, Duke of Portland; thence by descent.

LITERATURE: Goulding, *Welbeck*, p. 67 (22). V & A, 1947 (154).

ISAAC OLIVER

174 **Diana**, 1615

Victoria & Albert Museum (P.9–1940)
Gouache on sized cambric laid down on to a thin panel of limewood, oval, 86 × 64 mm, $3\frac{3}{8} \times 2\frac{17}{32}$ in.

Unique amongst Oliver's *oeuvre* both in technique and subject matter, this is a miniature of outstanding quality comparable to the one of his wife (no. 173) or the full length of Dorset (no. 276). The identity as Diana is secured by the crescent-moon in her head-dress. This is the only miniature in which Oliver embarks onto subject matter normally the preserve of his drawings. The stylistic source is Dutch mannerist mythological painting of the type stemming from Spranger via Goltzius, indeed, the miniature suggests that it is copied from part of a

mythological picture. This is perfectly possible as the Low Countries and Venice were the two sources drawn upon for the formation of picture collections in early seventeenth century England, the earliest of which were Prince Henry's and Robert Cecil's. The Prince's we know included substantial purchases of Netherlandish pictures. His mother also collected and a *Diana and her Nymphs* is recorded at Oatlands, a picture which may have been hers but might equally have come to her on Henry's death (O. Millar, *The Queen's Pictures*, London, 1977, p. 24). The edges have been trimmed in modern times.

INSCRIBED: To the right: *1615 /IO* (in monogram).

COLLECTIONS: H. Reynolds Solly sale, Sotheby's 27th June 1940 (lot 136); purchased with funds from the R. H. Stephenson Bequest.

LITERATURE: V & A, 1947 (193).

ISAAC OLIVER

175 **Head of Christ**, probably after c. 1610

Victoria & Albert Museum (P.15–1931)
Vellum stuck to plain card, oval, 53 × 43 mm, $2\frac{1}{8} \times 1\frac{23}{32}$ in.

One of the most extraordinary of all Oliver's miniatures, both in respect of style and subject-matter. The head is built up entirely in terms of light and shade without any linear effects which sets it apart as an extreme example of the artist's reaction to Hilliard's linear tradition and a vivid index of his own response to Italian Renaissance painting.

The dating of the *Head of Christ* is not easy, nor is it helped by any stylistic parallels. I would be inclined to date it after c. 1610. That religious works were coming back into fashion may be measured by Robert Cecil's decoration of the Chapel at Hatfield House. Indeed the closest parallel is the bust of Christ at Hatfield which was there before 1629, probably one of Robert Cecil's purchases, by an unidentified Italian artist of the early Baroque period (E. Auerbach and C. K. Adams, *Paintings*

177

178

179

and Sculpture at Hatfield House, London, 1971, p. 109 (119), pl. 94). The head is of a generalized North Italian type in the manner of Correggio, which would account for the very high esteem in which it was held in the eighteenth century, though modern taste prefers Oliver's portraits to what are now regarded as derivative religious pieces. There is slight abrasion on the cheek and beard and slight losses at the edge.

INSCRIBED: Signed to the right: *IO* in monogram.

COLLECTIONS: Dr Richard Mead (1673–1754); recorded by Vertue between 1736 and 1741 (*Notebooks*, IV, *Walpole Society*, XXIV, 1934–35, p. 187); recorded in *Musei Meadiani Pars Altera*, Langford, 1755 under the section *Picturae Minori Formae*: "CHRISTI caput longa caesarie flavescente promissa barbe et oculis occlusis, cui gratias omnes divinas circumfluit artiflex. *Isaaci Oliver celeberrimi pictoris opus praestantissimum*" (in the British Library's *Life of Dr Richard Mead. Catalogue of Dr Mead's Library, Museum*, etc, London, 1754–55); sold on the fourth day of the Mead sale, 14th March 1755 (lot 38); "Head of our saviour very capital, by Isaac Oliver"; purchased by Margaret Cavendish Harley, Duchess of Portland (d. 1785); op. cit., loc. cit.); sold by auction by Mr Skinner & Co, 24th April 1786 and following days, 24th May (lot 2947): "A *remarkable fine* MINIATURE HEAD of OUR SAVIOUR by *Isaac Oliver*, set in gold. Nothing can exceed the gracefulness, benevolence, and meekness, expressed in this picture. N.B. *It was purchased*

out of the well-known Collection of the late Dr Mead"; purchased by George 5th Earl of Stamford; sold by the 10th Earl of Stamford, Christie's 3rd March 1931 (lot 25); purchased for the V & A.

LITERATURE: V & A, 1947 (192).

ISAAC OLIVER

176 Unknown Lady, c. 1615

Victoria & Albert Museum (P.24–1932)
Vellum stuck to a playing card with two diamonds verso, oval, 55 × 44 mm, $2\frac{1}{8} \times 1\frac{3}{4}$ in.

A competent late miniature by Oliver suffering only noticeably from flaking on the picture box pinned to the sitter's dress. There is a tiny enamelled insect on her ruff. The miniature is still in the original locket, from which the lid has been wrenched. The sitter is unidentified, but as it was sold from the collections of the Earls of Moray, one of their ancestors is a possibility.

INSCRIBED: To the left of the head: *Aetatis Suae 50.*

COLLECTIONS: Sold from the collection of the 17th Earl of Moray Christie's 30 June 1932 (lot 131); purchased with funds from the Capt. H. B. Murray bequest.

LITERATURE: *Burlington Magazine*, LXIV, 1934, p. 233 (c).
Winter, *Elizabethan Miniatures*, pl. XIV (c).
V & A, 1947 (186).

ISAAC OLIVER

177 Unknown Lady, c. 1615

Victoria & Albert Museum (P.39–1941)
Vellum stuck to plain card, oval, 54 × 43 mm,
$2\frac{1}{8} \times 1\frac{11}{16}$ in.

A fussy, late miniature, Hilliardesque in mood, with a
greater concern for the details of the dress, lace and
embroidery than with any deep interpretation of character.
In good condition apart from very slight paint losses,
fading and oxidization. There is no substance to the
identity given to it as "Lady Hunsdon". This is a typical
instance of Oliver in an unadventurous mood when the
sitter clearly did not interest him.

INSCRIBED: Signed in monogram above the shoulder right: *IO*

COLLECTIONS: Given by Mrs S. S. Joseph, 1941, previous history
    unknown.

LITERATURE: V & A, 1947 (187).

ISAAC OLIVER

178 John Donne, 1616

H.M. The Queen
Vellum stuck to card, oval, 44 × 36 mm, $1\frac{3}{4} \times 1\frac{7}{16}$ in.

John Donne (1573–1631), poet and divine, Dean of St
Paul's from 1621.

A brilliant *ad vivum* miniature, although bearing the
perfectly authentic date of 1616, painted in Oliver's early
1590s manner, with a looseness in the brushstrokes and a
lighter Hilliardesque palette. Donne was ordained on 25th
January 1614/5 and appointed a royal chaplain almost
immediately. Painted in the year April 1st 1616 to March
31st 1616/7 Donne is recorded as divinity reader to the
benchers of Lincoln's Inn. It was engraved by Matthaus
Merian II for Donne's *LXXX Sermons* (1640). The
iconography of Donne is discussed at length by Sir Geoffrey
Keynes, *Bibliography of the Works of John Donne*, Cambridge,
2nd ed., 1932, pp. 182–84 and Strong, *Tudor and Jacobean*,
I, p. 66. There is a small restoration in the background at
the top edge.

INSCRIBED: To left of the head: ·*1616*·; and signed *IO* (in
    monogram) right.

COLLECTIONS: Lord Northwick sale, Thirlestane House,
    Cheltenham, 5th August 1859 (lot 740): "Portrait of the
    celebrated Dr Donne in a black dress with frill. Isaac Oliver";
    C. Sackville Bale sale 24th May 1881 (lot 1426); acquired for
    the Royal Collection.

LITERATURE: See above and also: V & A, 1947 (194).
Auerbach, *Hilliard*, p. 251, pl. 222; 331 (257).

ISAAC OLIVER

179 Madonna and Child in Glory, c. 1610–17?

Beaverbrook Art Gallery, Fredericton
Vellum laid down on panel, 27.64 × 20.32 cm,
$10\frac{7}{8} \times 8$ in.

One of the most puzzling and important of all Oliver's
miniatures. Edward Norgate records in his *Miniaturia* (ed.
Martin Hardie, Oxford, 1919, p. 55) that the miniaturist
spent two years on painting it which establishes not only his
obsession with subject miniatures but also that it was
unlikely to have been a commission. Its sources raise an
intriguing hypothesis: did Oliver return to Italy about
1610? The influences indicate that this is highly likely. The
mannerist Federico Barrocci's engraving, the *Madonna of the
Clouds* is the source from which is derived the general lines
of the composition and the placing, but in reverse, of the
figures. The second is more problematic, for the Madonna
and, above all, the child suggests that Oliver must have
seen Rubens' "Madonna della Vallicella" painted for the
church of the Oratorians in Rome in 1608 (Michael Jaffé,
Rubens and Italy, Oxford, 1977, pl. XII). In this miniature
Oliver moves on from mannerism and begins to experiment
with the baroque.

The contrast between this miniature, so pure an
expression of Counter Reformation Catholicism, and the
Oliver whose children were baptized at the French
Protestant Church is difficult to reconcile. Even more
extraordinary is that he was able, simultaneously, to paint
an iconic portrait in the manner of Larkin (no. 277) to
satisfy the tastes of a rich aristocratic client while
essaying for his own delectation a style and subject matter
so totally alien and remote from those of Jacobean
England. It is evidence of the enormous impact on him of
the new forms of Catholic religious art, one more familiar
in the literary scene with figures such as Richard Crashaw.
A copy by Peter Oliver is in the Royal Collection (A.
Oppé, *English Drawings . . . in the Collection of H.M. the King*,
London, 1950, p. 80 (470)). Richard Symonds records in
his *Notebook*, 1653, a miniature of a Madonna and child by
Oliver in the collection of Lady Anne Mary Howard,
eldest daughter of Edward Somerset, 2nd Marquess of
Worcester, wife of Henry Howard a grandson of the 1st
Earl of Arundel (Mary Harvey, *The life, correspondence and
collections of Thomas Howard, Earl of Arundel*, London 1921,
p. 251).

INSCRIBED: Lower right: *IO* (in monogram).

COLLECTIONS: A. Rofe collection; sold Sotheby's 18th November
    1959 (lot 16).

ISAAC OLIVER

180 Nymphs and Satyrs, 1610–15

H.M. The Queen
Black and white on brown paper, 20.5 × 35.7 cm,
$8\frac{1}{8} \times 13\frac{7}{8}$ in.

One of the most astonishing of Oliver's drawings, executed
with a high degree of finish as a work of art in its own

right. The subject-matter is without parallel in Jacobean
art, a scene of extreme eroticism with satyrs pursuing or
carrying off nymphs or engaging in amorous dalliance in a
woodland setting centered on a lake. The stylistic source
lies in the Netherlandish response to Italian mannerist art
as interpreted by Bartholomäeus Spranger (1546–1611).
The ingredients were violent contortions and
foreshortenings, particularly of elongated nudes, with a
sharp difference between the foreground and a distant
perspective. *Nymphs and Satyrs* particularly evokes the work
of Cornelis van Haarlem (1562–1638). The subject also
presupposes drawing from the nude model.

    Nymphs and Satyrs is Oliver's most accomplished drawing.
As with his other drawings the dating can only be
conjectural. Although its sources are Flemish artists
reacting to Spranger in the 1590s, it seems more reasonable
to place it in the Jacobean period. A related drawing of
Antiope is in the British Museum (Croft-Murray and
Hulton, *Catalogue*, I, p. 22 (7)).

INSCRIBED: Signed *Ollivier*; and on an inset: *Isac: Olivier Fec.*

COLLECTIONS: King James II, catalogue no. 638: "A drawing in
    black and white of Satyrs and women sporting. By Isaac
    Oliver".

LITERATURE: A. P. Oppé, *English Drawings . . . in the Collection of
    H.M. The King at Windsor Castle*, London, 1950, p. 79 (460).

ISAAC OLIVER

181 "The Entombment", post 1596, perhaps c. 1615

The British Museum, Department of Prints and Drawings
(1945-9-24-2)
Black chalk, pen and dark brown ink and wash,
heightened with white, 29.5 × 37.7 cm, $11\frac{5}{8} \times 14\frac{7}{8}$ in.

The drawing was made as a preliminary study for his large
limning of the same subject which was in the collection of
Charles I (O. Millar's *Walpole Society*, XXXVII, 1960,
pp. 103, 213; Edward Norgate, *Miniatures of the Art of
Limning*, ed. Martin Hardie, Oxford, 1918, p. 55). This is
now in the Musée d'Angers and was left, as van der Dort
records, unfinished at Oliver's death in 1617, subsequently
finished by his son, Peter. The miniature had no less than
twenty-six figures in it, more than in this drawing. The fact
that the limning was eventually acquired by Charles I
indicates that it was not a commissioned work. The
drawing perhaps may be dated c. 1615 to the period when
Oliver must have begun the limning, which was dated
1616, but we cannot necessarily draw that conclusion. It
re-works certain motifs from his 1586 *Lamentation* (no. 136),
presupposing that he still had that drawing in his
possession. As a composition *The Entombment* re-interprets
the earlier work in the light of his visit (or visits) to Italy.
The over-large figures are abandoned in favour of heroic
high Renaissance or sinuous Parmigianesque types placed
within a definable architectural space. The two *putti* to the
left introduce an oddly playful note into what is conceived
as a monumental religious scene.

INSCRIBED: In the lower right hand corner: *Isa: Ollivier*. On the
    reverse there are two notes by Vertue on its history.

COLLECTIONS: Theodore Russell (?); his son Anthony Russell;
    purchased by George Vertue; sold Ford, 19th May 1757
    (lot 81); Thomas Hollis I; Thomas Hollis II; sold Sotheby's
    30th April 1817 (lot 1688); Charles Carnegie, 11th Earl of
    Southesk; presented by N.A.C.F., 1945.

LITERATURE: Vertue, *Notebooks*, I, p. 130.
V & A, 1947 (202).
E. Croft-Murray and P. Hulton, *Catalogue of British Drawings*,
    London, British Museum, 1960, I, p. 23 (11).

Elizabeth I and the Limners

I HILLIARD, THE QUEEN'S PAINTER, 1572–c. 1580

The earliest portrait of Elizabeth by Hilliard is dated 1572 (no. 182). This marks the advent of a relationship between monarch and painter that was to last thirty years, but it was not to be a continuous one. From the very beginning of the reign government had been faced with the problem of controlling the quality of royal portraiture. A draft proclamation from 1563 indicates the process of control that was envisaged, the admission of an artist to the Queen's presence whose task was to produce a pattern that was then to be freely available for use by other artists. Such an arrangement certainly explains the fact that although portraits of Elizabeth I are clearly executed by a wide variety of hands, the face pattern always remains the same.

The relationship of Elizabeth and Hilliard falls into three distinct phases. The earliest lasted only a few years in the seventies prior to his departure for France. There was no question at that date of the systematic proliferation of her image to promote a cult as happened later. Instead it was individual portraits commissioned for a purpose, in particular for marriage or other diplomatic negotiations.

The 1572 miniature is far more assured already than any of those painted by Levina Teerlinc who died the year Hilliard left for France. But his large-scale portraits, based on the style emanating from the Master of the Countess of Warwick, are considerably less accomplished than, for instance, Hans Eworth's portraits of Mary I. They are flat and schematic, the face merely lines on a surface, and it is open to question as to how successful these were in fact regarded at the time. Hilliard's liaison with the Queen must have been far from settled in the 1570s. It was threatened firstly by the arrival of Federigo Zuccaro in 1575, a major Italian artist, brought over by Leicester during the summer that he staged his famous fêtes at Kenilworth. It is arguable that Zuccaro in fact is the painter of the celebrated Darnley Portrait (National Portrait Gallery), a revolutionary image in which the Queen is represented threequarter length turned to the right in a manner which must have emphasized to everyone the extreme provinciality of the Pelican and Phoenix Portraits by Hilliard (nos. 183, 184).

Even although Zuccaro had departed by the time that Hilliard went to France his effect must have been unsettling. There was also native competition in the shape of George Gower who was quickly emerging as a fashionable portrait painter. Indeed as far as the Queen was concerned it was an inept time for Hilliard to go abroad. As a result in 1577 she found herself unable to send a life-size portrait of herself to Don John of Austria because her painter was in France. She cannot have been pleased so that it is hardly surprising that in 1578–79 Hilliard had to re-establish his position at court. It was Gower and not

Hilliard who was appointed Serjeant Painter in 1581, although the latter was quite capable of fulfilling the role but had proved unreliable. A draft patent for 1584 suggests that Gower wished to consolidate his position even further by cutting Hilliard out of all forms of royal portraiture except for miniatures. He was, fortunately, not successful.

SELECT BIBLIOGRAPHY

Strong, *Portraits of Queen Elizabeth I.*
STRONG, *Renaissance Miniature*, pp. 81–92.

NICHOLAS HILLIARD

182 Elizabeth I, 1572

National Portrait Gallery (108)
Vellum stuck to a playing card with part of a queen showing at the reverse, oval, 52 × 47 mm, $2\frac{1}{16} \times 1\frac{7}{8}$ in.

Important though this *ad vivum* miniature is as the earliest portrait of the Queen, its condition is very poor. The face has been completely re-painted softening the image, whereas under ultra-violet light it is possible to discern remains of a more vigorous linear rendering of the Queen's features compatible with their treatment in the Pelican Portrait (no. 184). V. J. Murrell observes that the jewels are applied in opaque paint and that Hilliard had not yet established his resin technique which was in use by 1576 in his miniature of Leicester (no. 68). The ruff has been scraped off entirely and the present one is restoration.

The dress includes typical naturalistic decorative features, such as the white rose pinned to her left shoulder. The crowned *ER* echoes exactly the rose and fleur de lys in the Pelican Portrait (no. 184).

INSCRIBED: On either side of the head: *E | R* (crowned); *Ano Dni. 1572. | Ætatis suae 38*:-

COLLECTIONS: Purchased from a Mrs Sarah Mallet of St Helier, Jersey, via C. B. Hue, 1860.

LITERATURE: O'Donoghue, *Catalogue*, 1894, (3).
V & A, 1947 (6).
Auerbach, *Hilliard*, p. 63, pl. 21; 290 (19).
Strong, *Portraits of Queen Elizabeth I*, p. 89 (3).
Strong, *Tudor and Jacobean*, I, p. 101; II, pl. 190.

NICHOLAS HILLIARD

183 Elizabeth I, 1572–76

National Portrait Gallery (190)
Oil on Panel, 78.8 × 61 cm, 31 × 24 in.

When, in 1966, this and the Pelican Portrait (no. 184) were examined *in tandem*, there was no doubt that they were by the same painter and one face-mask can be superimposed onto the other, but in reverse. Infra-red photographs establish that the position of the lips was altered. As in the case of no. 184 this portrait gives us a glimpse of Hilliard's style in large-scale painting during the short period of four to five years from when he began to paint the Queen to when he left for France. The presentation is considerably stiffer than his approach as we know it from the miniatures. Later, influenced by French court art, it became far softer. The portrait takes its name from the Phoenix Jewel suspended from her carcanet, the phoenix being one of the Queen's most familiar emblems. ·

COLLECTIONS: Possibly bequeathed by Gabriel Goodman, Dean of Westminster (1529?–1601) with his household stuff to Christ's Hospital, Ruthin, which he founded in 1590; first recorded, 1839; acquired by the N.P.G., 1865.

LITERATURE: See Strong, *Tudor and Jacobean*, I, pp. 101–102 (190).
Strong, *The English Icon*, p. 160 (106).

NICHOLAS HILLIARD

184 Elizabeth I, 1572–76

Walker Art Gallery, Liverpool
Oil on Panel, 76.6 × 59.6 cm, 30¼ × 23½ in.
(Photograph)

This has long been attributed to Hilliard and, in the light of all the evidence that Hilliard produced oil paintings certainly down to at least 1600 (Strong, *Renaissance Miniature*, pp. passim), the attribution of this portrait is more than hypothesis. Infra-red examination of the repainted face of the 1572 miniature (no. 182) reveals it as very close to the schematic rendering of the Queen's features in this and in its companion, the Phoenix Portrait (no. 183). The approach has little to do with Hans Eworth or Steven van der Muelen but springs more directly out of the flat decorative style of a fashionable portrait painter of the 1560s whose work is fairly easily recognizable, the Master of the Countess of Warwick (no. 52). Hilliard places the sitter in the panel in the same manner but with the arms slightly cut into; the pose is rigid and upright and

the gesture of the hand holding gloves is a variant of ones in the Master's repertory (Strong, *The English Icon*, pp. 108 (55), 112 (60)). The unrepeated innovation is the *trompe l'oeil* gold fringe across the top of the picture.

The picture's name derives from the Pelican Jewel pinned to the bodice, a pelican being one of Elizabeth's most familiar emblems, alluding to her as the nursing mother of the Church of England. From these earliest portraits it is clear that Hilliard was faithfully recording what he actually saw in the way of the Queen's dress and jewels. The dating can now be more definite, as between 1572 and 1576, when Hilliard left for France.

COLLECTIONS: The Howards, Earls of Suffolk of Charlton Park; presented by E. Peter Jones to the Walker Art Gallery, 1945.

LITERATURE: See Strong, *Portraits of Queen Elizabeth I*, p. 60 (23) for previous bibliography.
Strong, *Tudor and Jacobean*, I, p. 110.
Strong, *The English Icon*, p. 161 (107).

NICHOLAS HILLIARD

185 Elizabeth I, c. 1575

Mrs E. Hamilton
Vellum stuck to plain card, oval,
18 × 15 mm, 23⁄32 × 19⁄32 in.

This and its pendant of Leicester (no. 186) show every sign of being *ad vivum* portraits on a minute scale that must have been painted for insertion into a jewel, conceivably as a gift from Leicester to the Queen. The presentation of the Earl as consort manqué indicates that these miniatures were once part of an object of extreme intimacy. This miniature must date to very shortly before Hilliard left for France and is of the utmost importance. The costume is virtually identical to that in the Darnley Portrait (Strong, *Portraits of Queen Elizabeth I*, p. 60, pl. VIII). The features are faded, the silver oxidized and there is slight flaking at the edges.

COLLECTIONS: R. H. Spurway, Fredericton, New Brunswick; sold Christie's 28th October 1970 (lot 124).

NICHOLAS HILLIARD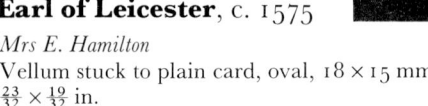

186 Robert Dudley, Earl of Leicester, c. 1575

Mrs E. Hamilton
Vellum stuck to plain card, oval, 18 × 15 mm,
23⁄32 × 19⁄32 in.
See no. 68.

See under no. 185. One of a pair of Elizabeth and Leicester with every indication that they were *ad vivum* and painted for insertion, probably into a jewel. There are some losses in the background due to water damage.

COLLECTIONS: See no. 185.

II THE CREATION OF THE LEGEND, c. 1580–90

There is a marked escalation in the production of royal portraits in all media in the 1580s. This is a direct reflection of the political confrontation with Spain as England moved towards the year of the Armada. More noticeably than ever before in the Tudor period was the potency of royal portraiture as political propaganda recognized and it is in this decade that the Elizabeth legend was manufactured. Statistically the numbers of oil portraits multiply, Hilliard, for the first time repeats miniatures of the Queen, and new media are explored, single engravings of her as votive images and medallions with rings for suspension around the neck.

There can be no doubt that all this must have been prompted by the government but it was Hilliard who carried out its visual expression. His presentation of Elizabeth becomes markedly different from the 1570s, increasingly iconic and stylized as he set about presenting her as a being sacred and set apart. Her robes can be lifted up by heavenly hands and celestial rays can encircle her head.

The Hilliard workshop cannot have been confined to producing a trickle of miniatures. The surviving images all point to the Gutter Lane workshop being the source for a wide range of royal portraits for which Hilliard drew the designs. Inevitably as these were carried out by artists whose work was inferior in quality the results are variable but the design remains firmly Hilliardesque.

SELECT BIBLIOGRAPHY
Strong, *Portraits of Queen Elizabeth I, passim.*
Strong, *Renaissance Miniature,* pp. 81–92.

NICHOLAS HILLIARD

187 Elizabeth I, c. 1580

The Trustee of the Will of the 8th Earl of Berkeley
Vellum stuck onto card, oval, 48 × 39 mm,
$1\frac{7}{8} \times 1\frac{9}{16}$ in.

The most outstanding portrait of the Queen by Hilliard, painted soon after his return from France, but the dramatic impact has been lessened by the oxidization of the dress which was once silver and shimmered, standing out against the chair upholstered in black and trimmed with gold. The draughtsmanship of the hands and the lute epitomize Hilliard at the height of his graphic powers. Apart from the oxidization, there is slight flaking.

The costume would indicate a date shortly after 1580 and is closely paralleled in a large-scale oil portrait, also probably by him (Strong, *Portraits of Queen Elizabeth I,* p. 60 (25)). There is no precedent for a portrait of a Tudor monarch playing a musical instrument; it may celebrate Elizabeth's own musical virtuosity as much as being an allegory on the harmony of the body politic. Its descent would indicate that it was painted for the Queen's cousin, Henry Carey, 1st Lord Hunsdon.

187

188

COLLECTIONS: Probably belonged to Henry Carey, 1st Lord Hunsdon; his grand-daughter, Elizabeth, married Sir Thomas Berkeley; recorded at Berkeley Castle in 1796 as "Queen Elizabeth playing on a Mandoline" (B.L. Additional MS 6391, f.58v).

LITERATURE: Auerbach, *Hilliard,* pp. 66, pl. 23; 290 (20). Strong, *Portraits of Queen Elizabeth I,* p. 89 (4).

NICHOLAS HILLIARD

188 Elizabeth I, c. 1580

H.M. The Queen
Vellum stuck to plain card, circular, 24.5 mm,
$1\frac{15}{16}$ in. diam.

As there is considerable restoration in the face and costume it is impossible to ascertain whether the miniature is *ad vivum.* The image, however, bears resemblances both to Hilliard's rendering of the Queen in the lost Prayer Book and to the Sieve Portrait at Sienna (Strong, *The English Icon* p. 157 (105)) suggesting a date in the very early 1580s. The costume and hairstyle cannot be as late as c. 1590 as suggested by Reynolds and Auerbach. There is slight flaking at the right edge and the highlights of the pearls have been re-painted.

The miniature is the earliest one of the Queen to survive in an original locket, a modest one compared with the elaboration which was to set in from the Drake Jewel, 1586/7, onwards. The locket is enamelled on the obverse and reverse in red with white enamelled sides very similar to a later one of James I (no. 238).

COLLECTIONS: Lowndes family; Wertheimer; given by Archibald, 5th Earl of Rosebery to Queen Victoria on the occasion of her Golden Jubilee, 1887.

LITERATURE: *Ceremonial of Her Majesty's Jubilee,* 1887, p. 56. V & A, 1947 (49).
Auerbach, *Hilliard,* pp. 92, pl. 60; 297 (55).
Strong, *Portraits of Queen Elizabeth I,* p. 90 (5); Edinburgh, 1975 (5).

?NICHOLAS HILLIARD

189 Elizabeth I, c. 1580

John Rylands University Library of Manchester
Woodcut, 11.8 × 8.9 cm, 4⅝ × 3½ in.

Added to a series of Kings and Queens of England published by Giles Godhed in 1560–62. The eulogistic verses point to a date well on in the reign and the costume is of the first half of the 1580s. An attribution to Hilliard is a distinct possibility; the arrangement of the figure with flanking crowned E and R recall Hilliard's 1572 miniature (no. 182) and the crowned rose and fleur de lys in the Pelican Portrait (no. 184). The position of the fingers holding the sceptre is identical with the mannerisms in the Emmanuel College Charter (no. 191). The head, ruff and costume are variants of those in the miniature formerly in the Bagot and now in the Royal Collection (Strong, *Renaissance Miniature*, pl. 96). A separate impression exists in the British Museum.

LITERATURE: H. Huth, *Ancient Broadsides and Ballads*, Philobiblon
    Society, London, 1867, pp. 52–53.
Strong, *Portraits of Queen Elizabeth I*, p. 124 (15).
T. F. Dibdin, *Aedes Althorpiae*, 1822, pp. 180–4

NICHOLAS HILLIARD

190 Elizabeth I, c. 1585

Victoria & Albert Museum (P.9–1943)
Pen and ink on vellum, rectangular, 13.7 × 11.6 cm, 5¹³⁄₃₂ × 4⁹⁄₁₆ in. (the borders have been chamferred).

There are only three surviving drawings certainly by Nicholas Hilliard, of which this is the earliest. The costume in this drawing, which was originally rectangular, is from a decade earlier and the silhouette and details of the dress can be closely paralleled in a series of dated images of Elizabeth I. The first is the illuminated charter for Mildmay College, 1584 (no. 191), the second the "Ermine Portrait" at Hatfield, 1585 and the third the "Armada Portrait", celebrating the defeat of the Spanish Armada in 1588, at Woburn Abbey (Auerbach, *Hilliard*, pl. 77). The formal bows across the shoulders and down the front of the dress are indeed identical to those in the "Armada Portrait". So spectacular are both dress and jewels that there can be no doubt that this drawing, until now regarded as being of a lady of the court, must be of Elizabeth I. The face, rendered in linear terms, is perfectly compatible with dated images from these years.

Pope-Hennessy cites this drawing as evidence for Hilliard's likely use of an optical device similar to that which must have been used by Holbein for executing this type of very precise drawing. All the technical evidence, however, excludes such a possibility: this is a drawing direct from life. He also locates the style as French which is not likely. Although Hilliard was familiar with the work of the Clouets, his drawing style stems from a direct imitation of Holbein linked with the copying of woodcuts, especially those by Dürer, both of which he specifically recommends as basic training in his *Treatise* and the treatment of the folds in the sleeves of the dress is directly Düreresque. Technical evidence would not support Pope-

Hennessy's assertion that "the painting of Hilliard's miniatures was almost certainly prefaced by careful graphic studies" and that a series of pattern drawings parallel to the Holbein series at Windsor must once have existed. On the contrary, all Hilliard's miniatures were conceived direct with no preliminary studies, making this drawing something quite exceptional. It is at this period, c. 1585, that Hilliard began to paint large, full-length miniatures, so perhaps this was a drawing in preparation for an especially splendid miniature of the Queen. There is however, another more likely possibility. In 1584, Hilliard designed a second Great Seal, for which the Queen's commission runs: "You shall embosse . . . patterns for a new Great Seal according to the last pattern made upon parchment by Our servant Hilliard'. The obverse of that seal is identical in silhouette to the drawing but clearly not the same. The commission, however, states that this was "according to the *last* pattern" meaning that others had been prepared and rejected. It can therefore be suggested that this drawing may be connected with the preparation of patterns for submission to the Queen. The drawing is clearly, even the face, from life and the placing of the figure outdoors fulfils exactly the Queen's famous choice of location to sit for her miniaturist: "in the open alley of a goodly garden, where no tree was near, nor any shadow at all" (Strong, *Portraits of Queen Elizabeth I*, p. 8).

Two full-length miniatures of Elizabeth did once exist; one is recorded in the will of his son, Laurence: "Queen Elizabeth drawn from head to foot in a small volume and in a jet box" and the second, referred to by De Piles, "a whole length of her sitting in her throne, which was deservedly esteem'd" (Auerbach, *Hilliard*, pp. 229–30).

COLLECTIONS: Francis Wellesley collection, sold Sotheby's June-
    July 1920 (lot 428); A. G. B. Russell; presented by the
    N.A.C.F., 1943.

LITERATURE: V & A, 1947 (106)
John Woodward, *Tudor and Stuart Drawings*, London, 1949, No. 6.
Pope-Hennessy, *Lecture*, 1949, p. 26, pl. XXV.
Auerbach, *Hilliard*, pp. 184–6, 320 (188).

NICHOLAS HILLIARD AND ASSISTANTS

191 Charter Authorising Sir Walter Mildmay to found Emmanuel College, Cambridge, 11th January 1584

The Master and Fellows of Emmanuel College, Cambridge

Nicholas Hilliard knew Sir Walter Mildmay (1520?–1589); a letter dated 28th June, presumably 1582, by his patron, Robert Dudley, Earl of Leicester, intervened for the miniaturist, who actually carried the letter himself to Mildmay who was Chancellor of the Exchequer, (Auerbach, *Hilliard*, p. 19). Mildmay was made Treasurer of the Household in 1558 and became Chancellor in 1566, a post that he held until his death. He was a man of puritan persuasion, a motivation behind the founding of Emmanuel College, Cambridge, the new building of which was opened in 1588.

The charter for the creation of the College is dated 11th January 1584. Auerbach, in 1961, wrote that "it seems possible that he had a hand in the Mildmay Charter" (*ibid.*, p. 88). A detailed examination of the Charter reinforces this, but makes it equally clear that such an illumination was a co-operative project. The overall design is Hilliard's but the figure of the Queen and the surrounding throne and canopy alone are painted by him. The degree of finish given to this area is unusually high and the technical tricks, drawing and brushwork are no different from those Hilliard uses on the portrait miniatures. The face-mask of the Queen is identical to that in the miniature formerly in the Bagot collection (Strong, *Renaissance Miniature*, pl. 96) and the general conception of the figure anticipates the second Great Seal (no. 193). The figures in the upright of the letter are Justice and Prudence.

As the colouring of the two decorative borders is by an inferior hand and more schematic in treatment, it can, of course, be argued that the figure of the Queen has been set into a border designed by another artist. Attribution to Hilliard for its design can only be argued on grounds of style and compositional motifs. The delicacy and lightness of its curving sprays of leaves and flowers, butterflies and insects and indented swags of drapery are in his manner. The source for this type of grotesque-work border as exemplified to the left was probably the decoration of Nonsuch Palace. A series of grotesque-work panels painted sometime after 1543 and attributed to Toto del Nunziata at Loseley House probably come from the demolished palace. They are exactly in the format of the left hand border. (E. Croft-Murray, *Decorative Painting in England, 1537–1837*, London, 1962, pp. 18, 165 (2), pl. 17–19)

Any reconstitution of Hilliard's work as a graphic designer depends largely on relating items stylistically to the idiosyncrasies here. The basic ingredient is always to embroider over a basic framework with serpenting detail.

In the same year a charter for Ashbourne Grammar School repeats the Emmanuel College design but is inferior in execution (rep. *Burlington Magazine*, CXX, 1978, p. 734 fig. 20).

COLLECTIONS: At Emmanuel College since its foundation.

LITERATURE: Auerbach, *Hilliard*, pp. 88–90; 323 (199).

NICHOLAS HILLIARD

192 Elizabeth I, c. 1586–87

Victoria & Albert Museum (P.23–1975)
Vellum stuck onto plain card, oval, 45 × 37 mm,
$1\frac{3}{4} \times 1\frac{15}{32}$ in.

About 1586–87 we have, for the first time, clear evidence of Hilliard multiplying the same miniature of the Queen. Three versions are extant of this face-mask, the second, in the Drake Jewel, contains the regnal year enabling us to date it to 1586–87 (Strong, *Renaissance Miniature*, pl. 98) and the third is in the Beauchamp Collection (Auerbach, *Hilliard*, pl. 57). None of the versions, including the V & A one, is from life. All, however, observe the Queen's dresses and jewels correctly. This version includes details such as the black picture box secured by an orange bow at her left

191

breast and, more important, a very early allusion to her as the moon-goddess, Cynthia or Diana, in the crescent-jewel nestling in her hair which is also scattered with tiny arrows (a further allusion to Diana, as goddess of the chase?). The other early dated visual allusion to the moon-cult is in the portrait of Sir Walter Raleigh, dated 1588, in the National Portrait Gallery (Strong, *Tudor and Jacobean*, I, pp. 256–57; II, pl. 505).

Basically the miniature is in good condition with minor losses, oxidization of the silver and a little damage due to moisture.

INSCRIBED: The miniature is set into a seventeenth century vellum mount with bands of lettering in black and gold; inscribed on either side: *ELISA.* | *BETHA; Regina* | *Angliae.*

COLLECTIONS: This miniature once belonged to a group of ten, five of which are now in the V & A. The earliest account of their history (Lord Ronald Sutherland Gower, *The Great Historic Galleries of England*, London, 1881, pl. xx) is highly romanticized and claims provenance from James II via Louis XIV which cannot be proved. Their certain history is as follows: acquired in Paris by James Edwards (1757–1816), bookseller and bibliographer, probably in the aftermath of the Treaty of Amiens; sold Christie's July 15th 1816 (lot 61); acquired by the Rev. Thomas Butt of Kinnersley, Shropshire, who married Edward's widow; by descent to Capt. H. Edwards-Heathcote, Belton Hall, Market Drayton; sold Christie's June 13th 1928 (lot 45); purchased by Mrs Doris Herschorn; bequeathed, 1975.

LITERATURE: V & A, 1947 (47).
Auerbach, *Hilliard*, pp. 109, pl. 85; 30 (83).
Strong, *Portraits of Queen Elizabeth I*, p. 90 (7).

195

DERICKE ANTHONY AND NICHOLAS HILLIARD
193 Second Great Seal of Elizabeth I, 1584–86

Victoria & Albert Museum (P48–1980)
Wax, 121 mm, 4¾ in. diam.

On July 8th 1584 a joint commission was issued to Nicholas Hilliard and Dericke Anthony, graver to the Mint, for a second Great Seal.

"You shall embosse . . . patterns for a new Great Seal according to the last pattern made upon parchment by you Our servant Hilliard . . . And by the same pattern you shall work, engrave, sink, finish and bring to perfection to be used a new Great Seal in silver". (Auerbach, *Hilliard*, p. 20).

The document makes it clear that Hilliard designed the seal by making a series of pattern drawings which were presumably submitted to the Queen to make her choice. It should be stressed that the survival of this warrant is unique and purely fortuitous, but through it one can establish that limners could supply patterns for seals. As everything worked according to precedent this is strong evidence in favour of attributing the design of earlier seals to Teerlinc and Hornebolte (nos. 19, 144). The fact that such a warrant was needed probably also sprang from the fact that Hilliard, unlike his predecessors, was not a salaried crown employee who would have provided such a design as part of his normal work. What is unusual about the arrangements is that Hilliard was to set about the actual making of three dimensional models and the final matrices jointly with Anthony. It must surely have been normal to have left these stages of manufacture entirely to the gravers at the Mint but Hilliard, being a goldsmith, was quite capable also of carrying out that process. The relationship was not a happy one as he recalled in a later letter. "For I had once envy enough about a Great Seal for my doing well in other men's offices". (*ibid, loc. cit.*)

The Great Seal was of immense importance, being attached to all major documents of state. The first Great Seal came into use with the new reign in 1558–59 (No. 44) and was therefore twenty-five years old and conformed to the standard seal image of the monarch which always depicted, on the obverse, the ruler enthroned and, on the reverse, riding on horseback. The second Great Seal still conforms to this but there is a radical enhancement of regal divinity coincidental with the cult of Elizabeth reaching its zenith in the pre-Armada years. On the obverse the Queen is seated enthroned, clasping orb and sceptre, flanked by royal coats of arms, crowned and encircled by the Garter and, above, by Tudor Roses. Divine hands, however, issue from clouds to lift up her mantle, a quite unprecedented iconographic innovation. This emphasis on the divinity of the Queen's rule is made even more forcefully on the reverse with another innovation in which her head is encircled by clouds and a burst of celestial rays. On either side of her float, crowned, are the Tudor Rose, the fleur-de-lys for France and the harp for Ireland. In these most formalized of state images Hilliard brings his linear powers of decoration to a third dimension as he evokes the perfect Spenserian image of Elizabeth as "a most royall Queene or Empresse". The second Great Seal image should be placed into the context of the progressively more formalized icons of Elizabeth with their increasing preoccupation with allegorical attribute that became the norm in the eighties.

It is suggested that the source for this image may have been the iconography devised for Henri III's Order of the Holy Spirit (no. 76).

LITERATURE: O'Donoghue, *Catalogue*, 1894 (2).
A. Wyon, *The Great Seals of England*, London, 1887, pp. 77–78.
Auerbach, *Hilliard*, pp. 181–84; 323 (208).
Strong, *Portraits of Queen Elizabeth I*, p. 148 (12).

NICHOLAS HILLIARD
194 Design for a Great Seal of Ireland, c. 1590

The British Museum, Department of Prints and Drawings (1912–7–17–1)
Pen and black ink, strengthened with wash, over black lead, on vellum, 12.9 cm, 5⅛ in. diam.

There is no documentation to associate Hilliard with the design of a new Great Seal of Ireland in the 1590's and it would be tempting to associate this drawing with the commission to make a third Great Seal of England, work upon which, begun probably in, or a little before, 1591, was still in hand in 1600 (N. Blakiston, "Queen Elizabeth's Third Great Seal", *Burlington Magazine*, XC, 1948, pp. 101–4; Auerbach, *Hilliard*, pp. 31–3). This possibility is eliminated by the Irish emblems indicated on the shields: the Harp and the Three Crowns.

The dating of the drawing can only be achieved from the costume and, in particular, the ruff. The knowledge of the third English Great Seal has tended to push the dating into the 1590's. The cut of sleeves, the ruff and still heart-shaped dressing of the hair are paralleled exactly as early as 1589 in Custodis's portrait of Elizabeth Brydges (Strong, *The English Icon*, p. 197 (149)). It might be more logical to place this drawing about 1590 and regard it as a sequential to the second Great Seal of England (no. 193) which was never carried out and pre-dating c. 1591 when it was found to be unsatisfactory and Hilliard was asked to design a

196

third. This would explain the virtual repetition of the iconography of the second Seal into this projected one for Ireland.

INSCRIBED: On the containing circular band, barely legible: *ELISABET D. G. ANGLIE FRAN. ET HIBERNIE REGINA.*

COLLECTIONS: Peter Gellatly; presented by his widow, 1912.

LITERATURE: C. Dodgson, *Burlington Magazine*, V, 1904, p. 574.
H. Farchar, "Nicholas Hilliard: Embosser of Medals in Gold",
  Numismatic Chronicle, 4th series, no. 32, 1908, pp. 342, 346–47.
V & A, 1947 (107).
J. Woodward, *Tudor and Stuart Drawings*, London, 1951, p. 44 (5).
Edward Croft-Murray and P. Hulton, *Catalogue of British Drawings*,
  I, *XVI and XVII Centuries*, British Museum, 1960, pp. 16–17 (1).
Auerbach, *Hilliard*, p. 320 (189).
Strong, *Portraits of Queen Elizabeth I*, p. 105 (12).

AFTER NICHOLAS HILLIARD

195 Medallion of Elizabeth I, 1585–90

> *The British Museum, Department of Coins and Medals*
> *(M6900)*
> Silver, 5.1 × 4.2 cm, 2 × 1⅝ in.

Traditionally associated with the defeat of the Spanish Armada in 1588 this medallion has no specific allusions to the event. It, together with no. 197, is better placed as an expression of the deliberate promotion of the royal image as an emblem of loyalty that was such a marked feature from the middle of the 1580's onwards. The important fact about these medallions is that they were

meant to be worn, as we know from the loop for suspension at the top. At the bottom a second loop enabled the recipient to add a pendant pearl. Miniatures and cameos of the Queen catered for the rich and aristocratic but mass-produced medallions of this kind proliferated the cult to classes lower in the social scale.

The execution and production of such an object would have been left to the Mint and the result is somewhat rough. Nonetheless the design should have come from Hilliard. The composition with its cartwheel ruff, heavily encrusted bejewelled dress and encircling celestial rays is closely related to that on the reverse of the Great Seal (no. 44) but with the face turned into profile.

The reverse again should be an interpretation of a Hilliard design: at the top there are formalized clouds and lightning above a stormy sea on which floats Noah's Ark as the symbol of the Protestant Church, whose destiny the Queen guides, with the motto: *SAEVAS. TRANQVILLA. PER. VNDAS.* The Ark is depicted as a house on a ship with smoke curling upwards from a chimney.

LITERATURE: E. Hawkins, *Medallic Illustrations of the History of Great*
  Britain and Ireland to the Death of George I, W. A. W. Franks and
  H. A. Groeber, London, 1885, (no. 119)
STRONG, *Portraits of Queen Elizabeth I*, p. 136 (11).

?NICHOLAS HILLIARD

196 Elizabeth I, frontispiece to

> Henry Lyte, *The Light of Britaine*, London, 1588
> *The British Library*
> Woodcut, 6.7 × 8.3 cm, 2⅝ × 3¼ in. *(Photograph)*

This exists in separate impressions and was also used for a frontispiece to *The Recantations as they were severalie pronounced by William Tedder and Anthony Tyrrell . . .*, (1588). The Queen is depicted encircled by two of her emblematic flowers, to the left the double Tudor Rose, to the right the single eglantine. The spirit is Hilliardesque and this could be after a design and even cut by him.

LITERATURE: Strong, *Portraits of Queen Elizabeth I*, p. 121; (17)

WORKSHOP OF NICHOLAS HILLIARD

197 Medallion of Elizabeth I, c. 1590

> *The British Museum, Department of Coins and Medals*
> *(1866–12–18–1)*
> Gold, oval, 5.1 × 4.5 cm, 2 × 1¾ in.

Although traditionally described as a Naval Award or the Armada Badge, there is no evidence to link it specifically with 1588. It is a medallion, cast and chased with a suspension ring indicating that it is meant to be worn and, like its predecessor (no. 195), extended the cult of wearing the royal image beyond the circles able to receive or commission miniatures. The costume places it firmly after 1588 and, indeed, with the hairdressing, is closely paralleled in the Ditchley Portrait, c. 1590–92 (National Portrait Gallery) and de Passe's engraving after Oliver dated 1592 (no. 200). I would therefore date in the very early 1590's but preceding the Mask of Youth miniatures.

Unlike no. 195 this shows every sign of being executed as

199

well as designed within the Hilliard workshop. The imagery is post-Armada in its imperialism: "No richer crown in the whole world, not even dangers affect it". On the reverse there is a bay tree arising from an island in the sea and a sun emerging from the clouds, imagery which continued into the Jacobean period: in Samuel Daniel's masque *Tethys Festival* (1610) Anne of Denmark and her ladies placed their gifts at a "Tree of Victory, which was a bay erected . . . upon a little mound" (Orgel and Strong, *Inigo Jones the Theatre of the Stuart Court*, I, p. 195 ll.252–53).

INSCRIBED: obverse: *DITIOR . IN. .TOTO .NON .ALTER CIRCVLVS ORBE*;
reverse: *E | RI; NON . IPSA . PERICVLA . TANGVNT .*

LITERATURE: Hawkins *Medallic Illustrations of the History of Great Britain and Ireland to the Death of George I*, W. A. Franks and H. A. Grueber, London 1885, (No. 130).
Strong, *Portraits of Queen Elizabeth I*, p. 138 (17) for previous bibliography.

WORKSHOP OF NICHOLAS HILLIARD

198 Medallion of Elizabeth I, c. 1588

The Fitzwilliam Museum, Cambridge
Gold, oval, 5.7 × 5.1 cm, 2¼ × 2 in.

A variant of the medallion (no. 197) of exceptional rarity and of such a quality, superior to the previous exhibit, as to indicate that the casting and chasing took place within the Hilliard workshop. The portrait of the Queen is a full-face frontal image. It seems probable that this is the earlier of the two, the cut of the sleeves at the top being late 1580's and of the type that appears in the Armada Portrait (Strong, *Portraits of Queen Elizabeth I*, pl. XIII). The reverse has considerably more detail, including buildings on the island and fish in the sea.

INSCRIBED: Obverse: DITIOR. IN. TOTO NON. ALTER. CIRCVLVS
Reverse: NON. IPSA. PERICVLA. TANGVNT.

COLLECTIONS: Charles Butler; given by A. W. Young, 1936.

LITERATURE: Strong, *Portraits of Queen Elizabeth I*, p. 138 (18) for bibliography.

III OLIVER AND THE QUEEN, c. 1592

Elizabeth sat for Isaac Oliver in or about 1592. The date can be reached by the fact that the face-pattern was forwarded to the Low Countries and used for an engraving dated that year (no. 200). It was a period when an attempt seems to have been made by the Queen to come to terms with a new generation of artists and a new aesthetic. At about the same time Oliver's future brother-in-law painted the Ditchley Portrait (National Portrait Gallery) in which he successfully married an accurate image of the fast ageing monarch to an icon of cosmic power. Gheeraerts was aided by the apparatus of allegory which detracts the eye away from the reality of the face. Oliver, confined to the tiny surface area of a miniature, was unable to produce the same effect. Although the encounter has left posterity with undoubtedly the most poignant portrait ever painted of Elizabeth, from the sitter's point of view it was a catastrophe. Immediately there was a return to Hilliard and government embarked on its deliberate suppression of any representation of the Queen as old.

SELECT BIBLIOGRAPHY

K. G. Boon, "De Passe's prent van Koningen Elizabeth I", *Bulletin van het Rijksmuseum*, I, 1958, pp. 3–9.

ISAAC OLIVER

199 Elizabeth I, 1590–1592

Victoria & Albert Museum (P. 8–1940)
Vellum stuck to a playing card with one club verso. The original rectangular card has been trimmed to an oval, leaving the squared edges at top and bottom, oval, 82 × 52 mm, 2$\frac{7}{16}$ × 2$\frac{1}{8}$ in.

Without doubt this miniature was painted from life. The evidence for this is not only the extraordinary directness of observation in the painting but also its actual shape which incorporates, at the top and bottom, the straight edges of the playing card mount enabling the miniature to be held in place while Oliver was painting it. This would have subsequently been trimmed to fit the miniature case. The fact that this was not done would suggest that it was kept for reference as a face-pattern and is not, as has often been suggested, merely an unfinished miniature.

That this was a pattern is reinforced by the remarkable series of images it influenced, Oliver certainly painted at least one known miniature from it, recently sold from the Heckett Collection (Sotheby's 24th April 1978 (lot 500)). The main reason for the sitting, however, was probably not for the multiplication of miniatures but for the purposes of engraving and the pattern connects directly with a series of engravings of Elizabeth commissioned by John Woutneel (worked in England from 1592–c. 1614), a book and printseller from the Netherlands who settled in London in 1592. There is also an engraving of Elizabeth I dated 1592 which, although it is now only known in later states (No. 200), directly relates to Oliver's miniature, by Crispin van de Passe I (born c. 1565–1637) two of whose sons, Simon and Willem, and a daughter, Magdalena, worked in England in the Jacobean period. There is no evidence that de Passe I, however, came in the 1590's but Woutneel either published, or acted as English agent for a number of his engravings (see Hind, *Engraving*, I, pp. 284 ff.). Of these one was the 1592 portrait of Elizabeth and the second the *Queen Elizabeth I between columns* dated 1596, almost certainly by him, which uses the same face-mask (*ibid*, I, pl. 144). Oliver would have been a natural choice of artist for drawing the Queen, belonging as he did to the reformist exile group in London. Evidence would point to the sitting taking place c. 1592 and being the result of a specific approach through the refugee colony in the form of Woutneel. The face-pattern was probably utilized by the English engraver William Rogers (worked c. 1589–1604) for his *Rosa Electa* (no. 202). The miniature is in good condition although faded.

This portrait of Elizabeth is virtually contemporaneous with Marcus Gheeraerts the Younger's Ditchley Portrait. The artists were, of course, closely related, Oliver later being Gheeraert's brother-in-law. There was no doubt a flow of ideas between them as, epitomizing a new generation of painters, they essayed the face of the ageing Queen. The result is reality, gently refined but catching all the intelligence and certainly providing us with an image matching the celebrated Hentzner description of 1598: "her face oblong, fair but wrinkled, her eyes small, yet black and pleasant, her nose a little hooked, her lips narrow . . . her hair . . . an auburn colour but false . . ." (W. B. Rye, *England as seen by Foreigners in the Days of Elizabeth and James I*, London, 1865, p. 104).

COLLECTIONS: The tradition that this was in the collection of Dr Richard Mead (1673–1754) can be discounted as there is no trace of it in the sale catalogue; first certainly recorded in the S. Reynolds Solly collection; sold by order of Mrs Edith Solly and the Trustees of the late Henry Reynolds Solly, Sotheby's June 27th 1940) (lot 33) purchased for the V & A from the funds of the R. H. Stephenson Bequest.

LITERATURE: O'Donoghue, *Catalogue*, 1894, p. 32 (no. 29). Winter, *Elizabethan Miniatures*, p. 28, pl. XII. V & A, 1947 (163). K. G. Boon, "De Passe's prent van Koningen Elizabeth I", *Bulletin van het Rijksmuseum*, I, 1958, pp. 3–9. Auerbach, *Hilliard*, p. 239 (no. 24). Strong, *Portraits of Queen Elizabeth I*, p. 92 (no. 12).

CRISPIN VAN DE PASSE I AFTER ISAAC OLIVER

200 Queen Elizabeth I, 1592

The British Museum, Department of Prints and Drawings (O. 7–218)
Engraving, 14.6 × 12.1 cm, $5\frac{3}{4} × 4\frac{3}{4}$ in. (border of subject), 18.1 × 12.7 cm, $7\frac{1}{8} × 5$ in. (near plate with lettering below).

Engraved in the Netherlands by Crispin van de Passe I (c. 1565–1637). In its third state it contains the inscription *procurante Joanne Waldnelio* which implies that John Woutneel (worked in England 1592–c. 1614) had obtained, printed and published the plate. Woutneel came from the Low Countries and was a book and printseller in London who either published or acted as the English agent for

engravings by de Passe. The connexion between this engraving and Oliver's portrait of the Queen (no. 199) must in some way be direct, postulating that Woutneel commissioned a design from Oliver which was forwarded for de Passe to engrave. Evidence to support this comes from the fact that this arrangement was more openly acknowledged in the case of the posthumous image of Elizabeth (no. 203).

LITERATURE: Hind, *Engraving*, I, p. 283–84 (2); 284(1). K. G. Boon, "De Passe's prent van Koningen Elizabeth I, *Bulletin van Het Rijksmuseum*, 1958, I, pp. 3–10. Strong, *Portraits of Queen Elizabeth I*, p. 43 (21).

WILLIAM ROGERS AFTER ISAAC OLIVER

201 Queen Elizabeth I Standing in a a Room with a Lattice Window, c. 1592

The British Museum, Department of Prints and Drawings (1901–4–17–35)
Engraving, 38.7 × 26 cm, $15\frac{1}{4} × 10\frac{1}{4}$ in. (Plate) 38.1 × 25.4 cm, 15 × 10 in. (border).

William Rogers (worked c. 1589–1604) is the first Englishman to sign and date a portrait engraving and, in one instance, boasted his patriotism by adding *Anglus et Civis Londinensis*. It was not the custom in the Elizabethan period to acknowledge the source for an engraving and the fact that we know this is after a design by Isaac Oliver is due entirely to Crispin van de Passe I's engraving of the Queen dated 1603 (no. 203) using the same figure and acknowledging its authorship. At one time it was believed that the original Oliver drawing was that in the Royal Collection at Windsor (Oppé, *English Drawings*, p. 78 (457)), but recent examination has established that this was worked up at a later date over a tracing from the engraving.

The verses beneath assume that the sitter is alive and the engraving must, therefore, have been issued before 1603. Costume is the only evidence for dating and the construction of the dress is identical with that in the famous Ditchley Portrait in the National Portrait Gallery, painted to commemorate either the Accession Day Tilt of 1590 or the Queen's visit to Sir Henry Lee at Ditchley in 1592 (Strong, *Cult of Elizabeth*, p. 154, pl. 74) which would place Rogers' engraving in the early 1590's. The face-pattern is Oliver's (no. 199), slightly softened to avoid emphasizing haggard old age. It is, of course, impossible to establish just where the engraver took over from the designer in the overall composition but it may be suggested that Oliver's hand can be traced in a substantial part. The perspective, for example, is accurate and, a startling innovation, the Queen is depicted by a window and in terms of *chiaroscuro* which is pure Oliver, totally at variance with the Queen's demands for open garden light with no shadow, the basis of Hilliard's aesthetic.

This is the only impression to survive of this portrait although the plate was reduced to a half-length of which many copies exist. It is arguable that this highly realistic presentation of the Queen as an old lady might have been one of the victims of the holocaust of royal portraits that was a feature of the 1590's. In July 1596 officers were

POSVI DEVM ADIVTOREM MEVM

ELISABET D.G.ANGLIAE, FRANCIAE, HIBERNIAE, ET VERGINIAE REGINA.
FIDEI CHRISTIANAE PROPVGNATRIX ACERRIMA. NVNC IN DNO REQVIESCENS.

203

ordered by the Privy Council to seek out and destroy all portraits of the Queen which were to her "great offence". Raleigh records a similar destruction and Evelyn writes that engravings were called in and used at Essex House for years for "*Peels* for the use of their Ovens" (see Strong, *Portraits of Queen Elizabeth I*, pp. 5, 9).

LITERATURE: Hind, *Engraving*, I, pp. 265–67.
Strong, *Portraits of Queen Elizabeth I*, p. 114 (30).

WILLIAM ROGERS PROBABLY AFTER ISAAC OLIVER

202 Queen Elizabeth I as Rosa Electa, 1590–95

The British Museum (Hind 7)
Engraving, 23.1 × 17.2 cm, $9\frac{1}{8} × 6\frac{3}{4}$ (outer border),
23.4 × 17.8 cm, $9\frac{1}{4} × 7$ in. (plate)

As no. 201 this makes use of a face-mask which is Isaac Oliver's (no. 199), realistic in depicting the Queen as advanced in years. The position of the eyes is changed to look to the left. The three quarter length formula with a decorative border is derived from Goltzius and was one adopted by Oliver for his earliest portrait miniature (no. 137). It is difficult to date exactly but the absence of gauze puffs lining the inside of the ruff and other details would place it in the first half of the 1590's. Any connexion with Oliver can only be conjecture, based on the one certain connexion he had with Rogers (no. 201) but the approach to the decorative border of roses and eglantine,

the Queen's flowers, is naturalistic and not stylized into a flat pattern in the Hilliard manner. There also is much use of light and shade.

LITERATURE: Hind, *Engraving*, I, pp. 264–65.
Strong, *Portraits of Queen Elizabeth I*, p. 114 (29).

CRISPIN VAN DE PASSE I AFTER ISAAC OLIVER

203 Queen Elizabeth I, 1603

Victoria & Albert Museum (E3288–1960)
Engraving, 31.7 × 22.5 cm, $12\frac{1}{2} × 8\frac{7}{8}$ in. (border).
34.9 × 22.8 cm, $13\frac{3}{4} × 9$ in. (plate)

The inscription *Mortua anno Miser | CorD | ae* indicates that this engraving was published soon after the Queen's death. As it was engraved by de Passe in the Low Countries it, unlike its English equivalents, acknowledged a source. The right of the verses there is inscribed: "*Isaac Oliver effigiebat. Crispin van de Passe incidebat. procurante Joanne Waldnelio.*" This is a unique record of the whole process: an Oliver design obtained by Woutneel and forwarded to the Netherlands for de Passe to engrave. It is significant that it repeats the figure of the Queen in William Rogers engraving of c. 1592 (no. 201). Certainly by 1603 the dress in the de Passe engraving was a decade out of fashion. On the Queen's death there must have been a ready market for prints of her and speed must have been of the essence. Oliver must have either sent his original drawing of c. 1592 or re-drawn it as there are slight variants in the dress and jewels though the figure is substantially the same. The great change is in the background which is new, but whether this was Oliver's or de Passe's invention there is no way of telling.

The Queen is depicted with her usual attributes of Bible (*VERBUM DEI*) and sword (*IVSTITIA*). This engraving was to be the most influential ever published of her and hundreds of derivatives exist.

LITERATURE: Hind, *Engraving*, I, pp. 282–3 (1).
K. G. Boon, "De Passes's prent van Koningen Elizabeth I",
    Bulletin van Het Rijksmuseum, 1958, I, pp. 3–10; 285 (3).
Strong, *Portraits of Queen Elizabeth I*, p. 152 (4).

IV THE RETREAT FROM REALITY: HILLIARD AND THE MASK OF YOUTH, 1593–1603

Over twenty miniatures survive by Nicholas Hilliard and his workshop of the face-pattern which we conveniently label, the Mask of Youth. As the evidence now emerges these can be tightly dated to the last decade of the reign. The dating depends not only on the evidence of the costume but on their style. Many have a folded velvet curtain as a background, a technical innovation whose earliest dated appearance is 1594 (no. 96). This neatly dates the beginning of the long series of Mask of Youth miniatures as *following* the Queen's disastrous encounter with Oliver. Unlike the latter these portraits deliberately

204

abandon any attempt to depict the reality of a woman in her sixties. Instead her features are rejuvenated back to those of a young girl by the simple process of reducing them to a few schematic lines, which would suggest that this formula was not the result of a sitting but a refinement by Hilliard of earlier images. The resulting portrait is one which mirrors exactly in visual terms the ecstatic extremes of Eliza-worship that are so characteristic a feature of the court in its final years. Festivals and poetic eulogies simultaneously celebrate her springtime beauty and eternal youth.

Beneath this poetic fancy, however, lay a deeper political reality because government would not have wished the physical decay of the monarch to gain public currency when the succession question lay in the balance. Portraits and engravings that were to her "great offence" were called in and destroyed. The Mask of Youth must have been laid down as the official image of Elizabeth to be made use of by all artists who wished to depict her regardless of media. We find confirmation of this in its appearance in works certainly not by Hilliard such as the Procession Picture (no. 204) and the Rainbow Portrait.

Although the rendering of the Queen's features is often perfunctory, that of the details of her extraordinary wardrobe remain nearly always as sparkling as ever. No payments for these miniatures have so far emerged but we know that she gave them to courtiers *without* a setting. The recipient was expected to commission a picture box and these lockets could become vehicles for an allegorical overlay in which a particular courtier was able to elaborate on his personal vision of the *Diva Elizabetha*.

SELECT BIBLIOGRAPHY:
Auerbach, *Hilliard*, pp. 142–46.
Strong, *Portraits of Queen Elizabeth I*, pp. 94–95.
Strong, *The Cult of Elizabeth*, pp. 46–48.
Strong, *Renaissance Miniature*, pp. 118–22.

ATTRIBUTED TO ROBERT PEAKE

204 **Eliza Triumphans**, c. 1600

Simon Wingfield Digby, Esq, Sherborne Castle, Dorset
Oil on canvas, 132 × 190.5 cm, 52 × 75 in.

This picture is in the style of Robert Peake (c. 1557–1619) whose certain work is typified by a characteristic manner of inscribing the date and age of the sitter (Strong, *The English Icon*, pp. 225–54). His style of painting was certainly influenced by Hilliard, it is linear, decorative in approach, and light in palette. *Eliza Triumphans* includes all these ingredients and is an important instance of another painter using the Mask of Youth face-pattern of the Queen.

Formerly known as *Queen Elizabeth going in Procession to Blackfriars in 1600*, this picture is a celebration of Elizabeth by her last Master of the Horse, Edward Somerset, 4th Earl of Worcester, the central figure in the picture standing immediately in front of the Queen, carrying a pair of gloves in his right hand.

Elizabeth is not sitting in a litter, as has always been assumed, but a chair on wheels, propelled by a groom, one of two that follow the chair, wearing black skullcaps and tunics with crowned Tudor Roses on the front. These are "grooms of our coaches or litters". Over her is a canopy (which has no structural connexion with the chair) carried by four young gentlemen. three are depicted actually carrying the canopy while the fourth, who would have been invisible, has been brought around to the front immediately behind the Earl of Worcester. The only certainly identifiable canopy bearer is the one on the extreme right, Worcester's son, Henry Somerset, Lord Herbert of Chepstow.

Before the Queen walk six Knights of the Garter who, reading from left to right, are: Edward Sheffield, 3rd Lord Sheffield, later Earl of Mulgrave; Charles Howard, Lord Howard of Effingham, later Earl of Nottingham; George

Elizabeth I and the Limners 127

Clifford, 3rd Earl of Cumberland; George Carey, 2nd Lord Hunsdon who carries the white wand of Lord Chamberlain; an unidentified Garter Knight, and Gilbert Talbot, Earl of Shrewsbury carrying the sword.

The route is lined with Gentlemen Pensioners holding halberds and these are clearly portraits. Behind the Queen follows a train of ladies, also portraits, but very difficult to identify, although conceivably members of the Somerset family.

The notion of such a picture being a reportage snapshot must be dismissed. As in the case of the miniatures the setting is symbolic and the vista to the two castles in the distance to the left should allude to Worcester's residences, Chepstow and Raglan Castles on the Welsh borders.

The picture is usually taken to be a record of Elizabeth's presence at the marriage of one of her Maids of Honour, Anne Russell, to Worcester's heir, Lord Herbert in June 1600. There could be allusions to this, but the picture is more likely to be a composite celebration of Worcester in his new role as Master of the Horse which he became in succession to Essex in 1601. In this sense he places himself as the escort of *Eliza Triumphans*, an Elizabethan re-interpretation of a Roman Imperial triumph.

COLLECTIONS: Presumably commissioned by Edward Somerset, 4th Earl of Worcester; Kildare, 2nd Lord Digby of Coleshill (d. 1693); by descent to William 5th Lord Digby and recorded by Vertue at Coleshill, 1737 (Vertue, *Notebooks*, I, p. 19); thence by descent.

LITERATURE: Strong, *Portraits of Queen Elizabeth I*, pp. 86–87 (for previous literature.

Strong, *Cult of Elizabeth*, pp. 19–55.)

NICHOLAS HILLIARD

205 Elizabeth I, c. 1600

Victoria & Albert Museum (4404–1857)
Vellum mounted onto a playing card with one spade showing at the reverse, oval, 62 × 48 mm, $2\frac{7}{16} \times 1\frac{27}{32}$ in.

As in the large-scale "Rainbow Portrait" (Strong, *Portraits of Queen Elizabeth*, I, pl. XV) this miniature is unique in showing the Queen with her hair flowing freely on to her shoulders in token of virginity. The concept of such a miniature would have been individual to the courtier who commissioned it and in this case the star-burst, which is such a striking feature of the lid, tells us that it is a celebration of Elizabeth as *Stella Britannis*. This astral apotheosis, which is constant, is perhaps best paralleled amongst the *Imprese* presented to the Queen at the tilts held annually on her Accession Day, November 17th, which were such rich founts of the mythology of the Elizabeth legend. William Camden records a knight who presented a shield on which was painted: "The Star called Spica Virginis, one of the fifteen which are accounted to be of the first magnitude among the Astronomers, with a scroll inwritten "Mihi vita Spica Virginis", declared there by haply that he had that Star in the Ascendent at his Nativity, or rather that he lived by the gracious favour of a Virgin Prince". (William Camden, *Remains concerning*

Britain, London, 1870, p. 378). Although there is no costume visible in this miniature it is an accurate record of a crown and a necklace set with gold, rubies and diamonds that was once part of her enormous collection of jewellery. The face, as usual, is a repetition.

The only two other surviving jewelled lockets containing miniatures of Elizabeth are the celebrated Drake and Armada Jewels. This one is unique in having an open-work front, although the same thing does occur on other miniature cases (see *Princely Magnificence*, 1980, (118), in particular the Lyte Jewel in the British Museum). The case is gold with the front both cast and chiselled with scrolling tendrils around the central star set with diamonds and rubies. The reverse of the case is enamelled black all over with a scrolling design in multi-coloured enamels, incorporating two dolphins, conceivably allusions to Elizabeth as Venus, "Queen of Beauty", as Venus was born from sea. As Anna Somers-Cocks points out the reverse, which is often referred to as being "after Daniel Mignot", who produced a series of engraved designs in Augsburg between 1593 and 1596, in fact only bears a general resemblance to his work.

COLLECTIONS: Purchased in 1857 from an unrecorded source.

LITERATURE: O'Donoghue, *Catalogue*, 1894, p. 13 (32). Winter, *Elizabethan Miniatures*, p. 24, pl. IV(a). V & A, 1947 (79). Joan Evans, *English Jewellery*, London, 1921, p. 101, pl. XX, Auerbach, *Hilliard*, p. 146, pl. 129, 310 (no. 132). Strong, *Portraits of Queen Elizabeth I*, p. 97 (21). Strong, *Hilliard*, p. 31; pl. 13. Strong, *The Cult of Elizabeth*, p. 49. *Princely Magnificence*, 1980 (36).

?STUDIO OF NICHOLAS HILLIARD

206 Queen Elizabeth I, probably 1599

The National Trust, Hardwick Hall
Oil on canvas, 223.2 × 165 cm, 88 × 65 in.

This should be the portrait of the Queen mentioned in the accounts as having been brought to Hardwick from London in 1599. Bess of Hardwick was a known patron of Nicholas Hilliard and his former apprentice, Rowland Lockey. There is a confusing series of payments both to Lockey and Hilliard in 1592 for pictures and definite payments to Lockey between 1609–13 for oil paintings, portraits and copies of portraits, for Bess's second son, Sir William, later Baron Cavendish, also for Hardwick (Auerbach, *Hilliard*, pp. 254–56). Several of the portraits relating to the second series of payments are identifiable.

The payments for 1592 imply that there was confusion between Lockey's and Hilliard's work but the final entry reads 40s to Hilliard for "one Pictur" and the same to Lockey for "one other pictur". There is a third payment to Hilliard of 20s for something unspecified, forty shillings was Hilliard's standard price for a miniature (*ibid*, p. 124), but we cannot exclude the possibility that one or all these pictures were large-scale as prices for them fluctuated so wildly according to size, work involved and framing.

Bess of Hardwick was over seventy in the 1590's and would have been conventional in her tastes. As a

206

commission it would have been an important one, designed to be by far the grandest picture in the long gallery. The portrait uses the official mask of Youth image of the Queen, as evolved by Hilliard, but is set, as in the case of the miniatures, into a totally original composition. Although this portrait is cruder than anything we would wish to attribute to the master himself the concept is Hilliardesque and the design could be his with the execution by Lockey or other assistants. The formula is that of the cabinet miniatures and can be compared to the unfinished full-length portrait of a Lady standing in front of a folded curtain background. The lack of understanding of perspective in the up-ended carpet, the flat frontal lighting and the accent on decorative detail are all in the Hilliard manner. The portrait is being especially cleaned for the exhibition which may confirm or otherwise the suggestions made here.

COLLECTION: Painted for Elizabeth Talbot, Countess of Shrewsbury (1520–1608); possibly identical with that mentioned as having been brought from London, 1599; presumably identical with one of the three portraits listed in the 1601 inventory; first certainly recorded at Hardwick, 1760 (*Walpole Society*, XVI, 1928, p. 30); transferred with the house to the National Trust, 1957.

LITERATURE: Lord Hawkesbury, *A Catalogue of the Pictures at Hardwick*, Liverpool, 1903, p. 41.
Strong, *Portraits of Queen Elizabeth I*, pp. 83–84 (95).
Mark Girouard, *Hardwick Hall*, National Trust, p. 83 (35).

AFTER NICHOLAS HILLIARD

207 Queen Elizabeth I, c. 1600

Visitors of the Ashmolean Museum
Woodcut, 48.8 × 36.8 cm, 19¼ × 14½ in.
This is the only print which makes use of the officially promoted Mask of Youth image of the Queen. The head, head-dress and first necklace are all identical with that in the Hardwick Portrait (no. 206) with the same ribbands jewels and flowers in the hair and the same pearl coronet, but minus the circle of stars in the woodcut. The ruff is lined with puffs of gauze, giving a date a year or two either side of 1600. The image it presents of the Queen is very different from that in prints derived from Oliver. The source for this wood-cut is Nicholas Hilliard and it is reasonable at least to suggest that he provided the design for it.

COLLECTIONS: Part of the "grangerised" edition of Clarendon's *History of the Rebellion* begun by Alexander Hume Sutherland in 1795 and continued by his widow who gave it to the Ashmolean Museum, 1837.

LITERATURE: Hind, *Engraving*, I, p. 10.
Strong, *Portraits of Queen Elizabeth I*, p. 126 (21).

NICHOLAS HILLIARD

208 The Heneage Jewel, formerly known as the Armada Jewel, c. 1600

Victoria & Albert Museum (M.81–1935)
Vellum stuck to card (the back cannot be seen as a slightly larger card has been stuck over it), oval, 39 × 30.5 mm, 17/32 × 1 3/16 in.

A layer of legend needs to be removed before any consideration of this Jewel, traditionally called the Armada Jewel because it is believed to have been given by the Queen to Sir Thomas Heneage (1556–1595), on the defeat of the Spanish Armada in 1588. Heneage was appointed, soon after Elizabeth's accession, Gentleman of the Privy Chamber and Chancellor of the Duchy of Lancaster and in 1589 succeeded Hatton as Vice-Chamberlain of the Household and Privy Counsellor. He was devoted to the Queen and, in his will, left instructions for a jewel to be made for her. There is no mention of the so-called Armada Jewel, however, although by tradition it passed to Heneage's brother, Michael (1540–1600), Sir Thomas Heneage having no male heirs. The Jewel does not appear in Michael's will (Somerset House, P.C.C., 3 Woodhall). In 1902 it was the property of Colonel Godfrey Walker-Heneage.

The Jewel is, in fact, far later than 1588 although it bears a spurious added date of 1580. The costume, with the tiny additional chin ruff, only appears in very late portraits of Elizabeth as the reign drew to its close of which the most famous instances are the "Rainbow Portrait" and the "Procession Picture", both c. 1600 (Strong, *The English Icon.*, pp. 299 (304); 240 (211)). Henceforth it would be far more accurately alluded to as the Heneage Jewel.

The miniature itself is one of the usual "Mask of Youth" repetitions. The features, however, severely damaged by

moisture are heavily restored and there is flaking and
scratch damages on the ruff, probably the result of repeated
opening. As in all these miniatures, Hilliard produces a
brilliant arrangement of tiny jewels in the hair and on the
ruff with a typical rose pinned to one side. V. J. Murrell
points to the remains of a gold line at the top and bottom
of the miniature which, if projected, would make it wider,
as a result the composition is slightly tighter than it should
be. There is no reason to believe that the miniature was
painted other than for this Jewel for it is the climax of its
iconography.

As was customary, the symbolism moves in the classic
manner from the external celebration of the Queen as a
"most royall Queene or Empresse" to the internal private
vision of her as "a most vertous and beautifull ladie". The
obverse exterior bears a profile image of her which was also
struck as a medal (Strong, *Portraits of Queen Elizabeth I*,
p. 136 (10)), bearing an inscription identifying her as the
ruler of her kingdoms. On the reverse there is the Ark
floating on the water and the motto: *Saevas tranquilla per
undas*. The Ark is a traditional symbol of the Church and
the allusion is to her as *Defensor Fidei* guiding it through
troubled waters. It frequently appears as a device on the
reverse of medals usually thought to commemorate the
defeat of the Armada (nos. 197, 198) and also on what was
probably another case for a miniature of Elizabeth now in
the Museo Poldi Pezzoli, Milan (*Princely Magnificence*,
V & A, 1980 (39)). Within, the progression is to a
paean on the Queen as the sonnet heroine. The reverse
of the lid bears a red Tudor Rose with the inscription:
*Hei mihi quod tanto virtus perfuse decore non habet eternos
inviolata dies*. The author of these lines is Walter Haddon,
the Queen's Master of Requests and they were published
in his *Poemata*, London, 1567, lib. ii. The rose, the
inscription and the 'Mask of Youth" image epitomize a
courtly celebration of her as "Beauty's Rose" of the kind
that appears in John Davies *Hymns to Astraea* (1599).

The Jewel is of gold, enamelled in white, black, opaque
pale blue, green, translucent red, green, blue, grey, orange
and yellow, set with diamonds and rubies. In style it is very
different from the Drake Jewel of 1587. Its pierced frame of
open strapwork of rectangular forms is more Jacobean than
Elizabethan and closer to the Lyte Jewel, c. 1610
(Auerbach, *Hilliard*, pl. 165) and therefore reminiscent of
the style associated with Arnold Lulls. Attribution to
Hilliard of the setting in this instance seems highly
unlikely.

INSCRIBED: Obverse exterior: under a convex glass enclosing a
profile bust: *ELIZABETHA DE G ANG FRA ET HIB
REGINA*; reverse exterior: *SAEVAS TRANQVILLA PER
VNDAS*; surrounding the rose on the obverse interior lid: *Hei
mihi quod tanto virtus perfuse decore non habet eternos inviolata dies*.

COLLECTIONS: The Heneage family; unrecorded until sold by
Colonel Godfrey Walker-Heneage, anonymously, Christie's
July 18th 1902 (lot 121); J. Pierpont Morgan collection; sold
Christie's June 24th 1935 (lot 99); presented by Lord
Wakefield to the V & A through the N.A.C.F.

LITERATURE: Williamson, *Catalogue*, 1906, I, p. 138.
H. Clifford Smith, *Jewellery*, London, 1908, pp. 255–56.
Joan Evans, *English Jewellery*, London, 1921, p. 91, pl. A.
V & A, 1947 (103).

209

Auerbach, *Hilliard*, pp. 188–91, pl. 181; 324 (211).
Strong, *Portraits of Queen Elizabeth I*, p. 97 (19).
Strong, *Hilliard*, p. 30, pl. 7.
Princely Magnificence, 1980 (38).

NICHOLAS HILLIARD

209 Elizabeth I, 1595–1600

Victoria & Albert Museum (Ham House 375)
Vellum which has been relaid onto modern card,
oval, 86 × 66 mm, $3\frac{3}{8} \times 2\frac{5}{8}$ in.

This is one of the finest of the surviving Mask of Youth
miniatures in remarkable condition, although the features
are very faded. The allegorical allusion is to the Queen as
Cynthia, the moon goddess, and a crescent jewel adorns
her hair. This is by far the largest of the series, including
much more of the figure than is usual and the rendering of
the dress, from life, is of exceptional brilliance.
The colours of the dress are subtle; ash-colour and white
adorned with braiding decorated with gold and pearls, the
whole set against the unusual foil of a blue velvet folded
curtain in the wet-in-wet technique.

The absence of a chin-ruff would suggest a date before
1600. There is also a unique relationship to an engraving,
Francis Delaram's portrait of Elizabeth after Hilliard,
issued between 1617 and 1619 (no. 212). Although reversed
in the process of engraving the pose, dress and jewellery are
virtually identical, except that the hand, which in the
miniature rests on the arm of a chair, is holding a fan. As
Hilliard did not do preparatory drawings for his miniatures
it presupposes access to this one by Delaram.

Ham House was built by one of Elizabeth's Gentleman
Pensioners, Sir Thomas Vavasour, a prominent figure at
the Accession Day Tilts who would be just the person to

210

211

commission such a cult image but there is no evidence that any of the contents of Ham passed with the house irrespective of owners.

INSCRIBED: A card at the back has a piece of paper inscribed: *Queen Elizabeth* and, later: *by Hilliard Pret: 5^{li}*; and, on a separate piece of paper the inventory number: *152* (damaged).

COLLECTIONS: First recorded c. 1679 when Ham House was in the possession of the Ham heiress, Elizabeth Murray, daughter of William Murray, 1st Earl of Dysart and wife of John Maitland, 1st Duke of Lauderdale; the inscriptions on the reverse refer to the "Estimate of Pictures" compiled c. 1679 in which it figures as "150. Queen Elizabeth, of Hilliard"; the discrepancy between 150 and 152 on the reverse implies a slight re-arrangement of the hanging between the listing and the actual numbering; descended via the Earls of Dysart with Ham House; the house was presented to the National Trust in 1948 to be administered by the V & A.

LITERATURE: O'Donoghue, *Catalogue*, 1894 (16).
C. Roundell, *Ham House, its History and Art Treasures*, London, 1904, 1, p. 142.
Auerbach, *Hilliard*, pp. 146, pl. 125; 309 (127).
Strong, *Portraits of Queen Elizabeth I*, p. 94 (13).
Reynolds, *Connoisseur's Complete Period Guides*, 1968, p. 226, pl. 72 (a).
Peter Thornton and Maurice Tomlin, *The Furnishing and Decoration of Ham House*, Furniture History Society, 1980, p. 131.

NICHOLAS HILLIARD

210 Elizabeth I, c. 1600

Victoria & Albert Museum (P.1–1974)
Vellum mounted onto card, with a lavender-coloured paper glued to the back, which may well be contemporary, oval, 64.5 × 49 mm, $2\frac{17}{32} \times 1\frac{29}{32}$ in.

Basically in good condition, although faded, the miniature is of vigorous autograph quality but the face is of the usual schematized Mask of Youth pattern. As in the case of all Hilliard's miniatures of the Queen, observation of the dress

is precise, to the sprigs of greenery tucked into her bodice and hair. The cascading ringlets and the additional chin-ruff occur only in portraits at the very close of the reign (Strong, *The English Icon*, p. 299 (304); 240 (211)). Thus Reynolds' and Auerbach's dating, c. 1590, is far too early. This is one of the five Radnor miniatures (see nos. 87, 93) which descended as a group, probably from Elizabeth Stafford, Lady Drury.

COLLECTIONS: See no. 87.

LITERATURE: Countess of Radnor and W. B. Squire, *Catalogue of the Collection of the Earl of Radnor*, London, 1909, II, pp. 108–11.
V & A, 1942 (42).
Auerbach, *Hilliard*, pp. 109–10; 301 (84)
Strong, *Portraits of Queen Elizabeth I*, p. 95 (15)
Strong, "*The Radnor Miniatures*", *Christie's Review of the Season 1974*, ed. John Herbert, 1974, pp. 254–57.

NICHOLAS HILLIARD

211 Elizabeth I, c. 1600,
possibly after a lost miniature by
Levina Teerlinc, c. 1559

Private Collection
Vellum stuck to plain card, rectangular, 91 × 56 mm, $3\frac{9}{16} \times 2\frac{3}{16}$ in.

Dated by Auerbach to c. 1569 and by Reynolds c. 1560–70, recent detailed examination establishes beyond a doubt that this miniature belongs to a group by Hilliard based on earlier portraits and painted c. 1600.

This miniature of Elizabeth in robes of state is painted in his typical late, somewhat mechanical manner. The inclusion of a wet-in-wet folded curtain background, is a feature decisive for dating. The use of ultramarine as well as blue bice in the curtain indicates the precious status of the object, reinforced by the insertion of an actual diamond into the cross of the orb. The fact that the curtain is blue relates it closely in date to the Ham House "Mask of Youth" portrait of the Queen (no. 209).

The new dating fits in exactly with the re-dating of the large-scale oil version now in the National Portrait Gallery (ex Warwick Castle) which, on tree-ring analysis, is from c. 1600–10. Although Janet Arnold in her study of the costume in both was unaware of the true dating of the miniature, it reinforces her conclusion that they both stem from "another picture, probably painted in 1559, or shortly afterwards, now missing". The Hilliard miniature ought to derive from one by Levina Teerlinc, recording the Queen in her coronation regalia, the basis for the official image on her Great Seal and state documents. Janet Arnold discusses the costume, which is that worn by Elizabeth for her state entry into London and her coronation, on January 14th and 15th 1559, in detail and points out that the crown is one which reappears later in the painting of *Queen Elizabeth I and the Three Goddesses*, 1569 (Strong, *Portraits of Queen Elizabeth I*, pl. VI). The later dating would also account for the distension of the bodice which relates more closely to fashions after c. 1590.

The condition is basically good, with the usual fading and oxidized silver, but there are some minute paint losses and scattered restorations in the background.

A similar rectangular miniature but in parliament robes, which were of crimson velvet, is recorded by van der Dort: "Inpris don upon the righte. lighte a full forward -/ faced Picture of Queene Elizabeth in her-/ Perliament Roabes with Scepter and Gloabe in / her hands in a little square Box woodden -/ frame wth a shiver /" (Millar, *Walpole Society*, XXXVII, 1960, p. 112 (40)). The $2\frac{1}{4} \times 2$ in. seems also to decisively eliminate any possibility that they are the same object.

COLLECTIONS: Edward Harley, 2nd Earl of Oxford (1689–1741);
   first recorded by Vertue, c. 1732 (*Notebooks*, IV, p. 41);
   Vertue's catalogue, 1743 (4); Oxford's daughter married
   William Bentinck, 2nd Duke of Portland; thence by descent.

LITERATURE: O'Donoghue, *Catalogue*, 1894, p. (1).
Goulding, *Welbeck*, pp. 59–60 (10).
V & A, 1947 (4).
Auerbach, *Hilliard*, pp. 57–58, pl. 13; 289 (13).
Strong, *Portraits of Queen Elizabeth I*, p. 89 (1).
Janet Arnold, "The 'Coronation' Portrait of Queen Elizabeth I", *Burlington Magazine*, CXX, 1978, p. 7.

FRANCIS DELARAM AFTER NICHOLAS HILLIARD

212 Elizabeth I, 1617–19

The British Museum, Department of Prints and Drawings (1849–3–15–1)
Engraving, 31.4 × 22.3 cm, $12\frac{3}{8} \times 8\frac{3}{4}$ (plate),
27.7 × 22.3 cm, $10\frac{7}{8} \times 8\frac{3}{8}$ (border)

In 1617 Hilliard was granted, by royal patent, the sole right to issue portraits of James I and other members of the royal family. From the wording of the patent this is a reassertion of an existing activity and not a novel departure. However normal it was for Hilliard to provide drawings for engravers, it was not the norm for them to acknowledge their source by including his name on the plate. This engraving is the sole exception with the acknowledgement: *Nic: Hillyard delin: et excud: cum privilegio Maiest:* The portrait of Elizabeth is a variant of the miniature at Ham House (no. 209) let down into a cloud vision more appropriate to a religious context. Francis Delaram (worked about 1615–24), it has been suggested, came to England with Cornelius Boel and his work is of the new wave stemming from the influence of Otto Vaenius. It is interesting to compare Delaram's interpretation of a Hilliard design with Elstracke's (nos. 251). He manages to convert the essentially flat, linear style of Hilliard into his own three-dimensional idiom. If it had not been for the 1617 patent to Hilliard, Delaram would surely have gone to Oliver.

LITERATURE: Hind, *Engraving*, II, pp. 219 (8).
Strong, *Portraits of Queen Elizabeth I*, p. 154 (9).

Tournaments and Masques

I HILLIARD AND THE ACCESSION DAY TILTS

The most important festivals of the Elizabethan age were the series of tournaments held annually on the Accession Day of the Queen, November 17th. These arose out of a vow made at the beginning of the reign by her Master of the Armoury, Sir Henry Lee, that he would meet all comers at the tilt on that day. As a result he became Queen's Champion at the Tilt and these events gradually came to be elaborated until, by the early 1580s, they had become the major public spectacle of the year. The tournaments, which were staged almost without exception in the tiltyard of Whitehall Palace, site of the present Horseguards, became an ideal vehicle for royalist propaganda. It was open to the public who flocked to see the Queen, seated in the tilt gallery, receiving the homage of her knights. As was customary throughout Europe in the late sixteenth century the actual fighting became increasingly overlaid by complicated stage-management involving scenery and costumes, allegorical plot and disguise, acting, music and singing. The surviving literary texts and descriptions together with poems celebrating the tournaments provide a vivid picture of these extravagant occasions. The mood was always heavily romantic, patriotic and Protestant. Each knight came in fancy dress, attended by his entourage in costume. They paid tribute to the Queen, an act formalized in the presentation of a pasteboard shield painted with the knight's *impresa* or device for that tournament. These were hung up afterwards in the Shield Gallery of the palace.

Hilliard's cabinet miniature of Cumberland (no. 216) shows one of these shields hung up on a tree behind him. The Earl's pseudonym was the Knight of Pendragon Castle and appearances at the tilt record his entrance astride a dragon laden with spoils and in a castle attended by Merlin. An earlier miniature of him (no. 214), also in tilt guise with a lady's favour tied to his arm, is probably the first instance of Hilliard's abandonment of the blue background. Behind the earl there is an emblematic stormy sky and a motto, in short his *impresa*. The tilts provided a focal point for the cult of emblematics and devices which became such a striking feature from the 1580s onwards reinforcing the anti-naturalistic tendencies already inherent in Hilliard's art. Although Cumberland succeeded Lee as Queen's Champion, an event almost certainly celebrated in Hilliard's miniature, his real successor was Essex. His tournament appearances were masterpieces of self-advertizement and royal flattery. In 1590 he entered the tiltyard in a procession looking like a funeral cortège and five years later dramatized himself in a script by Francis Bacon as Erophilus poised between Love and Self-Love or Philautia.

The miniatures are a vivid reflection of the Accession Day tilts but we cannot exclude the possibility that the Hilliard workshop could also have painted *imprese* shields or

otherwise assisted in the visual appearance of these occasions.

See also nos. 216,220.

SELECT BIBLIOGRAPHY

Frances A. Yates, *Astraea. The Imperial Theme in the Sixteenth Century*, London, 1975, pp. 88–111.
Strong, *The Cult of Elizabeth*, pp. 129–62.

213 *Tilt Cheque for Accession Day*, 1584

The College of Arms (MS Box 37)

The College of Arms contains a unique series of score cheques for Elizabethan tournaments and, in particular, those covering the tournament held annually to celebrate Elizabeth's Accession to the throne on November 17th. The cheque for 1584 is the earliest and records the tilters at Whitehall on that occasion: they ran in pairs against each other and the two opening runners had Hilliard connexions. Sir Henry Lee led the field as Queen's Champion and inaugurator of the tilts, and his will mentions what must be a miniature of himself tilting against Essex (Auerbach, *Hilliard*, p. 171). He ran against Sir Philip Sidney whom Hilliard mentions in his *Treatise* as a sitter (*Treatise*, p. 82). The second pair was Cumberland and Lord Thomas Howard. Cumberland was a noted patron of Hilliard and Howard possibly also. Each pair of knights ran six courses and these are recorded in the box by the score-keeper, the number of lances broken recorded by pen or the prick of a pin on the line issuing from the box.

The 1584 Tilt is also important because we have a description of it. The knights are described as making their separate entries on horseback or in triumphal cars attended by squires and pages. Some came dressed as savages, others with their horses disguised as elephants. A sonnet spoken or presented on behalf of a Blind Knight is extant (printed E. K. Chambers, *Sir Henry Lee*, Oxford, 1936, p. 271).

LITERATURE: Strong, "Elizabethan Jousting Cheques in the Possession of the College of Arms·II", *The Coat of Arms*, V, no. 35, 1958, pp. 63–4.
Strong, *The Cult of Elizabeth*, pp. 134–5, 150, 206.

NICHOLAS HILLIARD

214 George Clifford, 3rd Earl of Cumberland, 1585–89

The Nelson-Atkins Museum of Art, Kansas City
Vellum stuck onto card, oval, 71×58 mm,
$2\frac{3}{4} \times 2\frac{1}{4}$ in.

George Clifford, 3rd Earl of Cumberland (1558–1605), naval commander, succeeded as Earl in 1570, took part in numerous privateering expeditions, most of which ended in failure and lived extravagantly, taking a leading role in court festivals succeeding, in 1590, Sir Henry Lee as Queen's Champion.

This is the earliest portrait of Cumberland, dated by Auerbach c. 1590, but surely earlier. His hair is shorter

214

than in the likeness recorded in the family triptych, which is probably based on portraits painted in 1589 (Strong, *Tudor and Jacobean*, I, p. 57; II, pl. 104), and in the full-length miniature (no. 216). The portrait records his appearance in the Greenwich armour he wore at the Accession Day Tilts which he first attended in 1583 (Strong, *The Cult of Elizabeth*, p. 206). A date of 1585-89, but closer to 1585, would be more correct.

Dating is also helped by the innovation to the background, relating to the series of miniatures experimenting with the abandonment of the blue ground which belong to the years after c. 1587. This is conceivably the earliest example, the result, no doubt, of the sitter's demand that his *impresa* of a stormy sky, with a motto *Fulmen aquasque fero* (I bear lightning and water), replace the calm one. The lightning is formalized into the shape of a caduceus, an emblem that patterns the lining of the surcoat he wears in the full-length miniature at Greenwich (no. 216). The miniature probably records an appearance at an Accession Day Tilt when it was customary for a knight to present the Queen with his *impresa* painted on a pasteboard shield (see above; Strong, *The Cult of Elizabeth*, p. 140). Support for this is in the blue favour tied around his right arm.

This is a rare instance in which what the sitter wears still survives, reinforcing the technical evidence that Hilliard only painted what he saw.

INSCRIBED: The motto left: *Fulmen aquasque fero.*

COLLECTIONS: Lord Northwick sale, Thirlstane House, Cheltenham, 5th August 1859 (lot 779); bt. Whitehead; purchased by C. Sotheby, 1862; Sotheby of Ecton Hall sale Sotheby's October 11th 1955 (lot 74).

LITERATURE: V & A, 1947 (54).
Auerbach, *Hilliard*, pp. 115, pl. 90; 302 (88).
Strong, *Tudor and Jacobean*, I, p. 57.
Strong, *The Cult of Elizabeth*, pp. 141-42.

215 Tilt Armour for the Earl of Cumberland

Drawing in the Almain Armourers' Album, late 16th century
Victoria & Albert Museum (D605-1894)
Pen, ink and watercolour, 42.9 × 29 cm, $16\frac{7}{8} \times 11\frac{1}{2}$ in.

The Almain Armourer's Album contains a record of a whole series of suits made in the royal armouries at Greenwich during the Elizabethan period, including many that were made for and appeared in the Accession Day Tilts. Hilliard only ever painted what he saw and this armour is the one which appears in the miniature at Kansas (no. 214), decorated with bands interlinking Tudor Roses, fleur de lys and true lover's knots. The armour, moreover, survives virtually complete, and is now in the Metropolitan Museum of Art, New York (Strong, *The Cult of Elizabeth*, p. 142 (67)).

COLLECTIONS: Exhibited by Vertue to the Society of Antiquaries, 1723; Henrietta, Duchess of Portland; Spitzer collection, 1894; Stein of Paris; acquired, 1894.

LITERATURE: Viscount Dillon, *The Almain Armourers Album*, London, 1905.
F. H. CRIPPS-DAY, *Fragmenta Armamenta*, 1934, II, ii, pp. 121-36.

NICHOLAS HILLIARD

216 George Clifford, 3rd Earl of Cumberland, c. 1590

National Maritime Museum, Greenwich
Vellum stuck to a fruit wood panel, rectangular, 258 × 176 mm, $10\frac{1}{8} \times 6\frac{31}{32}$ in.
See no. 214

One of the most famous of all Hilliard's miniatures it depicts Cumberland dressed as he would have appeared at the fancy-dress tournament held annually on Elizabeth's Accession Day, November 17th. In 1590 he succeeded Sir Henry Lee as Champion at the tilt, an occasion marked by symbolic ceremonies in the tiltyard. It would seem natural, as Winter first suggested, that the miniature was commissioned to mark this advance by the Earl in the Queen's favour that was shortly to be overshadowed by the more brilliant Essex. In this office he sustained the role of the Knight of Pendragon Castle, the portrait therefore is a rare record of allegorical dress for the tournament. He wears Greenwich armour patterned with stars, a type for which pieces survive, over which is a tunic with sleeves banded with gold braid adorned with jewels in gold mounts. The lining is embroidered with a pattern of armillary spheres, branches of olive and *caducei*. The sphere, we know, was an image used by the Queen. Her bejewelled glove is also sewn onto his hat. The caduceus appears as an emblem in Hilliard's earlier miniature of Cumberland (no. 214). On the tree of chivalry to the right hangs a pasteboard shield of the type presented to the Queen at the Tilts bearing *Hasta quan (do)*. Previously this has been said to be a Spanish motto, *Hasta quan*, but the

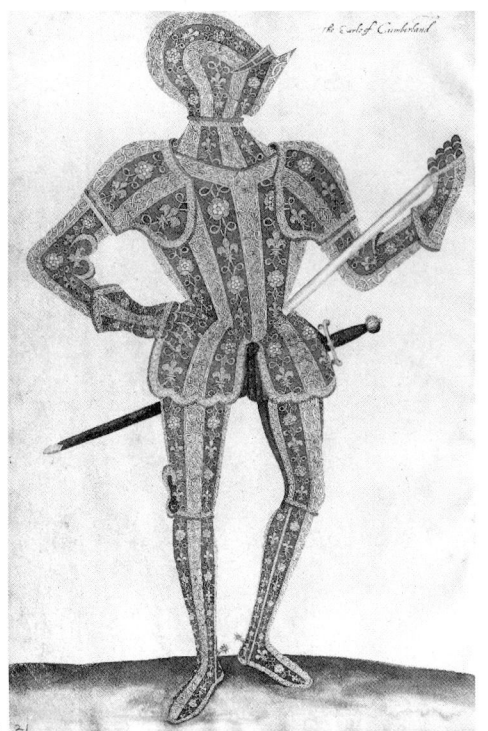

215

216

miniature has been slightly trimmed to the right and fragments of two other letters are clearly visible. The shield would originally have been complete. The meaning of the *impresa* would have been along the lines that Cumberland would wield the lance (*hasta*) as Champion until the sun, moon and earth went into eclipse. Examination of the view to the left under magnification establishes that it is intended as a panorama across the Thames from the south bank towards Westminster and Whitehall. From left to right it is possible to identify Westminster Hall, Westminster Abbey and the Tower with, on the south bank, Barnard's Castle. The allusion would be to his role in the tiltyard of Whitehall Palace and clinches the commemorative nature of the commission as celebrating his acceptance of the role of Champion on Accession Day, 1590.

The view of London should be from an unidentified engraved source, but the composition as a whole is taken from an engraving by Goltzius (1582) of a Pike-Bearer. The pose is identical, there is the same distant low-lying background view and there is even a tree to the right with an *impresa* shield suspended upon it. Although the miniature has suffered from fading, oxidization, and considerable flaking and repainting in the background areas it must rank as perhaps Hilliard's most successful large-scale miniature next to the *Young Man among Roses*.

INSCRIBED: On the shield to the right: *Hasta quan(do)*.

LITERATURE: Kennedy, *Buccleuch*, pl. 17.
Winter, *Elizabethan Miniatures*, pl. 5.
V & A, 1947 (54).
Pope-Hennessy, *Lecture*, 1949, pl. 31.
Auerbach, *Hilliard*, pp. 112–13, pl. 89; 302 (87).
Strong, *Tudor and Jacobean*, I, p. 57.
Strong, *The Cult of Elizabeth*, p. 156.

217 George Peele, *Polyhymnia*, London, 1590

(Photograph)

George Peele wrote two poems celebrating Accession Day Tilts, *Polyhymnia* in 1590 and *Anglorum Feriae* in 1595, valuable and rare sources, evoking something of the spectacle and pageantry of these occasions. In 1590 the leading participant in the tilts, Sir Henry Lee, resigned his post as Queen's Champion to Cumberland and this is probably the occasion commemorated in Hilliard's miniature of the Earl. Peele indicates some of the disguises of the tilters; Lord Strange on a pageant car with the Stanley eagle which stooped before the Queen; Lord Compton as the white knight; Sir Charles Blount as the Sun, Robert Knowles "Laden with golden boughs".

The tilting over, Lee made over his office to Cumberland in front of a reconstruction of the Temple of the Vestal Virgins erected before the gallery in which the Queen sat. He laid his arms at the foot of a crowned column embraced by an eglantine tree. The eglantine was one of Elizabeth's flowers and appears embowering in another context, Hilliard's *Young Man among Roses (no. 263)*.

WILLIAM SEGAR

218 **Robert Devereux, 2nd Earl of Essex**, 1590

National Gallery of Ireland, Dublin
Oil on panel, 113.1 × 87.7 cm, 44¾ × 34⅝ in.
(Photograph)

The portrait is dated 1590 and is the earliest certainly identifiable portrait of Essex, at the age of twenty-four.

Although the Earl was made a Knight of the Garter in 1588 it is significant that he is not even wearing the Lesser George which it was obligatory to wear with all forms of civil or military dress. Its absence only occurs in the case of portraits of sitters in fancy dress and, in this instance, it should record his appearance at the Accession Day Tilt of 1590. The occasion was used for an allegorical act of penance before the Queen for his marriage and Essex entered the tiltyard "all in sable sad" on a chariot pulled by black horses driven by Time.

The portrait was listed in the Lumley inventory as "done by Segar" and this connexion was first published by David Piper in 1957. Six portraits by him are listed in that inventory but his *œuvre* remains obscure. William Segar (fl. c. 1580/5–d. 1633), Portcullis Pursuivant in 1585, eventually became Garter King of Arms in 1603 and was knighted in 1617. His portrait of Essex reveals the influence of Hilliard in the calligraphic rendering of the features, the stylized drawing of the hands and the flat frontal lighting. If Hilliard's *Young Man among Roses* (no. 263) is Essex, this portrait depicts the same sitter three years later with a different hairstyle and a moustache.

INSCRIBED: On the *cartellino*, top left: *Robert Devereux Earle of Essex*.

COLLECTIONS: John, Lord Lumley; recorded in his inventory, 1590 (*Walpole Society*, VI, 1918, p. 23); recorded both in 1772 (B.L. Additional MS 5726 E.V. f. 18) and in 1776 by Pennant (*Walpole Society*, VI, 1918, p. 44) as a full length; referred to by Vertue when sent to London for repair, 1713 (*Notebooks*, IV, p. 42); sold, 1785 (lot 14) (*Walpole Society*, VI, 1918, p. 32); reappeared at the Earl of Stafford sale, Christie's 30th May 1885 (lot 380); acquired, 1886.

LITERATURE: *Catalogue of Pictures . . . in the National Gallery of Ireland*, 1928, p. 268.
D. Piper, "The 1590 Lumley Inventory", *Burlington Magazine*, XCIX, 1957, p. 231.
Auerbach, *Hillard*, pp. 276, 33 (276).
Strong, *Tudor and Jacobean*, I, p. 116.
Strong, *The English Icon*, p. 217 (175).
Strong, *The Cult of Elizabeth*, pp. 64, 152.

ARTIST UNKNOWN

219 Robert Radcliffe, 5th Earl of Sussex, 1593

The Armouries, H.M. Tower of London
Oil on canvas, 222.3 × 144.8 cm, 87½ × 57 in.

Robert Radcliffe, 5th Earl of Sussex (1569?–1629), known as Lord Fitzwalter until he succeeded his father in 1593; sent as ambassador extraordinary to Scotland for the christening of Prince Henry, 1594; accompanied Essex on the Cadiz expedition, 1596; Earl Marshal, 1597 and 1601; 1603 Lord lieutenant of Essex; sold Newhall to Buckingham 1622. During the 1590s he was a literary patron.

The portrait is dated 1593 and must record, in part at least, the sitter's first appearance at an Accession Day Tilt, held that year at Windsor, because plague had delayed the return of the court to Whitehall. Cumberland as

Champion appeared in his usual role of Knight of Pendragon Castle with his attendants dressed as sailors and Sir Robert Cary came as the Unknown Knight imploring forgiveness for his marriage.

Fitzwalter jousted at all the tilts until 1602. In 1595 Peele describes him wearing "ravens' feathers by the moon's reflex" and the year after Francis Bacon wrote a speech in which he made petition to retire from public life in order to study and acquire the virtues of his deceased father. As in the case of the miniatures large-scale portraiture vividly reflects this revival of chivalry. The bejewelled plume in the helmet on the table to the left is a quite astonishingly opulent object studded with pearls and precious stones. The motto dwelling on the ruin "awaiting those who are too loyal and loving" (*Amando Fidando Troppo sam rovinato*) might have been that he used for the tilt. It is contemporaneous with the full-length miniatures and the revival of the format went *in tandem*, in 1590s. No satisfactory attribution of this portrait has yet been made.

COLLECTIONS: John, Lord Lumley and recorded in the 1590 Lumley inventory (*Walpole Society*, VI, 1918, p. 22); sold from Lumley castle, 8th August, 1785 (lot 32); BT. Terry; Duke of Sutherland sale, Christie's, 8th February, 1908 (lot 53); Henry Harris; sold Southeby's 25th October, 1950 (lot 233); acquired by the tower armouries.

LITERATURE: L. Cust, "An Elizabethan Portrait", *Burlington Magazine* XXIV, 1913; pp. 4–10.
L. Cust "Marcus Gheeraerts" *Walpole Society*, 111, 1914, p. 43.
J. G. Mann, Armour in Essex, "*Trans. of the Essex Archaeological Society*, N.S. XXII, 1939, p. 294.
Strong, *The Cult of Elizabeth*, pp. 56, 208–11.

NICHOLAS HILLIARD

220 Robert Devereux, 2nd Earl of Essex, c. 1593–95

Private Collection
Vellum stuck onto card, 249 × 204 mm, 9$\frac{27}{32}$ × 7$\frac{1}{32}$ in.
See no. 263

The early portraiture of Essex as it has recently been established leads to a tight dating of the miniature. Its initial identification as Essex by David Piper was clinched by the emblematic device the sitter has embroidered on his bases. This is recorded by Camden in his *Remaines* (1605): "The late Earl of Essex took a Diamond only amidst his shield, with this about it, 'Dum Formas Minuis'. Diamonds, as we all know, are impaired while they are fashioned and pointed" (*Remains Concerning Britain*, London, 1870 ed., pp. 384–85). Camden is recording an *impresa* borne at a tilt and painted on a pasteboard shield of the type in the miniature of Cumberland (no. 216). This would not eliminate its incorporation into the costume and here it is embroidered on either side of his bases within a circle, a series of diamonds with the motto (damaged) on a scroll beneath. As a portrait of Essex it fits into the series of miniatures of knights at the Accession Day Tilts and he wears what must be the Queen's glove tied to his right arm. In the background an attendant clad in the Queen's colours of black and white leads on his horse.

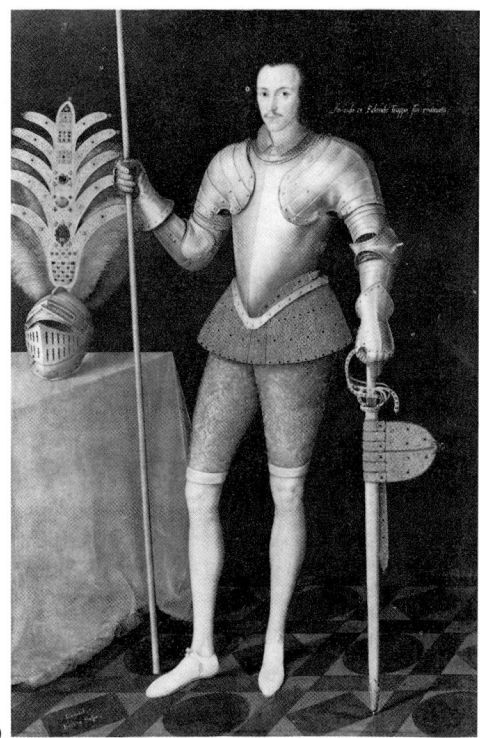

219

220

The dating must be between c. 1592/3 and 1595/6 as one of a series of portraits of Essex (discussed in Strong, *The Cult of Elizabeth*, pp. 64–5). It is conceivable that it commemorates the famous Accession Day Tilt of 1595. Elizabeth did, we know, bestow her glove on him on that occasion (ibid., p. 141). The background, which is of an army and an encampment, would support the earlier dating as an allusion to his involvement in the English campaign in Normandy in 1591.

This is one of Hilliard's most involved compositions, like the Cumberland conceived in sharp layers receding backwards. The large cavorting horse is probably derived in reverse from Goltzius' *Marcus Curtius* (c. 1586).

The present attribution of this to Hilliard is open to qualification, although the former one to Oliver cannot be sustained either. At precisely the period that this was painted Rowland Lockey was emerging as a miniaturist and painter. We know from *The More Family Group* (no. 267) that he did execute cabinet miniatures. The background panorama of tents and troops is far too impressionistic for Hilliard as is the painting of the cavorting horse and squire. There are also areas, such as the gold embroidery on the tent which are very feebly painted in a way that Hilliard never did even at his least inspired. The pose is one that recurs in Hilliard but the relationship between the figure, the tent and the horse is far from happy. The painting of the armour and the helmet is very close to the 1607 Prince Henry (no. 245). The collaboration of Lockey must be posed as a hypothesis.

The miniature is very damaged with large losses over the horse, left, considerable repainting on the table-cloth and flaking in the armour.

INSCRIBED: Fragmentary versions of the *impresa* motto on the bases either side: *DVM FORMAS*[*MINVIS*] / [*D*]*VM E*[*ieF*]*OR*[*MAS*] *M*[*INVIS*].

COLLECTIONS: First recorded by Vertue, c. 1750 when in the collection of James West (1704?–1772) (*Notebooks*, V, p. 84); James West Sale 27th February 1773 (lot 70) as Sidney by Oliver; Walpole states that it was in the collection of Philip Yorke, 1st Earl of Hardwicke.

LITERATURE: B. Siebeck, *Das Bild Sir P. Sidneys in der Englischen Renaissance*, 1939, p. 168.
British Portraits, R.A. 1956 (545).
D. Piper, "The 1590 Lumley Inventory: Hilliard, Segar and the Earl of Essex II", *Burlington Magazine*, XCIX, 1957, p. 303.
Roy Strong, "Queen Elizabeth, the Earl of Essex and Hilliard", ibid., p. 146.
A. C. Judson, *Sidney's Appearance*, Indiana U.P., 1958, pp. 34–35.
Auerbach, *Hilliard*, 1961, pp. 125–28, pl. 98; 304 (98).
Strong, *Tudor and Jacobean Portraits*, I, p. 116.
Strong, *The Cult of Elizabeth*, pp. 64–65.

HENRY PEACHAM

221 *Minerva Britanna, or a Garden of Heroical Devises*, London, 1612

"Impresa" of Robert Devereux, 2nd Earl of Essex p. 114)
The British Library (C.38.f.28.)

Henry Peacham's *Minerva Britanna* is one of the few English emblem books. Although published in 1612 and dedicated to Henry, Prince of Wales, it is backward looking and draws on devices and *imprese* from the previous reign: "some late dead, some living yet, / who serv'd ELIZA in her raigne, / And worthily had honour'd it" (p. 212). The margin is annotated with names including, Sir Philip Sidney, Cumberland and Lord Thomas Howard. The devices include one used by Essex at an Accession Day Tilt (p. 114), probably to signify his grief at the death of Sidney (Strong, *The Cult of Elizabeth*, p. 145), and which was amongst the decorative cartouche shields hung up in the Shield Gallery at Whitehall Palace. Comparison should be made between this tilt shield and that in the background of the portrait of Cumberland (no. 216). These were highly finished pieces of decorative painting and the Hilliard workshop could have produced such items.

The emblematic woodcut pictures in *Minerva Britanna* are believed to be by Peacham himself. Whoever their author, they are not lifted from continental emblem books but represent an indigenous tradition. Apart from the Accession Day *imprese* Peacham drew heavily on Ripa's *Iconologia* and, to a lesser extent, on Spenser's *Faerie Queene*. More important is that the aesthetic is anti-naturalistic and Hilliardesque.

LITERATURE: Rosemary Freeman, *English Emblem Books*, London, 1948, pp. 68–82.
Henry Peacham, *Minerva Britanna*, 1612, *English Emblem Books*, no. 5, ed. J. Horden, Scolar Press, 1973.

II OLIVER AND THE STUART COURT MASQUES

Under the Stuarts the focus shifted from outdoor to indoor court festivals epitomized by the court masques. The long series of court masques written by Ben Jonson and designed by Inigo Jones began in 1605 with the *Masque of Blackness* and were to continue virtually unbroken down to 1640. From the start they were, amongst other things, conceived to be deliberately visually revolutionary. Through these stage settings Jones over the years educated the court's vision as he taught them to look in terms of Renaissance optics and light and shade besides presenting the ideals of a new life graced by classical architecture and Italianate gardens. It is only, however, in Isaac Oliver's miniatures that we find direct reflections of the masques in the form of ladies sitting for their portraits wearing the extraordinary costumes created by Inigo Jones. Oliver and Jones would have been extremely sympathetic to each other, both having experienced Italy in the 1590s. Oliver was the older man, and his draughtsmanship was far more accomplished than anything Jones was to achieve until the 1630s. That they must have known each other is reflected in the fact that Jones preserved Oliver's drawing of Prince Henry (no. 259) and later gave it to Charles I.

The masques were a new and more insidious form of royalist propaganda. Through an alliance of verse, song, mime, dance and scenic spectacle Jones and Jonson aimed to present the court with visions in which the Queen and her ladies or the Prince and his companions became for a time their ideal Platonic selves come down from heaven to earth vanquishing vice and taming all opposition to the crown. The plots moved from disharmony to harmony and this was reflected in the settings in which the House of Fame would banish a witches' cavern or Oberon's Palace subject untamed rugged nature. In this way the masques continued to emphasize the essentially emblematic and symbolic nature of all pictured material even although that material was now depicted in accord with all the achievements of Renaissance painting.

SELECT BIBLIOGRAPHY
Stephen Orgel and Roy Strong, *Inigo Jones. The Theatre of the Stuart Court*, University of California Press, 1973.

John Harris, Stephen Orgel and Roy Strong, *The King's Arcadia: Inigo Jones and the Stuart Court*, Arts Council Exhibition Catalogue, 1973, pp. 35–55.

INIGO JONES

222 **Design for a Winged Masquer**, c. 1605

The Trustees of the Chatsworth Settlement
Watercolour, mostly opaque, heightened with gold and silver (now oxidized), 27.6 × 18 cm, $11\frac{1}{16} \times 7$ in.

There are two, virtually identical, designs for this costume. The quality of the drawing is extremely feeble and forms a striking comparison to the enormously accomplished work of Isaac Oliver twenty years earlier. As in the case of Jones's designs for the first masque, Ben Jonson's *Masque of Blackness* of 1605, it depicts the ground on which the figure stands, in this instance a verdant green. The costume format with its billowing veil, horizontally braided sleeves and layered striped skirt are all features repeated in those dresses. No certain identification can be suggested but it is important evidence for early Jacobean masquing dress in relation to Oliver's miniature of a lady (no. 223). The structure of the dress is identical with the breasts exposed beneath transparent gauze and a trailing veil falling from the elaborate head-dress.

COLLECTIONS: The artist to his assistant, John Webb; thence through a number of sources to Richard Boyle, 3rd Earl of Burlington, whose daughter, Charlotte, married William, 4th Duke of Devonshire; thence by descent.

LITERATURE: P. Simpson and C. F. Bell, *Designs by Inigo Jones for Masques and Plays at Court*, Walpole Society, XII, 1923–24 (418).
S. Orgel and R. Strong, *Inigo Jones. The Theatre of the Stuart Court*, University of California Press, 1973, I, p. 101 (5).

ISAAC OLIVER

223 **Lady Masquer**, c. 1605

The Rijksmuseum, Amsterdam (on loan to the Mauritshuis, The Hague, 1001)
Vellum stuck onto card, oval, 54 × 41 mm, $2\frac{1}{8} \times 1\frac{5}{8}$ in.

The sitter is wearing female masquing dress which frequently exposed the breasts beneath a transparent fabric. This type of attire with its elaborate dressing of the hair, falling loosely onto the shoulders, veil and mantle, and high waisted dress was standard for the early masques. Numerous early designs by Inigo Jones are variations on this format (e.g. no. 222 and see S. Orgel and R. Strong, *Inigo Jones. The Theatre of the Stuart Court*, University of California, 1973, I, pp. 101 (5–6); 146 (22); 149 (22); 153 (32); 326 (75)). There were few masques of ladies and none after 1613. All have designs or descriptions so that it is strange not to be able to identify which masque this miniature records. The dress and mantle are of a grey colour, shot with silver, and there is an elaborate belt below the breasts adorned with pearls. Her hair is decorated with pale pink roses and pansies. Stylistically this

222

223

224

miniature seems to pre-date the second masque miniature (no. 227) which is much more assured and eschews the flowery Hilliardesque approach to the decorative details of the dress. Its condition, apart from fading, is good.

COLLECTIONS: Dutch Royal Collection; first certainly recorded, 1815–21.

LITERATURE: V & A, 1947 (181).
All the Paintings in the Rijksmuseum, Amsterdam, 1976, p. 762 (A4347).

ATTRIBUTED TO JOHN DE CRITZ

224 Lucy Harington, Countess of Bedford as a Power of Juno in Ben Jonson's Masque, "Hymenaei", 1606

The Trustees of the Bedford Settled Estates
Oil on canvas, 213.4 × 129.5 cm, 84 × 50 in.

See no. 274

One of three full-length portraits of ladies dressed in the costumes Inigo Jones designed for *Hymenaei*, a masque danced on the occasion of the marriage of the Earl of Essex to the notorious Frances Howard, daughter of the Earl of Suffolk, on January 5th 1606. Jonson used the nuptials as a vehicle and image of a greater 'marriage', that effected by the King in the union of England and Scotland into Great Britain. The masque was a double one of both lords and ladies, the latter descending in clouds as "The Powers of Juno'.

None of Jones's designs for this masque survive but the pictures like Oliver's miniatures (nos. 223, 227) give us a glimpse of what they looked like. Jonson describes the costumes as follows: "'The ladies' attire was wholly new, for the invention, and full of glory, as having in it the most true impression of a celestial figure: the upper part of white cloth of silver wrought with Juno's birds and fruits; a loose under garment, full gathered, of carnation, striped with silver and parted with a golden zone; beneath that another flowing garment of watchet cloth of silver, laced with gold . . . The attire of their heads did answer, if not exceed;

their hair being carelessly . . . bound under the circle of a rare and rich coronet adorned with all variety and choice of jewels, from the top of which flowed a transparent veil down to the ground, whose verge, returning up, was fastened to either side in most sprightly manner. Their shoes were of azure and gold set with rubies and diamonds . . ." (Orgel and Strong cited below, l.l.578–95).

Lucy Harington, as a setter of fashion, reflects that the wearing of masque dress in portraits could also mean modifications. Unlike the sitters in the other two portraits she made two changes in her costume, dropped an over-arching circlet of pearl at the top of the coronet, certainly again painted in daylight, and replaced the two-tier dress with a single reddish-brown skirt with horizontal bands of gold and a pattern of alternate grey squares and white dots between the bands. This would not have been worn in the masque as she would have eclipsed the Queen. All three pictures are reproduced in Strong, *The English Icon*, pp. 261–62 (243–45).

COLLECTIONS: Presumably commissioned by the sitter and thence by descent.

LITERATURE: G. Scharf, *A Catalogue of the Collection of Pictures at Woburn Abbey*, 1899, pp. 53–4 (75).
L. Cust, "Marcus Gheeraerts", *Walpole Society*, III, 1914, p. 30.
Ben Jonson, ed, C. H. Herford and E. Simpson, Oxford, 1941, pp. XV–XIV.
Strong, *The English Icon*, p. 262 (244).
S. Orgel and R. Strong, *Inigo Jones. The Theatre of the Stuart Court*, University of California Press, 1973, p. 114 (8).

ISAAC OLIVER

225 Anne of Denmark in a Costume for the "Masque of Beauty" (1608) or "Love Freed", (1611)

H.M. The Queen
Vellum stuck onto plain card, oval, 52.5 × 42 mm, $2\frac{1}{16} \times 1\frac{21}{32}$ in. *(Photograph)*

A superb miniature presenting the Queen in *à l'antique* profile wearing a crimson mantle, lined with blue, over a white dress, both embroidered with gold. Her hair is intertwined with pearls and gauze with a large diamond jewel in the front. This belongs to the group of antique profile images current at this period. Although from the eighteenth century onwards called Queen Elizabeth I, its correct identity is Anne and the costume a masquing one. Anne only appeared in five masques: *Blackness* (1605), *Beauty* (1608), *Queens* (1609), *Tethys Festival* (1610) and *Love Freed* (1611) and certain designs for her costumes and head-dresses exist for *Blackness* and *Tethys* (Orgel and Strong, *Inigo Jones*, The Theatre of the Stuart Court, University of California 1973, I, p. 96 (1); 198 (55)). A highly likely design exists for *Queens* (ibid., p. 159 (29)) and, in any case, nothing in the head-dress in the miniature relates to Anne as Bel-Anna, Queen of the Ocean. In the case of *Love Freed*, the head-dress design of ostrich plumes reflects Jones's sketch for the costume in the scene-design (ibid., pp. 235 (74), 237 (76)). There is no description in the text and dress could be altered so that *Love Freed* cannot altogether be excluded as a possibility. The *Masque of Beauty* danced on January 10th 1608 had sixteen masquers but again there is no detailed description of the dresses beyond "the one half in orange-tawney and silver, the other in sea-green and silver; the bodies and short skirts of white and gold to both" (ibid., p. 95, 1.218–20). The bodice in the miniature is white and gold but the colours of the mantle do not fit.

As far as we know Jones did not design *Beauty*. The miniature, however, is a reflection of the series of fantastic head-dresses that he designed for Anne in the masques which were more elaborate and splendid than those for the other masquers and he made special drawings for them.

The condition is good, apart from a number of discoloured patches on the features, probably due to the contamination of the vellum by some copper product.

INSCRIBED: Signed to the left: *10* (in monogram); to the right: *Servo per regnare*.

COLLECTIONS: Dr Richard Mead (1673–1754), recorded by Horace Walpole (*Visits*, Walpole Society, XVI, 1927, p. 74); purchased by Frederick, Prince of Wales.

LITERATURE: Walpole, *Anecdotes*, ed. Wornum, 1849, p. 78.
Winter, *Elizabethan Miniatures*, pl. XIV(b).
V & A, 1947 (178).
Auerbach, *Hilliard*, pp. 249, pl. 217; 330 (253).
Strong, *Tudor and Jacobean*, I, p. 10, II, pl. 16.

INIGO JONES

226 Costume for Artemisia in Ben Johnson's "Masque of Queens", 1609

The Trustees of the Chatsworth Settlement
Pen and black ink washed with warm grey. The head has been traced with a point for transference, 30.5 × 18.7 cm, 12 × 7⅜ in.

The costume was designed for Elizabeth Somerset, Lady Guildford, eldest daughter of the 4th Earl of Worcester and wife of Sir Henry Guildford of Horsted Place, Kent. The *Masque of Queens* was danced on February 2nd 1609 and

was the first occasion of an anti-masque which was of witches and hags banished by a vision of twelve heroic queens led by Anne of Denmark as Bel-Anna, Queen of the Ocean. There were changes of cast and of character amongst the queens but all the costume designs are martial in their cut and accoutrements, exactly in the style of Oliver's miniature of a lady in what should be a costume in *Queens* (no. 227). Inigo Jones's designs are conceived in the same manner with the bodice, as in the miniature, cut on the lines of a cuirass with scrolled decoration both on it and the sleeves. Some ladies had cloaks and others veils floating from very elaborate head-dresses, all of which were different but exactly in the style of Oliver's portrait.

COLLECTIONS: See no. 222.

LITERATURE: P. Simpson and C. F. Bell, *Designs by Inigo Jones for Masques and Plays at Court*, Walpole Society, XII, 1923–24 (no. 22).
S. Orgel and R. Strong, *Inigo Jones. The Theatre of the Stuart Court*, University of California Press, 1973, I, p. 142 (20).

ISAAC OLIVER

227 ?Masquer in Ben Jonson's "Masque of Queens", 1609

Victoria & Albert Museum (P.3-1942)
Vellum stuck to plain card, 62 × 51 mm, 2⁷⁄₁₆ × 2 in.

Painted from life and perhaps the most striking of the three miniatures depicting ladies in allegorical masque costume (nos. 223, 225). This has always been referred to as a lady wearing a masque costume, probably after a design by Inigo Jones. Her hair is looped with pearls and ultramarine bows with a scrolled coronet from which a veil falls. The dress is pink with blue sleeves, again adorned with gold scrolling, and over which a green mantle lined with orange has been looped. All the masques from this period, c. 1610, are heavily documented and there is no doubt that this particular dress relates closely to the series of costumes designed for the *Masque of Queens* danced on February 2nd 1609 (for text and designs see S. Orgel and R. Strong, *Inigo Jones. The Theatre of the Stuart Court*, University of California Press, 1973, I, pp. 130–53). The masquers, led by Anne of Denmark, came as twelve heroic queens who had triumphed in war: Penthesileia, Camilla, Thomyris, Artemisia, Berenice, Hypsicratea, Candace, Boadicea, Zenobria, Amalasunta, Valasca and Bel-Arma. Designs for only seven costumes survive and one for Atalanta who did not appear, although Lady Arundel danced another role. No description of the costume is included in the text nor who danced which rôle. The costume design for each masquer was different, all vaguely, as in the miniature, military and all with differing, complicated head-dresses. From the annotations on the Jones designs we probably know who danced eight of the queens, although the rejected Atalanta design means that there were changes. The four queens for whom designs do not survive are Hypsicratea, Boadicia, Amalasunta and Valasca and four ladies left to play these parts, Lady Arundel, Lady Huntingdon, Lady Essex and Lady Cranborne. It is not, however, as simple as that since other designs connected

227   228

with *Queens* survive including a head-dress for Lady Blanche Somerset who, at one stage, was also probably one of the masquers. Thus we have no guarantee either that the designs that are identifiable were actually those used or even that they were not modified or altered by the participants and their tailors as we know did take place. Most of the participants can be eliminated on portrait evidence, but not all. A connection with *Queens* ought to be correct.

The miniature is in moderately good condition but has been restored.

INSCRIBED: Signed to the right: *IO* in monogram.

COLLECTIONS: Part of the collection formed by Walter Francis, 5th Duke of Buccleuch (1806–1884); purchased from that collection by the N.A.C.F. and presented, 1942.

LITERATURE: Kennedy, *Buccleuch*, pl. XIV.
Winter, *Elizabethan Miniatures*, pl. XIII (b).
V & A, 1947 (182).

INIGO JONES

228 Head-dress, probably for Anne of Denmark in Samuel Daniel's "Tethys' Festival", 1610

The Trustees of the Chatsworth Settlement
Pen and brown ink, 22 × 17.8 cm, 8¾ × 7 in.

Extremely elaborate head-dresses were a feature of all the early court masques designed by Inigo Jones for Anne of Denmark. So complicated were they that separate drawings were made, particularly for those to be worn by the Queen (Strong and Orgel cited below, I, pp. 151 (29), 198 (55), 237 (76)). The interest in these extraordinary confections is directly paralleled in Oliver's miniature of the Queen wearing one (no. 225).

Tethys' Festival was a maritime masque, danced in honour of the creation of Henry as Prince of Wales on 5th June 1610. Anne appeared as Tethys, Queen of the Ocean: "their head-tire was composed of shells and coral, and

from a great murex shell in the form of a crest of an helm hung a thin waving veil" (ll.236–38). The Queen's head-dress is an elaboration of those worn by her companions, with her hair loose to her shoulders, as in Oliver's miniature, and piled high in ringlets entwined with an arrangement of seashells, pearls and feathers.

COLLECTIONS: See no. 222.

LITERATURE: P. Simpson and C. F. Bell, *Designs by Inigo Jones for Masques and Plays at Court*, Walpole Society, XII, 1923–24 (39).
S. Orgel and R. Strong, *Inigo Jones. The Theatre of the Stuart Court*, University of California Press, 1973, I, p. 198 (55).

INIGO JONES

229 Helmet probably for Prince Henry in Ben Jonson's "Barriers", 1610

The Trustees of the Chatsworth Settlement
Pen and brown ink washed with brown,
22.5 × 17.2 cm, 8⅞ × 6¾ in.

The drawing depicts a youth wearing a splendid parade helmet. Inigo Jones was in the habit, at this early period, of doing separate designs for the elaborate head-dresses of royal masquers. The most likely occasion would be the *Barriers* performed in the Whitehall Banqueting House on 6th January 1610. The Prince and his six assistants were cast as revivers of ancient British chivalry, as lineal descendants of the knights of Arthurian legend and the martial heroes of the intervening Gothic centuries. Inigo Jones's scenery conceived of Ancient British architecture, which he was to restore, as being in the classical style. Prince Henry is described as "like Mars . . . in his armour clad" (ll.139–40) and his companions as like "old Grecian heroes" (l.142). These references indicate that they were dressed *à l'antique*. The mythology created in these entertainments is identical to that in Oliver's portrait miniatures (no. 230). The design for the helmet is conceived in the form of a classical antique profile form, encircled by a crown and surmounted with a sphinx, emblem of secret wisdom.

Tournaments and Masques 141

COLLECTIONS: See no. 222.

LITERATURE: P. Simpson and C. F. Bell, *Designs by Inigo Jones for Masques and Plays at Court*, Walpole Society, XII, 1923–24 (423).
S. Orgel and R. Strong, *Inigo Jones. The Theatre of the Stuart Court*, University of California Press, 1973, I, p. 185 (52).

ISAAC OLIVER

230 Henry, Prince of Wales, 1610–11

National Portrait Gallery (1572)
Vellum on card which has been glued onto a thin wooden panel, oval, 52 × 41.5 mm, $2\frac{1}{16} \times 1\frac{5}{8}$ in.

Three versions survive of Prince Henry presented in profile *à l'antique* silhouetted against a classical shell niche, the other two being in the Fitzwilliam Museum, Cambridge and in the Mauritshuis. The profile likeness may connect with the drawing Oliver did for the engraving by William Hole which depicts him armed for fighting at the barriers (no. 259).

The miniatures directly reflect Inigo Jones's presentation of the Prince in the *Barriers* of 1610 and the *Masque of Oberon* of 1611. No design for his costume in the Barriers survives but Jonson's text refers to him "like Mars . . . in his armour clad" (l.139–40). There is also the reference to Henry V "to whom in face you are so like" (l.280–81). Henry V's portraits are of the well-known profile type (Strong, *Tudor and Jacobean*, II, pl. 281–82), so the allusion in the use of the profile formula is also to a regal knightly hero of the Gothic ages.

Although unsigned, this miniature is certainly by Oliver himself. The architecture is crisply rendered and it is in good condition apart from substantial flaking on the cloak. Although the features are faded, it is clear that the portrait is a repetition rather than the initial *ad vivum*. It is, however, after detailed examination, considerably better in quality than the studio status I accorded it in 1969.

INSCRIBED: An old inscription on a piece of paper (now removed) on the back gives a mis-identification: *CNEIVS / POMPEIVS / MAGNVS*.

COLLECTIONS: Purchased from Sergius Thrasybulus Chalkiadi of Southend-on-Sea, 1910, previous history unknown.

LITERATURE: Strong, *Tudor and Jacobean*, I, p. 161; II, pl. 324.

INIGO JONES

231 Prince Henry as Oberon in Ben Jonson's "Oberon, The Fairy Prince", 1611

The Trustees of the Chatsworth Settlement
Pen and brown ink washed with grey accentuated in black ink, 29.5 × 14.19 cm, $11\frac{5}{16} \times 5\frac{7}{8}$ in.

Oberon was danced on January 1st 1611 and elaborated the themes begun in the *Barriers* the previous year. It presented Prince Henry as a combination of revived ancient British

chivalry and a prince ruling over a Spenserian land of fairy. Visually it was conceived as a Roman imperial triumph, the Prince entering in a chariot drawn by two white bears. An observer describes the masquers attired "as the Roman emperors are represented' (Orgel and Strong, cited below, p. 206). All the designs for the Prince and his companions (*ibid.*, nos. 68–73) are in the antique style. Those of Henry turn the head into classical profile exactly as in Oliver's miniature (no. 230), both reflecting the sitter's desire to present himself as a Roman *imperator*, reflective of his role as heir apparent to the newly revived Empire of Great Britain.

COLLECTIONS: See no. 222.

LITERATURE: P. Simpson and C. F. Bell, *Designs by Inigo Jones for Masques and Plays at Court*, Walpole Society, XII, 1923–24 (52).
S. Orgel and R. Strong, *Inigo Jones. The Theatre of the Stuart Court*, University of California Press, 1973, I, p. 220 (70).

INIGO JONES

232 Design for Oberon's Palace in Ben Jonson's "Oberon, The Fairy Prince", 1611

The Trustees of the Chatsworth Settlement
Pen and light brown ink washed with grey and reinforced with pen and black ink, traces of former squaring up, 33.3 × 39.3 cm, $13\frac{1}{8} \times 15\frac{1}{2}$ in.
See no. 231.

The first scene in Oberon was one of rocks which parted to reveal this palace which the text describes as being transparent. This can be reconciled with the account of an eye witness who states "the rock opened discovering a great throne with countless lights and colours all shifting, a lovely thing to see" (Orgel and Strong cited below, p. 206). The onlookers would have seen a development of the tableau in the *Barriers*, performed in the previous year, of the Prince and his companions in antique dress arranged in a group, glimpsed as a vision, in this instance assimilated to their ideal prototypes as Oberon, the Fairy King and his Knights as revivers of Ancient British virtue and chivalry. The aethereal evocation of antique knights in attendance upon their lord in the background of Oliver's great miniature of the Prince (no. 257) sprang from the same propaganda programme and had the same ideological connotation.

Jones's palace is a medieval gothic one with turrets and crenellation but overlaid with classical additions: Serlian windows and a dome based on Bramante's famous Tempietto. This accords exactly with the architect's life-long mission which superimposed onto the inherited buildings of the heroic British past the newly rediscovered classical ideals.

COLLECTIONS: See no. 222.

LITERATURE: P. Simpson and C. F. Bell, *Designs by Inigo Jones for Masques and Plays at Court*, Walpole Society, XII, 1923–4 (42).
S. Orgel and R. Strong, *Inigo Jones. The Theatre of the Stuart Court*, University of California Press, 1973, I, p. 216 (63).

The Stuarts and the Limners

I THE ROYAL FAMILY: HILLIARD, LOCKEY AND THE HILLIARD STUDIO

NICHOLAS HILLIARD was fifty-six in 1603 when James I succeeded to the throne. The new King had no interest in the visual arts and the deliberately reactionary style of the final phase of the old Queen's reign, instead of being swept away, was allowed to continue as the official manner. Hilliard was to remain unchallenged as limner to the crown until his death. Although he had agreed to paint a life-scale portrait of Elizabeth in 1600, there is no indication that he ever painted one of James I, although the flat flowery style he represented lived on in the work of so far unidentified artists (no. 233) and enjoyed a final fashionable flowering in the glossy icons of William Larkin (no. 277). Hilliard's activities centred on producing miniatures and medals and as a designer of engravings of members of the royal family. He also continued to contribute to the occasional illuminated royal manuscript (no. 234). During the first two decades of the reign the advent of a new dynasty, which included for the first time for more than half a century the novelty and security of a royal family with a queen, a male heir and a marriageable princess, resulted in a massive proliferation of royal portraits far in excess of the Elizabethan period and in every medium. In addition, James' enunciation of monarchy by Divine Right formalized a semi-divine role for the crown which portraiture, along with the other arts, was designed to promulgate. That there are far more miniatures of James I than Elizabeth in a reign half as long reflects that fact.

Hilliard was old and the work which could still be of the highest quality when confronted by a royal sitter such as the enchanting Princess Elizabeth (no. 247) or the pathetic Prince Charles (no. 248), is, in the main, pedestrian. What the exact mechanics were in the manufacture of these endless portraits we shall probably never know but the technical and stylistic evidence points to all kinds of combinations to keep up the production line. Some are just tired hasty work by Hilliard himself; others are by his pupil Lockey, to whom he may well have subcontracted; and there are those which, although they use his techniques, are by unknown hands, clumsy, awkward and schematic although often the basic outline drawing could only be by the master himself. By 1619, when he died, even for the King this aesthetic had run its course. The advent of the Spanish match of Prince Charles to the Infanta, stirred James to move on. In 1618 he sat to Paul van Somer followed, about three years after, by Daniel Mytens. That Hilliard's son Laurence became limner in succession could only have been the result of the office having been secured in reversion during his father's lifetime. Although he continued to produce, to order, miniatures of James

(no. 241), as soon as Charles I succeeded in 1625 he was abandoned in favour of John Hoskins and Peter Oliver.

SELECT BIBLIOGRAPHY

Graham Reynolds, "Portraits by Nicholas Hilliard and his Assistants of King James I and his Family", *Walpole Society*, XXXIV, 1952–54, pp. 14–26.
Auerbach, *Hilliard*, pp. 147–68.
Strong, *Renaissance Miniature*, pp. 122–27.

MANNER OF NICHOLAS HILLIARD

233 James I, c. 1615

University of Cambridge, Old Schools
Oil on canvas, 204.5 × 106.7 cm, 80½ × 42 in.

James I disliked sitting for his portrait and the one face-mask for life-size portraits was in use until 1618 when he sat for Paul van Somer. Hilliard had nothing to do with that first face-mask and the evidence would point to it being the result of a sitting to John de Critz (before 1552–1641) who, in 1605, was appointed Serjeant Painter jointly with Leonard Fryer. De Critz was certainly a portrait painter (Strong, *The English Icon*, p. 259) but his work is extremely difficult to disentangle. One fact is clear, the face-mask was not the monopoly of de Critz alone and Marcus Gheeraerts certainly also used it (Strong, *Tudor and Jacobean*, I, p. 179). The system followed was clearly the Elizabethan one of a single official face-pattern available for use by all painters. That pattern must have extended to the royal jewels depicted in these portraits, which alternate but which certainly go back to a specific repertory of items that it was laid down could appear. In the case of this picture the hat jewel is one known as the Feather (see R. Strong, "Three Royal Jewels: the Three Brothers, the Mirror of Great Britain and the Feather", *Burlington Magazine*, CVIII, 1968, pp. 350–52 and p. 351 note 15 for a list of other versions in which this appeared).

There is no evidence that Hilliard ever painted a large-scale portrait of the King. The University of Cambridge portrait of James was probably occasioned by his five day visit in 1615. It utilizes the official face-pattern but goes on to set it within a context stylistically very different from the numerous other extant versions (Strong, *Tudor and Jacobean*, II, pl. 346–47). It re-casts the image in Hilliardesque terms with a concern for decoration; the normally plain grey doublet is embroidered with flowers and the trunk hose, shoes and rosettes are embellished with spiralling embroidery in gold and jewels. The chair to left is similarly elaborated with pattern in gold and large tassels. No attempt at perspective is made and the carpet is literally presented up-ended vertically. Even when compared with the work of William Larkin (no. 277) this is a decidedly archaicizing approach for c. 1615 and must be the work of a painter heavily influenced by Hilliard.

COLLECTIONS: First recorded in possession of the University, 1776.

LITERATURE: J. W. Goodison, *Catalogue of Cambridge Portraits*, Cambridge, 1955, pp. 15–16.

234

NICHOLAS HILLIARD AND ASSISTANTS

234 James I, 1603

> Illumination in the "Liber Ceruleus" of the Order of
> the Garter
> *THE DEAN OF WINDSOR as Register of the (Most
> Noble) Order of the Garter*
> Vellum

The official books of the Order of the Garter are a rich
source of Tudor and early Stuart illuminations in a
document of the greatest importance to the monarch as a
record of the annual activities of the Order. Although
damaged the reign of James I is prefaced with a full length
portrait of him seated in robes of the Garter by Hilliard. As
in the case of the Emmanuel College Charter (no. 191) the
portrait and encompassing canopy are by Hilliard himself
while the border is probably his design but the work of
another, inferior hand. It is typically Hilliardesque, be-
sprinkled with a decorative arrangement of pansies,
honeysuckle, roses and strawberries.

NICHOLAS HILLIARD

235 James I, 1604–9

> *Victoria & Albert Museum (P.3–1937)*
> Vellum stuck onto a playing card with part of a
> spade at the reverse which has been concealed by
> painting a band of black watercolour across it, oval,
> 53 × 43 mm, $2\frac{3}{32} \times 1\frac{11}{16}$ in.

The miniature can be dated to after 1604 by the inscription
referring to James's assumption of the style of King of

Great Britain in November of that year. Graham Reynolds
in his classification of Hilliard's miniatures of the King
identifies three main groups stemming from three sittings.
The first, which must have occurred shortly after his
accession in 1603, lasted until 1609 and it is to this group
that the present miniature can be assigned. (See Strong,
Renaissance Miniature, pp. 114–119.) It depicts James at the
optimistic opening of the reign as described in the Venetian
relazione of the Ambassador Nicolo Molin in 1607 when the
King was forty-three: "He is sufficiently tall, of a noble
presence, his physical constitution robust, and he is at pains
to preserve it by taking much exercise at the chase" (*C.S.P.
Venetian 1603–1607*, no. 739).

The miniature is a repetition and not from life. The
costume, as in the case of those of Elizabeth, is, however,
directly observed and records a suit with a white slashed
and pinked doublet decorated with diamond buttons and
jewels on gold mounts and lavender trunk hose. The pale
grey hat has white and pale blue ostrich plumes secured by
a large hat jewel of diamonds.

The miniature has a companion, that of his daughter,
Elizabeth, Queen of Bohemia which is from life (no. 247).
One unusual feature of the miniature of James is the spade
on the playing card at the back being painted over, second,
a stylistic innovation, the introduction of the painted
border which is distinctively Jacobean.

INSCRIBED: In gold on a blue ground within the border: +
IACOBVS . DEI . G(RATIA) MAGNAE BRITAN(IAE)
FRAN . ET HIB (ERNIAE) REX. It is damaged.

COLLECTIONS: Purchased from Commandant F. Besançon, 14 Rue
Louis Grignon, Chalons Marne, France, along with pendant
miniature of Elizabeth, Queen of Bohemia (no. 247), 1937;
previous history unknown.

LITERATURE: V & A, 1947 (105).
Graham Reynolds, *Walpole Society*, XXXIV, 1958, pp. 17–18, A.1,
pl. V (a).
Auerbach, *Hilliard*, p. 148, pl. 132; 310 (no. 136).
Strong, *Hilliard*, p. 32, pl. 15 (a).

CHARLES ANTHONY FROM A DESIGN ATTRIBUTED
TO NICHOLAS HILLIARD

236 Great Seal of James I, 1603

> *Public Record Office (SC 13/N/4)*
> Wax, 150 mm, 5.9 in. diam.

The only surviving document for the making of James I's
seal is the warrant dated 9th May 1603 (B.L. Additional
MS 5751A. f.313) which orders the provision of gold and
silver to Charles Anthony, Graver at the Mint, for the
actual manufacture of the matrices. This does not mean
that Anthony designed it and it would be logical that this
seal should be the result of a relationship between Hilliard
and the Anthonys, father and son, in the making of the
Great Seals that stretched back to the 1580s. The survival
of the warrant which informs us that Hilliard prepared
patterns for Elizabeth's Second Great Seal is exceptional
(no. 193). The style of James's seal is typically
Hilliardesque: the obverse is close to that of Elizabeth with

235

236

the crowned heraldic emblems powdered across the background and the same bulbous formalized flowers and plants. The approach is considerably less adulatory than to Elizabeth and the semi-deification applied to her in the form of celestial rays and divine hands is dropped. On the obverse James is depicted enthroned, flanked by crowned coats of arms as in the case of Elizabeth. The treatment of the folds of robes of the King's cloak is identical in its articulation to that in the drawing for Elizabeth's abortive Irish Seal (no. 194). To the left is a lion sejant, crowned, supporting with his right paw a banner with the arms of Cadwallader, last King of the Britons. James by his accession was reviving Britain and he proclaimed the new style in 1604. To the right there is a unicorn sejant, supporting with the left fore hoof a banner charged with the arms of Edward the Confessor, the last Saxon King of England. The iconographic programme emphasizes James as the rightful successor not only to the post-Conquest monarchs but to the Saxon Kings and, before them, the legendary rulers of Ancient Britain.

LITERATURE: A. Wyon, *The Great Seals of England*, London, 1887, p. 79.

WORKSHOP OF NICHOLAS HILLIARD

237 Medal commemorating Peace with Spain, 1604

The British Museum, Department of Coins and Medals (1844-4-25-24).
Gold, 45 mm, 1¾ in. diam.

In a royal patent to Hilliard of 1617 he is refered to as "Imbosser of our Medallions of Gold" and in 1604 he was actually paid £64.10s for twelve gold medallions (Auerbach, *Hilliard*, pp. 39–40). There seems to be no reason to reject the attribution, made as long ago as 1790, of the present medal to him. As in the case of the medals of Elizabeth and of the royal seals, involvement varied from preparing designs to seeing the whole project through. In this instance the quality of the object is such that the likelihood is the medal was wholly the product of his

studio. The face-pattern is of the first type used by Hilliard in his miniatures of James (no. 235) with an inevitable change in response to medium and to the public nature of the image. Like the medallions of Elizabeth this bears a ring for suspension. A crown has been added, somewhat incongruously, above the brim of his hat which has been extended to meet the demands of the circular format.

The reverse gives interesting examples of Hilliard's treatment of allegorical figures: Peace stands to the left, a figure who embraces Victory as she holds a palm and Plenty as she also supports a cornucopia. Religion to the right holds the cross of faith but also a lighted cresset (? the light of the Gospel). The inscriptions and content confirm that this medallion should mark the treaty of peace with Spain in 1604.

Two more medals go on to re-use the obverse portrait, but are far inferior in quality, once again instances of a Hilliard design carried out by another hand at the Mint. One carries on the reverse the familiar Noah's Ark royalist emblem (Hawkins, *Medallic Illustrations*, pl. XIV nos. 17 and 96).

239

241

INSCRIBED: Obverse: *IACOBVS.D'.G'.ANG'.SCO' .FR'*
.ET.HIB.REX; reverse: *HINC.PAX.COPIA.CLARAQ.*
RELIGIO.; below: *A° 1604.*

LITERATURE: John Pinkerton, *The Medallic History of England to the*
Revolution, London, 1790.
Helen Farqhar, "Portraiture of our Stuart Monarchs on their
Coins and Medals", *Numismatic Chronicle*, 1909, pp. 160ff.
E. Hawkins, *Medallic Illustrations of the History of Great Britain and*
Ireland to the Death of George I, ed., A. W. Franks and H. A.
Groeber, London, 1904–1, pl. XLV (14–15).
Reynolds, *Walpole Society*, XXXIV, 1958, p. 18 (a).

HILLIARD STUDIO OR FOLLOWER

238 James I in a locket, 1609–14

Victoria & Albert Museum (M.92–1974)
The Portrait: vellum stuck to a plain card which is
4 mm larger in diameter; circular, 17 mm, $\frac{21}{32}$ in.
diam.
The Ark: vellum stuck to card, circular, 17 mm,
$\frac{21}{32}$ in. diam.

The portrait of James derives from the second face-mask in
use c. 1609 to 1614 as categorized by Reynolds. It is of
indifferent quality and very loosely painted, but the
addition of the sunburst indicates that its concept was close
to Hilliard who was at the same period introducing
decorative "jewelled" borders to his miniatures. The
sunburst encircling the monarch is a variant of a motif that
appears on the case of a miniature of Elizabeth (no. 188).
In this instance it celebrates the ruler as *Sol Britanniae*. The
complimentary device of the Ark sailing through the seas is
also Elizabethan in origin, for a discussion of its symbolism
see the "Armada Jewel" (no. 208). It was utilized by James
I on a number of commemorative medals but with a new
motto: *STET SALVA PER VNDAS*. Both miniatures have
suffered from flaking and the portrait is severely
craquelured in the costume and background.

This is a rare survival of a modest locket, very different
from the group of highly spectacular gem-encrusted ones,
of gold enamelled in white, opaque pale green and
translucent red and it once had a pendant, probably a
pearl. Anna Somers-Cocks points out that the bright,
translucent enamelling on a coffered ground also appears
on another miniature case, containing a miniature by Peter
Oliver, dated 1619 (V & A, Inv. no. 117–1888). Whether
this was the speciality of a particular goldsmiths' workshop
is not known.

INSCRIBED: Around the Ark: *STET SALVA PER VNDAS*.

COLLECTIONS: Given by Dame Joan Evans, 1974, previous history
unknown.

LITERATURE: *Princely Magnificence*, 1980 (117).

NICHOLAS HILLIARD AND ASSISTANTS

239 Letters patent creating James I's eldest son, Henry, Prince of Wales, 1610

The British Library, Department of Manuscripts
(Additional MS 36932)
Vellum

James I created his son Prince of Wales in June 1610, an
occasion not only for a formal ceremony in Westminster
Hall before both Houses but for a series of splendid
entertainments, including a tilt, a firework display and
Samuel Daniel's masque, *Tethys' Festival*. The ceremonial of
investiture on June 4th involved the reading of this patent
by Robert Cecil, Earl of Salisbury, after which the King
invested his son. The moment following the investiture is
depicted in the initial letter, the Prince is shown wearing a
mantle and hood of purple velvet. He has been invested
with "the cap of purple velvet edged with powdered

ermine having 4 gold laces, one each way like a cross upon it, and a prince's coronet upon the cap of rich stones", and the golden verge or rod. There was also a ring which is not visible. (See Wallace Notestein, *The House of Commons 1604–10* Yale University Press, 1971, pp. 95–8.)

The illumination is a striking example of Hilliard co-operating with a second, far inferior, hand who was responsible not only for the general design but its execution, apart from the actual faces of the King and Prince. In the case of the King the face is an autograph Hilliard of the usual second face-pattern but in reverse (see no. 238). In that of the Prince, the painting has all the liveliness of independent observation and Hilliard's interpretation of Henry's profile makes a striking comparison with Oliver's (no. 230).

ATTRIBUTED TO ROWLAND LOCKEY

240 James I, 1614

H.M. The Queen
Vellum stuck to a playing card with one diamond showing at the reverse, oval, 45 × 36.5 mm, $1\frac{25}{32} \times 1\frac{7}{16}$ in.

One of the many workshop productions of miniatures of James I, certainly not by Hilliard, although accepted as such by Auerbach. Several of these ought to be by Lockey and this shows many of the characteristics of his style. The date 1614 is on the reverse. Reynolds places this with his third face – pattern for the King but it is actually perfectly acceptable as an example of the second. The background is craquelured and slightly flaked in places and the silver slightly oxidized.

INSCRIBED: On the reverse in gold the date: *1614*

COLLECTIONS: It is difficult to disentangle the early history of miniatures of James I in the Royal Collection, but conceivably this or Vit. 1 no. 50 is that in the Charles II inventory, c. 1662–85 (422): "King James in a white Doublett. Ovall in an Ivory Box. In small Limbning, I.C.·2''; conceivably identical with one of those seen by Vertue at Kensington Palace in 1734: "K. James I of him two or three not very well". (Vertue, *Notebooks*, IV, p. 67).

LITERATURE: Reynolds, *Walpole Society*, XXXIV, 1958, no. A.12.
Auerbach, *Hilliard*, pp. 165, pl. 164; 317 (174).
Strong, *Tudor and Jacobean*, I, p. 180.

LAURENCE HILLIARD

241 James I, c. 1620

The Rijksmuseum, Amsterdam on loan to the Mauritshuis, The Hague (1022)
Vellum stuck onto card, heart-shaped, 51 × 34 mm, $2 \times 1\frac{1}{3}$ in.

Reynolds includes this miniature in the list of what he believes to be a third face-mask of James I originating with Nicholas Hilliard. Auerbach also accepts it as by him. The execution of the miniature, which is very faded, shows,

however, all the feeble schematic qualities typical of Nicholas's son, Laurence. The latter succeeded as King's limner on his father's death in 1619 and warrants exist paying him in 1624 for what were presumably miniatures of the King (Auerbach, *Hilliard*, p. 226). It would seem likely that James granted his incoming limner a sitting. The old and care-worn face accords far better with late portraits of James initiated in 1618 by Paul van Somer and subsequently by Mytens.

COLLECTIONS: The Dutch Royal Collection; first recorded, 1815–21.

LITERATURE: Reynolds, *Walpole Society*, XXXIV, 1958, p. 21 (A.14).
Auerbach, *Hilliard*, pp. 165, pl. 163; 317 (173).
All the Paintings in the Rijksmuseum, Amsterdam, Olivetti, 1976, p. 756 (A4322).

ATTRIBUTED TO ROWLAND LOCKEY

242 Anne of Denmark, 1605–10

Nationalmuseum, Stockholm (NMB2167)
Vellum stuck onto card, oval, 50 × 37 mm, $1\frac{15}{16} \times 1\frac{3}{8}$ in.

Anne of Denmark appears to have sat only once to Hilliard, presumably shortly after her arrival south in 1603. About eight versions exist of this face-pattern, in two instances conceived as pendants to ones of James, but few are directly from the hand of Hilliard himself (see Reynolds, *Walpole Society*, XXXIV, 1958, pp. 22–23). This example shows the mannerisms typical of Hilliard's pupil, Lockey, with fussy muddled brushwork and summary execution.

HILLIARD STUDIO OR FOLLOWER

243 Anne of Denmark, 1610–15

The Fitzwilliam Museum, Cambridge (3855)
Vellum stuck to a playing card with one club showing at the reverse, oval, 54 × 43 mm, $2\frac{1}{8} \times 1$ in.

This miniature is a studio work or by a follower and the costume is c. 1610–15. It utilizes the draped curtain background used by Hilliard after c. 1603, although Hilliard never used blue. The outline could be by him and then passed on to an assistant. The dress is light brown with pink rosettes on it, as is the hair. There are sprays of jewels on the ruff and a jewelled sash.

The miniature is still in its original locket of gold enamelled in white, translucent red and green, set with table diamonds. The design incorporates intertwined A for *Anna*, S for *Sophia* of Mecklenburg, her mother, and CAR for *Christianus*, her brother, Christian IV of Denmark, *Anna* and *Rex* or *Regina*. The features are faded and the silver oxidized. It was sold in 1922 with one of James I, both of which were conceivably given to or painted for Hugh, 5th Earl of Eglinton or his successor, Sir Alexander Seton, 6th Earl of Eglinton.

COLLECTIONS: The Earls of Eglinton and Winton; sold Christie's 13th July 1922 (lot 77); bequeathed by L. D. Cunliffe, 1937.

LITERATURE: Reynolds, *Walpole Society*, XXXIV, 1952–54, p. 22 (B1).
Joan Evans, *Jewellery*, London, 1970 ed., pl. 103 a + b.
Auerbach, *Hilliard*, p. 168, pl. 166; 318 (180).
Princely Magnificence, 1980 (118).

243

HILLIARD STUDIO OR FOLLOWER

244 **Anne of Denmark**, 1610–15

From the Castle Howard Collection
Vellum stuck to a playing card with diamonds overpainted with black verso, oval, 51 × 40 mm, 2 × 1 9/16 in.

This miniature is identical in composition to the previous one (no. 243), but far inferior in quality, even to sharing the same unusual blue curtain as a background. The dress, however, is slightly different: white with pink and blue rosettes; pink ones in the hair. There is also no jewelled sash. The miniature sheds an interesting light on the process of manufacture of these images. No. 243 is not by Hilliard, although he could have begun it and passed it on to a talented assistant or follower. In this instance the outline also has all the marks of Hilliard but the execution of the painting is feeble. This time it must have been passed on, perhaps to his son, Laurence, to finish. The result is extremely schematic.

The absence of a gold edgeline indicates trimming. Although faded and with oxidized silver, its condition is good. The Howard connexions could indicate that it was possibly painted for or given to Thomas Howard, 1st Earl of Suffolk and 1st Baron Howard de Walden (1561–1626).

COLLECTIONS: First recorded by Lord Hawkesbury in 1903.

LITERATURE: Lord Hawkesbury, *Catalogue of the Portraits, Miniatures Etc. at Castle Howard*, 1903, p. 70 (6).

ATTRIBUTED TO ROWLAND LOCKEY

245 **Henry, Prince of Wales**, 1607

H.M. The Queen
Vellum stuck to card, oval, 61 × 51 mm, 2 3/8 × 2 in.

Although ascribed to Hilliard by van der Dort and accepted by all scholars until now as being by him, this is highly likely to be a candidate for attribution to Lockey. Weak and uncertain in composition, its technique displays none of Hilliard's unflagging virtuosity, especially when painting an *ad vivum* royal likeness. A comparison with Hilliard's portrait of Prince Charles (no. 249) would confirm the immense superiority of such an autograph work, the same applies to his earlier one of Henry (no. 246) in which the same armour is worn (Sir Guy Laking, *Catalogue of the Armoury of Windsor Castle*, no. 786 and 802).

Van der Dort's catalogue is marked by an extreme ignorance of Tudor and Jacobean painters.

INSCRIBED: On the curtain::: *Ano Dni.1607.Ætatis Svae 14.* On the reverse in van der Dort's hand: "*56 In the cubborde within y*e *Cabinett . . . White hall.*"

COLLECTIONS: Recorded by van der Dort: "Item done upon the right light a defaced -/ Picture of Prince Henry upon an ovall -/ redd Curteine ground Card in a white silver / and gilded Armor his left hand in a Gantlett / houlding the dame at his side, and on his right / side upon the Table standing a head peece -/ wth a white feather Bush:"; "Done by ould Hilliard:" (Millar, *Walpole Society*, XXXVII, 1960, p. 108 (20)); presumably sold in the Commonwealth sale and recovered at the Restoration and recorded in the Charles II inventory, c. 1662–85 (no. 439); James II inventory (no. 614) as "A limning of a man in gilt armour to the waste, with a feather in his headpiece", Stowe MS 567, temp. George I inventory when at Kensington: "Le Prince Henry en Cuirasse et son Casque aupres"; Fraser Tytler, *List*, 1851, p. 7 (no. 26).

LITERATURE: Reynolds, *Walpole Society*, XXXIV, 1958, C.I., pl. VI(E).
Auerbach, *Hilliard*, pp. 156, pl. 152; 314 (158).

NICHOLAS HILLIARD

246 **Henry, Prince of Wales**, 1607–10

H.M. The Queen
Vellum stuck to a card the back of which is painted with crest of the Prince of Wales and the monogram P.H., oval, 34 × 28 mm, 1 × 1 1/8 in.

The only known *ad vivum* miniature by Hilliard of Prince Henry, depicting him wearing a suit of French armour, still in the Royal Collection (Sir Guy Laking, *Catalogue of the Armoury at Windsor Castle*, nos. 786 and 802) which reappears in a second miniature dated 1607, not by him, but tentatively assigned to Lockey (no. 245). The physiognomy is less boyish than in the 1607 portrait and it can therefore reasonably be dated between 1607 and 1610 when the Prince established his own household and began his patronage of Oliver. The feathers on the reverse could argue for the later date of 1610, the year of his creation as

244   245   247

Prince of Wales. Although faded the portrait is in good condition. The back, however, is badly flaked.

INSCRIBED: On the reverse beneath the Prince of Wales' coronet and feathers the monogram *PH* and on a scroll beneath: *ICH DIEN*.

COLLECTIONS: See no. 245 until Capt. J. H. Edwards-Heathcote sale, Christie's June 13th 1928 (lot 48); Harry Seal collection; sold Christie's February 16th 1949 (lot 102); purchased for the Royal Collection.

LITERATURE: Reynolds, *Walpole Society*, XXXIV, 1958, no. C.2, pl. VI.
V & A, 1947 (85).
Auerbach, *Hilliard*, pp. 151–52, pl. 143; 312 (149).

NICHOLAS HILLIARD

247 **Elizabeth, Queen of Bohemia**, 1606–9

Victoria & Albert Museum (P.4–1937)
Vellum stuck onto a playing card with four diamonds at the reverse, which have been painted black, oval, 53 × 43 mm, $2\frac{3}{32} \times 1\frac{24}{32}$ in.

This miniature is of fine autograph quality painted *ad vivum*. It forms one of a pair with her father (not from life, no. 235). When acquired it was called "A Lady of the family of James I", but, as Reynolds pointed out, is obviously Elizabeth, Queen of Bohemia as a girl. On costume the portrait is c. 1605 and much of the jewellery is identical to that in the full-length portrait attributed to Robert Peake in the Metropolitan Museum of Art, New York (Strong, *The English Icon*, p. 242 (214)). The items, in particular, which appear to be the same are the looped pearl coronet, the pearl necklace and the chain swagged across the shoulder. Its companion of James I cannot have been painted later than 1609. Elizabeth would have been ten in 1606 and thirteen in 1609, somewhere between those two dates would fit the age of the sitter.

Although it has suffered from a little flaking, oxidization, and is very faded, the miniature is characteristic of late Hilliard, with his use of a crimson velvet curtain as a background and his delight in naturalistic touches such as the bluebell tucked into a rosette on her bodice.

Conceivably the miniature was executed in connexion with marriage proposals.

COLLECTIONS: See no. 235.

LITERATURE: V & A, 1947 (88).
Reynolds, *Walpole Society*, XXXIV, 1958, p. 25, pl. VI (d).
Auerbach, *Hilliard*, p. 162, pl. 161; 316 (169).

NICHOLAS HILLIARD

248 **Charles I as Duke of York**, 1605–8

Victoria & Albert Museum (P.10–1947)
Vellum stuck to a plain card, oval, 33 × 27 mm, $1\frac{5}{16} \times 1\frac{3}{32}$ in.

The earliest surviving portrait of Charles I from life. It must date before May 1611 when he was created a Knight of the Garter and has been dated by Reynolds c. 1603 and by Margaret Toynbee c. 1608–9; three certainly seems too young and somewhere between 1605 and 1608, i.e. between the ages of five and eight, would be more suitable.

Charles came to England in the summer of 1604 and was placed in the charge of Lady Cary. Although he was a weak child, with a speech impediment, Hilliard records him as an upright, healthy figure with sparkling grey-blue eyes. The formal curtain with gold embroidery and fringing is unusual. A similar hanging occurs in his *Sir Robert Dudley* (no. 265). It is interesting to compare Hilliard's approach with that of Robert Peake, whose portrait, although considerably more wooden, captures the pathetic ailing face and sad haunted eyes more accurately (Strong, *The English Icon*, pl. 216 now identified as the Prince).

COLLECTIONS: See no. 245 until sold in the Capt. J. H. Edwards-Heathcote sale, Christie's 13th June 1928 (lot 47) as by Isaac Oliver; purchased by E. Peter Jones and bequeathed to the V & A, 1948.

LITERATURE: V & A, 1947 (86).
M. R. Toynbee, "Some Early Portraits of Charles I", *Burlington Magazine*, XCI, 1958, pp. 4–9.
Reynolds, *Walpole Society*, XXXIV, 1958, no. D1.
Auerbach, *Hilliard*, pp. 151–52, 313 (no. 150).

NICHOLAS HILLIARD

249 Charles I as Prince of Wales, c. 1613

Victoria & Albert Museum (P.150–1910)
Vellum stuck to a playing card with spades at the
reverse. The back of the card has been overpainted
with bands of opaque pink and green watercolour,
oval, 51 × 41 mm, 2 × 1⅝ in.

Although faded, a superb *ad vivum* likeness of the young
Charles I. He wears the Lesser George of the Order of the
Garter with which he was invested in May 1611. It must
therefore be after that date but precede Hilliard's portrait
of 1614 at Belvoir (Auerbach, *Hilliard*, pl. 158). It is
tempting to associate it with the payment to Hilliard for a
portrait of the Prince on November 3rd 1613 (Toynbee
cited P.R.O. Declared Accounts Roll 544, f.32). In
composition it is strongly reminiscent, as Reynolds has
pointed out, of two other miniatures; of James (no. 235)
and Elizabeth of Bohemia (no. 247) which both depict the
sitters in light coloured costumes against crimson velvet
curtains. It differs from them, however, in the introduction
of a decorative border of patterned gold over smalt (blue),
a compositional innovation of precisely this period. It is
basically in good condition, although the background and
jewel in the hat have craquelured and the silver oxidized.

Framed at an early date with miniatures of James I,
Anne of Denmark, Prince Henry, Frederick, Elector
Palatine and Elizabeth of Bohemia (Auerbach, *Hilliard*,
pl. 160).

COLLECTIONS: On a label on the back of the frame is written:
*"Sheriff Hutton Park | 23ʳᵈ July 1866 | Miniatures by Isaac Oliver |
Family of King James 1ˢᵗ | Leonard Thompson"*; George Lowther
Thompson, Sheriff Hutton Park; sold Christie's 5th July 1894
(lot 65); bequeathed by George Salting, 1911.

LITERATURE: V & A, 1947 (89).
Margaret Toynbee, "Some Early Portraits of Charles I",
    Burlington Magazine, XCI, 1949, p. 14.
Reynolds, *Walpole Society*, XXXIV, 1958, no. D.2, pl. VI (c).
Auerbach, *Hilliard*, pp. 158, pl. 157, 159; 315 (165).

RENOLD ELSTRACK POSSIBLY AFTER NICHOLAS
HILLIARD

250 Elizabeth, Queen of Bohemia and Frederick, Elector Palatine and King of Bohemia, c. 1613

*The British Museum, Department of Prints and Drawings
(1864–12–10–490)*
Engraving, 25.8 × 20 cm, 10¼ × 7⅞ in. (plate).

In 1617 Hilliard, at the age of seventy, was granted a
twelve year monopoly to make, engrave and print Royal
portraits. The solitary documented example is one of
Queen Elizabeth by Francis Delaram (see no. 212) but the
grant was made in view of his "extraordinary Art and Skill
in Drawing Graving and Imprinting of Pictures . . . of us
and others" (quoted Auerbach, *Hilliard*, p. 40). This means
that he had been producing designs for royal portraits to be
engraved all the time. One of the most prolific engravers of

250

portraits of James I and his family was Renold Elstrack
(1570–worked as an engraver 1598–1625). He was brought
to England as an infant and his work is entirely in the
isolationist style of Hilliard, indeed, his engraved full-
length engravings include all the mannerisms and short-
comings of Hilliard's large-scale miniatures. In the case of
a design supplied to an engraver, allowance always has to
be made for his stylistic reinterpretation and for possible
alterations and additions. The double portrait of the
Elector Palatine and the Princess Elizabeth must have been
issued on the occasion of the marriage in 1613. A
relationship between Elstrack and Hilliard seems likely.

LITERATURE: Hind, *Engraving*, II, p. 175 (22).

RENOLD ELSTRACK POSSIBLY AFTER NICHOLAS
HILLIARD

251 Henry, Prince of Wales, c. 1612

*The British Museum, Department of Prints and Drawings.
(1870–5–14–2895)*
Engraving, 39.6 × 30.1 cm, 15⅝ × 11⅞ in.

Issued, as the verses indicate, after the Prince's death in
1612, Hind's attribution of this to Elstrack is surely correct.
There is an indication that, at one stage, it was
contemplated giving the Prince a hat. The face-mask is
derived from one of the many portraits of the Prince by
Robert Peake (Strong, *The English Icon*, pp. 250 (228), 251
(224)), but the overall design could have been supplied by
Hilliard to Elstrack (for a possible relationship see no. 250).

LITERATURE: Hind, *Engraving*, II, pp. 178–79 (33).

252

NICHOLAS HILLIARD

252 Elizabeth, Electress Palatine, later Queen of Bohemia, and her son, Frederick Henry, c. 1615

The British Museum, Department of Prints and Drawings (T–15–18)
Pen and ink over graphite, on two slips of vellum, the one pasted over the other to enlarge the composition, 12.7 × 8.9 cm, 5 × 3½ in.

The attribution of the drawing to Hilliard depends on the inscription, bottom left, of the initials NH. Croft-Murray observes that "The tightness of its handling suggests that it might have been intended as an engraver's design . . ." The fact that no known engraving survives need not exclude this as the logical purpose of the drawing and it is extremely close in compositional formula to the full-length engraved portraits by Elstrack (no. 250). In style it is consonant with other drawings certainly by Hilliard, the only difference being the purposeful use of cross-hatching, supplemented by fine and strong lines in accordance with the demands for engraving.

In 1837 the drawing was described as "Mary Queen of Scots and her son" which is certainly incorrect. The lady passes to her son a sceptre tipped with a fleur de lys and he carries an orb in his left hand and wears a coronet. His doublet is patterned with Tudor Roses. In the years around 1615, the date of the dress, this could only be James I's daughter, Elizabeth, Electress Palatine and her first born, Frederick Henry (1614–1629). With the death of Henry Prince of Wales in 1612 and until the marriage of Charles I in 1625, that child was next in succession to the throne of Great Britain. The hopes of Protestant England in the

years leading up to the outbreak of the Thirty Years War focussed on the Palatine Court. The likeness of Elizabeth is older than in Hilliard's only miniature of her (no. 247) but close to how she appears in Elstrack's engraving of c. 1613 (no. 250). The child is young, perhaps a year old, which would date the drawing to c. 1615.

The drawing was presumably abandoned before the setting, in which the figues stand, was filled in. Conceivably the sarcophagus, beside which the child stands is that of his namesake, Elizabeth's brother, Henry Frederick. That there was great interest in the child in England is reflected in the engravings of him as an infant by Francis Delaram (Hind, *Engraving*, II, pl. 125 (a), and as a boy by anonymous engravers (ibid., pls. 23 (a), 232 (c)).

INSCRIBED: In the lower left hand corner: *N.H.*

COLLECTIONS: Provenance unknown; first recorded in the British Museum, 1837.

LITERATURE: Edward Croft-Murray and P. Hulton, *Catalogue of British Drawings, I, XVI and XVII Centuries*, British Museum, 1960, p. 17 (2).
Auerbach, *Hilliard*, pp. 196–97; 321 (190).

II OLIVER, ANNE OF DENMARK AND PRINCE HENRY

On 22nd June 1605 Isaac Oliver was appointed limner to the new Queen, Anne of Denmark. Unlike her husband, she was passionately interested in the arts, in building and gardening, picture collecting and court festivals. In all these spheres she personally patronized artists of the new wave and she was particularly Italianate in her tastes. Initially she had to get her bearings on arriving south in the summer of 1603 but she quickly abandoned Hilliard for Oliver in the case of miniature portraits and de Critz for Gheeraerts in that of life scale portraiture. The latter's position always remained precarious. It was threatened first in 1611 by the arrival of a Florentine painter and architect, Constantino de' Servi, for whom she sat, and, subsequently, in 1617, by Paul van Somer who effectively replaced him. Inigo Jones, another of her protégés nearly suffered a similar fate. He was so threatened by de' Servi that he re-visited Italy with the Arundels and, on his return, was able far better to satisfy Anne's taste for all that was novel. The French hydraulic engineer, Salomon de Caus, carried out for her elaborate gardens both at Somerset House and at Greenwich which included grottoes and automata. Oliver belongs firmly in this *avant garde* milieu and his portraiture of her from the start has no connexion with Hilliard's votive images of Gloriana. Anne must have sat frequently, for the miniatures, in which she is celebrated both as lady and queen, are nearly all *ad vivum*.

Even more than with Anne, Oliver was to respond to her eldest son, Henry, Prince of Wales. Created Prince in 1610 for three years this young man set out to create a brilliant court which far eclipsed that of either of his parents.

255

256

MARCUS GHEERAERTS

253 **Anne of Denmark**, 1614

H.M. The Queen
Oil on panel, 109.4 × 87.3 cm, 43½ × 34⅜ in.
(Photograph.)

An autograph version by Gheeraerts of his official portrait
of the Queen of which the full-length at Woburn Abbey,
painted for the Queen's friend Lucy Harington, Countess
of Bedford, is the prime original (Strong, *The English Icon*,
p. 299 (305)). This version is dated and inscribed in
calligraphy of a type which regularly appears in Gheeraerts
portraits.

Gheeraerts was, for a short time, Isaac Oliver's brother-
in-law and undoubtedly must have been influenced by the
miniaturist's approach to painting the Queen. It is
noticeable how very sharply his work declined and became
archaic after Oliver's and Anne's deaths in 1617 and 1619.
Already in 1617 the Queen had sat for Paul van Somer, an
indication that by then she was coming to regard
Gheeraerts as old-fashioned, but in this 1614 version of his
standard portrait of her he works in a style and a manner
which is far in advance of the parallel portraiture of the
King (no. 233).

As in James's portrait certain jewels recur: the C4 for
her brother Christian IV of Denmark, the crown letter S
on her ruff for her mother Sophia of Mecklenburg, the
double cross of Lorraine and the picture box pinned to her
bodice. The latter is important evidence for the new style
of locket for miniatures, in which the exterior of the case
consists of a bold arrangement of table diamonds. The only
surviving locket in this manner is the Lyte Jewel in the
British Museum (Auerbach, *Hilliard*, pl. 165).

INSCRIBED: Dated *1614* and with the motto: *La mia grandezza dal
eccelso.*

COLLECTIONS: Apparently first recorded in the collection of James
II, 1687.

LITERATURE: O. Millar, *The Tudor, Stuart and Early Georgian Pictures
in the Collection of Her Majesty the Queen*, London, 1969, I, p. 79
(98).

O. Millar, "Marcus Gheeraerts the Younger," *Burlington Magazine*,
CV, 1963, p. 534.

Strong, *The English Icon*, p. 283 (275).

Although he had sat for Hilliard as a child (no. 246) the
Prince never patronized him. Oliver became his limner too
and for the Prince he produced perhaps his supreme royal
portrait (no. 257). The Prince, like his mother, also had
problems over finding a satisfactory life-scale portrait
painter. As a minor the Hilliardesque Robert Peake had
been appointed as his painter and indeed continued to be
so until Henry died but this did not preclude a serious
search for a painter who could depict the prince in the new
manner. He, of course, also sat for Constantino de' Servi
but negotiations in earnest went on to secure the Dutch
artist Miereveldt. These ended in failure early in 1612 and
in the Prince's funeral procession in the December of that
year Oliver figures not as his limner but as his painter. A
new limner is listed, a protégé of Sir Henry Wotton's
Mark Bilford. Oliver did we know paint on a large scale
and this would indicate that after the failure of the
Miereveldt negotiations Oliver was induced to become
court painter.

The atmosphere surrounding the Prince must have been
one of intense aesthetic stimulation for his collections
ranged from the masters of the Netherlandish and
Venetian schools to a picture by Beccafumi and bronzes by
Giovanni Bologna. Oliver was to articulate visually the
image adopted by the heir to the throne: a warrior hero
not only in terms of the lost classical world of Ancient
Britain but in those of the chivalry of the Gothic centuries
The ethos was redolent of Rudolfine Prague overlaid with
a fiercely Protestant theological stance. The death of the
Prince in November 1612 removed a powerful impulse and
direction in the arts that was never to be recovered. The
court around the new Prince of Wales was but a shadow by
comparison. Oliver's final miniatures of Charles reflect the
enormity of the tragedy (nos. 260, 261).

SELECT BIBLIOGRAPHY

Millar, *The Queen's Pictures*, London, 1977, pp. 22–24.
Strong, *The Renaissance Garden in England*, London, 1979,
    pp. 87–97.
Strong, *The Lost Renaissance. A Biography of Henry, Prince of Wales*
    (forthcoming).

ISAAC OLIVER

254 **Anne of Denmark**, c. 1605

National Portrait Gallery (4010)
Vellum stuck to plain card, oval, 52 × 41 mm,
$2\frac{1}{16} \times 1\frac{5}{8}$ in.

Oliver was appointed limner to Anne in 1605 (Edmond,
Limners and Picturemakers, Walpole Society, XLVII, 1980,
p. 75) and this must have been painted *ad vivum* shortly
after. Auerbach's dating of it c. 1610 seems far too late on
costume and in relation to Oliver's late 1609 portrait. The
features are delicately and sensitively observed. It is
basically in good condition, apart from slight flaking in the
background and the dress, faded flesh and oxidized silver.
The S-shaped pendant suspended on the ruff alludes to her
mother, Sophia of Mecklenburg. This, and the picture-box
on her left breast, are familiar features of her portraits.

COLLECTIONS: Purchased by James Sotheby of Ecton (whose
    monogram is on the back of the gilt case) from Parry Walton,
    dealer and restorer, in 1691 for £1.16s.od (Sotheby Notebooks,
    Victoria & Albert Museum); seen by Vertue, c. 1742
    (*Notebooks*, V, p. 11); sold at the Sotheby sale, Sotheby's 11th
    October 1955 (lot 72); purchased with the aid of a
    contribution from the N.A.C.F., 1957.

LITERATURE: V & A, 1947 (183).
Auerbach, *Hilliard*, p. 249, pl. 220; 330 (255).
Strong, *Tudor and Jacobean*, I, p. 8; II, pl. 15.

ISAAC OLIVER

255 **Anne of Denmark**, 1605–10

The Trustee of the Will of the 8th Earl of Berkeley
Vellum stuck onto card, laid down on a later
mount, oval 72 × 52 mm, $2\frac{7}{8} \times 2\frac{1}{16}$ in.

The largest known miniature of Anne, *ad vivum* and of the
finest quality. The Queen is placed before a crimson velvet
curtain wearing a yellow and brown dress, with her hand
extended in a typical Oliver pose. As George Carey, 2nd
Lord Hunsdon died in 1603, it is likely that it was painted
for his daughter, Elizabeth, Lady Berkeley. It is faded,
with slight flaking in the background and oxidized silver.

COLLECTIONS: Elizabeth Carey, daughter and heiress of George,
    2nd Baron Hunsdon, married Sir Thomas Berkeley.

ISAAC OLIVER WITH ADDITIONS PROBABLY BY
BERNARD LENS

256 **Anne of Denmark**, 1609

Private Collection
Vellum stuck to card, the painting extended on to
another, later, card stuck to the back, oval,
50 × 40 mm, $1\frac{31}{32} \times 1\frac{9}{16}$ in.

The only part of this miniature by Oliver is the face and
hair, the remainder being by a later hand, executed
presumably at the same time as the enlargement. The

relative crudity of the later work obscures what is one of
Oliver's finest characterizations. If the additions were
removed we would be left with an object resembling the
pattern miniature of Elizabeth I (no. 199). As the
miniature is in a Bernard Lens pear-tree frame and is
inscribed, by him, on the back *Queen Elizabeth.Hiliard*, it
would be reasonable to conclude that it was he who
completed it and added the false signature.
  Beneath the present surface there are visible fragments of
the underdrawing for a different costume. George Vertue
in his list of Lord Oxford's miniatures c. 1732 records it as
"Qu. Anne of Denmark 1609" (*Notebooks*, IV, p. 41).
Vertue probably saw the miniature before it was remounted and "extended". I see no reason to doubt his
word that it was dated 1609, conceivably on the original
reverse now stuck down onto the extension. It is likely,
therefore, that this could be a pattern miniature made in
1609. No miniatures utilizing this face-mask, however, have
so far come to light. As a likeness of Anne it is closely
related to Gheeraerts' full-length of the Queen at Woburn
in which she faces the same direction and is clearly older.
The dressing of the hair, with ringlets falling downwards
on the left shoulder, recurs only in Larkin's portrait of her
wearing mourning on the occasion of the death of Prince
Henry (Strong, *The English Icon*, p. 323 (34)).

INSCRIBED: A false signature of Hilliard to the right: *NH*. On the
    back in the hand of Bernard Lens: *Queen Elizabeth. Hiliard*.

COLLECTIONS: Edward Harley, 2nd Earl of Oxford (1689–1741);
    first recorded by Vertue, c. 1732 (*Notebooks*, IV, p. 41);
    recorded again by Vertue, 1743 (*Catalogue*), as Anne of
    Denmark but with the addition of Hilliard's cipher; Oxford's
    daughter married William Bentinck, 2nd Duke of Portland;
    thence by descent.

LITERATURE: Goulding, *Welbeck*, p. 65 (19).

ISAAC OLIVER

257 **Henry Frederick, Prince of Wales**,
c. 1612

H.M. The Queen
Vellum stuck onto card, rectangular, 134 × 102 mm,
$5\frac{1}{4} \times 4$ in. *(photograph)*

One of Oliver's most spectacular miniatures, arguably his
masterpiece and certainly his supreme royal portrait. The
whole is encompassed by an ochre frame with a gold line
over which he projects the Lesser George of the Garter.
The use of ultramarine for the blue Garter sash emphasizes
the importance of the commission. In technique there is a
marked difference in handling between the main portrait
and the inset scene. The former is in his tight manner,
whereas the latter is loosely painted. It heightens its elusive
dream-like quality, in which *à l'antique* warriors holding
lances, shields and spears are grouped before a pale yellow
tent. The allusion is to the heroic, chivalric antique dream
world which is the major theme of the Prince's image as
revealed above all in the *Barriers* (1610) and the *Masque of
Oberon* (1611) (see no. 230). Considering the vicissitudes of
its history, the miniature is in remarkable condition.

258

259

INSCRIBED: On the reverse a CR and crown and an old label: *le vieil Isac Oliver*.

COLLECTIONS: Recorded by van der Dort: "Don by Isack / Olliver"; "Inpris done upon the righte lighte the biggest / lim'd Picture that was made by Prince -/ Henry being lim'd in a sett laced Roofe in a -/ gilded Armo^r and a Landskip by wherein some / Souldiers and Tents are made, in a square / frame with a shuting Glass over it" (Millar, *Walpole Society*, XXXVII, 1960, p. 107 (17) and again, p. 215 (2)); reappears in the Charles II Inventory, c. 1662–85 (no. 417); passes out of the Royal Collection and reappears again when purchased by James West (1704?–1772) in a sale in April 1751 (Vertue, *Notebooks*, V, p. 84); re-acquired for the Royal Collection by George IV from Rundall, 7th August 1807: "A fine large Picture of Henry Prince of Wales by Isaac Oliver an undoubted Original" (Windsor, Royal Archives, Georgian Papers, 25780); again lost from the Royal Collection and returned in 1863.

LITERATURE: V & A, 1947 (175).
Strong, *Tudor and Jacobean*, I, p. 164; II, pl. 325.
O. Millar, *The Queen's Pictures*, London, 1977, p. 25, pl. IV.

ISAAC OLIVER

258 Henry Frederick, Prince of Wales, c. 1612

The Marquess of Anglesey (on loan to the National Museum of Wales, Cardiff)
Vellum stuck to a playing card with two spades verso, oval, 66 × 53 mm, $2\frac{5}{8} \times 2\frac{1}{16}$ in.

A repetition of the same head pattern as no. 257, autograph and of fine quality but depicting the Prince in a different suit of armour, which strengthens the supposition that there was once a pattern head from which these portraits were multiplied. It is reinforced here by the tracing lines that are visible under magnification on the eye-lids, lip-line and nostrils. Dating is difficult as portraits

must have been manufactured posthumously; on the other hand the vibrancy would perhaps indicate that the miniature was executed before the sitter's death. The condition is good, apart from slight paint losses around the edge and smudging of the gold edge-line and monogram. The silver is oxidized. It is in its original turned ivory box.

INSCRIBED: Signed to the left; *IO* (in monogram).

COLLECTIONS: Pierpont Morgan coll; no previous history; Pierpont Morgan sale 24th June 1935 (lot 167).

LITERATURE: Williamson, *Catalogue*, 1906, I, p. 45.

WILLIAM HOLE AFTER ISAAC OLIVER

259 Henry, Prince of Wales, 1612

Michael Drayton, *Polyolbion*, London, 1612
British Library (C.116.G.2.)
Engraving, 19.1 × 12.4 cm, $7\frac{1}{2} \times 4\frac{7}{8}$ in. (border)

This is a rare instance of a documented source for an engraved royal portrait. The original drawing for this engraving was given by Inigo Jones to Charles I: "Item a drawing in little of Prince / Henry where hee is playing wth a lance / beeing side faced in a black frame / with a shiver" and in a second entry in phonetic English: "Wit a . . . pijck stading tu a strijff . . . at lengt don bij isak oliffers vor a patron tu bij bin in bot in blak and Wijt . . ." (Millar, *Walpole Society*, XXXVI, 1960, p. 153 (23) and note 4).

260

This engraving appears in two versions in 1612, one by William Hole and one by Simon van de Passe. In the case of the latter there is a background added with landscape, building and military exercises in the tiltyard, something added only in state V of Hole's plate. The absence of any mention of this background in van der Dort's entry must make Hole's engraving the earlier version. William Hole (d. 1624) was chief engraver of the mint and moved in a circle that included the *literati* of the day, in particular those we associate with the intellectual circle around the young Prince of Wales; George Chapman, Michael Drayton, Thomas Coryate and Angelo Notari (Hind, *Engraving*, II, pp. 316–17).

The engraving is signed *William Hole sculp:* and but for Inigo Jones holding on to the original drawing we would have had no way of proving Oliver's authorship. The relationship to the profile likenesses *à l'antique* (no. 230) is only too apparent. Hind records no less than five states and admits the relationship of the first three remains unclear.

LITERATURE: Hind, *Engraving*, II, p. 321 (9).

ISAAC OLIVER

260 Charles I as Prince of Wales, 1615–16

Private Collection
Vellum stuck to plain card, oval, 51 ×40 mm, $2 \times 1\frac{9}{16}$ in.

Perhaps the most outstanding of the early portraits of Charles I to survive; the breadth of its treatment establishes its *ad vivum* status and suggests strong influences from Venetian painting of the type arriving in England for Prince Henry's picture collection. It joins Oliver's miniature of Queen Elizabeth (no. 199) in a class on its own, not as unfinished, but certainly painted as a pattern (see no. 261). The type is not discussed in M. R. Toynbee's article on the early portraits of Charles I but is closest to the engraving by Francis Delaram dated 1616 (her fig. 9) which was presumably based on a pattern slightly earlier in date. Although the features are finished, the collar, armour and Garter ribbon are only partially worked and areas of bare vellum are still visible. It is in excellent condition.

COLLECTIONS: Edward Harley, Earl of Oxford (1689–1741); recorded by Vertue, c. 1732: "Prince Charles. Young" (*Notebooks*, IV, p. 41); Vertue's (*Catalogue*), 1743 (no. 103); Oxford's daughter married William Bentinck, 2nd Duke of Portland; thence by descent.

LITERATURE: Goulding, *Welbeck*, p. 72 (33).

ISAAC OLIVER PROBABLY ASSISTED BY PETER OLIVER

261 Charles I as Prince of Wales, 1615–16

Nationalmuseum, Stockholm (NMB 978)
Vellum stuck onto card, oval, 50 × 43 mm, $1\frac{15}{16} \times 1\frac{11}{16}$ in.

This is the only known finished version derived from the previous pattern miniature (no. 260). The head is certainly by Isaac Oliver and of fine quality but the summary and schematic treatment of the doublet suggests another hand, which ought, logically, to be that of the miniaturist's son and eventual inheritor of the business, Peter Oliver. The miniature is in good condition, apart from oxidized silver.

COLLECTIONS: C. R. of Ugglas collection.

ISAAC OLIVER

262 Elizabeth, Queen of Bohemia, c. 1610

H.M. The Queen
Vellum stuck onto card, oval, 51 ×41 mm, $2 \times 1\frac{5}{8}$ in.

A charming *ad vivum* portrait by Oliver with loose brushstrokes, in a return to his free Hilliardesque manner. Her dress is white and gold and her hair adorned with flowers and leaves enamelled in pastel colours. There is flaking and fading.

INSCRIBED: Signed to the left: *IO* (in monogram).

COLLECTIONS: First recorded by van der Dort as "Don by Isack / Olliver by the / life"; "Item don upon the right light more upon -/ an Ovall blew grounded Card the Picture / of your Ma^{ts} Sister when she was younger / in her high time past fashioned haire / dressing adorn'd at her head wth some single / Eglentine Roases wth Jewell about her / neck and her habbitt adorn'd all over wth / Carnation and white Ribbons in a white / Ivory Box with a Christall over it" (Millar, *Walpole Society*, XXXVII, 1960, p. 117 (54)); reappears in James II's Inventory (613): "A limning or a woman's head with flowers upon it in an ivory frame"; William III's Inventory in the King's Great Closet (79): "A women's head with flowers upon it; in an Ivory frame. Isaac Oliver"; reappears in the 1870s list of miniatures in the Royal Library.

LITERATURE: V & A, 1947 (158).
Reynolds, *Walpole Society*, XXXIV, 1958, p. 25.
Auerbach, *Hilliard*, pp. 249, pl. 219; 330 254).

264

The Cabinet Miniatures

THE large-scale miniature appears with all the suddenness of a novelty at the close of the 1580s. They form, from the outset, a quite separate genre from the usual head and shoulders or half-length portraits. The sitters, virtually all of whom are identifiable, establish that this was an immensely expensive form of portraiture: Essex, Cumberland, Northumberland, Dorset, Lord Herbert of Cherbury and the Countess of Bedford. All these sitters were noted for their wealth, ostentation and concern with their own image. The miniatures must have involved a great deal of time and labour. One of parallel size, Oliver's *Madonna and Child* (no. 179) is recorded as having occupied the artist on and off for two years.

What is most marked, however, when these are considered collectively is the difference between the two artists. In the case of Hilliard the cabinet miniature is a genre which forms an isolated episode that ends in failure. His earliest, the *Young Man among Roses* (no. 263) is easily his best. Its shape is one never repeated, an elongated oval, which must have been necessitated by a specific setting. The format all too quickly revealed Hilliard's essential limitations in handling both linear and aerial perspective

and by about 1595 he abandoned the format and never returned to it. Oliver in comparison returns to it again and again throughout his career. It evoked from him indeed some of his finest and most adventurous work. From the start he had a total mastery of Renaissance optical principles which Hilliard lacked. This is abundantly clear from his first cabinet miniature of a young man seated beneath a tree in an attitude of melancholy (no. 268), even although it is still close to Hilliard in mood. His miniatures form a far more astonishing series than those of his master. They reveal the enormous range of the man from the *Allegorical Scene* (no. 270) in the vein of late sixteenth-century Netherlandish landscape painting to the mysterious aristocratic ladies emerging smiling in the half-light that stem from the work of Leonardesque painters of the Milanese school. These are astounding works in European terms and even more so when placed into the context of late Elizabethan and Jacobean England. It is clear, however, that these highly *avant garde* and sophisticated ones were not to everyone's taste. When it came to sitters such as Lord Herbert of Cherbury (no. 273) and the Earl of Dorset (no. 276) he was able to abdicate his knowledge of what was happening in painting on the mainland of Europe and revert to the bright colours and iconic formality of the native school.

SELECT BIBLIOGRAPHY
Strong, *Renaissance Miniature*, pp. 102–11, and for others *passim*.

NICHOLAS HILLIARD

263 Young Man Among Roses, possibly Robert Devereux, 2nd Earl of Essex, c. 1587

Victoria & Albert Museum (P.163–1910)
Vellum stuck onto card, oval, 135.5 × 73 mm,
$5\frac{5}{16} \times 2\frac{27}{32}$ in.

Robert Devereux, 2nd Earl of Essex (1566–1601), the eldest son of Walter Devereux, 1st Earl of Essex and Lettice Knollys, was educated at Trinity College, Cambridge, and introduced to the court in 1584 where he immediately attracted the Queen. He fought in the Low Countries campaign and was knighted at Zutphen. In 1587 he married Sir Philip Sidney's widow, a secret kept from the Queen until his wife's pregnancy in 1590 brought it into the open. During those years he established himself as royal favourite and, from 1590 onwards, embarked on a career as a military commander and sought, with Francis Bacon's aid, to achieve "domesticall greatness". He led an English expedition in aid of Henry of Navarre (1591), attacked and sacked the town of Cadiz (1596), embarked on the abortive Azores expedition (1597) and, finally, wrecked his fortunes in Ireland (1599). He attempted to stir up Londoners in rebellion (1601) and was subsequently tried and executed.

The most famous of all Elizabethan miniatures, a *chef d'œuvre* of Hilliard's art and the perfect evocation of Elizabethan Arcady. As the miniature has virtually no history before the present century the identity of its sitter and its meaning must, necessarily, remain speculative. I cannot, however, accept Dr Leslie Hotson's identification of the sitter as a certain William Hatcliffe, a gentleman of the Inns of Court and identified as Mr W.H. of Shakespeare's sonnets (see Leslie Hotson, *Mr W.H.*, London, 1964, esp. pp. 21–23, 204–15). There is no real evidence for such an identification and its possibility is ruled out by the miniature itself.

What follows is a summary of the only detailed study of the miniature which I made in *The Cult of Elizabeth*, pp. 56–83, in which I developed the proposition, first made in 1959 by David Piper, that the *Young Man* was Robert Devereux, 2nd Earl of Essex. The identity rests on comparison with the earliest authentic portrait of the Earl, dated 1590, by William Segar (no. 278), depicting him at the age of twenty-four with a moustache. Two other miniatures by Hilliard, one dated 1588, could also be the *Young Man*. One is dated 1588 and gives the right age of twenty-two.

The portrait evidence has to be accepted or rejected subjectively although, in my view, it is right and the eyes throughout are brown. Leaving aside that there is the interpretation of the emblems which can only relate to the Queen: (i) the *Young Man* is embowered in eglantine, the single white five-petalled rose which recurs in the Elizabeth mythology. In its most extended form it took the shape of a full-length poem *Eglantine of Meryfleur* by the courtier, Sir Arthur Gorges; (ii) he is wearing black and white, the Queen's colours, worn by knights in the tiltyard and dancers in court masques. At Sandwich, in 1573, for example, the whole town was hung in black and white in her honour; (iii) the tree against which he leans is a standard emblem of constancy.

All these would point to the sitter, hand in heart, presenting himself as a devotee of Elizabeth. The motto, as Miss Carolyn Merion pointed out, is a half-verse from a famous speech out of Lucan's *De Bello Civili* in which the eunuch Pothinus counsels Pompey's death:

> *Dat poenas laudata fides, dum sustinet inquit,*
> *Quos fortuna premit . . .*

Translated by Ben Jonson as:

> . . . a praised faith
> Is her own scourge, when it sustains their states
> Whom fortune hath depressed.

The general drift would seem to be that faithful love and loyalty bring their own pain and suffering. There is, as Leslie Hotson points out, an implied identification of the sitter with Pompey. This would fit the ambitious role in which Essex deliberately cast himself as successor to Sir Philip Sidney, for Pompey was a great military commander, a general at twenty-three, awarded two Roman triumphs by the age of twenty-five, besides being a popular hero of the citizens of Rome.

The miniature without doubt both on costume and in respect of the evolution of Hilliard's work is late 1580s. To be of Essex it should date between the return of the Earl from the Netherlands in the autumn of 1586 and 1590. The years 1587 and 1588 saw him establish himself as prime favourite and this would fit the *Young Man* exactly.

The contents of the miniature would have been dictated by the sitter but the pose with legs crossed must relate to Hilliard's memories of the art of the School of Fontainebleau and can be paralleled exactly in the work of

Primaticcio, the source being ultimately antique. Its sinuous elegance and its flower bedecked surface also echo the work of the Maitre de Flore.

The large elongated oval shape of this miniature is never repeated in Hilliard's work and must relate to the purpose of the object, which is hardly likely to have been a jewel on this scale. Conceivably it was incorporated into an object such as looking-glass worn at the end of a chain suspended from the waist. It has flaked slightly and been restored.

INSCRIBED: On either side of the head: *Dat | poenas laudata fides.*

COLLECTIONS: A Dutch Bourgeois family, who had owned it for several generations, sold it to Fritz Lugt, who in turn sold it to George Salting; bequeathed by him to the V & A, 1910.

LITERATURE: C. H. Collins Baker, *British Painting*, London, 1931, p. 40, pl. 31.
Winter, *Elizabethan Miniatures*, p. 26, pl. vii.
V & A, 1947 (38).
Pope-Hennessy, *Lecture*, 1949, p. 20, pl. 15.
D. Piper, "The 1590 Lumley Inventory II", *Burlington Magazine*, XCIX, 1957, pp. 300–301.
Auerbach, *Hilliard*, pp. 103–109, 300 (no. 78).
Strong, *Hilliard*, p. 30 (pl. 8).
Strong, *The Cult of Elizabeth*, pp. 56–83.

NICHOLAS HILLIARD

264 Sir Anthony Mildmay, 1590–93

Cleveland Museum of Art, Ohio
Vellum stuck onto card, rectangular, 245 × 185 mm, $9\frac{1}{4} \times 7$ in.

Sir Anthony Mildmay (d. 1617) was the eldest son of Sir Walter Mildmay Hilliard's patron (see no. 191), Chancellor of the Exchequer and inheritor of the family estate at Apethorpe. He entered Gray's Inn in 1579 and was knighted in 1596 on this appointment as ambassador to Henry IV.

Both Reynolds and Auerbach's dating c. 1595 seems far too late, and Pope-Hennessy's of post 1596 even more untenable. The costume silhouette, with very abbreviated trunk-hose and peascod doublet are all but identical with the *Young Man Among Roses* (no. 263), and a late instance of it is dated 1593 (Strong, *The English Icon*, p. 202 (159)). In any case, the free painting of the hair would be more likely before 1593. This is one of Hilliard's most ambitious miniatures, for which he draws on the conventions of large-scale formal portraiture, placing the figure in a shallow space bounded by a tent with the customary attributes of armour, table and chair. The perspective, as usual, is misunderstood, with no single vanishing point, so that, although the figure is viewed front on, the furniture and ground are viewed from above.

Pope-Hennessy rightly pointed out its relationship to François Clouet's full-length drawing of Henri III (no. 71): (Pope-Hennessy, *Lecture*, 1949, p. 18). He did not know, however, that the final version of this drawing, now only known by a study, was sent to England in July 1571 to Elizabeth I (Jean Adhémar, *Le Dessin Francais au XVIe siecle*, Lausanne, 1954, pp. xxi–xxii).

265

The miniature, as with several of the other large-scale ones, depicts Dudley attired as a knight, the upper half of his body in armour with a large jewel tied as a favour to his left arm. Noted for his horsemanship, he appeared at most of the Accession Day Tilts during the last decade from 1591 onwards (Strong, *The Cult of Elizabeth*, pp. 208–11). In 1591 he was just seventeen and it is conceivable that the miniature was painted to commemorate that event, fitting neatly into the series of portraits that sprang out of these occasions. The hair is painted in the free pre-1593 manner which gives the miniature a tight dating. As in the case of Mildmay the figure is viewed front on, but the table, left, is tipped up at an impossible angle. This, almost more than any of the other large-scale miniatures, reveals Hilliard's swift decline in this genre. The work is, at best, summary and the face very poorly painted. Its condition is good, apart from fading, flaking in the feathers, mat and elsewhere and some retouching on the face.

COLLECTIONS: The Lords de L'Isle at Penshurst; Bertram Currie collection; sold Christie's 27th March 1953 (lot 22).

LITERATURE: Reynolds, *Connoisseur's Complete Period Guides*, 1968, pl. 71.
Auerbach, *Hilliard*, pp. 112, pl. 88; 302 (86).

NICHOLAS HILLIARD

266 Henry Percy, 9th Earl of Northumberland, 1590–95

The Rijksmuseum, Amsterdam
Vellum stuck to a later piece of card, rectangular, 257 × 173 mm, 10⅛ × 6¾ in.

Henry Percy, 9th Earl of Northumberland (1564–1632), the "Wizard Earl", was early interested in literature and the sciences; served under Leicester in the Low Countries, 1585–86; K.G., 1593; general, 1599. Received with favour by James I but fell from it in the wake of the Gunpowder Plot resulting in life imprisonment in the Tower. Released in 1617, he lived in retirement at Petworth.

One of the most abstruse of all Hilliard's miniatures. The Earl patronized the miniaturist extensively and Auerbach (*Hilliard*, p. 124) prints the entries from the Household Accounts: one for 1585/6, a second for 1587/88: "for your *Lordship's Picture to Hillyard L × s*" and a third for the period March 1594/5 to Feb. 1595/6: "to Mr Hilliard for his Lp Picture L × s". The final payment would fit this miniature exactly although the amount is that for the usual head and shoulders portrait.

In 1595–96 Northumberland was just over thirty and in 1595 he married Essex's sister, Dorothy Devereux, widow of Sir John Percy. During the 1590s it is generally accepted that Northumberland was one of a group of noblemen and their friends, of whom the key member was Raleigh, who devoted their time to deep philosophical and mathematical studies but were imbued with Renaissance occultism and Hermetism. The programme for Hilliard's miniature must have been drawn up by the Earl and presents him in this light. In 1593 he was invested with the Garter and George Peele dedicated the Honour of the Garter to him in which he evokes this ambience:

COLLECTIONS: Sir Anthony Mildmay's daughter and heiress, Mary, married Francis, 1st Earl of Westmorland; their grandson, Henry Fane, married secondly Anne, daughter of John Wynn, Bishop of Bath and Wells; their daughter and heiress, Mary, married Sir Thomas Stapleton, 5th Bt., of Greys Court (1727–1781); thence by descent to Sir Miles Stapleton, 9th Bt.; sold Christie's 11th May 1926 (79).

LITERATURE: V & A, 1947 (57).
Pope-Hennessy, *Lecture*, 1949, pp. 18–19.
Auerbach, *Hilliard*, pp. 116–117, pl. 93; 303 (93).
Strong, *Hilliard*, pl. 11.

NICHOLAS HILLIARD

265 Sir Robert Dudley, styled Duke of Northumberland and Earl of Warwick, 1591–93

Nationalmuseum, Stockholm (NMB. 1669)
Vellum stuck onto card, 190 × 115 mm, 7½ × 4½ in.

Sir Robert Dudley (1574–1649) was son of the Earl of Leicester by Douglas Sheffield but his legitimacy was never legally established. Leicester left him the Kenilworth estates and in the 1590s he was in favour at court. Failure to gain recognition of his legitimacy led to an elopement abroad with Elizabeth Southwell where they settled in Tuscany and became Roman Catholic. Under the patronage of the Medici he enhanced their fleet and published his *Arcano del Mare* (1646–47).

(Renowmed Lord, Northumberlands fayre flower)
The Muses love, Patrone, and favoret,
That artizans and schollers doost embrace,
And clothest Mathesis in rich ornaments,
That admirable Mathematique skill,
Familiar with the starres and Zodiack.
(To whom the heaven lyes open as her booke)
By whose directions undeceiveable,
(Leaving our Schoolemens vulgar troden pathes)
And following the auncient reverend steps
Of Trismegistus and Pythagoras,
Through uncouth waies and unaccessible,
Doost passe into the spacious pleasant fieldes
Of divine science and Phylosophie,

The Life and Minor Works of George Peele, ed. David H. Horne, Yale
U.P., 1952, p. 245.)

The last few lines re-echo the miniature closely. The Earl
reclines in a rectangular garden, enclosed by a clipped
hedge on the summit of a mountain with vistas of ascents in
the distance. The location must in one sense be "the
spacious pleasant fieldes / Of divine science and
Phylosophie to which he has gained entrance "Through
uncouth waies and unaccessible".

He reclines attired in black, his shirt and doublet
undone, his hat and gloves cast to one side. Although this is
almost certainly painted after 1593, he is not depicted
wearing the Garter which was mandatory and which only
fails to appear when a sitter is in symbolic guise (e.g.
no. 218). Both the reclining pose and negligent dress are
attributes of the melancholic and the image is an
expression of the Ficinian revaluation of the Saturnian
influence. This is one of a series of portraits from the 1590s
depicting men in the fashionable attire of the melancholic
(see Roy Strong, "The Elizabethan Malady. Melancholy
in Elizabethan and Jacobean Portraiture", *Apollo*,
LXXIX, 1964, pp. 164–9 and bibliography). In
Northumberland's case he is presented as a philosopher
and thinker. Chapman's *The Shadow of Night* published in
1594 mentions Northumberland in the preface as one of the
noblemen devoted to deep studies. The poem is a
celebration of the Saturnian humour in the profound
contemplations of night.

Normally the melancholy man seeks the shade of the
greenwood tree *outside* the confines of the formal garden as
in Isaac Oliver's miniature of a *Young Man* (no. 268).
Northumberland is, in contrast, placed within the orbit of
cultivated nature: a clipped rectangular hedge, a path,
grass, and a sloping bank followed by a second rectangular
hedge. Mathesis, to which Peele refers, is one of the four
"guides in religion", of which the others are Love, Art and
Magic, to the last of which it is most closely aligned.
Northumberland's concern was the mathematical arts in
this sense which meant that diagrams and geometrical
shapes, not only embodied the symbolic Pythagorean and
numerological approach of the middle ages but reinforced
it with all the ramifications of Renaissance occultism, as
expressed in Hermetism and Cabalism (see Frances Yates,
Giordano Bruno and the Hermetic Tradition in the Renaissance,
University of Chicago Press, 1964, pp. 295). Hilliard's
perspective is so inadequate that it is likely that
Northumberland is really reclining in a square. The square
is above all the hieroglyph of wisdom signifying its firmness

and constancy (Piero Valeriano, *Les Hieroglyphes*, trans.
J. de Monteyard, Lyons, 1615, pp. 518–19). There is no
doubt that these straight enclosures have a significance of
this kind complemented by the *impresa* suspended from a
tree in which a feather or quill-pen outweighs a sphere or
canonball(?) with the motto TANTI.

In terms of composition this is Hilliard's most ambitious
venture demanding an aerial view dependent on the
principles of single-point perspective. In this he has failed.

The miniature is unusual in having no containing gold
line. The features have faded and the greens and browns of
the foreground have flaked and been restored. A half-
length version is by Lockey (no. 122).

COLLECTIONS: Descended from the sitter to Charles Seymour, 6th
Duke of Somerset recorded by Vertue when in his collection at
Northumberland House, 1738: "a Lord Percy a limning lying
on the ground. dyd about 1585. in Syon Gardens". (*Notebooks*,
IV, p. 152); his daughter Charlotte married Heneage, 3rd Earl
of Aylesford, 1750; thence by descent; sold Christie's 23rd July
1937 (lot 45); Dr Beets, Amsterdam, sold 9th to 11th April
1940 (lot 66); Dr M. E. Kronenberg, Rotterdam; acquired by
the Rijksmuseum, 1980.

LITERATURE: Pope-Hennessy, *Lecture*, 1949, pl. 32.
A. C. Judson, *Sydney's Appearance*, Indiana U.P., 1958, pp. 32–33,
pl. 4.
Auerbach, *Hilliard*, pp. 119–20, pl. 94; 303–4 (94).
Strong, Nicholas Hilliard's Miniature of the Wizard Earl, *Bulletin
van het Rijksmuseum* 31, 1983. I, pp. 54–62.

ROWLAND LOCKEY

267 Sir Thomas More, his father, his household and his descendants, 1593–94

Victoria & Albert Museum (P.15–1973)
Vellum stuck onto card, rectangular,
24.6 × 29.4 mm, $9\frac{11}{16}$ × $11\frac{9}{16}$ in., in a walnut cabinet
with double locking doors

From left to right and as identified by the gold letters on
their clothing: *A: Sir John More* (?1451–1530), a barrister,
Serjeant at Law (1503), Judge of the Court of Common
Pleas (1518) and of the King's Bench (1523); *B: Sir
Thomas More* (1477/8–1535), Humanist and Chancellor;
C: John More (?1509–47), Sir Thomas's youngest child and
only son; *D: Anne Cresacre* (1511–77), the only daughter
and heiress of Edward Cresacre of Barnborough, Yorkshire,
ward of Sir Thomas, whose son, John, she married in 1529;
E: Thomas More II (1531–1606), son of John More and
Anne Cresacre, who probably commissioned, from Lockey,
the miniature; *F: Mary Scrope* (1534–1607), niece of Lord
Scrope of Bolton and wife of Thomas More II; *G: John
More* (1577–1599?) and *Cresacre More* (1572–1649), sons of
Thomas More II; *H: Cecily Heron* (b. 1507), *Elizabeth
Dauncey* (b. 1506) *Margaret Roper* (1505–1544), the three
daughters. The figure in the background lifting the curtain
is the More family jester, Henry Patenson.

The miniature depicting Sir Thomas More, his family
and descendants is a unique visual document which can

267

only be understood by reference to the original Holbein painting of Sir Thomas and his family and to the other paintings connected with it, commissioned at the same time as the miniature by Thomas More II in the late Elizabethan period. The most complete discussions of this are in S. Morison and N. Barker, *The Likeness of Thomas More*, London, 1963, pp. 18 ff. and Strong, *Tudor and Jacobean*, I, pp. 345–51 and what follows is based on those accounts with an emphasis on the miniature.

One of Holbein's earliest commissions when he arrived in England in 1527 was the famous, lost, Family Group of the More family. It was executed in the fragile medium of distemper and is known to us best by Holbein's sketch sent to Erasmus as an interim report before the picture was finished in 1528. This picture was presumably confiscated along with More's other chattels on his fall from power and we next hear of it in the possession of the Holbein collector, Andreas de Loo. He died in 1590 and Van Mander records that it passed to a nephew of Sir Thomas More who was also called More. This must have been More's grandson, Thomas More II. It is next recorded in the collection of Thomas Howard, Earl of Arundel, to whom it may have passed by way of John, 1st Lord Lumley, the Elizabethan collector who was also a Catholic.

Albeit that the history of its early descent is somewhat patchy there is no doubt that it belonged to Thomas More II in the 1590s and that it was he and his relatives who probably commissioned Rowland Lockey to execute three paintings: (i) the life-size copy of the picture as it was which, signed by Rowland Lockey, is now in the collection of Lord St Oswald. This descended via the Ropers who could have commissioned the copy. It has recently been cleaned revealing the date, 1592. (ii) a second life-size copy of the picture which introduced, to the right, Sir Thomas's descendants and which, bearing the date 1593, is now in the National Portrait Gallery (2765). This we know was painted for Thomas More II and passed

to his surviving son, Cresacre. (iii) the miniature version of (ii) but again with further slight variants, in particular the introduction of a view of a garden through an arch to the right.

The miniature seems to have been in the possession of a More descendant before it entered the Sotheby collection and its portrait content establishes that it must have originated directly with Thomas More II. In date it must be slightly later than the oil version in the National Portrait Gallery because here Cresacre is shown clean shaven whereas he has a slight beard and moustache in the miniature. This would suggest a date about 1594.

Thomas More II married Mary Scrope, the niece of Lord Scrope of Bolton, in 1553. They lived on the Cresacre estates in Yorkshire until they moved south early in the 1580s, taking up residence on their Essex estate at Lower Leyton. From 1582 to 1586 Thomas More II was imprisoned for recusancy, after his release the More family continued to live quietly as recusants in the country (see D. Shanahan, "The Family of St. Thomas More in Essex", *Essex Recusant*, I, pp. 62–74; 95–104; II, pp. 76–85).

Both large-scale picture and miniature transmute what Holbein had conceived with daring originality as the first family conversation piece north of the Alps, into a genealogical family tree brought to life, accentuated by the introduction of coats of arms. In the miniature these float before the canopy over the buffet and, although on a minute scale and damaged, recording (left) those of More (Quarterly; 1 and 4 Argent a Chevron engrailed between three Moorcocks Sable crested Gules; 2 and 3, Argent on a Chevron between three Unicorns' Heads erased Sable as many Bezants) and (right) those of Cresacre (of three Lions rampant guardant Gules) quartering those of More.

The main difference from the large version is the dropping of the portrait of Anne Cresacre on the right in favour of a garden view, which Vertue states, was More's Chelsea garden. The panorama in the distance certainly

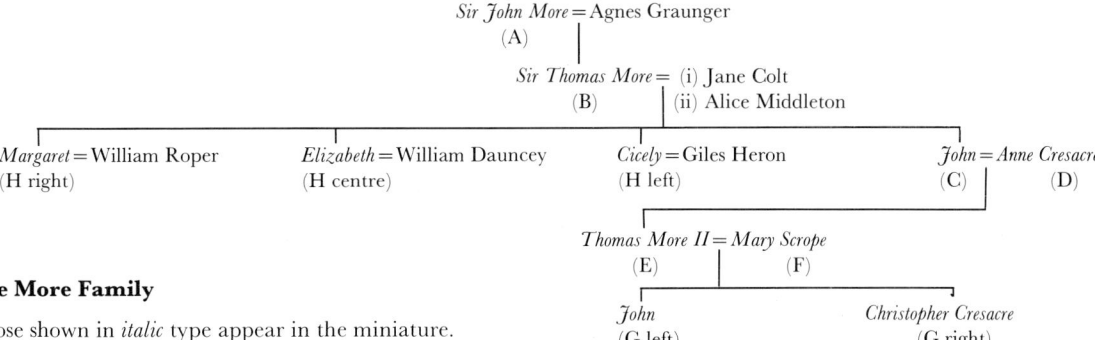

Sir John More = Agnes Graunger
(A)

Sir Thomas More = (i) Jane Colt
(B)　　　　　　(ii) Alice Middleton

Margaret = William Roper　　Elizabeth = William Dauncey　　Cicely = Giles Heron　　John = Anne Cresacre
(H right)　　　　　　　　　(H centre)　　　　　　　　(H left)　　　　　(C)　　　(D)

Thomas More II = Mary Scrope
(E)　　　　　(F)

John　　　　　　　　　　Christopher Cresacre
(G left)　　　　　　　　　　(G right)

The More Family

Those shown in *italic* type appear in the miniature.

seems to be London with Old St Paul's in the centre, but it is difficult to know what sources existed c. 1593–94 that could possibly provide an accurate view of Sir Thomas More's celebrated Chelsea garden half a century earlier: "A portion of this garden was left to the care of each of the many servants . . . He would have no idle retainer in his service . . . they were expected to occupy their leisure with gardening, music or books" (see Miles Hadfield, *A History of British Gardening*, 3rd revised ed., London, 1979, pp. 38–39). All one can say is that it is a rare view of a Tudor garden, enclosed by walls with a banqueting house in one corner and the centre laid out in knots surrounded by low clipped hedges.

The attribution of the miniature follows from the documentation of the large group being by Lockey and our knowledge that he was a pupil of Hilliard and practised as a miniaturist. This group must be the cornerstone for any further attributions to him. It does establish Lockey as an artist who never rose much above being a mediocre follower of the Hilliard manner.

The miniature is in the frame that was made for it on its acquisition by the Sotheby family in 1715. The features have flaked and been restored. There is scattered flaking both in the background and the landscape. The paint surface is generally soiled by ingrained dirt and the silver has oxidized.

INSCRIBED: Across the top in gold: *A. Johañes Morus eques auratus et iudex; B. Tho. Mor⁵ eques aur. Dñs. Canc. Ang. et fil. et haer, dti; C. John More Ar. fil. et haer. Dti. Tho.; D. Anna Jois sola fil, et haer. Ed. Cresacre Ar. Vxor Joh. Mor Ar. E. Tho. More (II) Arm. fil et haer. Dictor. Joh. Mor. Ar. et An Vx. eius; F. Maria fil Joh. Scroope, Ar. frat. Henrici Dni. Scroope,; G. Duo Filij dictor Tho Mor. et Mar. Vx. eius* (i.e. John and Cresacre More); *H. Tres filiae Tho. Mori Dni Cancellarij Angliae* (i.e. Cicely Heron, Elizabeth Dauncey and Margaret Roper).

On a label in the lower left-hand corner in gold: *Thomas Morus Londini | An. Do. 1480. est natus | Scaccarij primu. tum A.D. | 1529. totius Angliae | Cancellarius est tactus | Henrici: 8. iussu decollatus | interijt A.D. 1535. 6 non. Jul.*

COLLECTIONS: Purchased by James Sotheby, 1705, from an unidentified Lady Gerrard, a More family descendant, for £10.15 sh; seen by Vertue in 1742 at Ecton Hall in the possession of James Sotheby's son: "another Curious limning. being the family peece of Sʳ Thomas More and his Father son and 3 daughters. his sons wife. Cresacre – his grandson Thomas More. & his Lady Scroope & their two Sons. standing – a

prospect of his Gardens at Chelsea appears part of his Gallery & chappel at the distance. London spires very small. above this is the names of each person writ in small – the father of Mʳ. Southbys. bought this limning many years ago of a Gentlewoman who was under some necessity. – and was as I heard before (sold to him by a) daughter of one of the Mores family . . ." (Vertue, *Notebooks*, V, Walpole Society, XXVI, 1937–38, pp. 10–11); thence by descent in the Sotheby family; sold Sotheby's October 11th 1955 (lot 67) bt the Rev. J. E. Strickland; bequeathed by his widow, Anne Louise Strickland, to V & A in memory of her husband, 1973.

LITERATURE: Horace Walpole, *Anecdotes*, ed. Wornum, 1849, I, pp. 145–46.
O. Kurz, "Rowland Lockey", *Burlington Magazine*, XCIX, 1957, p. 15.
Auerbach, *Hilliard*, pp. 258–61, pl. 227, 331 (no. 262).
Strong, *Tudor and Jacobean*, I, pp. 345–51.
The King's Good Servant. Sir Thomas More, 1977 [170].
　National Portrait Gallery

ISAAC OLIVER

268　Unknown Melancholy Man, 1590–95

H.M. The Queen
Vellum stuck onto card, rectangular, 118 × 83 mm, 4⅝ × 3¼ in.

Painted, in the main, in Oliver's free Hilliardesque manner, accentuated by the naturalistic wild flowers observed in the foreground. The tradition that it depicts Sir Philip Sidney, which goes back to the early eighteenth century, can be discounted. It must, however, be a sitter of some eminence who portrays himself as a melancholic seeking the shade of the greenwood tree as opposed to the walks of the formal garden in the distance. The large floppy black hat, the folded arms and the pose in a "dump" are all attributes of the fashionable melancholic gallant (Strong, *The English Icon*, pp. 352–53). It has been pointed out that the garden is close to a series engraved by Vredeman de Vries (*Hortorum viridariorumque elegantes et multiplicis formae*, 1583), consisting of turfs laid in geometric patterns with the whole enclosed by an arcaded pergola. Gardens of this type did exist in Elizabethan England and the possibility that both house and garden are records of reality cannot altogether be excluded.

Carl Winter states that the composition as a whole is based on Dürer's engraving of the *Madonna of the Pear* but in reverse. There seems, however, to be little connexion between the two.

INSCRIBED: Signed on the rock of the bank to the right: *IO* (in monogram).

COLLECTIONS: First recorded as Sir Philip Sidney by Vertue, c. 1725 with information from a "M^r . . . Correy" who perhaps is the person in whose hands "this picture has been . . . time out of mind" (*Notebooks*, I, p. 153); acquired by Dr Richard Mead (1673–1754); engraved by Vertue, 1745; recorded in *Musei Meadiani Pars Altera*, Langford, 1755 under the section *Picturae Minori Formae* (in the British Library's *Life of Dr Richard Mead. Catalogue of Dr Mead's Library, Museum, etc*, London, 1754–55); purchased by Frederick, Prince of Wales.

LITERATURE: Walpole, *Anecdotes*, ed. Wornum, 1849, I, p. 178. Winter, *Elizabeth Miniatures*, pl. VIII; V & A, 1947 (124). A. C. Judson, *Sidney's Appearance*, Indiana U. P. 1958, pp. 30–32; Auerbach, *Hilliard*, pp. 240–41, pl. 202; 328 (237). Strong, *The English Icon*, pp. 36, 353. Strong, *The Renaissance Garden in England*, London, 1979, pp. 54, 216.

ISAAC OLIVER

269 Unknown Lady, c. 1596–1600

Collection V de S.
Vellum, which has lost its original backing, circular, 120 mm, $4\frac{11}{16}$ in. diam. cut at each side and at the bottom.

Painted in Oliver's tighter post-Italian style, this is an exceptionally large, unpublished miniature from the same period as the unknown lady formerly called the Countess of Somerset (no. 271). The sitter is not of the gentry, but citizen class, wearing a simple dress, minus any jewellery. It has, however, suffered clipping and other damage, including considerable repainting in the costume and background.

INSCRIBED: Signed to the right: *IO* (in monogram).

COLLECTIONS: Purchased at the F. Muller sale, Amsterdam 31st March 1896 (lot 548).

ISAAC OLIVER

270 Allegorical Scene: Virtue Confronts Vice, 1590–95

The State Museum of Art, Copenhagen
Vellum stuck onto card, rectangular, 110 × 170 mm, $4\frac{3}{8} \times 6\frac{3}{4}$ in. *(Photograph)*

Stylistically this belongs to the early 1590's and establishes Oliver immediately as superior to Hilliard in his handling of the large-scale miniature. It is his most ambitious and complex surviving composition with twenty-five figures. As a work it has no precedent within Hilliard's *oeuvre* and its

271

roots are not in England but in the Netherlands, in the large-scale pictures of artists such as Gillis van Coninxloo and Lucas van Valckenborch. The landscape setting with its twisted tree trunks, fantastic mountains and bird's eye vistas stem directly from this tradition. It is unique amongst Oliver's work, giving an insight into his enormous talents at a young age.

The miniature is full of incident: in the background the pleasures of the chase are depicted, reading from left to right: hawking, boar hunting and duck shooting. The main action to the right in the foreground is a scene of wanton revelry accentuated by luxurious costumes which, in the case of the women, expose the breasts. Couples engage in dalliance in the wood, while in the foreground centre, a couple embrace. The main action focuses on a young man reclining on the ground, his doublet undone and his hat beside him, resting against a lady playing a lute with a flautist behind her. A female figure in fancy dress takes him by the right arm and points to the group to the left; a gentleman leading in a lady attended by two other women. The costume in the miniature belongs to the middle class or City and not to the court.

The event depicts a moralistic denouement, familiar from the group pictures of Elizabeth I reversing the Judgement of Paris (Strong, *Portraits of Queen Elizabeth I*, pl. VI) or that depicting the Protestant succession in which her arrival ushers in peace and plenty (ibid, p. 79 (82)).

The movements and gestures of the chief figures argue a number of interpretations. The figures on the left could be husband and wife and epitomize a celebration of virtuous marriage. On the other hand the man gestures and draws the lady's attention to the reclining man on the right, whose attention in turn is about to be drawn to her by the gesturing lady enveloped in veils. Conceivably this embodies a return to virtue. The theme of virtue confronting vice is heightened by the colour range and clothes, the virtuous on the left in sombre attire of blue and purple and the vicious in pastel colours elaborately bejewelled and embroidered. The iconographical tradition is that of the Garden of Love (cf. Pourbus's *Allegorical Love Feast*, Wallace Collection).

That the composition is Oliver's own is stressed in the form of the signature that incorporates the word *in (venit)*.

INSCRIBED: Signed bottom left: *IO* (in monogram) *in*.

COLLECTIONS: Possibly identical with the miniature of a May Day "made after the life in England" by Oliver in the collection of Baeker, a Leiden lawyer, in 1622; first certainly recorded when in the collection of Christian Eberhard Voss, privy counsellor and counsellor of justice, who settled in Denmark in 1758; purchased in his sale, 1791, for the Ledreborg Collection; the Counts Holstein-Ledreborg Collection until acquired by the Museum.

LITERATURE: T. H. Colding and J. Andersen, "An Elizabethan LOVE-THEME", *Burlington Magazine*, XCII, 1950, pp. 326–27.
T. H. Colding, *Aspects of Miniature Painting*, Copenhagen, 1953, p. 104, fig. 114.
Auerbach, *Hilliard*, pp. 242–43.

ISAAC OLIVER

271 Unknown Lady, 1596–1600, formerly called Frances Howard, Countess of Somerset

Victoria & Albert Museum (P.12–1971)
Vellum stuck to plain card, circular, 130 mm, $5\frac{1}{8}$ in. diam.

This miniature is one of Oliver's largest and finest painted from life. From its first appearance at the close of the 18th century it was identified as Frances Howard, Countess of Essex and later Countess of Somerset (1593–1632), the notorious beauty whose career came to an end at the discovery of her murder by poison of Sir Thomas Overbury. Her iconography is thin but the oil portraits that depict her do agree in terms of the grey eyes and fair hair. To be her, however, the costume would have to be not earlier than 1609, when, at sixteen, she took up her role in court life in Jonson's *Masque of Queens*. Enveloping veils similar, but not identical, to these occur in pictures about 1615 (e.g. Gheeraerts Catherine Killigrew, Lady Jermyn, dated 1614, Strong, *The English Icon*, pl. 285 (no. 278)). This is deceptive for the real dating of the miniature depends on the dress beneath which can only be 1590's. The line of the sleeves and oversleeves, with their narrow lace cuff and the farthingale, are paralleled exactly in the Ditchley Portrait of Elizabeth I, c. 1590–92 (ibid, p. 289 (285)). It is a silhouette which lasts throughout the 1590's but which is suddenly abandoned with the new reign, when sleeves went tight upon the arms. The hair, which is composed almost into a halo surrounding the head with tiny ringlets near the ears, is similarly a feature of the 1590's (e.g. ibid, p. 278, (no. 265), 295 (nos. 296–297)). The miniature is no doubt intended as a love-token because her hand is placed on her heart as in Hilliard's *Young Man Among Roses* (no. 263). The veils may be a fashionable form of "undress" because to complete her formal attire she would discard the veils and add a fan-shaped ruff and adorn her hair with a jewelled head-dress.

Until now the dating of the miniature has always been to the Jacobean period, based on the inaccurate identification of the sitter and on a parallel miniature of another lady of the same size, that of Lucy Harington, Countess of Bedford, (no. 274), the costume for which, however, is correct for 1615.

There is no reason why Oliver should not have repeated the effect a decade later. His style and technique did not change and it is no argument as to date. The V & A miniature is one of Oliver's masterpieces, revealing the infinite variability of his work far beyond the narrower confines of Hilliard who produced nothing comparable in the 1590's. It is faded which, to an extent, must be taken into account for, originally, the impact of the carnations of the face and rose of the lips must have been even more striking in contrast to the virtuoso *chiaroscuro* essay that dominates the image, conceived in terms of grey into grey-black with touches of white and highlights of gold and silver. The sitter was clearly a lady of a high rank but we have no clues so far as to her identity.

The concern with *chiaroscuro*, the figure emerging from the shadows, the elegance and sophistication of the composition and the elusive half-smile of the sitter would indicate that it was painted shortly after Oliver's Italian visit of 1596 and with a strong recollection of North Italian painting in the form of Leonardo, his followers and Correggio. This is one of the first works of English art to respond directly to the art of the Italian Renaissance since Holbein. In this miniature we have surely the Elizabethan response to a tradition that stems from Leonardo da Vinci's *Mona Lisa* through the works of his followers in the Milanese School.

The features have faded and the silver has oxidized in some areas.

INSCRIBED: Signed bottom left: *10* in monogram; inscribed on the reverse in the hand of Horace Walpole: *The Lady Frances Howard Countess of Essex and Somerset, by Isaac Oliver; from the collection of James West, president of the Royal Society. H. W. 1773.*

COLLECTIONS: James West (1704?–1772); sold at Langford's 27th February 1773 (lot 74): "A large and remarkable fine haead of the Countess of *Somerset*"; bought Morgan, £3.17.6.; Horace Walpole at Strawberry Hill (*Description of the Villa . . . at Strawberry Hill*, 1774, p. 98); sold Strawberry Hill sale, May 9th 1842 (13th day) (lot 52); bought by the 13th Earl of Derby for 18gns.; Earls of Derby at Knowsley Hall; sold Christie's June 8th 1971 (lot 80); purchased by the V & A with the aid of the N.A.C.F. and the Pilgrim Trust.

LITERATURE: George Scharf, *A Catalogue of the Collection of Pictures at Knowsley Hall*, 1875, p. 131 (no. 234).
V & A, 1947 (18).
Pope-Hennessy, *Lecture*, 1949, pl. XXVII.
Auerbach, *Hilliard*, p. 248.
Strong, *Tudor and Jacobean* I, p. 298.
Graham Reynolds, "A Masterpiece by Isaac Oliver", *Victoria & Albert Museum Yearbook*, IV, 1974, pp. 7–10.

ISAAC OLIVER

272 The Three Brothers Browne, 1598

The Governors of Burghley House Preservation Trust
Vellum stuck onto card, rectangular, 240 × 260 mm,
9 × 10 in.

The miniature depicts the three grandsons of Anthony
Browne, 1st Viscount Montague (c. 1528–1592). They are
Anthony Maria Browne, 2nd Viscount (1574–1629) in the
centre flanked by his two brothers, John and William,
(1576–1637), sons of Anthony Browne and Mary, daughter
of Sir William Dormer. Due to his father pre-deceasing his
grandfather, Anthony Maria succeeded at the age of
eighteen. The Montagues were loyal Catholics and Queen
Elizabeth visited them at Cowdray in 1591. The second
Viscount continued the tradition, being imprisoned in the
Fleet for his vigorous speech against the new recusancy
laws in 1604 and remaining perpetually in difficulties
under James I. John Browne married Anne Gifford and
from their son, Stanislaus, the 9th and last Viscount
Montague was descended. William became a Jesuit lay
brother in 1613 at the College of St Omer.

The composition must have been as Vertue remarks
(*Notebooks*, VI, p. 54), at the behest of the patron.
Conceivably Oliver knew Du Val's engraving of 1579 of
the three Coligny brothers (*Coligny*, Archives Nationales,
Hotel de Rohan, 1972 (no. 452) rep.) but the placing of
three figures with arms intertwined in this way derives
more directly from groups of the Three Graces, although in
their case one normally stands with her back to the
onlooker. Presumably the allusion is the same as in the case
of the Graces, to concord and unity, in this instance not
only to each other but to the Catholic faith. The motto
Figurae conformis affectus corroborates this. This figure
entering to the right is also clearly a portrait. Although he
has removed his hat there seems no reason to describe him,
as is usually done, as a servant, as his age is given and he is
dressed as a gentleman.

The colour range is close to that of the so-called
"Countess of Essex" (no. 271), monochromatic moving
through black, grey and brown with touches of silver. It is

272

painted with an all over attention to detail unusual for a
miniature on this scale. The vellum is cracked and the
silver oxidized.

INSCRIBED: Top left: *Ano Dom. 1598*; below left to right the ages:
Ætatis.21.; Ætatis 24; Ætatis.18.; Aetatis 21; top centre the
motto: *FIGVRAE CONFORMIS AFFECTVS*; age of sitter to
the right: *Ætatis.21*. On a pilaster: IO (in monogram)

COLLECTIONS: By descent in the family of Browne, Viscounts
Montague, Cowdray; first recorded by Vertue on a visit to
Cowdray, c. 1730 (*Notebooks*, LL, p. 82); by the marriage of
Isabella, daughter of William Stephen Poyntz of Cowdray
House, in 1825, to Brownlow, 2nd Marquess of Exeter;
recorded, (W. H. Charlton, *Burghley*, Stamford, 1847 (81).
Walpole, *Anecdotes*, ed. Wornum, 1849, I, p. 179; Mrs Charles
Roundell, *Cowdray*, London, 1884, pp. 46–47); thence by
descent.

ISAAC OLIVER

273 Edward Herbert, 1st Baron Herbert of Cherbury, 1610–14

The Earl of Powis, Powis Castle
Vellum stuck onto card, rectangular, 180 × 230 mm,
7⅛ × 9 in.

Edward Herbert, 1st Baron Herbert of Cherbury
(1583–1648), philosopher, historian and diplomat,
accomplished fencer, musician and horseman. Toured the
continent, 1608–10; volunteer at capture of Julich; joined
the Prince of Orange's army, 1614; ambassador to Paris,
1619 and 1622–24. He was created baron, 1629 and
attended Charles I to Scotland, 1639–40. Attempted to
remain neutral in the Civil War. His chief philosophical
work was *De Veritate* (1624). Author of a famous
autobiography.

The miniature can only initially be dated by the
costume: the backcombed hair, high, flat collar and baggy
breeches can be paralleled in a series of portraits dated
1613 and 1614 (Strong, *The English Icon*, pp. 274 (nos.

273

276–77); 323 (no. 341); 324 (no. 342)). This is corroborated by the sitter's own movements. In July 1610 he went to the continent to serve under Sir Edward Cecil in the attack on Julich and returned in September leaving England again in 1614 as a volunteer in the army of the Prince of Orange. The miniature can therefore be firmly assigned to the years 1610–14.

Lord Herbert had a sustained interest in his own portraiture which he records in his Autobiography. In 1604 he sat to Peake in the robes in which he was created Knight of the Bath (Strong, *The English Icon*, p. 245 (220); *Autobiography*, ed. W. H. Dircks, London, 1888, p. 55), an event which created a great impression and reinforced his role as the epitome of Jacobean chivalry. In the passage on his return from France he refers to a picture of himself on horseback (ibid, p. 74) to commemorate a favourite horse. About 1609–10 he records sitting to William Larkin (ibid, p. 86) for the picture now at Charlecote (Strong, *The English Icon*, p. 315 (no. 325)), copies of which he states were procured from Larkin by Richard Sackville, 3rd Earl of Dorset (see no. 276) and "a greater person" (apparently Anne of Denmark). Lord Herbert's portrait was also borrowed by Lady Ayres who "gave it to Mr Isaac Oliver, the painter in Blackfriars, and desired him to draw it in little after his manner". This she placed in an enamelled locket and wore (*Autobiography*, ed. cit, p. 86). It is clear that the Powis miniature cannot be this one.

The Powis miniature celebrates Lord Herbert as knight and philosopher. His knightly prowess is alluded to in the distant tableau in which his armour is being hung up on the tree of chivalry. The lance rests against the tree, an attendant bears a plumed helmet and an elaborately caparisoned horse stands to the right. His intellectual preoccupations are developed in the presentation of him as a melancholic in a pose taken up from Hilliard's Northumberland (no. 266) and relating to a whole series of portraits utilising the attributes of Ficinian *melancolia*. In this instance the attributes are the wood and trickling stream. The linking symbol is the *impresa* on his shield which is a heart rising from flames (?) or wings (?) with smoke and golden sparks arising from the heart and the motto *Magica Sympathia*, referring to the doctrine of sympathetic magic. All *imprese* are open to purely personal interpretation but the allusion must be to some sort of ascent. George Wither's *Emblemes* (1635), although later, contains a number of flaming heart emblems, one of which is a winged heart on a book upon which the divine rays emanate downwards. The heart represents "the *Reasonable-soule*" as aspiring "to clime / To *Mysteries*, and *Knowledge*, more sublime". This must be close to the general intent of Lord Herbert's *impresa*, in which he casts himself as philosopher, poet, intellectual and man-at-arms.

It is conceivable that Oliver was aware of Giulio Campagnola's engraving of the river god type of Kronos.

INSCRIBED: On the shield: *MAGICA SYMPATHIA*.

COLLECTIONS: By descent; on the death of the 4th Lord Herbert in 1691 it passed to his sister and co-heir, Florentia, wife of Richard Herbert of Oakley Park, Montgomery; their grandson became 1st Earl of Powis.

LITERATURE: Pope-Hennessy, *Lecture*, 1949, pl. XXX. Auerbach, *Hilliard*, pp. 251, pl. 224; 331 (259).

274

Strong, *The English Icon*, pp. 35–36, 353.
D. Piper, *The Genius of British Painting*, London, 1975, p. 96.
Roy Strong, *The Renaissance Garden in England*, London, 1979, pp. 216–17.

ISAAC OLIVER

274 Lucy Harington, Countess of Bedford, c. 1615

The Fitzwilliam Museum, Cambridge (3902)
Vellum stuck onto card, circular, 127 mm, 5 in. diam.

Lucy Harington, Countess of Bedford (1582–1627), daughter of John, 1st Lord Harington of Exton, married Edward Russell, 3rd Earl of Bedford, in 1594. An heiress, through the death of her brother, she lived extravagantly, collecting, building, laying out notable gardens and patronizing poets and men of letters.

The miniature can only be dated from the costume. Embroidered waistcoats and dresses of this kind worn with enveloping veils are recorded in two dated Gheeraerts portraits, Lady Jermyn, 1614 and Lady Scudamore, 1614/15 (Strong, *The English Icon*, p. 285 (nos. 278–79)). An undated version of this attire, with a low-cut neckline, is the portrait of the Countess of Rutland (ibid., pp. 301–302 (nos. 310–11)) also by Gheeraerts. Other variants occur in portraits by Larkin (ibid., pp. 330 (no. 354), 331 (no. 356), 334 (no. 363)) from the same period. These are evidence of a vogue for embroidered dresses and veils during these years and the date c. 1605 given by Reynolds and Auerbach is too early.

In this miniature Oliver is repeating the effect, two decades on, of his unknown lady (no. 271) and the stylistic and iconographic impulses are the same.

The oxidization of the silver considerably diminishes the present impact of the miniature which must have been a tissue of shimmering highlights. The extensive damage to the background through erroneous "cleaning" is greatly to be regretted. Her hand is placed upon her breast. Although

275

doubts have been cast on its identity as Lucy Harington, the long face and nose seem perfectly acceptable as her and the extravagance of a miniature on this scale entirely in character (see no. 224). Uniquely among Oliver's works there is a compositional sketch (no. 275).

COLLECTIONS: In the collection of the Dukes of Buckingham at Stowe; sold at the Stowe sale, March 15th 1849 (lot 63); purchased by Walter Francis, 5th Duke of Buccleuch; purchased by the Fitzwilliam Museum, 1942.

LITERATURE: Kennedy, *Buccleuch*, pl. 5.
V & A, 1947 (165).
Auerbach, *Hilliard*, pp. 248; pl. 216; 330 (251).

ISAAC OLIVER

275 Composition Sketch for Lucy Harington, Countess of Bedford, c. 1615.

The Fitzwilliam Museum, Cambridge (2753)
Pen and brown ink on paper, 149×11 mm,
$5\frac{7}{8} \times 4\frac{3}{8}$ in.

In the 1947 V & A exhibition this was accepted as being by Oliver, but, subsequently, it was suggested that it was a sketch done after the miniature by Mathys van den Berg (c. 1617–1687). There seems, however, good reason for accepting this as a composition sketch by Oliver. Although Oliver worked within the limning tradition in painting from life on to the vellum as Hilliard and Hornebolte before him, he did, unlike them, do composition studies. Vertue records seeing a book of these bearing the dates 1609 and 1610, at the very period of this miniature: "many Sketches. postures &c done with a Silver pen" (*Notebooks*, II pp. 73–4). This is followed by a list of sitters including Anne of Denmark, the Countess of Arundel and Sir Henry Roe. The sketch would suggest that the miniature of Lucy Harington was initially conceived as rectangular in format. If this were a copy after the miniature the copyist would have surely followed the basic *tondo* form of the finished object rather than make it rectangular.

LITERATURE: V & A, 1947 (200).

ISAAC OLIVER

276 Richard Sackville, 3rd Earl of Dorset, 1616

Victoria & Albert Museum (721–1882)
Vellum stuck to plain card, rectangular,
239×157 mm, $9\frac{7}{16} \times 6\frac{3}{16}$ in.

Richard Sackville, (1590–1624), who succeeded as third Earl in 1609 was categorized as "a man of spirit and talent, but a licentious spendthrift". He married Anne Clifford, daughter of George Clifford, 3rd Earl of Cumberland and her diary records his extravagances, so that by his death he had mortgaged Knole.

One of the biggest and most important of all Oliver's large-scale miniatures. Dorset's prodigality was famous and is here reflected, as V. J. Murrell has observed, in the use of the three most important blue pigments: the costly ultramarine (lapis lazuli) for the trunk hose; blue bice (azurite) for the side curtain, pelmet and stockings; and smalt (a pigment made from cobalt-coloured glass) for the greyish curtain behind the sitter.

This miniature is a rare instance where the clothes worn can actually be identified in a contemporary inventory. In 1617 "An Inventorie of the rich wearing Apparrell of the right honorable Richard Earle of Dorset" was compiled, in which Sackville's attire is identifiable:

"Item one paire of Bullen hose of Scarlett and blew velvett the panes of Scarlett laced all over with watchett silk silver and gold lace and the puffs of blew velvett embroadered all over with sonnes Moones and starres of gold
Item one paire of longe watchet silke stockings embroadered".

The suit in the inventory consists of only five items, whereas normally it would have been made up of eleven. By 1617 parts of it must have already been given away or dismantled for upholstery at Knole, as was the case of most of the clothes and caparisons in the inventory.

Dorset was a prominent figure in the tiltyard and his interest in chivalrous pastimes is reflected in the pieces of armour on the table and floor. No other miniature corresponds so closely with the formalized portraits ascribed to William Larkin (no. 277). The miniature, however startling a feat of virtuosity, is so uncharacteristic of Oliver in its composition and multicoloured tonality that it must reflect the dictates of the sitter. It is in remarkably brilliant condition, apart from losses to the curtains and helmet crest and the inevitable oxidization which, in the case of the armour, has resulted in the unsightly highlights.

INSCRIBED: Signed bottom right: *Isaac. Olliuierus. fecit.; and: 1616.*

COLLECTIONS: Presumably commissioned by the sitter; first recorded in the collection of Jeremiah Harman; C. Sackville Bale collection; sold 24th May 1881 (lot 1424); acquired by John Jones; bequeathed by him, 1882.

LITERATURE: A. Waagen, *Art Treasures in Britain*, 1854, II, p. 332.
V & A, 1947 (195).
Winter, *Elizabethan Miniatures*, pl. XV.
E. K. Waterhouse, *Painting in Britain 1530 to 1790*, London, 1962 ed., p. 27, pl. 24.
Peter and Ann MacTaggart, "The Rich Wearing Apparel of Richard, 3rd Earl of Dorset", *Costume*, XIV, 1980, pp. 41–55.

276

277

WILLIAM LARKIN

277 Richard Sackville, 3rd Earl of Dorset, 1613

The Ranger's House, Blackheath (GLC)
Oil on canvas, 206.4 × 122.3 cm, 81¼ × 48⅛ in.

For the sitter see no. 276

William Larkin (b. early 1580s – d. 1619) must have emerged out of an apprenticeship as a practicing painter in the first years of the seventeenth century. The documentation on him is thin, two portraits from c. 1609–10 (Edward Herbert, 1st Baron Herbert of Cherbury and Sir Thomas Lucy at Charlecote (National Trust)) and a number of payments from the years 1617–19 (for Larkin see J. Lees-Milne, "Two Portraits at Charlecote by William Larkin", *Burlington Magazine*, XCIV, 1952, pp. 352–56; Strong, *The English Icon*, pp. 313–34; Edmond, *Limners and Picturemakers*, pp. 127–29).

This portrait, together with a companion of his brother, has been attributed by Waterhouse to Isaac Oliver but it would be difficult to reconcile their archaicizing tendencies with the *avant garde* work of Oliver during the same period. They fit neatly, however, into a long series of iconic formalized full lengths that seem to form a reasonable nucleus for Larkin's *oeuvre*. Larkin belongs to the Hilliardesque style in its final phase and his work is seen to be far more old-fashioned when set against Gheeraert's contemporary portraits. It is a conceivable hypothesis that Larkin was apprenticed to Hilliard in the 1590s.

There were, however, links between Larkin and Oliver: Lady Ayres commissioned Oliver to make a miniature of Larkin's portrait of Lord Herbert (see no. 273), and Dorset patronized them both. The relationship between this picture and Oliver's full length of 1616 (no. 276) has been pointed out before, the Oliver miniature is a Larkin with all the perspective and compositional errors removed. What needs to be stressed is not the influence of Larkin on Oliver but the role of the patron. Dorset was conservative in his tastes and must have dictated to the miniaturist that he wished to be depicted in all the costume splendour of a Larkin full length.

It has been plausibly suggested that this is the dress Dorset wore at the wedding of the Princess Elizabeth to the Elector Palatine on February 14th 1613. The clothes he wears are recorded, as in the case of those in the Oliver miniature, in an inventory of 1617: "One doublett of Cloth of silver embroadered all over in slips of sattin black and gold", "one Cloake of uncutt velvett blacke laced with seaven embroadered laces of gold and black silke and above the borders powdred with slipps of sattin embroad(ered) with gold and lyned with shagg of black silver and gold"; "one paire of white silke stockinges embroadered with gold silver and black silke".

INSCRIBED: Top left: *1613 Ætis suae 24 | Aul nunquam tentes: aut perfile*; below right on the tablecloth (inaccurately) a later inscription: *Sr Edward Sackvill Brother | to Rich^d : Earle of Dorset | who Succeeded him in ye Earldom.*

LITERATURE: E. K. Waterhouse, *Painting in Britain 1530–1790*, London, 1953, pl. 25.
Strong, *The English Icon*, p. 323 (341).
The Suffolk Collection. Catalogue of Paintings, GLC, 1974 (3).
P. and A. MacTaggart, "The Rich Wearing Apparel of Richard, 3rd Earl of Dorset", *Costume*, 14, 1980, pp. 41–55.

Index

Numbers refer to Catalogue entries

ABERGAVENNY, George Neville, Lord 25, 26
Anjou, Francis, Duke of 72
Aragon, Catherine of 6, 8
Audley, Elizabeth Grey, Lady 31, 32

BARBOR?, William 143
Beaufort, Margaret, Countess of Richmond and Derby 13, 123
Bedford, Lucy Harington, Countess of 224, 274, 275
Benninck, Simon VI
Bodley, Sir Thomas 50
Bohemia, Elizabeth, Queen of 247, 250, 252, 262
Boleyn?, Anne 14
Brandon, Alice, Mrs Hilliard 77
Browne, the three brothers 272

CHARLES I 248, 249, 260, 261
Charles V 11
Cherbury, Edward Herbert, 1st Baron Herbert of 273
Cleveland, Barbara Villiers, Duchess of I
Cleves, Anne of 30
Coningsby, Jane, Mrs Boughton 63
Cumberland, George Clifford, 3rd Earl of 214, 216

DARR, Leonard 91
Denmark, Anne of 225, 242, 243, 244, 253, 254, 255, 256
Donne, John 178
Dorset, Richard Sackville, 3rd Earl of 276, 277
Drake, Elizabeth Sydenham, Lady 85
Dudley, Sir Robert 265

EDWARD IV 23
Edward VI 18, 108
Effingham, Charles Howard, 2nd Baron of and 1st Earl of Nottingham 66, 129
Elizabeth I 40, 42, 44, 45, 46, 109, 182, 183, 184, 185, 187, 188, 189, 190, 191, 192, 193, 194, 195, 196, 197, 198, 199, 200, 201, 202, 203, 204, 205, 206, 207, 208, 209, 210, 211, 212
Essex, Robert Devereux, 2nd Earl of 154, 155, 218, 220, 263

FRANÇOIS, Dauphin 4

HATTON, Sir Christopher 89
Henry, Prince of Wales 230, 231, 245, 246, 251, 257, 258, 259
Henry VIII 2, 5, 7, 12, 16, 19, 20, 21, 22
Hertford, Katherine Grey, Countess of 38
Hertford, Edward Seymour, 1st Earl of and 1st Duke of Somerset 51, 110
Hilliard, Nicholas 49
Hilliard, Richard 48
Holbein, Hans V
Howard, Catherine 33
Howard, Frances, Duchess of Richmond and Lennox 114
Howard, Thomas, Lord 83
Hunsdon, George Carey, 2nd Lord 162

JAMES I 233, 234, 235, 236, 237, 238, 239, 240, 241

KYTSON, Elizabeth Cornwallis, Lady 62

LEICESTER, Robert Dudley, Earl of 68, 186
Lennox, Margaret, Countess of 64

MARY I 9, 39, 43
Mary Queen of Scots 79
Medici, Catherine de 70
Mildmay, Sir Anthony 264
Molle, Mrs, Elizabeth 117
Molle, John 97
Montague, Anthony Browne, 1st Viscount 54
Montgomerie, Jane, Duchess of Richmond and Lennox 165
More, Sir Thomas and family 267

NEVERS, Henriette de Cleves, Duchess of 75
Nevers, Louis de Gonzague, Duke of 75
Nottingham, Catherine Carey, Countess of 131
Northumberland, Henry Percy, 9th Earl of 122, 266

OLIVER, Elizabeth Harding, Mrs 173
Oliver, Isaac 133, 134

RALEIGH, Sir Walter 81
Richmond, Henry FitzRoy, Duke of 15
Roper, Margaret 28
Roper, William 27

ST CATHERINE, by Veronese 151
St John of Bletso, John, 2nd Lord of
Salisbury, Robert Cecil, 1st Earl of 166
Salisbury, Margaret Pole, Countess of 24
Seymour, Jane 17, 107
Slingsby, Sir Henry 98
Sonoy, Diederik 140
Southampton, Henry Wriothesley, 3rd Earl of 96, 119
Suffolk, Charles Brandon, 1st Duke of 10
Suffolk, Henry Brandon, 2nd Duke of 34
Suffolk, Charles Brandon, 3rd Duke of 35
Sussex, Robert Radcliffe, 5th Earl of 219

TALBOT, Sir Arundell 152
Throckmorton, Margaret, Mrs Robert Pemberton 29

VAN EGMONT, Lady Françoise 138
Valois, Marguerite de 73, 74

WALSINGHAM, Lady 61
Willoughby D'Eresby, Elizabeth, Lady 170
Willoughby D'Eresby, Peregrine Bertie, Lord 142